New Histories of the Andaman Islands

This innovative, multidisciplinary exploration of the unique history of the Andaman Islands as a hunter-gatherer society, colonial penal colony and state-engineered space of settlement and development ranges across the theoretical, conceptual and thematic concerns of history, anthropology and historical geography. Covering the entire period of post-settlement Andaman history, from the first (failed) British occupation of the Islands in the 1790s up to the year 2012, the authors examine imperial histories of expansion and colonization, decolonization, anti-colonialism and nationalism, Japanese occupation, Independence and Partition, migration, commemoration and contemporary issues of Indigenous welfare. *New Histories of the Andaman Islands* offers a new way of thinking about the history of South Asia, and will be thought-provoking reading for scholars of settler colonial societies in other contexts, as well as those engaged in studies of nationalism and post-colonial state formation, ecology, visual cultures and the politics of representation.

CLARE ANDERSON is Professor of History at the University of Leicester. She has written widely on the history of penal transportation, including most recently *Subaltern Lives: Biographies of Colonialism in the Indian Ocean World, 1790–1920* (Cambridge University Press, 2012).

MADHUMITA MAZUMDAR is Associate Professor at the Dhirubhai Ambani Institute of Information and Communication Technology. Much of her published work derives from her early researches into science and the cultural politics of nationalism in colonial Bengal.

VISHVAJIT PANDYA is Professor of Anthropology at the Dhirubhai Ambani Institute of Information and Communication Technology, and is also the founder and honorary director of the Andaman and Nicobar Tribal Research Institute. He is the author of *Above the Forest* (Oxford University Press, 1993) and *In the Forest* (University Press of America, 2009).

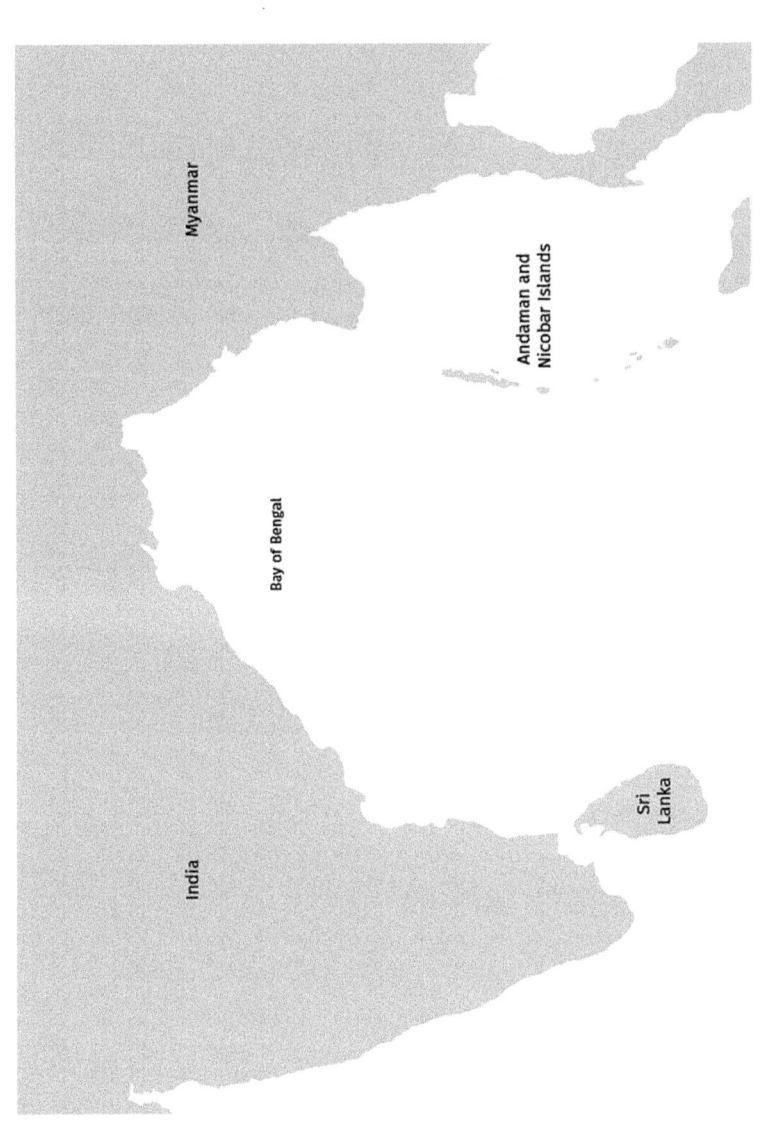

New Histories of the Andaman Islands

Landscape, Place and Identity in the Bay of Bengal, 1790–2012

Clare Anderson
University of Leicester

Madhumita Mazumdar
and
Vishvajit Pandya
Dhirubhai Ambani Institute of Information and Communication Technology

CAMBRIDGE
UNIVERSITY PRESS

University Printing House, Cambridge CB2 8BS, United Kingdom

One Liberty Plaza, 20th Floor, New York, NY 10006, USA

477 Williamstown Road, Port Melbourne, VIC 3207, Australia

314-321, 3rd Floor, Plot 3, Splendor Forum, Jasola District Centre, New Delhi-110025, India

79 Anson Road, #06-04/06, Singapore 079906

Cambridge University Press is part of the University of Cambridge.

It furthers the University's mission by disseminating knowledge in the pursuit of
education, learning and research at the highest international levels of excellence.

www.cambridge.org
Information on this title: www.cambridge.org/9781107434028

First published 2016
First paperback edition 2018

A catalogue record for this publication is available from the British Library

Library of Congress Cataloging in Publication data
Anderson, Clare, 1969–
New histories of the Andaman Islands : landscape, place and identity in the
Bay of Bengal, 1790–2012 / Clare Anderson, University of Leicester, Madhumita
Mazumdar, Dhirubhai Ambani Institute of Information and Communication
Technology and Vishvajit Pandya, Dhirubhai Ambani Institute of Information
and Communication Technology.
    pages cm
Includes bibliographical references and index.
ISBN 978-1-107-07679-2 (hardback : alk. paper)   1. Andaman Islands
(India)–History.   2. Andaman Islands (India)–Historiography.
3. Ethnicity–India–Andaman Islands.   I. Mazumdar, Madhumita.
II. Pandya, Vishvajit.   III. Title.
DS486.5.A5A58 2015
954'.8803–dc23   2015014380

ISBN   978-1-107-07679-2   Hardback
ISBN   978-1-107-43402-8   Paperback

Contents

Figures

Acknowledgements

We are grateful to the Economic and Social Research Council (ESRC) for funding our research project, *Integrated Histories of the Andaman Islands*, during the period 2009–13 (grant no. RES-000-22-3484). We are also further indebted to the ESRC which, jointly with the British Academy and Arts and Humanities Research Council, resourced Madhumita Mazumdar's visiting fellowship to Britain in summer 2008 to undertake the project *Refugee Resettlement in the Andaman Islands: Colonial Precedents, Post-Colonial Predicaments* (grant no. RES-067-27-0001). Her visit laid the foundation for the development of this research, which was the principal intent of our collaboration during that period.

We thank also the many people who provided inspiration and support as our research progressed: our ESRC peer reviewers and assessors, and archivists, curators, scholars, interlocutors and friends. They include Zubair Ahmed, Hasan Ali (Andaman and Nicobar Administration Archives, Secretariat Complex, Port Blair), Rahaab Allana (Alkazi Collection of Photography, New Delhi), Sunil Amrith, Michaela Appel, Eileen Arnell, David Arnold, Sheikh Farooq Alam, Felix Driver, John Falconer (British Library), David Hardiman, Hugh Duffield, Frank Heidemann, Ashley Givens (V&A), Viv Golding, Kevin Greenbank (Centre for South Asian Studies, University of Cambridge), James Hamill (British Museum), Rashida Iqbal (Cellular Jail Museum), Fiona Kerlogue (Horniman Museum), Hari Kishen, Mukeshwar Lal, Alan Lester, John Lobo, Lester Lobo, Margaret Makepeace (British Library), Francis Neelam, Joy Neelam, Kathy Prior, Mahomed Abdul Qadir, (Ahmad) Mujtaba-sir, Vicky Pearce (Horniman Museum), Shirin Rai, Nigel Rigby (National Maritime Museum), Agata Rutkowska (Royal Collections Trust), Jonathan Saha, Satadru Sen, Uditi Sen, Sujit Sivasundaram, Carolyn Strange, Sarah Strong (Royal Geographical Society), Akshaya Tankha (Alkazi), Julian Warren (Bristol Record Office), Joy Wheeler (Royal Geographical Society), Claire Wintle and Philipp Zehmisch.

Clare Anderson also thanks her colleagues at the University of Warwick (especially in the Department of Sociology and the Global

History and Culture Centre), where this project began, and the School of History at the University of Leicester, where it was completed. She thanks particularly Leicester's former Vice-Chancellor, Professor Sir Robert Burgess, for granting study leave during 2011–12. She is also indebted to the staff in the libraries and archives of the Alkazi Collection of Photography, New Delhi; Anthropology Library, British Museum; Bristol Record Office; India Office Library; Horniman Museum; The National Archives; National Maritime Museum; Royal Geographical Society; Victoria and Albert Museum; Queen's Collection, Windsor Castle; Department of Manuscripts, Cambridge University Library; National Library of Australia, Canberra; and the Archives and Special Collections of the School of Oriental and African Studies. A special note of thanks to genealogists Eileen Arnell and Keith Wilson, who shared stories of their fascinating connections with the Islands; and to Clare's many friends among the Islands' local-born community, with whom she worked during repeated field visits. Francis Neelam and Rashida Iqbal and her team at the Cellular Jail Museum bear special mention for their invaluable support and assistance at these times.

Vishvajit Pandya would like to extend a special debt of gratitude to the Andaman and Nicobar Administration and the AAJVS staff, particularly Anup Mondal, Bisheswar Das, Pronob Sircar, Dipu and Swapan. Stationed in different parts of Jarawa territory, their kind assistance was invaluable in making it possible for him to work among the Jarawas as old family friends.

Madhumita Mazumdar would also like to thank especially George Weber of the Andaman Association, and the members of the Bengali Matua community in Port Blair, Kadamtalla and Rangat for their valuable inputs into research in these areas. She is also grateful to Samir Acharya, founder of the Society for Andaman Nicobar Ecology (SANE). Mazumdar would also like to thank the faculty and members of the Department of Sociology at the University of Warwick for extending their fullest cooperation to her as Visiting Fellow to the Department. She thanks her mother and her family for always being there and encouraging her throughout.

Finally, we thank Dr Emma Battell Lowman for her assistance in finalizing the manuscript, our copy editor Kevin Eagan, project manager Ezhilmaran Sugumaran, and at Cambridge University Press, Assistant Editor in History Rosalyn Scott and our ever-patient Commissioning Editor, Lucy Rhymer.

Abbreviations

Archives

A&N Archives	Andaman and Nicobar Administration Archives, Secretariat Complex, Port Blair
J&R	Judicial and Revenue
CJML	Cellular Jail Museum Library, Port Blair
CSAS	Centre of South Asian Studies, University of Cambridge
IJC	India Judicial Consultations
IOR	India Office Collections, British Library
NAI	National Archives of India, New Delhi
MLPC	Personal Collection of Mukeshwar Lal
PCKW	Personal Collection of Keith Wilson
RGS	Royal Geographical Society
TNA	The National Archives, Kew
V&A	Victoria & Albert Museum

Abbreviations

AIA	Andaman Indian Association
AA	Andamanian Association
AAJVS	Andaman Adim Janjati Vikas Samiti
IIL	Indian Independence League
INA	Indian National Army
JTR	Jarawa Tribal Reserve
LBA	Local Born Association
OBC	Other Backward Castes

Glossary

allamey	heat inducing red clay (Jarawa)
als	narrow pathways along rice fields
atma	spirits
Azad Hind	Free India
Azad Hind Fauj	The Indian National Army founded by Subhas Chandra Bose
balidan kar na	to make a sacrifice
balidan vedi	sacrificial altar
bash	home/abode
bhakt	devotee
bhakti	devotion, faith
bhakti-r pukur	pools of faith
bal jar, bou tar	the assertion that 'whoever had the strength to take a wife by force could do so'
Bharat	India
bone	light (Jarawa)
boneye	illumination (Jarawa)
chaddha	shelter or a place to reside (Jarawa)
charpoy	bed
Dalit	literally meaning 'oppressed', a self-ascribed political name embraced by communities considered 'untouchables' within the Hindu caste structure
desh	land, country, native village, etc.
dhobi	washerman, often a caste or occupational group in Indian society
durbar	court
Dvadosh Ajna	Twelve Commands
edang	amulet (Jarawa)
enen	outsiders (Jarawa)
Hamari Awaz	Our Voice

haathe kaam,	a lifelong commitment to work and devotion to
mukhe naam	the name of Hari or God
Harinam	the name of the Lord
heyolo	forest (Jarawa)
Harimandir	the temple of the Lord
inaka	middle-of-nowhere (Japanese)
Isai Sena	local name for Salvation Army
Jai Hind	Victory to India! A salutation
jaydaad	inherited property
junglee	literally forest dweller but also connotes savage or uncivilized
kaidi	prisoners
kala pani	black waters (Andamans as a place for shameful banishment)
khadee/khari	mangrove creek
khatarnak zindagi	dangerous life
khilafat	literally from 'khilaf' (to rebel or go against) but also refers to the Khilafat Movement in India in the early twentieth century, where Indian nationalists expressed solidarity with the movement for the restoration of the sovereign rights of the Islamic caliphate following the defeat of Ottoman Turkey in World War I
kirtans	devotional chants or songs sung by a group of believers
kisans	peasants
kul	lineage
kuchcha	raw or mud-built when referring to houses
kuwey	wild bore/pig (Jarawa)
Lok Sabha	the lower House of the Indian Parliament
maati	soil
machan	scaffolding/platform
malik kashtkar	compound of two terms: 'malik', meaning owner or proprietor, and 'kashtkar', meaning tenant thus referring to tenant proprietors.
mandir	temple
Mariamman	local mother goddess bearing semblance with the more widely worshipped goddess Durga
Matuas	an anti-caste Hindu sect founded in East Bengal in the late nineteenth century committed to values of egalitarianism, community solidarity and devotion

Matua Mahasangha	the Matua great congregation
Mazar	commemorative site associated with a holy Muslim individual
mehtars	sweepers
Messcott	from the English word 'mess' and 'kot' (house): mess house
mitti	soil/clay
Mukti Fauj	another local name for the Salvation Army
Mukti Tirtha	pilgrimage of salvation
muluk	native land, village, country
padas	neighbourhoods
palan poshan	nurturing and upbringing
panchayats	local assemblies or councils
paramananda	eternal bliss, God
patwari	local rural land record holder
peti afsar	petty officer
poribaar	family
pradhan	local village headman
pranam	salutations
punya bhoomi	sacred land
pukka	brick built
purdah	veil/curtain
rashan	ration
ruuh	soul/sprit
Shaheed Dweep	Martyr Island
sahitya	literature
sanskriti	culture
samaj	society
sanads	deeds of occupancy
sepoys	soldiers
shikar	hunting
Shinbun	newspaper (Japanese)
Swaraj Dweep	Self-ruled Islands
sher sahib	derived from 'tiger' (sher), to mean European overseer
sikāman	sick man or convict in hospital
talabdar	orderly
tapu	island
tehsil	local administrative unit
tikatliv	ticket-of-leave
tikatwallah	self-supporter

uppa chaddha	invisible space where dead and spirits live (Jarawa)
utsav	celebration
vigrahas	religious icon
waye-dama	light/heat (Jarawa)
wilpo	thatch/shelter (Jarawa)
zameen	ground/land
zamindar	landlord

1   Introduction

Clare Anderson, Madhumita Mazumdar
and Vishvajit Pandya

Tucked away in the Bay of Bengal, some thousand miles from the great city of Kolkata, the Union Territory of the Andaman Islands is a relatively isolated and marginalized part of the Republic of India, constituting a long chain of 204 islands, some 40 of which are inhabited. In recent times, the catastrophic tsunami of December 2004 brought the Islands under the glare of national and international media. Suffering some of the worst damage unleashed by the earthquake, the Islands acquired new forms of visibility and attracted unprecedented interest both in mainland India and across the world. News reports driven by both humanitarian and commercial interests, for instance, sought to generate new forms of appreciation of the Islands as a tropical paradise replete with forests, beaches and 'exotic natives' that desperately demanded conservation. Such texts complemented previous knowledge of the islands as *kala pani*, the black waters over which the British transported thousands of convicts and freedom fighters to a life of exile or forced labour. However, despite the post-tsunami national and international interest in the Andamans, little has been done to change or even to question the enduring stereotype of the Islands as no more than the home of 'tropical exotica' and nationalist martyrdom. The larger historical, social and cultural context of the Islands has remained quite apart from debates on island tourism, conservation and development, as well as symbolic acts of remembering the freedom struggle. This book seeks to correct this partial image of the Andaman Islands and to bring into focus the story of the complex multicultural society encompassed within its territorial bounds.

Our approach is one of integration, with respect to our disciplinary focus and the subjects of our concern. We propose chapters that start from the vantage points offered within the disciplines of History, Sociology and Anthropology in order to bring the past to the centre of present-day issues and concerns. In part, we want to show the importance of understanding how society, culture and political economy in the Andamans have been historically constituted. But we also offer interpretations of how history is understood in the Islands today and how it has been deployed (and contested) in the making of nation, community and identity. Our conceptual tools turn on ideas of landscape and space, and in particular on the importance of human intervention in the making of place. The book is strongly island-centred. Though it is necessarily engaged with the relationship between the Islands, the British Empire and the Indian mainland, we look outwards, deliberately, from within. In each of these ways, *New Histories of the Andaman Islands* offers a fresh perspective to studies of India and the Bay of Bengal, as well as to scholarship on other post-colonial spaces forged through indigenous marginalization and migration – coerced or free.

Entangled histories

Situated along the sea routes to Southeast Asia and the South China Sea, the pristine islands of the Andamans have long attracted a range of people to their shores: sailors, traders, pirates, colonizers and settlers from various parts of India, Burma and Malaysia. Previously uncolonized, the British first became interested in the Islands in 1789, when the Governor-General of India, Lord Cornwallis, dispatched Lieutenant Archibald Blair on a survey mission, instructing him to raise the Union Flag and to set up a harbour where merchant and navy ships might be refreshed and refitted. At this time, it was widely believed that the Islands were inhabited by ferocious cannibals with dog-like faces and tails. There was scant contemporary knowledge of the Andamans, and what the British knew was drawn largely from the writings of the second-century Mediterranean astronomer and geographer Ptolemy as well as the seventh, thirteenth and early eighteenth-century travellers I-Tsing, Marco Polo and Alexander Hamilton. Lieutenant Blair was the first visitor to offer a more nuanced commentary on the Andamanese, writing that though he once noted their hostility and 'rude and uncivilized state'. he also found them to be of happy disposition and 'susceptible of the most tender impressions'.[1]

In his report to the East India Company in 1789, Blair recommended that the colonial settlement be established at the mouth of the large harbour of South Andaman. This was quickly effected; the site was named Port Cornwallis, and Blair took charge of about two hundred labourers, sepoys and settlers who he put to work on Chatham Island. They cleared land of jungle, built huts and storehouses, and planted fruits and vegetables on the island; within a few months, they had constructed a road

---

[1] Selections from the Records of the Government of India (Foreign Dept), 24, John Gray, 'Calcutta Gazette' Office, 1858, Survey of the Andamans, Report of Archibald Blair, 27 May 1793, 92–3, RGS.

between what are now Phoenix and Navy bays. So successful were they that many sent for their families. Blair, meanwhile, believed that a second harbour in the northeast of North Andaman had great potential, and in 1792 the Company ordered that the Chatham settlement move, with Major Alexander Kyd replacing Blair as officer in charge. He was ordered to report on the comparative advantages of Port Cornwallis and Prince of Wales Island as naval stations.[2] Although the settlers duplicated the labours of South Andaman, and the workforce was augmented with convicts from Bengal, the new settlement, also named Port Cornwallis, was a disaster. This was because when Britain went to war against France, Kyd was forced to divert resources from colonization to fortification. Moreover, the settlers and convicts quickly fell ill with fevers, sores and scurvy, and many died. After the surgeon succumbed, the East India Company decided to abandon the Andamans altogether. It transferred the surviving convicts to its penal colony in neighbouring Prince of Wales Island (Penang), and sent the free settlers back to Calcutta.

Because of their central position in the Asian trading routes that criss-crossed the Bay of Bengal, the Company remained interested in the Islands during the years that followed, and its ships occasionally anchored there. This maritime traffic increased as Company interests penetrated South India, the Burmese coast, and the littorals of Singapore and the Malacca Straits. During the 1840s and 1850s, however, stories of Andamanese attacks on prospectors and shipwrecked sailors and passengers began to circulate. Though Governor-General Charles Canning was initially sceptical, the Company began to reconsider settling the Islands, bolstered by the positive reports of the Commissioner of neighbouring Arakan, Henry Hopkinson.[3] Their view was only strengthened when shortly afterwards a group of Andamanese killed eight Chinese traders when they landed on the Islands in search of fresh water.[4] '[I]t appears highly discreditable in a civilized Government to allow such a state of things to exist within a sea', the Magistrate of Tenasserim

---

[2] Copy of the first part of a report from Major Kyd relative to the Settlements at Prince of Wales Island and the Andamans with its appendix, 4 March 1795, Reports of the surgeons at Port Cornwallis during the years 1793 and 1794, IOR G/34/1 ff. 379–518.

[3] W. Grey, secretary to government Bengal, to J. W. Dalrymple, under secretary to government of India, 29 February 1856; Henry Hopkinson, commissioner of Arakan, to Grey, 8 February 1856, cited in M. V. Portman, *A History of Our Relations with the Andamanese, vol. I* (Calcutta: Superintendent of Government Printing, 1899), 189–97.

[4] Governor-General Canning to the Court of Directors, 22 April 1856, enc. A. Bogle, Commissioner Tenasserim and Martaban Provinces, to G. Edmonstone, secretary to government of India, cited in Portman, *A History of Our Relations, vol. 1*, 197–204.

wrote, 'bounded by its own territories and on the high road to many of its chief emporia'.[5]

Governor-General Canning remained sceptical, and set up a survey party under the direction of Bengal army surgeon F. J. Mouat to gather further information.[6] His planned survey was quickly overtaken by events, for in the middle of these discussions much of North India broke out in revolt. There were mass jailbreaks, following rebel attacks on Company prisons. The British government had no means of securing the many thousands of escaped prisoners who they were able to recapture, or the rebels and mutineers tried, convicted and sentenced by special tribunals. By the time Mouat left Calcutta, therefore, he was issued with new instructions: he was not to gather information but to select the best site for a penal colony.[7] As officer-in-charge of the Andamanese M. V. Portman wrote later, if the cause of colonization was the British desire to dominate and pacify Islanders, its catalyst was the 1857 Revolt.[8]

The first batch of 200 convicted mutineers and rebels arrived in the Andamans in March 1858, and they were landed at Chatham under the charge of J. P. Walker, who had previously been the Superintendent of Agra Jail, which was at the time one of the largest prisons in the world. They were joined by almost 4,000 transportees convicted in the aftermath of the 1857 Revolt. Death rates during the first eighteen months of colonization were appalling, and about one-third of the convicts then transported died. But as the jungles and swamps were cleared and convicts were moved from canvas shelters to wooden barracks, the health of the settlement improved. Through the exertions of convict forced labour, the Andaman settlement expanded year on year, and the British continued to use it as a penal colony.[9] They transported some 80,000 criminal convicts to the Islands during the period to the 1930s, and about 1,000 political prisoners, most famously about 350 nationalist agitators during the period 1910 to 1916 and again in 1932. Ordinary convicts were put to

---

[5] J. C. Haughton, Magistrate Tenasserim and Martaban Provinces, to Bogle, 3 March 1856, cited in Portman, *A History of Our Relations, vol. 1*, 198.

[6] Canning's Minute; Canning to the Court of Directors, 8 April 1857, cited in Portman, *A History of Our Relations, vol. 1*, 203–4, 206–7.

[7] C. Beadon, secretary to government of India, to F. J. Mouat, G. F. Playfair and J. A. Heathcote, 20 November 1857, IJC 15 January 1858, IOR P.188.49.

[8] Portman, *A History of Our Relations, vol. I*, 186. For a detailed account of the 1857 survey and the decision to recolonize the Andamans in the aftermath of the Indian revolt, see Clare Anderson, *The Indian Uprising of 1857–8: Prisons, Prisoners and Rebellion* (London: Anthem, 2007), chapter 5.

[9] Anderson, *The Indian Uprising*, chapter 5; Satadru Sen, *Disciplining Punishment: Colonialism and Convict Society in the Andaman Islands* (New Delhi: Oxford University Press, 2000); Aparna Vaidik, *Imperial Andamans: Colonial Encounter and Island History* (Basingstoke: Palgrave, 2010).

forced labour on various developmental projects; political prisoners were punished through exile and isolation. Many of the latter were incarcerated in the Islands' notorious Cellular Jail, a panoptican structure with a central watchtower and radiating three-storey wings that was opened in 1906.[10]

With the penal colonization of the Andamans began the decimation of the Islands' indigenous peoples. From the first years of British settlement, they were made subject to violent kidnaps and confinement, and subjected to various forms of industrial training, for the purpose of 'civilization'. Populations dwindled, partly after violent colonial incursions and indigenous retaliation, and partly due to the spread of disease, including high rates of stillbirth probably caused by syphilis. During the period after 1858, the British veered between policies of tribal incorporation, separate containment and non-contact. The changing ideas about indigenous–settler relations might be seen as the historical background to post-colonial forms of reservation, and the debates around them, which are one focus of this book and continue into the present day.[11]

Over the years, there were various government inspections of the Islands, underpinned by extensive correspondence and productive of voluminous reports. In the years prior to the construction of the Cellular Jail, these were Charles Napier (1865), H. Nelson Davies (1867), J. S. Campbell and H. W. Norman (1874), A. Mackenzie (1886), C. J. Lyall and A. S. Lethbridge (1890). After 1906, there were reports in 1913 (Reginald Craddock), 1920 (Indian Jails Committee), 1925 (Alexander Muddiman), 1933 (F.A. Barker) and 1935 (Henry Craik). These reports made various interventions into the management of the penal colony, as well as over time suggesting how it might become more penal in character, how it might strive for economic productivity and self-sufficiency, and how it might encourage convict rehabilitation and permanent settlement.

---

[10] A. N. Aggarwal, *The Heroes of Cellular Jail* (Patiala: Publication Bureau, Punjabi University, 1995); L. P. Mathur, *Kala Pani: History of Andaman and Nicobar Islands with a Study of India's Freedom Struggle* (New Delhi: Eastern Book Corporation, 1985), 73–125. Many political prisoners wrote accounts of their incarceration in the Andamans. See David Arnold, 'The Self and the Cell: Indian Prison Narratives as Life Histories', in David Arnold and Stuart H. Blackburn (eds.), *Telling Lives in India: Biography, Autobiography, and Life History* (Bloomington: Indiana University Press, 2004), 29–53.

[11] Vishvajit Pandya, *In the Forest: Visual and Material Worlds of the Andaman Islanders 1858–2000* (Lanham, MD: University Press of America, 2009). See also Clare Anderson, 'Colonization, Kidnap and Confinement in the Andamans Penal Colony, 1771–1864', *Journal of Historical Geography* 37, 1 (2011), 68–81. Satadru Sen, *Savagery and Colonialism in the Indian Ocean: Power, Pleasure and the Andaman Islanders* (New York: Routledge, 2010); UNESCO, *The Jarawa Tribal Reserve Dossier: Cultural & Biological Diversities in the Andaman Islands*, Pankaj Sekhsaria and Vishvajit Pandya (eds.), (Paris: UNESCO, 2010), 212; Claire Wintle, *Colonial Collecting and Display: Encounters with Material Culture from the Andaman and Nicobar Islands* (Oxford: Bergahan, 2013).

Ultimately, following the critical tone of the report of the Indian Jails Committee (1920), the British decided to abolish the penal colony. However, there was insufficient jail capacity on the mainland for this policy to be effected, and transportation continued. More than 1,000 Moplah convicts were transported to the Islands' capital Port Blair after the Malabar Rebellion of 1921, and given land around Bamboo Flat. They were joined by 'volunteer' convicts, who chose transportation under relatively favourable conditions over continued incarceration in mainland jails. After serving a limited term, they were released as near-free settlers.[12]

A few hundred non-convict settlers were shipped to the Andamans during the colonial era too, primarily to plug labour gaps. Though they were neither criminally convicted nor sentenced to transportation, these settlers were certainly coerced migrants. In 1920, Karen people from Bassein (Burma) were shipped to the Islands under the Baptist missionary Reverend Lugyi. They settled in Webi, in North Andaman, and worked as forest labourers.[13] A few Ranchis from Chotanagpur in Bihar were also recruited at about this time, and also as labourers in the forest department.[14] The Bhantus were a tribe of supposedly hereditary criminals from North Central India. Between 1926 and 1928, almost 300 of them were shipped to the Islands under the purview of the Salvation Army, which was paid to oversee the Bhantus by the government of India. They settled down as agriculturalists in the villages of Caddelgunj and Aniket.[15] By the 1930s, then, the Islands had become quite socially complex. Living there were the indigenous inhabitants, convicts, ex-convicts, convict descendants (the local born) and these various other coerced migrant groups.

In 1937, following a mass hunger strike, the last political prisoners were repatriated to India.[16] Just two years later, the world went to war. When Japan entered the war in the east in 1941, they invaded Burma, and it was not long before they occupied the Andamans. The

---

[12] Taylor C. Sherman, 'From Hell to Paradise? Voluntary Transfer of Convicts to the Andaman Islands, 1921–1940', *Modern Asian Studies* 43, 2 (2009), 367–88.

[13] Palash Chandra Coomar, *Tradition and Transformation in an Immigrant Island Society: The Karen of Andaman Islands* (New Delhi: Abhijeet Publications, 2009).

[14] O. P. Verma, 'The Working Composition of the Ranchi Tribal Labourers in Andaman and Nicobar Islands: A Case Study of Baratang Island', *Journal of Social Research* 19, 2 (1976), 114–24.

[15] Palash Chandra Coomar, *Migration and Social Change: A Study of the Bhantu of Andaman Islands* (Calcutta: Anthropological Survey of India, 1997); Palash C. Coomar and Manis K. Raha, 'Family among the Bhantu of Andamans', *Journal of the Indian Anthropological Society*, 24, 2 (1989), 122.

[16] Pramod Kumar Srivastava, 'Resistance and Repression in India: The Hunger Strike at the Andaman Cellular Jail in 1933', *Crime, History and Societies* 7, 2 (2003), 81–102.

British evacuated Rangoon and Port Blair on the 7 and 13 March 1942, respectively, and the Japanese invaded on 23 March 1942. They released all the convicts and arrested the two remaining British officials, Chief Commissioner Charles Waterfall and his assistant A. J. Bird. Initially, the population assisted the Japanese, collaborating with them in the administration of the Islands as well as their larger anti-British imperial and pan-Asian agenda. Importantly, Islanders set up a branch of the Indian Independence League. It was not long, however, before the occupation turned sour. The Japanese publicly executed Bird, and arrested hundreds of ordinary people, on trumped-up charges of spying for the British. The British had during 1942 through 1943 managed to land four missions on the Islands, and from there directed air and submarine raids against Port Blair. They had been assisted by villagers in Ferrargunj and Wimberleygunj, as well as Ranchi forest labourers. Against this backdrop, in October 1943, the leader of the Provisional Indian Government, Subhas Chandra Bose, visited Port Blair.[17] He was received as a hero, though the Japanese kept him away from the locals, and he was seemingly unaware of their brutal treatment, which included death by torture and mass executions. By the time the Japanese surrendered in a formal ceremony on 7 October 1945, the Islands had been reduced to a state of extreme privation and near starvation.[18]

The British returned to the Islands to oversee their rehabilitation. Under Chief Commissioner N. K. Paterson, they abolished the penal colony and liberated all remaining convicts. The eventual transfer of power came when the first chief commissioner of independent India, Imam-ul-Majid, was appointed in 1947. Although the Islands acquired notoriety under the British colonial regime and were devastated by the Japanese occupation, the stigma attached to them perhaps wore off sooner than expected. In the aftermath of Indian Independence and Partition in 1947, about 500 refugee families, fleeing the communal violence that broke out on the subcontinent, readily agreed to be 'rehabilitated' into a region they had hitherto feared.[19] They were joined

---

[17] For a fascinating recent biography, see Sugata Bose, *His Majesty's Opponent: Subhas Chandra Bose and India's Struggle Against Empire* (Cambridge, MA: Harvard University Press, 2012).

[18] B. B. Lall, *A Regime of Fears and Tears (History of the Japanese Occupation of the Andaman Islands)* (New Delhi: Farsight Publishers, 1992); Rabin Roychowdhury, *Black Days in Andaman and Nicobar Islands* (New Delhi: Manas Publications, 2004).

[19] Swapan Kumar Biswas, *Colonization and Rehabilitation in the Andaman Islands* (New Delhi: Abhijeet Publications, 2009); Sabyasachi Basu Ray Chaudhuri, 'Exiled to the Andamans: The Refugees from East Pakistan', in Pradip Kumar Bose (ed.), *Refugees in West Bengal: Institutional Processes, Contested Identities* (Calcutta: MCRG, 2000), 131–9; Sabyasachi Basu Roychowdhury, 'Exiled in the Andamans: The Refugees of East

by other batches from East Bengal in the 1950s. Indeed, they came to make their homes in a place they perceived to be free of the social hierarchies, prejudices and conflicts of mainland India – social gradations that had been dissolved and remade by the social and cultural syncretism effected through the transportation of convicts from all over the subcontinent. Meantime, however, the local-born population – many of whom had been economically ruined by the war – began to resent the seemingly favourable conditions that the new settlers enjoyed. This drew a line of distinction around the local borns – the descendants of convicts – who began to call themselves 'pre-42' settlers. In the 1960s, free settlers began to migrate in greater numbers from the mainland, and so more housing was needed in and around Port Blair, in particular.[20] As land and forest clearance and infrastructure work progressed and expanded in the 1950s and 60s, during this period we find the historical roots of one of the biggest social issues in the Islands today: the encroachment of settlers onto reserved tribal land.[21]

The Andaman Islands, then, have a complex and entangled history: they constitute and remain a place at the centre of networks of governance, coercion and mobility that span the Bay of Bengal, South and Southeast Asia and beyond; where the colonized could also be colonizers; and where old hierarchies could give way to the making of new social structures. Its geographical situation in the Bay of Bengal has, over time, given rise to particular geopolitical relationships with the colonial metropole (Britain), the mainland (as Islanders call continental India), Burma, the Straits of Malacca and Japan. As is often recognized, colonization and settlement –

Pakistan', in Pradip Kumar Bose (ed.), *Refugees in West Bengal: Institutional Processes and Contested Identities* (Calcutta: Calcutta Research Group, 2000); and Uditi Sen, 'Dissident Memories: Exploring Bengali Refugee Narratives in the Andaman Islands', in Panikos Panayi and Pippa Virdee (eds.), *Refugees and the End of Empire: Imperial Collapse and Forced Migration in the Twentieth Century* (Basingstoke: Palgrave Macmillan, 2011), 219–44.

[20] Kumar Suresh Singh (ed.), *People of India: Andaman and Nicobar Islands, Volume XII* (New Delhi: Anthropological Survey of India, 1994).

[21] For general overviews of migration and settlement, see S. K. Bhattacharya, *Sagarkanya Andaman* (Calcutta: Swati Prashani, 1983); S. K. Bhattacharya, P. C. Dutta and S. Bhattacharya, 'The Migrant Oraon in the Andaman: Demographic Aspects', *Journal of Indian Anthropological Society* 20, 1 (1985), 86–92; Sabyasachi Basu Ray Chaudhuri, 'Exiled to the Andamans: The Refugees of East Pakistan', in Pradip Kumar Bose (ed.), *Refugees in West Bengal: Institutional Practices and Contested Identities* (Calcutta: Calcutta Research Group, 2000); Kiran Dhingra, *The Andaman and Nicobar Islands in the Twentieth Century: A Gazetteer* (New Delhi: Oxford University Press, 2005); Rabin Roychowdhury, *The Untold Andaman and Nicobar Islands* (New Delhi: Manas Publications, 2011); A. K. Joshi, *Emigration and Social Change: A Sociological Study of Early Emigrants of the Andamans* (New Delhi: Rawat Publications, 2005); Kailash, 'Peaceful Coexistence: Lessons from Andamans', *Economic and Political Weekly* 35, 32 (2000), 2859–65; Singh (ed.), *People of India*.

even that effected through the exploitation of some of the most marginalized peoples of Empire – has ushered in profound environmental and
human degradation and devastation. And yet, at the same time, the
seemingly peaceful coexistence in the Islands of people from all over South
Asia has led to the often-cited notion that they are a 'mini India', a place of
'unity in diversity'. But what is less well understood are the ways in which
indigenous peoples and settlers alike have made sense of colonialism and
its aftermath; and how they express their relationship to the land, to
Empire or nation, and to each other. Such an appreciation will assist us
in understanding whether 'mini India' as a social form has been produced
out of nationalist or statist narratives, or has developed out of the Islands'
inner history and social dynamics, rather than through any easy replication
of mainland social formations. How, we ask in the chapters that follow, are
ethnicity, caste, cultural distinction, historical memory and a sense of
belonging articulated in the Islands, and how do they relate to the transformation of space into place?

Collaboration, integration, relationships

The aim of this book is to develop a historicized analytical approach that
addresses these gaps in understanding, and unpicks the nature and
meaning of some of the contemporary problems, issues and debates
related to the complexities of the social and cultural formation of the
Andaman Islands. We contend that such an analysis requires scholarly
collaboration and integration at a number of levels. First, we bring
together the island spaces of the Andamans with the Indian mainland
and beyond, and we ask questions about what work a Bay of Bengal–
centred cartography of the British Empire and its aftermath in South Asia
can do. Second, we foreground in our analysis the making of historic and
contemporary relationships between the various communities that constitute the Islands' population today, rather than seeing particular groups
of people as necessarily distinct or isolated from each other. This enables
us to think beyond the categories of state governmentality, and to centre
the peoples of the Islands rather than their political interlocutors in our
analysis. Third, we seek to cross the invisible line of scholarly convention
that frequently separates the 'colonial' from the 'post-colonial'. Here, it is
not just that we wish to stress the ongoing economic, social and cultural
effects of the British Empire, as we certainly do, but that we want to show
how and for what purpose since Indian Independence the 'colonial' has
been invoked in the Islands, and what the nature of that invocation has
meant for the way in which history in the Andamans is understood,
interpreted and represented.

In each of these respects, our integrative approach has compelled us towards a multidisciplinary engagement – with theory, with archives and with ethnographic research. We have considered in the same frame of analysis histories, sociologies and anthropologies of the Islands; historic papers, texts, photographs and inscriptions; and monuments, memorials and other sites of memory and commemoration. We have thought about the relationship between these literatures, material traces and representations of Empire, and what the descendants of convicts and other settlers have told us about the past, and their individual and collective family genealogies. We have listened to the stories and narratives of the indigenous peoples and refugees of the Islands, to reflect upon their construction of history in the world today. Our research has included work in colonial and post-colonial archives in India, the Andamans, North America and Great Britain. It has incorporated interviews, anthropological work and ethnographic observation. Our point in working with people living in the Islands has neither been to verify or to add nuance to the always partial and incomplete archive, nor to seek out the roots or 'truth' of our anthropological and ethnographic observations in written texts, but rather to explore what history means in the Andamans and how that meaning has been constituted historically and in the present day.

In this sense, the collaboration that underpins this book is a productive engagement between ourselves as scholars, with our distinct areas of research expertise, and between history, ethnography and anthropology. *New Histories* will be of obvious interest to scholars of the Andamans, and of South Asia and the Bay of Bengal; however, it seeks to make further contributions even more broadly: to the history and contemporary politics of *inter alia* indigenous–settler relations, colonization, land, migration, environment, labour, penal transportation, refugees and tribal welfare, in India and other national or imperial contexts.[22] It shows also, we hope, the value of a collaborative and multidisciplinary approach to other

[22] Sunil S. Amrith, *Crossing the Bay of Bengal: The Furies of Nature and the Fortunes of Migrants* (Cambridge, MA: Harvard University Press, 2013); Sunil Amrith, 'Tamil Diasporas across the Bay of Bengal', *American Historical Review* 114, 3 (2009), 547–72; Tracy Banivanua Mar and Penny Edmonds (eds.), *Making Settler Colonial Space: Perspectives on Race, Place and Identity* (Basingstoke: Palgrave, 2010); Joya Chatterji, 'Dispositions and Destinations: Refugee Agency and "Mobility Capital" in the Bengal Diaspora, 1947–2007', *Comparative Studies in Society and History* 55, 2 (2013), 273–304; Tim Harper and Sunil Amrith (eds.), 'Sites of Asian Interaction', *Modern Asian Studies* 46, special issue 02 (2012), 273–304; Stuart Macintyre and Anna Clark, *The History Wars* (Melbourne: Melbourne University Press, 2003); Sujit Sivasundaram, 'Ethnicity, Indigeneity, and Migration in the Advent of British Rule to Sri Lanka', *American Historical Review* 115, 2 (2010), 428–52; Bruce Tranter and Jed Donoghue, 'Convict Ancestry: A Neglected Aspect of Australian Identity', *Nations and Nationalism* 9, 4 (2003), 555–77.

geographically or thematically different studies of colonial history and their post-colonial afterlives.

The kernel of our intellectual framework came out of a realization that in large part, previous scholarship on the Andamans (including our own) has been historically, sociologically or anthropologically grounded, and has split the Islands' various communities into discrete entities according to the particular disciplinary or thematic interests of its author. The historiography of the Islands is quite typical of this, for it has focused on particular periods of colonial rule and on the experiences of specific communities, notably convicts, tribals, settlers and refugees. Though not completely absent, these works often hint at but rarely pursue the interconnections between colonial practices as they played out across communities. For instance, despite an interest in the sociology of migration in the Andamans, literatures of colonization, punishment, modernity and governmentality have not been linked systematically to those of imperial expansion, settlement and 'development'. Neither have they been understood as part of a connected history of practices of containment and confinement that work across communities, and stretch across colonial and post-colonial regimes. Arguably, in this respect, penal transportation, coerced migration, settler rehabilitation, the 'double displacement' of refugees and tribal reservation can all be linked together in important ways. Of particular interest in this regard are the hierarchies among the constitutive social groups in the Islands formed by the successive policies of settlement and resettlement. These hierarchies relate to the varying privileges granted to each group in terms of land holdings, forest resources, taxes, and access to employment in government. A major concern of this study is to understand how such hierarchies were instituted under the colonial regime, and how they continue to be negotiated under the political dispensation of the Indian state.

Of further interest in this respect is the relationship between the Islands and the mainland. Although the 'view from the mainland' is an important element of the book, its critical focus will be on the 'view from within the Islands'. We seek to situate the Andamans not solely within the historical narratives of colonial and post-Partition politics on the Indian mainland but within the larger history of the development of the Andaman Islands: from penal colony, to self-supporting colony, to directly administered Union Territory of the Indian state. Bringing together these two perspectives – mainland and island centred – will help unravel the structural continuities in the historical experience of the Islands from colonial to present times, to understand their relationship with the mainland and to offer new possibilities in approaching their complex social formations.

Our point of entry is an attempt to forge an integrated understanding of the peoples of the Islands, during the colonial and post-colonial periods, in order to address the ways in which the population of the islands understands land, society and history. The communities we will focus on include the Islands' indigenous peoples (known locally as 'tribals'); the colonial official establishment; convicts and their descendants (called 'local born'); other colonial era settlers including the Bhantu 'criminal tribes' of north India, Karen and Ranchi forest labourers from Burma and India, Moplah 'rebel' deportees from south India; and the Bengali refugees who went to the Islands after Independence. Previously, these communities have been represented as separate social and cultural groups, and scholars have carved boundaries around them accordingly, transforming them into unconnected 'anthropological', 'transported', 'deported', or 'settler' subjects and/or citizens. Each group has been viewed as a social enclave, and there has been little attempt to conceptualize them as interrelated components of a complex plural society with a shared – or imagined as shared – history. Though several commentators have highlighted the continuities between tribal experiences of colonial and post-colonial settlement,[23] a more socially inclusive discussion on their relationships with convicts, local born, settlers and refugees has been lacking. Further, because of the relatively recent colonization and early history of the Andamans as a penal colony, it is today widely assumed that Indian mainland social hierarchies and distinctions are completely irrelevant in the Islands. Whilst they have certainly been transformed, neither this belief nor the relationship between the islands and the mainland has ever been subject to rigorous analysis.

This failure to make connections across Andamans communities, and between the Islands and the mainland, emerges in part because scholars have known relatively little about important areas of the Islands' human history. We have not historicized the development of local-born (convict descended) communities and their political associations; and only very recently have we learned something of programmes of refugee resettlement in the post-Bengal Partition years (1949–76). Meanwhile, Japan's wartime occupation of the Andamans has been entirely written out of the larger history of the Second World War, despite two good, locally written studies.[24]

---

[23] Vishvajit Pandya, *Above the Forest: A Study of Andamanese Ethnoanemology, Cosmology, and the Power of Ritual* (New Delhi: Oxford University Press, 1993); Sita Venkateswar, *Development and Ethnocide: Colonial Practices in the Andaman Islands* (Copenhagen: IWGIA, 2004).

[24] Lall, *A Regime of Fears and Tears*; Roychowdhury, *Black Days*.

This book presents a new social and cultural history of the Islands that looks outwards from this empirical and disciplinary myopia and will be of relevance today. We explore relations between tribal peoples and settlers, and the relationship between mainland and islands. We interrogate the relationship between the past and the present. Our historical analysis works out of contemporary concerns, but we stress the importance of history in the way in which Islanders make political and cultural sense of their everyday lives. Those same, present-day concerns have formed the basis of our framework of analysis, use and sharing of research tools from history, ethnography and anthropology. Our work spans the colonial and post-colonial periods. We draw on historical archives, including for the first time those held in Port Blair, both by the Andaman and Nicobar Administration, as well as privately. We conducted extensive fieldwork and interviewing in the Islands during the period 2010–3.

Thus we address issues of tribal 'reservation', forest labour, and refugee rehabilitation schemes, from our insights into regimes of penal labour on the Islands. Explorations of the relations within and between the penal colony and later settlements similarly draw upon our understanding of social identity and community formation among the convicts and their families. Anthropological research on the Islands' indigenous communities strives to understand their troubled relations with Bengali refugees in the areas bordering tribal reserves. We stress, again, that our goal is to move beyond area studies, and to suggest future possibilities for integrated histories of other spaces of transportation, migration, and settlement in similar colonial frontier zones across the Bay of Bengal, the Indian Ocean, and beyond. In this endeavour, we hope to open up research questions that go beyond our immediate frame of inquiry.

Landscape, space and place

Having outlined a brief history of the Andamans and dwelled at some length on the nature and significance of our integrated approach, we turn now to an elaboration of two of the structuring themes that scaffold the chapters that follow. The first is landscape, and the second is space. The use of these structuring themes has allowed us to write an overlapping narrative that traverses the broad spectrum of theoretical approaches to landscape and space and brings them into productive dialogue. The study of landscape has in recent times developed into a truly interdisciplinary field of inquiry in geography, architecture, archaeology, anthropology, philosophy and history. This development is largely attributed to the seminal works of the human geographer Denis Cosgrove.[25] Cosgroves's *Social Formations and Symbolic Landscapes* is still cited as a path-breaking text in its application of a cultural Marxist approach to the study of landscape. Cosgrove departed from a narrow confining view of landscape as an artistic or literary response to the visible scene to argue that 'landscape' is not a neutral term but an ideologically charged and geographically contingent way of seeing whose development paralleled the transition to capitalism in Europe from the fifteenth to late nineteenth century.[26] The visual ideology of landscape, in other words, was complicit with physical acts of appropriation, colonization and settlement of landscapes. Cosgrove was keen to draw attention to the complex relationships between cultural production and material practice. It was important to address the visual aspect of landscape interpretation particularly to focus on ways in which it facilitated acts of territorial appropriation and colonization; however, Cosgrove maintained that landscape as a 'way of seeing' could not be confined to mediated representations in art and literature alone. Landscape had to be understood as a broader concept pertaining to how we view, interpret and configure space in contingent political, social, economic and cultural contexts.[27] Following Cosgrove, the idea of landscape was positioned squarely within the sphere of political economy, social and cultural practice. Barabara Bender, for instance, explored the idea of landscape as a medium through which dominant ideologies and political power could physically express presence. Landscape was about entrance and exclusion, about many voices mobilizing different histories in a constantly changing environment.[28]

In short, the new approaches to landscape drew attention to the inherently dialectical nature of landscape as a physical and built environment, as a context for human economic, social and political activity, and at the same time, as a symbolic system offering rich interpretative templates for such activities.[29] Other more pronouncedly 'non-representational' and phenomenological approaches to landscape sought to include interpretations of our practical uses of the physical environment as nature and territory, and simultaneously our understanding of these as sites of

---

[25] Denis Cosgrove, *Social Formation and the Symbolic Landscape,* 2nd edn. (Madison: University of Wisconsin Press, 1998).

[26] Cosgrove, *Social Formation*, 1.

[27] Denis Cosgrove, 'Modernity, Community and the Landscape Idea', *Journal of Material Culture* 11 (2006), 49–66.

[28] Barbara Bender, *Landscape, Politics, Perspectives* (Oxford: Berg, 1993), 3–10.

[29] For a detailed survey of these approaches, see John Wylie, *Landscapes, Key Ideas* (London: Routledge, 2007).

'embodiment', 'inhabitation' and 'dwelling'.[30] As Emma Waterton puts it, 'the new theoretical turn has firmed up and fleshed out a series of longer standing assumptions that had already rendered landscapes affective, embodied, sensuous and material'.[31]

Our book draws upon both representational and phenomenological approaches to landscape to explore sites and contexts within which the relationship between mainland India and the Andaman Islands remains entangled in complex ways. These entanglements are often asymmetrical and steeped in relationships of power, but are also sites that are generative of spaces of contest, collaboration and negotiation. Our focus on entangled landscapes seeks to interface narratives of colonization, development and appropriation of the Island space with narratives of belonging, dwelling, agency, imagination and identity.

We locate our study of landscape within larger studies of space, spatiality and place making that have generated a vibrant common ground for interdisciplinary scholarship. Edward Soja's notion of the 'socio-spatial dialectic', in this context, remains central to an understanding of space as a social product rooted in practices, disciplinary power and ideology.[32] Such an approach marks a significant move away from earlier absolutist notions to more constructivist conceptualizations.[33] These approaches to space focus on developing perspectives on the social construction of space and also on people's sense of places.[34] The intersection with landscape studies occurs at the point of understanding not space *per se*, but on 'spatialization' or 'spatial practices' – the different processes by which space comes to be organized, experienced and represented. As Paul Carter describes in the classic *The Road to*

---

[30] Such studies drew upon philosophical and critical writings of Martin Heidegger, Maurice Merleau Ponty and Michel de Certeau, among others. For a detailed discussion, see Emma Waterton, 'Landscape and Non-Representational Theories', in Peter Howard, Ian Thompson and Emma Waterton (eds.), *The Routledge Companion to Landscape Studies* (London: Routledge, 2013), 66–75.

[31] Waterton, 'Landscape and Non-Representational Theories', 73.

[32] Edward W. Soja, 'The Socio-Spatial Dialectic', *Annals of the Association of American Geographers* 70, 2 (1980), 207–25.

[33] David Harvey, *Spaces of Global Capitalism: Towards a Theory of Uneven Geographical Development* (London: Verso, 2006); Henri Lefebvre, *The Production of Space* (Oxford: Blackwell, 1991); Doreen Massey and Pat M. Jess, *A Place in the World? Places, Cultures and Globalization* (Oxford: Oxford University Press, 1995); Philip J. Etherington, 'Placing the Past: "Groundwork" for a Spatial Theory of History', *Rethinking History: The Journal of Theory and Practice* 11, 4 (2007), 465–93.

[34] Alan Lester, 'Spatial Concepts and the Historical Geographies of British Colonialism', in A. Thompson (ed.), *Writing Imperial Histories* (Manchester: Manchester University Press, 2013), 118–42; C. W. J. Withers, 'Place and the "Spatial Turn" in Geography and in History', *Journal of the History of Ideas* 7, 4 (2009), 637–58.

Botany Bay, there can be no history but spatial history.[35] The transform-ation of space into place, as is now widely understood, is the inevitable outcome of various interactions involving the manipulation of nature through agriculture, architecture and landscaping, and symbolically through activities such as depicting, narrating and remembering.

The argument that follows from this is that all these activities involve territorial claims, reorganization of livelihoods, spatial segregation and struggles, the categorization of 'insiders' and 'outsiders' and the invoca-tion and invention of traditions and cultural practices reinforcing notions of Self and Other. These in turn index different levels of territorial and social stratification, identity claims, power relations and contesta-tions. The challenge in the multidisciplinary initiative represented in this book has been to explore these spatial dynamics through attention to their material social and symbolic implications. The use of the analytical tropes of landscape and space has allowed us to elaborate a running thematic of this book, that of the making of the Andaman Islands as a distinctive social space on the margins of the Indian nation state.

This focus on the relational dynamics between the Islands and the mainland has allowed us to re-examine the Island space both in the context of the Indian subcontinent as well as within a larger Indian Ocean framework. Our book seeks to deploy the spatial lens to study the Andaman Islands for the critical implications it has in understanding both its colonial past and its contemporary history. Recent studies on 'Islands' as units of historical or geographical study have drawn attention to the need to critically engage with the structural and discursive inter-ventions that underpin our common assumptions about islands as dis-crete, territorially bounded units marked by isolation and distance.[36] Godfrey Baldacchino and Eric Clark, in a remarkably critical vein, pro-pose that if Islands provoke imagination, of a particular understanding of 'islandness', there is a corresponding action of 'islanding' that creates and sustains it. In their own words, '[B]y adding the verb to island, islanding, to our theoretical instruments, we are better equipped to maintain perspectives on islands as historical processes of "weaves of existence", as currently ongoing and commonly contested process of creation and becoming, with largely indeterminate futures'.[37] Elaborating the argument further, Baldacchino and Clark write:

---

[35] Paul Carter, *The Road to Botany Bay: An Exploration of Landscape and History* (Chicago: University of Chicago Press, 1987).

[36] Sujit Sivasundaram, *Islanded: Britain, Sri Lanka and the Bounds of an Indian Ocean Colony* (Chicago: University of Chicago Press, 2013).

[37] Godfrey Baldacchino and Eric Clark, 'Guest Editorial Introduction: Islanding Cultural Geographies', *Cultural Geographies* 20, 2 (2013), 129–32, 130–1.

We need this verb [islanding] to mediate and attenuate dizzying oscillations between paradise and prison, openness and closure, roots and routes materiality and metaphor. For grasping the rich weave of relational space and place, such lurid dichotomies oblige constant vigilance.[38]

Clearly, then, the methodological focus of our book dwells on the need to build upon relational approaches to spaces that see them as constituted through interactions, as Doreen Massey puts it, 'from the immensity of the global to the intimately tiny'.[39]

We have drawn inspiration from these studies of space and of islands, in particular within larger national or imperial formations, as well as within the specificities of their local histories, politics and society.[40] Within Indian Ocean studies more specifically, two especially relevant trends have emerged: one charts the history of the sea as a zone of movement and connectedness; the other looks to the colonial politics of 'islanding' spaces in the context of these crossings.[41] These studies are hugely relevant to our understanding of the Andamans as a place of mobility and migration, and of social distinction.

In this context, we draw attention to two new histories of the Andaman Islands that have used the 'spatial lens' to develop new ways to understand the projects of colonization and settlement under the aegis of British rule. In *Imperial Andamans*, Aparna Vaidik has sought to reckon with the 'discursive and captive power of the popular historical narratives in order to reclaim the history of the Andamans from its confinement with colonialist nationalist frameworks and its consequent mythicization as natural prison'.[42] Inspired by the work of scholars David Harvey, Paul Carter, Henri Lefebvre and Derek Gregory, Vaidik has been inspired 'to write a historical narrative of the Andamans in which the Islands appear as the space, the palimpsest where the historical plot unfolds as a space which was constituted by history'.[43] By doing so her book seeks to extricate the Andamans from their foundational metanarratives, associated with the 1857 Revolt, and the construction of the Cellular Jail, which she argues has kept it confined within the bounds of penal history.

---

[38] Baldacchino and Clark, 'Guest Editorial Introduction', 129.
[39] Doreen Massey, *For Space* (London: Sage, 2005), 9.
[40] Godfrey Baldacchino, 'Studying Islands: On Whose Terms? Some Epistemological and Methodological Challenges to the Pursuit of Island Studies', *Island Studies Journal* 3, 1 (2008), 37–56; S. A. Royle, 'Postcolonial Culture on Dependent Islands', *Space and Culture* 13, 2 (2010), 203–15.
[41] Amrith, *Crossing the Bay of Bengal*; Sivasundaram, *Islanded*.
[42] Vaidik, *Imperial Andamans*, 9.   [43] Vaidik, *Imperial Andamans*, 187–91.

While agreeing with Vaidik's methodological focus on 'space', we argue that there are no single narratives that can retell the story of the Andamans as either a colonial or a post-colonial space. The production of the Andaman Islands as an historical space is bound up in multiple narratives of the colonial cultural encounter with tropical wilderness and savagery, of the Revolt of 1857, of the Cellular Jail, and of the Partition of India in 1947. In all these narratives, the Island space has been variously conceptualized, imagined or even mythicized as the pestilential tropics, as natural prison, or more importantly as *terra nullius* or simply empty space. It is these 'mainland' imaginings of the islands, that have configured the material landscape of the Andamans and mediated its sense of place. We argue that islands are poly-semiotic spaces that acquire different meanings from the different vantage points, both of history and of location. What we wish to explore in the chapters that follow are the complex socio-historical relationships that tie the Indian mainland to the Andaman Islands. It is a history of entangled mainland–Island relations from colonial to contemporary times. We try to understand how these entanglements ordered the Island landscape, generated feelings of belonging within it, and created a distinctive visual and discursive vocabulary through which it was viewed and represented by those living outside.

One of the compelling themes brought out through recent writings on the Andamans is that of the failed colony. Vaidik explores this theme in some detail, arguing that while the British may have effectively 'islanded' the Andaman Islands, they failed to 'colonize' them on their own terms.[44] Administrative experience on the Islands brought into focus the facile assumptions about the Islands as a natural prison. The colonizers operated under the misconception that the Islands with their tropical jungles, climate and the presence of ferocious cannibals rendered them a natural prison. However, it was soon found that the Islands' geography worked against the project of adapting the Islands into a penal colony and deeply compromised the meanings of punitive transportation. In fact, the entire penal framework was pulled in contradictory directions – different administrators understood the objectives of penalty differently. Contrary to general assumptions the Andaman system was defined less by coherence and consistency and more by internal fissures and contingent responses by the colonial administration. Settling the colony was inextricably tied to the penal colony. Vaidik argues that it was difficult to develop a colony that was covered with tropical jungles

---

[44] Vaidik, *Imperial Andamans*, 16–34.

and swamps, and was yet to benefit from the development of steam shipping, communication networks and telegraph lines. Both the terrain and the location of the Andaman Islands – in a corner of the Bay of Bengal that lay outside the main commercial routes – made it unattractive in terms of investment initiatives. The added difficulty of procuring adequate and regular supplies of labour made it clear that decades of hard work would be required for any economic project to accrue dividends. Thus, as Vaidik argues, in the long term, the British were not able to transform the Andamans into either a flourishing agricultural colony or a commercial outpost. Nor did the Islands live up to the expectations of a penal judicial space. The failure of the colonial enterprise had to be located in the structural failures of colonization.

The second recent history of the islands that we wish to discuss here is Satadru Sen's *Savagery and Colonialism in the Indian Ocean*. If an intractable terrain militated against the successes of British colonization and development of the Andaman Islands, the relentless intransigence of its indigenous population engendered a deeply ambivalent colonial enterprise. Sen attributes its ceaselessly shifting strategies to its inherent failure to either transform the savage into potential labour or to civilize and tame it on its own terms. He writes:

In the closing decades of the nineteenth century Andamanese savages were not the Calibans that greeted Marco Polo or even Mouat. They were simultaneously dwindling and thriving, but in a great proliferation of mutations . . . Produced by multiple, disjointed and relentlessly experimental British Indian encroachments into the jungle and by the parallel dynamics of exposure (to the scientific/ administrative gaze) and secrecy (distance from civilization, insularity) the savage was a symptom not only of power failures and cross-purposes within the colonial regime but of remarkably successful compromises on its margins.[45]

Sen also draws attention to the ambivalences of the colonial project in the Andamans by arguing that, unlike Australia where penal colonies were established during the period 1787–1868, the settler colonial agenda in the Andamans was informed and mediated by the agenda of British colonialism in the Indian subcontinent. This meant that it ran contrary to what anthropologist Patrick Wolfe has theorized as the organization of the settler-colonial savage encounter. This was marked by phases of confrontation, incarceration and assimilation.[46] According to Sen, the improvised settler colonial model drew upon the colonial project on the Indian mainland and based itself on 'the articulation, management and

---

[45] Sen, *Savagery and Colonialism*, 209–10.
[46] See Patrick Wolfe, *Settler Colonialism and the Transformation of Anthropology* (London: Cassell, 1999).

preservation of social compartments rather than wholesale mergers'.[47] Yet even this model proved ridden with contradiction and compromise.

When the newly independent Indian state acquired control and administrative authority over the Andaman Islands it was thus burdened with the legacies of two ambivalent colonial projects. Notwithstanding the bequest of failure that it had to contend with, the Indian state was evidently enthused by the prospect of beginning all over again. Colonization and development were to begin afresh and the Island space nationalized. It was this new agenda on the Islands, often undergirded by old colonial practices that shaped the relationship between the Islands and mainland India during the years after Independence.

New Histories seeks to understand the emerging contours of the Island–mainland relationship by focusing on the landscape of the Islands as an historical archive bearing the imprints of the legacy of colonial failure on the one hand and the inscription of a nationalist agenda on the other. We ask a series of related questions. How did the dialectics of failure and promise play out on the Island landscape? How was the landscape reordered to define nationalist agenda? How was the nationalist promise perceived within the Islands by the communities whose lives and livelihoods were being reconfigured in the process? How did the Island landscape bear out the numerous quotidian struggles that went into the making of a new sense of place and home in the Islands? And, finally, how does the Island landscape continue to operate as an embattled terrain where mutually contradictory agendas are imagined and represented and perpetuated? How is the mainland–Island relationship sustained through coercion and compromise?

Our focus on 'landscape' of the Andamans is an exercise founded on a cartographic metaphor of 'mapping' as well as a geological metaphor of 'excavating' – involving both an exploration and charting of new terrains of historical research as well as delving into already sedimented histories and memories to understand how the past becomes manifest in the present and has implications for the future. A series of themes that spin around the history of colonization and settlement in the Andamans are woven into this book. We think historically through the politics of settler-indigenous and island–mainland relations, most especially with respect to debates about access to land, natural resources, welfare and employment. We focus on broad questions, to ask why the colonial and post-colonial states assigned convicts and forced settlers to different types of labour and to separate spaces of settlement. We explore how these forcibly

---

[47] Sen, *Savagery and Colonialism*, 56.

segregated communities viewed each other and 'tribal' spatial exclusivity and exclusion over time. We unpack the relationship between colonization, settlement and economic development. We examine how convicts and their descendants, settlers and the state imposed order on the Andamans landscape, and how the natural and built environment has been represented and defined their experiences, including through the 'rule of difference' around gender, race and ethnicity. In sum, the book poses the question: does an integrated history of the Andamans reveal the Islands as socially and culturally contiguous to the mainland, or fundamentally different in some way?

The book's structuring themes of landscape and space will, we hope, enable us to make sense of a range of economic, social and cultural relationships that straddle communities, traverse the colonial and post-colonial periods, and move multi-directionally between islands and mainland across the Bay of Bengal. Here, we would like to return to cartography. How, we wish to ask, does colonial history and its aftermath look when bringing a geographical, social and cultural periphery to the centre of our analysis? Viewed from the Bay of Bengal, the Andaman Islands become an integral part of a history of colonial formations in the Indian Ocean. It offers new ways of understanding the Bay as the context for myriad histories of movement and confinement of 'crossings' and moorings of flows and of boundaries. More significantly, it brings into focus the histories of colonial aftermaths and legacies that significantly alter the imaginative and epistemic frames that inform our understanding of Islands. We will show how Islands reconfigure themselves into new spaces of connectedness and flows once the colonial structures of 'Islanding' are abandoned. We will articulate how people in the Andaman Islands have sought to redefine their peripherality by turning their backs on the Indian mainland and developing new forms of belonging and a new sense of place, home and dwelling within its own bounds.

Contentious, affective and imagined landscapes

We address these questions and issues through the eight chapters that follow. The book is divided into three sections, each centred on a particular theme: contentious landscapes, affective landscapes, and imagined landscapes. Together, the chapters focus on a set of interrelated issues pertaining to indigeneity, migration, the penal colony, war, community formation, development and representation. We offer distinct vantage points, but complementing perspectives, on how these speak to the large issues of mainland–Island relations, the making of place, and understandings of history.

We open the first section with Madhumita Mazumdar's chapter on the troubled legacies of a colonial improving vision in the Andaman Islands (Chapter 2). She looks at the shaping of this vision of improvement through the policies of Chief Commissioner Michael Lloyd Ferrar (1923–31); to argue that the improving ideals embedded in Ferrar's initiatives to make the penal colony into a free settlement in the aftermath of the Great War gave shape to a new socio-spatial order in the Islands. The massive programme of swamp reclamation, agrarian extension, quasi-coerced settlements, and the relentless punitive expeditions against the Islands' indigenous people bequeathed a troubled legacy to the Islands as it came under the rule of the independent Indian state. She concludes that Ferrar's 'improving vision' legitimated a distinctive 'mainland' imagination of the Islands that continues to configure its landscape, manage its social relations, interpret its history and determine its political future.

In Chapter 3, Clare Anderson moves on to explore the ongoing claims of ex-convicts and their descendants (known locally as 'local born') to 'freedom fighting' status, following the Japanese occupation of the Andaman Islands during the Second World War. The chapter seeks both to inject the Andamans into histories of the war in Southeast Asia and to explore their role as an occupied space in the making of a shared history for the new Indian nation in the aftermath of Independence in 1947. It explores the many lines of fracture that opened up between the Islands and the mainland during the 1950s. These were centred on wartime relief, reparation and compensation, and Islanders' political status and identity. A complex history of belonging both to the Islands and to the nation is revealed; and the chapter argues that this is reflected in the history of the production of monuments and memorials, and debates about them by government and Islanders, and across Islands and mainland. This has been underpinned, Anderson suggests, by a complex working-through of local political identities that turn on a broad definition of nationalism and resistance to Empire, and this has produced a heavily contested material landscape through which local and state generated histories of freedom fighting have emerged.

Vishvajit Pandya closes the section with Chapter 4, an exploration of the possibilities of developing an understanding of the Andaman Islands through its 'landscape', as it constitutes itself through memorial sites that invoke notions of sacrifice and martyrdom. Through a multi-sited ethnographic study conducted at five memorial sites, he tries to understand how statist discourses and practices of memorializing, as well as people's own ritual observances of significant events in their collective lives on the Islands, invest the landscape with multiple and often contradictory historical meanings. The chapter focuses on the dialogical relationship between the statist discourse of 'nation making' on the Island and the people's discourse of 'place-making'. The discourses are different yet interconnected by negotiations and compromise revealing in the process inherent mainland–island tensions that continue to define the nation-building project in the Andaman Islands. Chapter 4 elaborates some of themes from the earlier chapters in this section but focuses centrally on the political and cultural logic mediating place-making and nation making projects on the Andamans and tries to understand how multiple regimes of memorializing coexist and interface to constitute the Island landscape as an inherently rhizomatic space with multiple, heterodox and contingent relationships with the politics, history and culture of mainland India.

Section two, 'Affective landscapes', opens with Chapter 5, Anderson's consideration of the historical evolution of the convict-descended population of the Andamans, the local born. Anderson discusses their remarkable success in acquiring land during the penal colony era and shows that the Islands' disciplinary regime produced profound cultural and social changes, relating to mainland norms about labour practices, gender relations and religious affiliations. Associated with this were government efforts to boost local-born community esteem and morale, which were in part effected through the creation of a Local Born Association. The legacies of the penal colony in this respect, Anderson argues, underpin the economic, social and cultural landscape of the Islands today and are central to how local-born people articulate claims of belonging. The ways in which they make sense of their convict history, she suggests, lie at the heart of representations of the Andamans as a place of national distinction – a 'mini India' or place of 'unity in diversity'. They also urge the Islands' incorporation into the India's national history, and as such are a key element of the contemporary articulation of the relationship between the Islands and the mainland.

In Chapter 6, Mazumdar engages with recent revisionist writing on refugee memory and identity in the Andaman Islands to understand why post-Partition Bengali refugee narratives in the Islands do not always resonate with themes dominant in mainland India. She explores why instead of ready expressions of pain at the experience of violence, and displacement and lost homes, one encounters engaging narratives of belonging and dwelling in the Islands. Her chapter draws upon fieldwork conducted amongst Bengali refugee families who came to the Andaman Islands under various rehabilitation schemes of the Government from 1949 to 1976 and focuses on the area of Port Blair and the Middle Andaman region. She argues that Bengali refugee narratives of early life in the Islands came to be dominated by discussions of community life, faith and the Matua sect. Mazumdar looks at the early history of this anti-caste Hindu sect and shows how its community of believers brought their faith into the Islands and made it a critical point of reference in their stories of survival in an alien landscape. The chapter argues that it is in these narratives of faith, devotion and the immersive space of community life that Bengali refugee experience and identity in the Andaman Islands could be rethought and understood.

Chapter 7 is based on Pandya's ethnographic research among two groups of Jarawa elders and young men in the Reserve Territory located on the fringes of Bengali settlements in Tirrur and Kadamtalla, and brings together indigenous narratives of dwelling in the forest that have critical implications for policy-makers keen on mainstreaming Jarawas to settled forms of life. It tries to retrieve the voices of members of the Jarawa community struggling to articulate the dilemmas of their life choices vis-à-vis the policies of tribal welfare. Although expressed in symbolic and metaphoric language, the chapter tries to glean the Jarawa community's larger argument against life in a 'cleared' space outside the forest. It shows how the Jarawa deploy a discourse of light and luminosity to distinguish the existential challenges that face them in the space of the forest on the one hand and that of the settlement on the other. Although steeped in a language of affect and expressed in deeply nuanced metaphors, the Jarawa arguments against the settlement are indicative of their predicaments of living on the borders of settlements which are perceived as spaces that forge new points of contact with the 'outsider' but spaces that also threaten the structure and practice of life in the forest.

In the final section of the book, 'Imagined landscapes', Anderson and Mazumdar explore issues of visual and textual representation, both historically and in the present day. Chapter 8 takes as its focus visual representations of the penal colony. It suggests that paintings, photographs and lithographs of the Andamans were key to creating metropolitan ideas about the suitability of the Islands as a place of colonization and 'civilization', and especially after the dramatic convict assassination of the Viceroy of India in 1872 as a colony underpinned by orderliness, discipline and control. Anderson draws out the interrelationships between photographs and their derivative images (lithographs), texts and objects, and also proposes that images have important meanings beyond representation *per se*. She argues that sometimes photographs presented images of the Islands that are textually unavailable in archives. Photographic albums in particular could be sites for the constitution of kinship, remembering and identity formation.

Mazumdar, in Chapter 9, turns attention to the visual and textual representations of the Andaman Islands in contemporary contexts and argues that these constitute new battle zones wherein contending perspectives on Island development and its environmental implications are fought out and resolved. She outlines the contours of such a debate around ideas about the Islands' tropicality as it played out in state-produced environmental reports on the one hand and state-sponsored popular travel books on the other. She looks into the visual and textual exchanges between these reports and coffee table books to understand how an argument for environmental conservation could transform into an argument for the promotion of ecotourism, or how proposals to publicize the Islands' tropical ecosystems could lead to its commodification for purposes of tourist consumption. The chapter concludes by arguing that the visual representations of the Islands' tropicality, with its shifts, erasures and silences on the one hand and its excess and eloquence on the other, are indicators of the struggles of the Islands to chart out a coherent developmental strategy that ensures its survival and sustains its economic relevance for mainland India.

New Histories of the Andaman Islands thus works across disciplines and draws on a range of archives and ethnographic fieldwork to explore a series of relationships: between Andaman communities, between the Islands and mainland India, between history and the present, and between conservation and development. The chapters that follow seek to understand the historical constitution of society and culture; to explore community 'belonging'; and to tease out how history is used and contested as a means of nation and identity making. The concepts of landscape and space are central to our analysis; and it is our ambition to present the view from within the Islands, to look outward across the Bay of Bengal to the Indian mainland. Indigenous marginalization, penal colonization, and migration: these are the threads that weave through the heart of each chapter. And so it is to Mazumdar's analysis of one of the key moments in the making of the Andaman landscape, Colonel Ferrar's improving vision, which we first turn.

Part I

Contentious landscapes

2 Improving visions, troubled landscapes: the legacies of colonial Ferrargunj

Madhumita Mazumdar

Introduction

Recent historical writing on the Andaman Islands has sought to move beyond the study of the colonial penal settlement and explore the shifting trajectories of the colonial project on the Islands and its ambivalent legacies on the lives of those who were forced to make their homes there.[1] Anthropological writing, on the other hand, has focused more compellingly on the British colonial encounter with the Islands' indigenous peoples. One study has underscored the embedded projects of 'ethnocide' in the colonial encounter, while another has sought to understand the complexity of the colonial encounter by looking at it from the perspective of the Islands' indigenous communities themselves.[2] Other scholars have begun to study the lives of the Islands' migrant communities, many of whom came to the Andamans either as forest labour or as post-Partition refugees from erstwhile East Pakistan, and later from Sri Lanka. There are stories of many others who migrated more freely from the rest of mainland India in search of better livelihoods.[3] In all these connected histories of colonial and post-colonial projects of colonization and development of the

[1] On the penal settlement in the Andaman Islands, see Clare Anderson, *Legible Bodies: Race, Criminality and Colonialism in South Asia* (Oxford: Berg, 2004); Clare Anderson, *The Indian Uprising of 1857: Prisons, Prisoners and Rebellion* (London: Anthem, 2007), chapter 5; Satadru Sen, *Disciplining Punishment: Colonialism and Convict Society in the Andaman Islands* (New Delhi: Oxford University Press, 2000); Satadru Sen, *Savagery and Colonialism in the Indian Ocean: Power, Pleasure and the Andaman Islanders* (Oxford: Routledge, 2010); and Aparna Vaidik, *Imperial Andamans: Colonial Encounter and Island History* (Basingstoke: Palgrave, 2010).
[2] Sita Venkateswar, *Development and Ethnocide: Colonial Practices in the Andaman Islands* (Copenhagen: IWGA, 2004). Vishvajit Pandya, *In the Forest: Visual and Material Worlds of the Andaman Islanders, 1858–2000* (Lanham, MD: University Press of America, 2009).
[3] Swapan Kumar Biswas, *Colonization and Rehabilitation in the Andaman Islands* (New Delhi: Abhijeet Publications, 2009); Sabyasachi Basu Roychowdhury, 'Exiled in the Andamans: The Refugees of East Pakistan', in Pradip Kumar Bose (ed.), *Refugees in West Bengal: Institutional Processes and Contested Identities* (Calcutta: Calcutta Research Group, 2000); and Uditi Sen, 'Dissident Memories: Exploring Bengali Refugee Narratives in the Andaman Islands', in Panikos Panayi and Pippa Virdee (eds.),

Andaman Islands, one finds the workings of a singularly 'mainland' imagination. More precisely, perhaps, it is a distinctively settler colonial imagination that derives its ideological legitimacy from a broadly implied notion of improvement. Although never explicitly stated in these terms, arguments and the idea of 'improvement' find expression in the myriad ways in which the Islands have been imagined as *terra nullius* or empty space and the radical terms on which its landscape has been shaped, altered and selectively populated. Vishvajit Pandya argues that the idea of *terra nullius* lay at the heart of the colonial imagination of the Islands from its very inception in the eighteenth century. Unlike in other British settler colonies, such as Australia where the doctrine was enshrined in law, the notion of *terra nullius* in the Andaman Islands was subtly and insidiously invoked through survey reports, administrative policies and schemes for colonization and development.[4] This chapter draws upon this argument to put the colonial developmental imaginary that took shape in the interwar years into larger historical perspective.

It argues that after the 1920s, when it was decided to abolish the penal settlement and initiate a free colony, there was a distinctive push towards developing the Islands through a vigorous programme of agricultural extension and a search for suitable colonists. This new colonial agenda became the cornerstone of all subsequent development projects on the Islands and the harbinger of a political, economic and spatial order that redefined the Islands' social relations forever. This overarching argument frames the broad terms of this chapter, yet it looks more specifically into the shaping of a colonial 'improving' vision as it took shape through the policies of Colonel Michael Lloyd Ferrar, Chief Commissioner of the Andaman and Nicobar Islands between 1923–31. It focuses on the trajectory of Ferrar's policies for the colonization and development of Islands and the clues it offers in exploring the ideological charge of 'improvement' and 'agrarianism' in the interwar years. It builds upon both archival and ethnographic resources to understand the legacy of the Ferrar years on the contemporary history of the Islands.

In her explorations of governmentality, development and practices of post-colonial politics in the highlands of Indonesia, Tania Murray Li argues that 'the will to improve' embodied a distinctive governmental rationality underpinned by a notion of 'trusteeship'. 'Trusteeship' is

---

Refugees and the End of Empire: Imperial Collapse and Forced Migration in the Twentieth Century (Basingstoke: Palgrave, 2011), 219–44.

[4] Vishvajit Pandya, 'In Terra Nullius: The Legacies of Science and Colonialism in the Andaman Islands', Public Lecture Series, 'Science, Society and Nature' (New Delhi: Nehru Memorial Museum and Library, Teen Murti, 22 May 2013).

defined as 'the intent which is expressed by one source of agency to develop the capacities of another'. It included programmes to rationalize the use of land, to move populations from place to place, to divide farms from forest and to introduce larger programmes of education and modernization.[5]

The chapter argues that from the mid 1920s it was the 'will to improve' and the certitude of 'trusteeship' that informed mainland India's colonial relations with the Andaman Islands and legitimized its contentious interventions in its landscape, history, memory and identity. It argues that the 'will to improve' articulated itself in complex and even conflicting ways. It mobilized what Li describes as both calculation and *bricolage*.[6] Its programmes could be planned as well as be contingent. The 'will to improve' could be both benign and violent. To govern, as Li quotes Foucault, was to seek not one dogmatic goal 'but a whole series of specific finalities'.[7] The 'will to improve', in other words, included radical interventions on the land on the one hand and the formulation of projects aimed at the settlement, containment and management of populations on the other. It fitted in well with what Satadru Sen describes as a specifically British 'Indian' model of settler colonialism (see Chapter 1).

The chapter's initial focus is on the early 1920s, the period soon after the publication of the Jail Committee's recommendations and the changes wrought by the decision to close the penal settlement. It explores the political changes on the Islands during this period through the career of Ferrar, who presided over a major change in the Islands' land regulations. It draws attention to the durbar of 1926 wherein Ferrar handed over *sanads* or deeds of occupancy, to more than 2,000 self-supporters (convict ticket-of-leave holders) and free colonists in the hope of inaugurating a new phase of agrarian expansion in the Islands. It then follows Ferrar's pursuit of an 'improving' agenda on the Islands premised on the notion of a 'redemptive rurality', understood as the power and reach of a project of agricultural colonization into the moral discourse of the redemption of 'fallen subjects' – in the case of the Andamans, the convict population and their descendants.[8] While the chapter follows whatever

---

[5] Tania Murray Li, *The Will to Improve: Governmentality, Development, and the Practice of Politics* (Durham NC: Duke, 2007), 1.

[6] Li here invokes the arguments of James C. Scott in *Seeing Like the State: How Certain Schemes to Improve the Human Condition Have Failed* (New Haven, CT: Yale University Press, 1998).

[7] Li, *The Will to Improve*, 9.

[8] Ferrar's 'improving vision' invoked a whole range of ideas and sensibilities associated with the agricultural revolution, industrialization and the Age of Reform in England in the eighteenth and nineteenth centuries. For a discussion of some of these ideas, see Asa Briggs, *The Age of Improvement 1783–1867* (London: Longman, 1959); Richard Drayton,

remains of the official records of Ferrar's developmental projects on the Islands, it looks more closely and comprehensively at his personal correspondence with his mother during these years. It may be noted, however, that what goes by the name of Ferrar correspondence in the archival collection at the Cambridge South Asian Studies are largely letters from Ferrar to his mother and not his mother's letters to him. The letters constitute a window into the mind of a colonial administrator on the Islands at a critical period of transition. Ferrar's letters to his mother during these years testify to what Ferrar himself described as the five major projects that absorbed his mind: 'colonization, malaria, lumber sales, dredgers and Jarawas'.[9]

The chapter moves on to explore the legacy of the Ferrar years as they played out in the plans for the colonization and development of the Andamans in the aftermath of the Partition and the renewed claims for a deeper penetration of the Islands through an extension of the agrarian frontier. It concludes by suggesting that the pushing of the agrarian frontier, changes to land regulations and the vision of redemptive rurality ushered in by the colonization and development programmes of the 1920s has had enormous implications in shaping ethnic relations on the Islands today. Indeed, the project embodied violence, for both the redrawing of the agrarian landscape and the agenda of colonization legitimized the forced relocation of the indigenous communities of the Islands and the fixing of territories along ethnic lines. The forest and field today constitute not merely two segments of a seamless landscape but operate as historical markers of a colonial developmental agenda marked by violence, segregation and prejudice. The colonial development project, as it took shape in Ferrargunj, was paradigmatic of the making of new spatial configurations whose troubled legacies continue to define the political relations between the Islands and the Indian mainland.

The penal colony in transition

There is little memory, historical or otherwise, of a man who lent his name to the largest *tehsil*, or local administrative unit, in the Andaman Islands. Few in the Islands today remember either Chief Commissioner

Nature's Government: Science, Imperial Britain and the Improvement of the World (New Haven, CT: Yale University Press, 2000). Also, see R. A. C. Parker, 'Coke of Norfolk and the Agricultural Revolution', *Economic and Social History Review*, 2, 8 (1955), 155–66; and more recently, Susanna Wade Martins, *Coke of Norfolk, 1754–1842* (Woodbridge: Boydell Press, 2009).

[9] Ferrar to his mother, 20 November 1926, Ferrar Collection, (small box collection 10), CSAS.

Figure 2.1 Colonel Michael Lloyd Ferrar, Chief Commissioner of the Andaman Islands 1921–33. Ferrar collection, courtesy of Centre of South Asian Studies, University of Cambridge.

Ferrar or the history of the village and district that bear his name, Ferrargunj, in South Andaman. This is partly due to the fact that the original inhabitants of the erstwhile Ferrargunj village have been pushed to the margins of the village where they were once settled. Although technically the original inhabitants, the Bhantus live within the administrative bounds of the larger Ferrargunj *tehsil*, and their settlements are no longer identified with the name of Ferrar. The original village named Ferrargunj is now in the possession of Bengali refugee settlers who came to the Islands in 1949 in the aftermath of the Partition of India, most under a refugee rehabilitation scheme meant specifically for those from East Pakistan.[10]

In December 2009, I visited Ramtibai, then in her late eighties and one of the few old timers in her community who remembered not Ferrar, but

[10] Ferrargunj today is the largest *tehsil* of the Andaman Islands. According to the 2001 Census of India, its population was 48,626. Andaman and Nicobar Administration, 'Basic Statistics of Andaman and Nicobar Islands 2010–1', www.and.nic.in/stats/BasicStatistics/basicstat%20PDF/03%20Demography.pdf.

a certain Francis Sahib, Chief Officer of the *Mukti Fauj* (the Salvation Army). On prodding her rapidly faltering memory, she told me that Francis Sahib had brought her and several other families from a village in Gorakhpur in the United Provinces to be settled in what she remembers as *kala pani*.[11] She was a very young girl at the time of her arrival in the Andaman Islands, and remembers little of the circumstances that made her family follow the Sahib across the Bay of Bengal.[12] Yet it is in the diffuse memories of Ramtibai's early life in the Islands and Adjutant Sheard of the Salvation Army that there emerge possibilities of locating the links that tie up the story of Ferrargunj to the histories of the shifting imperatives of the colonial penal settlement, the agenda of agrarian colonization and the making of a contemporary refugee diaspora in the Andamans. For one of the things that Ramtibai remembered clearly about her family's eager acceptance of the arrangements made for their new life in the Andamans was the promise of possessing land. After years of being hounded by the colonial police, and fleeing from village to village, her family was promised land, occupancy rights and material assistance in cultivation, if they accepted settlement in the Andaman Islands under the protection of the Salvation Army. Ramtibai's failing memory could not remember the actual year of their arrival to the Islands, but her insistence on the 'land question' made it clear that her family was brought in as part of a larger scheme of agrarian colonization that was being tentatively worked out by Chief Commissioner Michael Lloyd Ferrar in the years between 1923 and 1926.

The ravages of the Japanese occupation of the Islands (1942–5) and the destruction of the colonial headquarters in Ross Island has meant that virtually nothing remains of Ferrar's papers. Fragments of the record of Ferrar's fairly long tenure have, however, survived in the short biographical pieces and memoirs written by those who either knew him personally or through their families, and by a smaller group of natural historians, who remember Ferrar less for his achievements as colonial administrator and more for his enormous collection of butterflies.[13] The biography of Ferrar as it takes shape in this historical archive reveals an interesting trajectory. Ferrar, we are told, 'was a slightly built man' with a

---

[11] The 'Francis Sahib' Ramtibai mentions probably referred to Brigadier Francis of the Salvation Army, who came later to the Islands and not exactly at the time Ramtibai seems to suggest. The Bhantu settlement in the Andamans in the 1920s, as we know, was undertaken by Edwin H. Sheard of the Salvation Army.

[12] Conversation with Ramtibai, 17 December 2009. Ramtibai died in 2012.

[13] Prashanth Mohanraj and K. Veena Kumar, 'Lt. Colonel M. L. Ferrar: The "Butterfly Mad" Chief Commissioner of the Andaman and Nicobar Islands', *Current Science*, 87, 10 (2004), 1467–9.

passion for 'languages and butterflies'.[14] Born in 1876, Ferrar was a contemporary of Winston Churchill at Sandhurst, and joined the Indian Army at the age of twenty. He soon opted for a transfer to the Civil Service and was inducted into the Punjab Commission. During the five years he spent in the army, Ferrar acquired proficiency in Urdu, Persian, Punjabi and Pashto. Thus he earned distinction as a linguist during his early career.[15]

Ferrar won reputation among colonial naturalists as an avid butterfly collector. His collection was hailed not merely for it size, but because of the range of new species he was able to identify during his travels with the army and later in his capacity as a civil administrator in the Punjab. The scale of his collection was said to have grown rapidly during his stint as Chief Commissioner of the Andaman Islands. It was during this period that Ferrar was able to add nearly 4,000 new species to his collection. He travelled extensively along the length and breadth of the Islands and developed a deep understanding of its terrain and topography.[16]

It was perhaps fortuitous that his knowledge of the Andaman landscape intensified precisely at a time when the British penal settlement was poised for a major structural shift. The event that marked this historical conjuncture in the administrative records as well as in the personal files of the Chief Commissioner was the institution of a new policy of settlement on the Islands. This was a response to the recommendations of the Jails Committee that visited the Islands in 1920 and proposed a new land rights regime. Soon after Ferrar's arrival, the land reform programme acquired momentum. The impact of these reforms, as I will argue later, was felt not just in the Andamans, but far away in a small village in eastern United Provinces, from where Ramtibai along with other Bhantu families set sail in the hope of acquiring land and a new home in the Islands – or what Ramtibai noted as 'the promise of *zameen*.'[17]

In March 1921, Sir William Vincent, member of the Viceroy's executive council, proposed the formal abandonment of the penal colony, but gave no clear indications about the future of the Islands. Although the causes for such a decision remain varied and open to debate, the process of implementation, as Taylor Sherman argues in a recent study of this phase of penal liberalization in the Andamans, was halting and uncoordinated.[18] The process was marked by tensions, particularly

---

[14] Raleigh Treveleyan, *The Golden Oriole: The Two Hundred Year History of an English Family in India* (London: The Long Rider's Guild Press, 2007), 230–32.

[15] Treveleyan, *The Golden Oriole.*   [16] Treveleyan, *The Golden Oriole.*

[17] Conversation with Ramtibai, 17 December 2009.

[18] For details of these new government policies for the Islands, see, Taylor. C. Sherman, 'From Hell to Paradise? Voluntary Transfer of Convicts to the Andaman Islands,

over conflicting demands of imperial development and punishment. Provincial governments put pressure on penal policies that had little to do with imperial strategies or disciplinary objectives. Sherman argues that the practice of transportation was somewhat anomalous in the 1920s, and there was little ideological justification for the retention of the penal colony. The settlement at Port Blair, she proposes, 'remained in use not because of its exemplary disciplinary regime, but because no compromise could be found between the centre and the provinces which would facilitate the transformation of the settlement into a free colony.'[19]

A two-fold process was contemplated, firstly the evacuation of those convicts who wished to return to India and the construction of a free colony from a nucleus of self-supporters augmented by voluntary convicts from India and Burma. It was part of a pragmatic solution offered in the context of official anxieties over the proposal for the summary abandonment of the penal colony. At the time of the proposed closure of the settlement, the convict population was 11,532, of whom 1,168 were self-supporters. In October 1925, Sir Alexander Muddiman, member of the Executive Council of the Governor General, was sent to review the condition of this population as a sort of preparation for the next stage of colonial policy on the Islands. Muddiman witnessed a vast change in convict demographics. In December 1925, out of a total convict population of 7,740, there were 2,105 self-supporters drawing wages from the government, and 2,272 self-supporters employed in agriculture and other occupations. Moreover, the proportion of self-supporters in the Islands' population had increased dramatically in a period of just five years.[20] This development would have important implications on colonial thinking on agricultural development in the interwar years.

But by the time Ferrar assumed office in 1923, the optimism that framed the Home Department's call for 'voluntary colonization' seemed to have receded considerably. The recourse was to generate conditions for those who were already in the Islands and persuade them to make it their permanent home. It is in the context of this administrative dilemma that the push for a 'free colony' in the Andamans in the 1920s needs to be understood. The idea of forming a free colony on the basis of colonization by the 'unfree' meant that the political initiative of these years had to be redefined, directed and deployed by the state over

1921–40', *Modern Asian Studies*, 43, 2 (2009), 357–68. See also, Vaidik, *Imperial Andamans*, 161–86.

[19] Sherman, 'From Hell to Paradise?', 375.

[20] Sherman, 'From Hell to Paradise?', 375.

multiple sites of intervention. From physical interventions in the landscape to moral investments in patterns of land use, the ideology of the new course of colonization demanded the simultaneous deployment of a whole new range of material and discursive tools of persuasion and control. The disciplinary agenda of colonization, in other words, had to be dispersed more widely and entrenched more deeply into the Island landscape. It is here that the role of Ferrar and the making of Ferrargunj assume historical significance.

Although the idea of abolishing the penal settlement was welcomed by the colonial authorities, Ferrar was clear that the establishment of a free colony required the provision of various incentives to potential settlers. Considerable press was given to debates about settling the Islands with domiciled Europeans and Anglo-Indians, yet it was clear the Government of India was apprehensive of these schemes.[21] The model of colonization it had in mind required a different kind of colonizer. The government said that it would encourage applications from European or Anglo-Indian communities, but also carried a warning that the climate of the Islands was tropical, agriculture would be possible only through hard labour, and so it would not be congenial for those not used to such physical exertion in moist heat.

Ferrar was prepared to take the view that if he failed to bring in genuine settlers, his administration would be inclined to initiate a process of what could be described as 'colonization from within'. To consolidate this model of colonization it was necessary to formulate a new land regime and to encourage the expansion of the self-supporter base. More importantly, it was necessary to persuade well-behaved convict volunteers from the mainland to undergo their sentences in the Islands by creating the conditions for agricultural development and announcing family emigration schemes.

Ferrar presided over the promulgation of the historic Andaman and Nicobar Islands Land Tenure Regulation III of 1926 that conferred security of tenure on small as well as large landholders, and enabled convicts to acquire occupancy rights on release.[22] That he was an enthusiastic votary of the land reforms was clear from the very outset. In a letter to his mother written shortly after the promulgation of the new land regulations, he wrote:

---

[21] For a discussion of these schemes and the political economic argument that informed them, see Vaidik, *Imperial Andamans*, 161–86.

[22] For a full official report on the 'Ferrar durbar', see: *Report of the Administration of the Andamans and Nicobar Islands and the Penal Settlement for 1925–6* (Calcutta: Government of India Publications Branch, 1927), 3–4. A total of 290 *sanads* or deeds of occupancy were given away on this occasion.

The Government Of India having approved of my land proposals, I yesterday held a durbar, really more an organized public meeting, out [at] Garacharma about six miles from here, to about [a] thousand free and ticket of leave men [self-supporters], moneylenders and local born [convict descended] government servants and delivered a long speech in Urdu which was followed with rapt attention. Also I had handbills distributed with a resume of concessions. They amount to giving everyone occupancy rights over their land and secure incentives to improve their land and houses. I hope good will come of this. It certainly has created a stir but the whole settlement is only about forty odd villages, a potty little show from the agricultural point of view.[23]

In his formal speech delivered at the durbar and attended by a range of economic and political stakeholders in the Islands, Ferrar delineated the advantages of the new regulations. The durbar was a huge congregation of gazetted and commissioned officers, plantation lessees, village heads and prospective tenants. In a speech delivered half in Urdu and half in English, Ferrar began by stating that although the penal settlement would be converted into a free settlement, it was clear that until a sufficient free population had come into being, well-behaved convicts of the casual and accidental class were to be encouraged to volunteer to undergo their sentences in the Andamans and were encouraged to bring their wives and families. All those with wives would have a definite promise of land within five years of their arrival, many of them sooner if convenient for the government. In the meantime, the severe restrictions with regard to land which were necessary formerly but which constituted an insurmountable barrier to agricultural progress would be removed. Two classes that would benefit most by its provisions would be the lessees of plantations, who would obtain a tenure of sixty years, and small tenants, who would obtain occupancy rights on very simple terms. The rates of land revenue on plantation land would be brought in line with those obtained in Burma.[24] In his own words:

It is my sanguine hope that with the security thus obtained coupled with easier land revenue terms would bring in capitalists from outside into these Islands and would induce tenants to develop their holdings and improve their dwellings. This would lead to great improvements in the methods and standards of agriculture and add to wealth and happiness of the King's subjects in Port Blair.[25]

---

[23] Ferrar to his mother, 22 March 1926, Ferrar Papers, CSAS.

[24] 'Proceedings of the Durbar Held by the Chief Commissioner', 13 March 1926, *Andaman and Nicobar Gazetteer Extraordinary*, No. 3, Port Blair, 18 March 1926, 11–12, Ferrar Papers, CSAS.

[25] 'Proceedings of the Durbar', Ferrar Papers, CSAS.

Beneath Ferrar's optimism at the durbar, however, there lurked a deep sense of anxiety about the successful outcome of the new regulations. For the problem was not only the availability of labour to work the land on terms of occupancy, but the capacity of the land itself to respond to the demands of agrarian expansion. In a *Memorandum on Agriculture* written soon after the promulgation of the new land regulations, Ferrar reflected on the causes of the limits of agriculture in the Andamans. The Islands, he observed, prior to the founding of the penal settlement in 1858, were covered by a 2,508 square mile area of unbroken tropical forest. After the establishment of the penal settlement in Port Blair in South Andaman, and after almost sixty-eight years of occupation, only 250 square miles were declared developed 'for the use of civilized men'. Adding a more significant observation, he wrote that the early days of the penal settlement agricultural operations were carried out by convict labour. But such convict labour proved to be of uneven use as convicts came from various parts of India with varied aptitudes for agricultural work.[26]

In the following paragraphs, Ferrar documented the initiatives undertaken by Lord Mayo, the Viceroy of India, who had taken up the question of agriculture in the Andamans with a remarkable sense of purpose. This was particularly evident in the several agricultural experiments undertaken during this period. The results of such experimentation were startling. About 520 acres were put under tea, 1,400 under coffee, and about 500 acres under Hevea rubber. Apart from this plantation phase, the settlement gardens also experimented with cultivating a range of tropical fruit and vegetables.[27]

Many of these agricultural experiments were supported by the introduction of new structures of land holding for the convict population. The ticket-of-leave men, who were often employed in these activities, were themselves allowed to hold land as 'tenants at will' of the government. The usual holding was two to five acres of valley land on which the tenant could grow enough paddy and not only subsist but also sell to the government, which bought locally approximately Rs 100,000 worth of agricultural produce per annum. Despite these conditions of land holding much agricultural activity and enterprise occurred in fits and starts. At times the more energetic among the self-supporters would take up hill land in the blocks and plant these with sugarcane, maize and turmeric. After making a degree of profit from such land for three to four years, they would abandon it. In the early years, these abandoned fields

---

[26] See Ferrar, 'Memorandum on Agriculture', March 1926, Ferrar Papers, CSAS.
[27] Ferrar, 'Memorandum on Agriculture', CSAS.

would turn to grass, but later on the increasing prevalence of weeds both indigenous and exotic would prevent the formation of grass, leaving the plot almost unsuitable for recovery. Thus all the effort put into the land for the previous three to four years would be rendered useless. Ferrar rationalized the behaviour of these 'enterprising' yet 'unreliable' agriculturalists in terms of the prevailing land rights regime. An improving agriculture was not possible, he believed, within the constraining conditions of a penal colony.[28]

Yet the necessity for safeguarding the interests of the government in a penal settlement made it imperative that no rights adverse to the government of a penal settlement should accrue to any tenant. For Ferrar, therefore, the institution of a new structure of land rights amenable to the disciplinary imperatives of the penal regime had to be the primary precondition for the new programme of colonization. The pre-reform penal system with its crowds of 'bachelor convict cultivators' merely awaiting release and its many restrictions on the free population created what Ferrar saw as 'make believe' settlements. He hoped that with the great change in conditions, visibly improving the status, self-respect and general well being of Port Blair agriculturalists, there would necessarily come an improvement in agriculture. It was this 'improving impulse' that was to drive the agricultural agenda under his tenure and generate a new moral and political aesthetic investment in the Island landscape. His interventions into the Andaman landscape might be interpreted as a new phase in the relocation and moral/productive organization of the Islands' local-born population earlier in the 1910s, described by Clare Anderson in Chapter 5. Both phases drew on knowledge of canal colonization in the Punjab – in Ferrar's case, acquired through his prior membership of the Punjab Commission.[29]

Letters written to his mother during the early months of his arrival in the Islands are replete with references to the richness of the Island landscape. Shortly after he took over as Chief Commissioner he remarked that the settlements and rice fields were far hidden from view, and it was the dense forests that dominated the view from his summer residence at Mount Harriet:

The view from here is wonderful, the harbor and its creeks all running up into the mainland. Outside the mouth of the harbor, Ross Island, half a mile from the

---

[28] Ferrar, 'Memorandum on Agriculture', CSAS.

[29] William J. Glover, 'Objects, Models, and Exemplary Works: Educating Sentiment in Colonial India', *Journal of Asian Studies* 64, 3 (2005), 539–66; Ian Talbot, 'The Punjab Under Colonialism: Order and Transformation in British India', *Journal of Punjab Studies* 14, 1 (2008), 3–10.

shore. The mainland is all forest and indented with creeks, and beyond again, small islands, the three thousand or so hectares of cultivated areas are invisible from here.[30]

The comment acquires special significance in the context of Ferrar's later interventions in the landscape, when the mangrove swamps and the rice fields would become the constitutive sites of his vision of improvement. For Ferrar as much as for many of his generation of administrators who were either in charge of reviving national communities or overseas colonies, the vision of an Arcadian rurality was often creatively invoked as a counterpoise to the disillusionment with urban decay.[31] Although far removed from the reach of industrial modernity and therefore ostensibly unsuited for comparison with the more obvious sites of the Western imagination, the investment in the vision of a rural utopia in the Andamans acquired specific meaning in this phase of colonization. For the focus of colonization was agriculture and the creation of permanent bonds with cultivation. Ferrar was aware of the fact that the aim of sustaining an improving agriculture in a terrain as complex as the Andamans was a challenge that he would have to accept.

The improving vision

At the heart of Ferrar's vision lay the search for flat lands for rice cultivation. In the Andamans this was a critical challenge, for much of the terrain was hilly. Lord Mayo's 1870 minute on the penal settlement had directed that efforts were to be made to develop the Islands' agricultural resources in all possible ways in order to make the settlement self-supporting.[32] In furtherance of that object and in the absence of sufficient flat land above sea level, successive administrations cleared many hundreds of acres of mangrove swamp, built protective bunds and sluices and brought the land so reclaimed under rice and coconut cultivation. These early efforts at swamp reclamation however, died out as the tides, rain and crabs damaged the breaches and allowed water to collect in the rice fields and convert the newly cleared land into malarial marshes.[33]

---

[30] Ferrar to his mother, 11 April 1923, Ferrar Papers, CSAS.
[31] For an interesting recent discussion on the subject, see Kate Murphy, 'The Modern Idea is to Bring the Country to the City: Australian Urban Reformers and the Ideal of Rurality, 1900–1918', *Rural History* 20, 1 (2009), 119–36.
[32] Ferrar, 'Memorandum on Agriculture', Ferrar Papers, CSAS.
[33] M. C. C. Bonington, *Census of India, 1931, Volume II: The Andaman and Nicobar Islands*, Part 1-A 'Reclamation Works: Report on the Andamans' (Calcutta: Government of India, Central Publication Branch, 1932).

In this context, Ferrar's anxiety about the new scheme was not misplaced. For even among those groups who were to be brought to the Islands as part of the settlement schemes and with the promise of occupancy rights over land, the response to the offer was deeply ambivalent. Apart from the stigma of *kala pani* that discouraged any voluntary colonization, prospects for any long-term settlement remained constrained by the reputation of the insalubrious airs of the Islands. The scourge of malaria and the high rates of mortality during these years were key to the negative propaganda that the Islands received from people who remained opposed to the new schemes of convict colonization. Ferrar's engagement with the epidemiological literature on malaria is well known.[34] His specific response to the challenges malaria represented to his agenda of colonization was his early realization of the need to invest greater amounts of capital and technology in the draining of swamps and the reclamation of land for agriculture. Malarial morbidity in the Andaman Islands remained a recurring concern within colonial administrative circles and continued to pose huge challenges to any attempts at Island improvement. Administrative recommendations for malarial control were made in five major reports, including the Napier report of 1865, the Cadell Committee report of 1880, the Lyall Lethbridge report of 1890, the Christopher Covell report of 1911 and the Indian Jails Committee of 1919–20. Most made recommendations to drain the swamps and reclaim land for agriculture.[35]

The investigations of Colonel Covell proved that the *anophelene ludlowii*, the primary malaria-carrying mosquito in the Islands, bred in these brackish swamps.[36] Commenting on the significance of Covell's visit to the Islands, Ferrar wrote to his mother:

I spoke to you of Mr. Covell the 'malaria man'. He works from 6 am to 11 pm. He is entranced with his opportunity here. He finds overwhelming confirmation of Colonel Christopher's theory regarding malaria in the Andamans published in 1912. We are in the singular and fortunate position of having no fresh water mosquitoes that carry malaria. Our only carriers are the *ludlowii* that breed in the brackish water and this is the kind of swamp we are eliminating from all important areas by the dredger.[37]

---

[34] The Ferrar papers include a heavily marked copy of Major C. Covell's paper, 'The Anopheles Mosquitoes of the Andaman Islands', 1926, Ferrar Papers, CSAS.

[35] For a detailed discussion of these reports, see G. Dennis Shanks and David J. Bradley, 'Island Fever: The Historical Determinants of Malaria in the Andaman Islands', *Transactions of the Royal Society of Tropical Medicine and Hygiene* 104, 3 (2010), 185–90.

[36] Ferrar's own thoughts on the subject were reflected in a typescript, 'Swamps and Reclamations in the Andaman Islands', 4 April 1931, Ferrar Papers, CSAS.

[37] Ferrar to his mother, 14 August 1926, Ferrar Papers, CSAS.

Ferrar was certain that what was clearly needed for the new plan of colonization was the generation of a sustained moral and material investment in land. The rice fields hidden behind the wooded forests that he had earlier spoken of needed greater visibility and the deadly swamps that surrounded them along the coastline needed to be drained. The free colony required a new generation of productive labour and healthy conditions to ensure its steady reproduction. In a letter to his mother during the early days of his arrival in the Islands, he had observed:

> There are no horseflies here in Ross and no malaria. But there is a mosquito that lives in salt water and breeds in tidal mangrove swamps of the mainland. Where possible these have been filled . . . that particular mosquito cannot fly more than a mile. But works like swamp clearing can never be undertaken by convict labour and of course the provision of labour is going to be one of great difficulties in future.[38]

By the time the new land regulations were promulgated, and Ferrar more confidently ensconced in his position, he presented to the colonial authorities in Delhi a proposal to station a dredger in the Islands for a sustained period of two to three years and engage in a systematic process of swamp reclamation. He would often complain to his mother that, his best intentions notwithstanding, the Home Department seemed to be interested in the Andamans only in a 'patronizing way'. In one of his letters to her he wrote:

> They ought to be pleased to have little real administration in the province . . . but they prefer thinking how best they can please Gandhi or Lajpat Rai and placate some other implacable. Of course I may be a bit too slow and move in fits and starts after periods of apathy or disgust culminating in anger. Were I Frank Swettenham or George Lloyd, I would have now got the Government really galvanized into developing this place and I would have sized up the position here much quicker.[39]

Ferrar's invocation of Frank Swettenham (Resident General of the Federated Malay States, 1896–1901) acquires significance in the light of the similarities they shared in their engagement with the tropical landscapes under their control. As one scholar observes, Swettenham's evaluation of the Malayan landscape was essentially based on its potential economic rewards, its natural resources and its remunerative returns.[40] His appreciation of scenes could be likened to the appreciation of a

---

[38] Ferrar to his mother, 14 August 1926, Ferrar Papers, CSAS.
[39] Ferrar to his mother, 28 June 1925, Ferrar papers, CSAS.
[40] See Robert S. Aiken, 'Images of Nature in Swettenham's Writings: Prolegomenon to a Historical Perspective on Peninsular Malaysia's Ecological Problems', *Asian Survey* 11, 3 (1973), 135–49; H. S. Barlow, 'Swettenham, Sir Frank Athelstane (1850–1946)', *Oxford Dictionary of National Biography* (Oxford: Oxford University Press, 2004).

landscape painting; a visual representation of forms, colours and textures. While there is no doubt that Swettenham was attracted to landscape aesthetics, it did not distract him from what he saw to be the ultimate end of colonialism: landscape changes and 'improvements'. Hence, even while he aesthetically enjoyed the tropical forests, he was emotionally detached from them, equating them with 'fallow' land awaiting agricultural replacement. Ferrar admired Swettenham's capacity to work through his projects of improvements with great success.[41]

Taking recourse to a spirit of self-deprecation, Ferrar would often look at the outcome of his own efforts with a tinge of sadness. On 12 December 1925, he expressed his deepest misgivings about the project at hand. He wrote:

This morning I have had to send a two hundred and forty word telegram to Delhi, over the dredger scheme which they are trying to shelve for another year and make contingent on a good monsoon – another way of letting the whole thing drop. I find it difficult to settle for anything until I get an answer – I feel pretty sure that if I don't get a dredger this year then it will never come ... how I long to see those flat raised lands emerging from the black and stinking swamps![42]

The dredger did arrive a couple of years later and Ferrar was able to convince before authorities in Delhi that it needed to be stationed in the Andamans initially for one year. In that time Ferrar believed that 120 million cubic feet of silt would be sapped through its pipes and almost 700 acres of swamps turned into flat paddy land. And more importantly, he added, malaria would be eliminated from large tracts of land adjoining the harbour.[43]

By the end of 1929, the 'good old Ronaldshay', as Ferrar put it, had changed the face of the harbour. More than twenty-five malarial swamps around Port Blair, including Aberdeen, Phoenix Bay, Janglighat, Dhanikhari, Mithakhari, Chouldhari, Port Mouat East and Stewartgunj, had been reclaimed and converted to flat paddy land.[44] On 3 March 1929, Ferrar wrote triumphantly: 'I have got my fourteen lakhs again for swamp reclamation and that will make a total of twenty lakhs in my time'.[45] Almost a year later, the mood was more introspective:

Fifty-four I am today and we have exactly one more year in front of us and so much left undone and much of the progress rather dubious. However my name is not mud but rather will rest in the future on the millions of cubic feet of mud that

---

[41] Barlow, 'Swettenham, Sir Frank Athelstane (1850–1946)', 146–7.
[42] Ferrar to his mother, 14 December 1925, Ferrar Papers, CSAS.
[43] Ferrar to his mother, 11 December 1928, Ferrar Papers, CSAS.
[44] Ferrar to his mother, 11 December 1928, Ferrar Papers, CSAS.
[45] Ferrar to his mother, 3 March 1929, Ferrar Papers, CSAS.

is being dug out of the harbour and poured on the swamps to render great areas of this settlement safe to live and prosper in. When I first took up my trip around the harbour road just seven years ago and saw those dismal derelict swamps, I never thought I should be here to see them wiped out, many hundred scores of then forever and changed into high land.[46]

And then, more evocatively, writing from his desk at Mount Harriet: 'From up here, I watch the good Ronaldshay five and a quarter miles away and twelve hundred feet below me pouring a huge black jet of mud and water on the Mithkhari swamp, she is doing very well, though much behind her time'.[47]

Notwithstanding the delays, Ferrar could feel a certain degree of satisfaction at the way in which his larger project of improving the Islands by the institution of a whole range of public works was shaping up. If improving the health of the colony and expanding agriculture were two of the major projects he undertook during the first half of his tenure, then the improvement of road communication vied for his attention during the later years. Real life villages, bustling bazars, busy traffic and the ceaseless flow of goods and people between the Islands and the mainland were to him the true signs of development.

Ferrar was convinced that in order push the Islands beyond self-sufficiency in food production, he would have to adopt a model of development from other successful tropical possessions of the British Empire. Commenting on an article he read in the *Journal of The Royal Society of Arts*, that made the comparison between the developmental achievements of British Guiana and British Malaya, Ferrar wrote that the article made him think a great deal on the development of the Andamans.[48] In his own words:

There is a school of thought which says no tropical country can run any big developmental schemes without minerals and another which says Ceylon, Jamaica, Uganda and Sumatra none of which owes much to minerals. We have nothing conceivably exportable beyond timber and forest produce (cane, resin, oil) and plantation products, tea, coffee, coconuts and rubber. Of these coconuts have grown in quantity – tea and coffee at about one hundred and fifty acres each, rubber unworked at present. We get a few thousand rupees on tortoise shells, bird nest, trepang and green snail – otherwise nothing to be got from the sea. Pearl oysters do not exist here and conches and green snail, which in Mergui and Madras fetch some revenue, are not sufficiently abundant ... There is a marble quarry long neglected and I have sent blocks to be evaluated in Calcutta – may get

---

[46] Ferrar to his mother, 13 April 1930, Ferrar Papers, CSAS.

[47] Ferrar to his mother, 13 April 1930, Ferrar Papers, CSAS.

[48] This argument was elaborated in Ferrar's letter to his mother, 28 June 1925, Ferrar Papers, CSAS.

the quarry taken over by private enterprise. Have thought of lime ... the coral affords an unlimited yet limited source. It is hard to say what it would cost to produce large quantities. Anyhow the immediate certain products are coconut and timber. It seems we have to increase the peasant holders of rice land and increase local staples of food – rice and dal and a get a bigger rural population ... The local people want something more than my promise and I'm longing to convey the first gift of occupancy with my own hand. Once they really have it, there will be a great fillip to agriculture. Also we have to get the convict villages to look like real villages with lots of women and children about the place.[49]

It was this vision of a rural arcadia that prompted the search for the good colonists and the making of a new settlement in his name. The idea was to create the appearance of what was evocatively described as 'real villages' on the Islands with happy homesteads, and men, women and children all working together in the great collective enterprise of developing the Islands. Colonel Ferrar's papers are replete with references to these images of rural development. He wanted to reinvigorate the family emigration scheme for convicts using new incentives and to encourage more convict volunteers and their families.

The search for colonists

The family emigration scheme initiated many years before the arrival of Ferrar proved to be a deeply ambivalent exercise both at the level of official thinking and the response it generated among the convict population. In her study of the scheme during its early period of operation, Aparna Vaidik argues that family emigration was part of official thinking from the very early years of the penal settlement.[50] The success of the colonial enterprise in the Andamans, it was argued, rested on transforming the transported felons into 'law-abiding and gainfully employed citizens of the empire and converting the island space into a flourishing agricultural colony'. The outcome of this enterprise, however, depended on the success of the government's efforts to persuade convicts to make the Islands their permanent homes. It was important to try and create a life somewhat akin to their earlier lives on the mainland. Within the colonial administration it was believed that matrimony and domesticity were two redemptive institutions that worked to eliminate the possible social anomalies that might arise in the predominantly male penal settlement.[51] The family emigration scheme was meant to strengthen the

---

[49] Ferrar to his mother, 28 June 1925, Ferrar Papers, CSAS.
[50] Aparna Vaidik, 'Settling the Convict: Matrimony and Domesticity in the Andamans', *Studies in History*, 22, 2 (2006), 221–50.
[51] Vaidik, 'Settling the Convict'.

self-supporter system and sustain the productive base of the settlement particularly in agriculture. The importation of convict families was thought to be the most prudent mode of ensuring a regular supply of labour in the colony. The government, however, had to walk a tricky tight rope while introducing the scheme. Initially it encouraged the scheme for all; however, in course of time it was widely acknowledged that in order to sustain the identity of the Islands as 'a penal settlement' rather than 'a colony of emigrants', it was important to institute the emigration scheme judiciously for those with proven character.[52]

Notwithstanding the promises that the government held out in favour of the scheme most convicts remained unconvinced and the motivation to bring in families was very low. Even when some of them did try to bring in their wives and children, the response from the mainland was most often discouraging.[53] By the early 1920s, when the decision was taken to abolish the penal colony and to encourage its conversion into a free colony, the family emigration scheme was revived with a new sense of urgency. The demand for voluntary emigration and the expansion of agriculture meant a renewed effort at encouraging convict families to settle on the Islands, not merely for the duration of the penal sentence but permanently.

Ferrar's first initiative in this direction came in response to the challenge of encouraging the voluntary settlement of Moplah (Mappilas) transportees on the Islands. The Moplah Uprising had taken place in Malabar (Kerala) in the context of the Khilafat agitations. The Moplahs were Muslim peasants of the region who periodically took to armed resistance against their exploitative landlords. Their uprising in 1921 acquired a wider resonance as it invoked the political discourse of the all-India Khilafat movement led by Gandhi. After six months of decisive guerrilla assaults on the government, the Moplah rebels were brutally subdued and the movement died out.[54] It may be noted at this point that the attempt to 'settle' the Moplah convicts in the Islands, notwithstanding the official position on the abolition of the penal settlement and the

---

[52] Vaidik, 'Settling the Convict', 225. See also Satadru Sen, 'Domesticated Convicts: Producing Families in the Andaman Islands', in Indrani Chatterjee (ed.), *Unfamiliar Relations: Family and History in South Asia* (New Brunswick: Rutgers University Press, 2004), 261–91.

[53] Vaidik, 'Settling the Convict', 226.

[54] For a meticulously researched history of the Moplah Uprising, see K. N. Panikkar, *Against Lord and State: Religion and Peasant Uprisings in Malabar* (New Delhi: Oxford University Press, 1990). See also Conrad Wood, 'The First Moplah Rebellion Against British Rule in Malabar', *Modern Asian Studies* 10, 4 (1976), 543–56, and P. K. Zubair Ahmed, http://vehicleferry.blogspot.in/2012/09/the-moplah-rebellion-and-andamans_2.html.

abandonment of the policy of transportation, was eventually based on a compromise. Indeed, it was at the request of the Madras government that a decision was taken to encourage the Moplah to serve their sentences on the Islands. This move proved to be controversial because of an organized opposition to the policy staged by sitting legislators of the Madras Legislative Council. In the debates that raged within the Council, it was insinuated that the government had resorted to false propaganda in their desire to induce the project of Moplah colonization. References were made in particular to a series of articles written for the *Madras Mail* by Colonel James Barker, an officer of the Indian Medical Service who had visited the penal settlement in the early 1920s and who had prepared a note on its overall climatic and health conditions. Major Barker's report was placed before the Council for discussion on the ground that it was biased and therefore open to debate.[55]

According to the Barker report, the adverse observations of the Jail Committee's report on the Andamans needed to be interrogated in the light of the many steps taken to introduce new and better health and sanitary conditions on the Islands. Barker also pointed out that the Andamans would be an ideal location for the Moplah settlers on account of the similarities of the weather in the Andamans and in Malabar. On the specific issue of the recurrence of malarial mortality on the Islands, he made it clear that it varied over time and was contingent upon the availability of medical facilities. He also pointed out that there was nothing peculiar to the malarial fevers in the Andamans as malaria was a common scourge across the Indian subcontinent and the Malabar in particular. The only difference was, he claimed, that 'malaria in the Malabar being inland at the foothills of the Wynaad whereas that of the Andamans was on the sea!' On the specific issue of livelihood opportunities in the Andamans, Barker maintained that the rich valleys lying within the virgin forests in the Islands were waiting to be cultivated by a range of agricultural produce. The Moplahs would have the opportunity to engage in fishing and forest work and hence carry on similar subsistence activities as they did in Malabar.[56]

Barker's report, however, scarcely impressed the members of the Madras Legislative Council and, as Sherman writes, the debate on settling the Moplahs continued until the government was forced into a compromise.[57] In a letter to his mother, Ferrar responded angrily to the

---

[55] Major Barker's Report, 20 July 1925, Law (General) Acc. No. 485, A&N Archives.
[56] Major Barker's Report, A&N Archives.   [57] Sherman, 'From Hell to Paradise?', 384.

delaying of the Moplah immigration project by over eighteen months. He wrote:

The Indian politician is a parrot and a dishonest man. Yet it (the Moplah immigration) has started again with renewed strength as it is purely voluntary and 840 free people have chosen to come here and live with their convict relatives. The politician may as well go shut up and acknowledge himself to be wrong.[58]

On 4 October 1926, the Moplahs in the Andamans were given the choice to return to jails in Madras while those imprisoned in Madras were offered the opportunity of serving their sentences in Port Blair. Notwithstanding the early discomfiture he might have felt at this proposal, Ferrar was relieved to report that 448 convicts in Madras had elected to settle in the Islands while the option to return to Madras was made use of by only eighty single men.[59] The Moplah settlement, however, continued to generate debate and reflected the misgivings that prospective convict volunteers had about life in the Andamans. Ferrar's desire to transform the dull villages of the settlement into a full-fledged rural society meant that a new ideological investment had to be made in the promotion of the image of the Islands as a place for healthy habitation. At the end of his first term as Chief Commissioner, he sought another five-year extension. He conveyed this to his mother in a letter soon after:

There is a great deal of ploughing in the sand here, but the place progresses and I have the excitement of being here long enough to see whether my policy is going to be a success even if a modified success. There are plenty of times when I have felt we are getting on rather indifferently with the fixing of a permanent population but we are steadily eliminating the dread of this place by the rest of India.[60]

Ferrar's letters to his mother during this phase reveal an undercurrent of frustration at the slow progress of his schemes, yet there was a sense of achievement too. It is important to note in the paragraph quoted above his express conviction that the 'dread' associated with *kala pani* was being gradually eliminated. It was a key condition for the establishment of the free colony in the Islands. Yet notwithstanding this optimism, the search for voluntary convict colonists remained elusive. Ferrar had to evolve a different strategy.

---

[58] Ferrar to his mother, 8 February 1927, Ferrar Papers, CSAS.
[59] Ferrar to his mother, 8 February 1927, Ferrar Papers, CSAS.
[60] Ferrar to his mother, 25 May 1927, Ferrar Collection, CSAS.

The birth of Ferrargunj Colony

Ferrar turned to another group of convict-colonists and encouraged them to settle on the Islands. Several letters to his mother reflect the anxieties and hopes he had pinned upon his pet schemes of dredging the marshes of Mithakhari and settling the community of the Bhantus under the aegis of the Salvation Army. The formulation of a rehabilitation scheme for the Bhantus, an officially designated criminal tribe, marked one of the high points of his schemes of improvement. The Bhantus may not have proved to be the ideal agriculturalists Ferrar wished them to be, but he celebrated the perceived success of his scheme by naming the Bhantu colony, Ferrargunj. The 'successful' settlement and moral rehabilitation of a 'criminal tribe' through agriculture was meant to underscore the ultimate legitimacy of his 'improving' vision.

The Bhantus were an officially designated 'criminal tribe' from the United Provinces. For at least fifty years, these so-called hereditary criminals had been rounded up and resettled in specially designated mainland colonies, where they were supposed to be reformed and taught productive labour, frequently under the auspices of the Salvation Army.[61] Descriptions of the Andaman Bhantu colony as they are revealed through accounts in both the Ferrar papers and the Andaman administrative records reveal the character of the colonization process as an extension of this correctional, rehabilitative project, carefully instituted to address the chronic shortage of labour on the Islands and to attempt to reorganize/reform the penal regime according to the demands of productive expenditure.[62] Apart from the official record of the early Bhantu settlement, the memories of a people forced to relocate and redefine their lives as a settled community are few and fragmentary.

As I spoke to old Ramtibai, prodding her to tell me more about her family's arrival on the Islands, she said she had scarcely known of the momentous decision her family was to take in 1926. She was a very

---

[61] Sanjay Nigam, 'Disciplining and Policing The "Criminals By Birth", Part 1: The Making of a Colonial Stereotype – The Criminal Tribes and Castes of North India', *Indian Economic and Social History Review*, 27, 2 (1990), 131–64; Sanjay Nigam, 'Disciplining and Policing the "Criminals By Birth", Part 2: The Development of a Disciplinary System, 1871–1900', *Indian Economic and Social History Review*, 27, 3 (1990), 257–87; Meena Radhakrishna, *Dishonoured by History: 'Criminal Tribes' and British Colonial Policy* (New Delhi: Orient Blackswan, 2001); Rachel J. Tolen, 'Colonizing and Transforming the Criminal Tribesmen: the Salvation Army in British India', *American Ethnologist*, 18, 1 (1991), 106–25.

[62] See also Major Edwin H. Sheard, 'Reforming Robbers in the Andamans', *The Officers' Review* (November 1937), 535–40; Edwin H. Sheard, *Sergeant-Major in the Andamans: Kanhaiya Gariba* (St Albans: Campfield Press, 1957).

young girl at that time and remembered little of their first few years on the settlement. Her father and uncles were perhaps more aware of what their new life would entail. They had, she recalled, known of the *Isai Sena* or the Mukti Fauj, the name they used to refer to the Salvation Army. It had brought many of their brethren under their settlement schemes elsewhere in mainland India and introduced them to the correctional habits of cultivation and prayer. Her family was ready for their new life; perhaps, as she said, they were the descendants of the fiercely courageous Sultana Daku, a famous early twentieth-century Indian *dacoit* (gang robber).

Ramtibai's genealogical claims find corroboration in a 'Note on the Bhantus' prepared by a government official in 1946. According to this document, the majority of the Bhantus were 'Hindus' belonging to the Beria, Aheria, Sainsi, Dom, Kanjar and Karwal castes. In the United Provinces all these are castes classified as Criminal Tribes, and for them Criminal Tribes Settlements existed at Moradabad, Lucknow and Bijner. According to the note, they claimed to be descendants of Rana Pratap of Chittor (a sixteenth-century Rajput ruler) or descendants of the Pindaris (eighteenth-century Maratha plunderers). In 1922, a large gang under the leadership of one Sultana, known also as Jungle King, was arrested. Subsequently the whole gang was convicted. Sultana was sentenced for capital punishment and hanged. In 1926 the Government of India decided to send his followers, these Bhantu convicts, with their families to Port Blair with a view to settling them permanently under a Salvation Army Officer.[63]

The charge of settling the Bhantus in the Andaman Islands provided the Salvation Army with a new port of entry to their expanding field of operations in British India. In her discussion of Salvation Army work among other 'criminal tribes', Meena Radhakrishna writes that settlement for the Yerakulas of Guntur district was set up under one of the provisions of the Criminal Tribes Act of 1911.[64] Similar settlements for the other notified 'criminal tribes' were formed in the United and Central Provinces, in accordance with one of the clauses of the act, which stated that a section of those declared criminal could be interned in special settlements set up under a special government-approved agency. In the 1910s, when the criminal tribe settlements were established in the Madras Presidency, itinerant communities were singled out for settling by policy. The official directive was that 'worst characters especially

---

[63] Note on the Bhantus, File No. 11–4–49, A&N Archives.
[64] Meena Radhakrishna, 'Colonial Constructions of a Criminal Tribe: Yerakulas of Madras Presidency', *Economic and Political Weekly*, 35, 28/29 (15–21 July 2000), 2553–63.

wandering gangs must be settled'.[65] The Salvation Army was entrusted with itinerant communities and sedentary criminals were to be responsibility of the police.

Stuartpuram, as Meena Radhakrishna writes, became the literal site where the British administration and the Salvation Army together decided to have what they called an 'experiment in criminocurology'.[66]

The Bhantus who were brought to the Andaman Islands in 1926 were the objects of a similar experiment, although the project to settle them was part of penal reform and internal colonization in the Islands. In accordance with these objectives, an officer of the Salvation Army was deputed to take charge of the Bhantu settlement in the Andamans. Chief Commissioner Ferrar's enthusiasm for the project was evident and land was allotted for the settlement in the outskirts of Port Blair. Writing to his mother in 1927, Ferrar expressed deep satisfaction at the thought that the new settlement for the Bhantus would be named after him. He mentions this categorically in the letter, where he writes, 'I have agreed to the Bhantu village, a real life village of seventy families being called Ferrargunj. There is a place by the same name in Gorakhpur. (the name being given there by my father, M. L. Ferrar).'[67]

The understanding between him and Adjutant Sheard, the officer in charge of the settlement, was that Ferrargunj would be primarily agricultural in its orientation. Although other skills would be imparted to the settlers, the main objective would be to train them into becoming good cultivators. At the end of Ferrar's tenure there were several hundred families in the settlement. Unlike the controversy and the problems that accompanied the Moplah emigration scheme during the same period, the Bhantu family emigration was relatively smooth. Under the stewardship of Adjutant Dr Sheard and his wife, the Bhantu settlement evolved into a sort of Boothite farm colony, based on what was generally believed to be the Bible's Ten Commandments combined with common sense and socialism. Its aim, in Boothite terms, was in 'redeeming men by the eternal remedies of labour and discipline'.[68] Although the initial flow of

---

[65] Radhakrishna, 'Colonial Constructions', 2556–57.

[66] Radhakrishna, 'Colonial Constructions', 2557. See also Frederick Booth-Tucker, *Criminocurology or the Indian Crim, and What to Do with Him: Being a Review of the Work of the Salvation Army amongst the Prisoners, Habituals and Criminal Tribes of India* (Simla: Liddell's Printing Works, 1916).

[67] Ferrar to his mother, 5 June 1927, Ferrar Papers, CSAS.

[68] H. Ausubel, 'General Booth's Scheme of Social Salvation', *American Historical Review*, 56, 3 (1951), 519–25. William Booth was the founder of the Salvation Army. See D. C. Lamb, 'Booth, (William) Bramwell (1856–1929)', Rev. L. E. Lauer, *Oxford Dictionary of National Biography* (Oxford University Press, 2004; online edn, September 2012), www.oxforddnb.com/view/article/31969, accessed 17 September 2014.

Bhantu settlers in 1926 was relatively slow, it picked up momentum in 1928 when women and children joined their husbands. Women in particular were said to have added value to the settlement by involving themselves in a range of agricultural, craft and artisanal work. They took to weaving and became, in course of time, the prime suppliers of hand-woven fabric for use in the prison establishment. Bhantu men took great pride in their agricultural skills. Not only were they able to clear forests and prepare the soil for cultivation, they succeeded in fulfilling their paddy production targets in little time.

In yet another letter to his mother, Ferrar observed with much satisfaction

Ferrargunj prospers. There are 260 inhabitants, no unmarried men, 61 children of school age and 350 more are to arrive in January and two more smaller villages on each side of Ferrargunj are to be built. They are starting a drum and fife band and I am going to present them with a big drum![69]

Ferrar took great pains to see that the colony not only prospered but was also protected. This was because the security of Ferrargunj colony and the surrounding areas that were being reclaimed for agriculture had become the targets of attacks by the Islands' indigenous people, the Jarawas; Ferrar's letters to his mother during this period are replete with references to the Jarawas who, according to Ferrar, seemed to be at that point the greatest enemies of the settlement. In one of these letters written soon after the dredging operations had begun and the new villages in the South Andaman were being settled, he wrote:

There are two thousand square miles of country teeming with food for the Jarawas and unoccupied by any human being. Why must they keep coming over to our hundred square mile settlements and keep killing our wretched convicts?[70]

Ferrar genuinely believed that Jarawa attacks on the settlements were wanton acts of mischief, or what he described as a 'sport and a pastime'. The Burmese and other convicts were for them easy prey for their targets of *shikar* (hunting as a sport). He was convinced that such attacks had to be retaliated with equal amounts of force, and the Jarawa quelled if the settlement was to survive. In a letter on May 1930, he wrote:

The Jarawas have at last had their go at Ferrargunj and killed a man at about midnight in a sugarcane machan. The arrow fastened his arm to his side and

---

[69] Ferrar to his mother, 13 September 1927, Ferrar Papers, CSAS. The two villages referred to in this note would be present-day Aniket and Caddelgunj.
[70] Ferrar to his mother, 15 March 1926, Ferrar Collection, CSAS.

passing through the lung, the sharp wooden point was embedded in his spine. I have sent out a party of some six rifles, forty slug guns to beat up their rains quarters and kill as many as possible during a week's hunting. There is nothing else to do. They are implacable and their outrages without any object of sense.[71]

A whole series of punitive expeditions against the Jarawa marked the term of Ferrar's chief commissionership. Although the campaigns were often brutal and generated controversy in British administrative circles, Ferrar remained unapologetic. The colonization scheme had to be carried through and Ferrargunj, its showpiece, had to be protected at any cost.

As administrative reports of the period noted, after a decade the colony of a 'notorious criminal tribe' had indeed proved to be a definite success. Although there remains little in contemporary administrative records describing the steady growth of the settlement during these years, an Andaman administration report of 1936 is quite explicit in its positive appraisal of the Bhantu settlement. According to its assessment, Bhantu settlers at Ferrargunj for that year numbered 466, of whom 88 were convicts, 75 free men, 108 free women, 91 boys and 104 girls.[72] In their new homes, the colonists had shown no inclination towards indulging in any criminal practices and had developed into 'hardworking' members of the community engaging in agriculture, hand weaving and forest clearance work.[73] The report goes on to say that it was understood that when the colony was established it was intended to move most of India's Bhantus to it. There was a considerable area of vacant arable land in the three villages in the colony and a dozen families of newcomers could be absorbed easily.[74] At the time of his departure from the Andamans, Ferrar was happy to see the colony flourish and the Bhantus apparently reformed. His push for an agricultural colony and a moral space within the degraded environs of the penal settlement seemed to have borne fruit.

But what about the Bhantus themselves? The Ferragunj colony that gave them a new life on the Islands faced a period of severe crisis in the years following the Japanese occupation between 1942 and 1945. The Bhantus were amongst many of the settlers who remained in the Islands during the most difficult times of the occupation. Although their

---

[71] Ferrar to to his mother, 18 May 1930, Ferrar Collection, CSAS. A *machan* was a platform erected in a tree, for the purpose of hunting.

[72] *Report on the Administration of the Andaman and Nicobar Islands and the Penal Settlement of Port Blair for 1937–38* (New Delhi: Government of India Press, 1938), 1–2.

[73] *Report on the Administration of the Andaman and Nicobar Islands and the Penal Settlement of Port Blair for 1936–37* (New Delhi: Government of India Press, 1937), 2.

[74] *Report on the Administration of the Andaman and Nicobar Islands and the Penal Settlement of Port Blair for 1936–37*, 3.

economic situation declined drastically during these years, many Bhantu families continued to hold on to their homes in Ferrargunj with few expressing the desire to return to the mainland. In 1946, soon after the end of the Japanese occupation, however, the British administration decided to repatriate the Bhantus to the mainland. Several Bhantu survivors of the Japanese occupation welcomed this decision and left their homes in Ferrargunj to return to their villages in the United Provinces. Within a year of their departure, however, a veritable tide in favour of their return became evident. The administration received hundreds of petitions pleading to take them back. It is in these petitions that the Bhantus sought to represent themselves as the icons of settlement schemes of the 1920s.[75] The irony of their tryst with life in the Andamans, however, was that notwithstanding their ardent petitioning, they were received back into the Islands with a certain degree of scepticism.

An official note commenting on the Bhantus' desire to be resettled on the Islands in the wake of the reoccupation of the Islands following the Japanese aggression made it clear that Bhantus would no longer be fit for the new schemes of settlement on the Islands then being considered:

[I]f the idea is that the Andamans be made a colony of middle-class and other people having no taint of crime, then the Bhantu settlement would not be in consonance with such scheme ... When the Bhantus were sent to the Andamans between 1924–7 some of them had life or lesser sentences. Taking into account one-third remission usually given to convicts who went to the Andamans the ex-convict Bhantus must have become free men by the time the Japanese came. Like other free convict settlers they may continue to remain in the Islands, but it is clear that no fresh Bhantu settlers will be taken. In 1927 it was Lieutenant Colonel Ferrar then Chief Commissioner who was mainly responsible for the experiment of settling the Bhantus has sent a note saying that the scheme had been a success.[76]

The changing fate of Ferrargunj

It was on the strength of this reputation that the repatriated Bhantus were allowed to return to the Islands. It was with one such returning group of Bhantus that Ramtibai's family came back to the Islands in late 1947. The irony of their return, however, lay in their discovery that the lands they cultivated in the Ferrargunj settlement were no longer theirs.

---

[75] For a cache of these petitions see, 'Bhantu Petitions for Return', File No. 11–4–49, A&N Archives.

[76] Note from District Commissioner Kishen Singh, 20 July 1945, File No. 11–4–49, A&N Archives.

Their homes, their lands and the houses and workshops built by the Salvation Army had now been taken over by the Local Born Association. A note from the Deputy Commissioner's office recorded this change of hands vis-à-vis the Bhantu lands in a spirit of bureaucratic detachment. It said that the Bhantus were brought to the Andamans in 1926 and settled in Ferrargunj and two other neighbouring villages of Aniket and Caddelgunj. In a group, they surrendered their holdings in June 1946 and on their 'persistent' request were repatriated to the mainland in March 1947. It was further noted that as a class they had a good reputation as cultivators and expert weavers. On their return to the Islands they were seemingly 'advised' by the government to settle on the land in the whole of Manglutan and Craikabad but not Ferrargunj. This was because, as the note said, 'the whole of Ferrargunj colony (which included Aniket and Caddelgunj) had been allotted to the Andaman Indians on license for thirty years on a cooperative basis.'[77]

The Bhantus responded to this with several petitions demanding the restoration of their lands. They felt that notwithstanding their surrender of these lands in terms of the repatriation programme of 1946, their attachment to these remained as deep as before. 'Kindly go through our tales of sorrow and take action', wrote one petitioner. 'We got this land in 1926 and had to undergo many difficulties in clearing the jungle and making the land cultivable. Many of our men died for the sake of this land.'[78]

There were negotiations with the Andaman administration, but the land issue for the Bhantus remained unresolved. They had to give up their claims on Ferrargunj. The 'good colonists' who had reformed themselves and cultivated the lands allotted to them were now deemed unfair claimants on a right they had willingly forfeited. For the Andaman administration, however, the land issue in general remained a huge source of concern. All that was achieved in terms of clearance and cultivation in the pre-occupation era had to begin all over again in the changed circumstances. The search had to begin for a new class of colonists and a new plan of colonization put in place. On 4 February 1946, the *Hindustan Times* carried a news item that suggested that the British government was planning to invest Rs 1.5 crore (million) to reconstruct the Islands following the Japanese occupation. The newspaper asked if the investment of such a huge sum of money was necessary and whether alternative ways could be thought of to make the Islands

---

[77] Note from District Commissioner Kishen Singh, A&N Archives.
[78] Petition for the restoration of lands, 1946, File no. 11–4–49, A&N Archives.

self-supporting.[79] Although the archives of this period are scant and largely fragmentary, a cache of petitions from private businessmen to the Chief Commissioner of the Islands during this time seem to indicate that there were plans of leasing land to private developers for plantation work as well as other infrastructural developmental work.[80]

By all indications, however, plans for the reconstruction of the Andaman Islands on the lines conceived by the colonial government in the immediate aftermath of the reoccupation remained unfulfilled. With the formal departure of the British, the political turmoil in the subcontinent and the large influx of refugees into India in the aftermath of Partition provoked the developmental discourse on the Andaman Islands to take on an entirely new turn. A new trajectory of colonization was proposed in the wake of the plans for refugee rehabilitation on the Islands, though it would be different from the one proposed by the colonial government under Viceroy Lord Wavell. Instead of leasing out lands for agriculture to private capitalists, the new colonization plan would be premised upon the new supply of refugee labour.

In October 1948 an exploratory party headed by the Minister in Charge of Refugee Rehabilitation visited the Andaman Islands with a view to examine the possibility of resettling displaced families from East Pakistan in the Islands. After a careful survey the party was unanimous in its opinion that the Islands were admirably suitable for colonization by displaced persons.[81] Part of this favourable appraisal for colonization by Bengali refugees from East Pakistan was based on the fact that most of the families were agriculturalists. A more formal statement on the colonization of the Andamans was prepared a year later by H. Shivdasani of the Department of Home Affairs, Government of India. Many of the recommendations of this report were based on an internal consideration of the possibilities of colonization prepared by the Chief Commissioner of the Andamans. The Shivdasani Report, as it came to be known, endorsed the view of the local administration: that the refugees who were to be brought in to colonize the Andaman Islands were to be given special concessions. Apart from free passage from Calcutta, each head of family would be given ten acres of land free of cost with remission of revenue for the first two years. Additional incentives would be the grant of plough cattle, milch cattle, seed paddy, agricultural implements, and manure

---

[79] Clipping from the *Hindustan Times*, in File No. 1–225–46, A&N Archives.

[80] These petitions are from businessmen based both in India and Burma. Copies of their letters are available in File No. 1–34–46, A&N Archives.

[81] Kiran Dhingra, *The Andaman and Nicobar Islands in the Twentieth Century: A Gazetteer* (New Delhi: Oxford University Press, 2006), 69–120.

free of cost. Non-agricultural families would be given half an acre of land for construction of houses and financial assistance admissible to agriculturalists for a period of three months.[82]

The most significant aspect of these plans for refugee rehabilitation scheme as worked out in the Shivdasani report was the view it held about land-holding rights. On the specific subject of local tenure laws, it said:

Provision will have to be made to ensure that in course of time, the zamindari system does not grow up. Cultivators should be proprietors of their land which should be heritable, transferable but limitations will have to be imposed on transfers and sub-leases as to prevent the cultivator acquiring in course of time so much land that his sub-leasees become his tenants and he becomes a landlord paying taxes to the government.[83]

It was also decided that in order to impart a feeling of security to the cultivator, it would be desirable to introduce a term such as *malik kashtkar* instead of occupancy tenant. But the report made elaborated 'it should be made perfectly clear that this right has been given away in perpetuity on certain conditions. The ultimate proprietary right was vested in the state.'[84]

Clearly, then, the plans for refugee rehabilitation took over some of the key ideas of the colonization scheme of the mid 1920s. For the scheme not merely included a programme of rehabilitation based on the extension of agrarian expansion through use of quasi-coerced labour, but it also instituted a regime of limited land rights aimed a creating a society of peasant proprietors tied to the land but enjoying no sovereign ownership rights over it.

It was on the basis of this report that the Andaman Administration welcomed hundreds of refugee families on to the Islands, particularly in the years after 1949, when large-scale riots in the deltaic districts of East Pakistan forced a huge exodus of agrarian labouring families into refugee camps in West Bengal in central and eastern Indian states.[85] It was during this period that Ferrargunj district, including the former Ferrargunj settlement, went into the possession of the families from East Pakistan. The Local Born Association that had taken over the settlement on lease evidently moved elsewhere. For the first few batches of Bengali

---

[82] H. Shivdasani, 'Report on the Possibilities of Colonization and the Development of the Andaman and Nicobar Islands', Government of India, Ministry of Home Affairs, 5 March 1949, 60, IOR V/190/65.

[83] Shivdasani, 'Report on the Possibilities of Colonization and the Development', 61.

[84] Shivdasani, 'Report on the Possibilities of Colonization and the Development', 5–6.

[85] Joya Chatterji, 'Dispositions and Destinations: Refugee Agency and "Mobility Capital" in the Bengal Diaspora, 1947–2007', *Comparative Studies in Society and History*, 55, 2 (2013), 273–304.

refugees, it was the Ferrargunj region along with a few other areas in South Andaman that appeared to be cleared and somewhat ready for cultivation. The Bhantus who had worked on large swathes of those lands were resettled in villages on the fringes of the earlier settlement. Several petitions followed in which they expressed their resentment of the new arrivals on their lands, but much of these were ignored on the grounds that arrangements had been made for their settlement elsewhere in the vicinity of their former lands. The 'good colonists' who had once set up the village of Ferrargunj were now forced to live outside it.

Old Ramtibai was witness to the changed circumstances of her life as well as those of several others of her community, but she remains grateful for the fact that they were given the opportunity to return to the Islands. Her memories of the Ferrargunj settlement were kept alive through the impression she retains of Mr and Mrs Francis of the Salvation Army (who came to the Settlement soon after the Japanese surrender), of the relics of Ferrar's guest house in the village and of the newly spruced-up church wherein they received their social entry into a world from which they had been politically and socially excluded. The improving ethos of Ferrargunj had pushed the Bhantus out of their original settlement. But

Figure 2.2 The late Ramtibai in her home in Aniket village near the erstwhile Ferrargunj Colony, the only person who vaguely recalled the times associated with Ferrar. Photograph: Madhumita Mazumdar.

the new scheme of colonization and development demanded a new agrarian order and a new and more rigorous pace of settlement that perhaps the Bhantus would find hard to keep pace with.[86]

Conclusion

If the new will to improve shunted the Bhantus out from their lands in Ferrargunj on the plea that the new agriculturalists from erstwhile East Pakistan would make even better colonists, the schemes for colonization and development drawn up in the early 1950s and 1960s also made the implicit argument that the Islands' indigenous peoples too would have to give up their present locations and move deeper into the forest recesses. The 1949 Shivdasani Report betrayed a remarkable continuity with the scheme of colonization of the Ferrar era in its implicit espousal of a renewed 'will to improve'. It underscored the pressing need to initiate a fast track programme of forest clearance and a rapid extension of agriculture with the labour of Bengali refugees. In the Ferrar years, such a programme hit a roadblock as a result of irregular supplies of labour and the ambiguities surrounding official thinking on the penal settlement. It also had to contend with what Ferrar unequivocally described as the 'Jarawa menace'.[87] Ferrar's response to what was perceived to be a serious impediment to his schemes of improvement was a resort to a campaign of unrelenting violence. Although at one point he was placed in the embarrassing predicament of having to explain and subsequently delete the term 'extermination' as the objective of one of his campaigns against the Jarawa to the Viceroy in Delhi, he remained firm in his resolve. In the aftermath of Independence, this policy of violence was completely and decidedly abandoned by the Indian state, but the demands of the post-colonial scheme of colonization were based on a similar ideological premise that saw the indigenous peoples of the Islands as an ambivalent presence in a predominantly settler society. The carving out of an agrarian landscape from the pristine forests of the Islands introduced a new cultural cartography wherein the boundary between the historical/civilized and the prehistoric/primitive is perpetuated by both the politics of tribal welfare and the unceasing reserves of social prejudice. It is this element of the Ferrar legacy that survives, even today, in the very place that bears his name. It is here that the Jarawas residing in the Tirrur area

---

[86] For a detailed study of the shifts in Bhantu society in the Andamans, see Palash Chandra Coomar, *Migration and Social Change: A study of the Bhantus of the Andaman Islands* (Calcutta: The Anthropological Society of India, 1997).

[87] Treveleyan, *The Golden Oriole*, 238–39.

on the fringes of the Ferrargunj settlement live uneasily with the peasant refugees of erstwhile East Pakistan and the Bhantus of Aniket.

The project of colonization and settlement initiated by Ferrar saw its logical conclusion in the political regime of the Indian state, which supported the slow and gradual ruralization of an overwhelmingly forest space, and the peasantization of its social fabric. Within a span of forty years a large segment of the virgin forests of the South and Middle Andamans were cleared and thousands of acres put under the plough. Swamps were drained, mangroves dredged, coconut plantations carved out from reclaimed land and paddy fields extended all along the valleys and the terraced slopes. And within these reclaimed landscapes were planted a community of settlers and 'colonists' who were meant to supply the Islands with a permanent labour force and unique ethnic identity.

Apart from the uneven consequences this has had on the Island ecology, the inscription of an agrarian landscape in the depths of the forest has created deep and irrevocable divides between the local-born community (convict descendants), the Islands' indigenous people and peasant settlers. The redistribution of the physical space in the forest between the tribal reserves and the settler villages has meant the demarcation of two potentially conflicting 'temporal spaces' – one marked by the seemingly 'frozen' time of the indigenous hunter-gatherer communities, and the other, the 'continuous' time of sedentary settler culture. As Vishvajit Pandya argues in Chapter 7, this demarcation has produced three further consequences: the positioning of the inhabitants of the tribal reserve as unchanging primitives, the settlers and local borns as their civilized 'other' and the state as a constant presence and arbiter between the two. The stories of their quotidian struggles of existence may go unrecorded in the historical archives of the state but remains forever etched on the borders of the paddy fields and forest reserves of South Andaman Island.

If Ferrar wanted to 'improve' the Islands into an ideal self-supporting agricultural settlement with a steady supply of labour and a healthy moral environment, the Indian state perpetuated that policy by integrating the project of 'improvement' with that of 'nationalization'. Such projects of nationalization not only sought to reappropriate and improve the Islands' territorial space but also to define its historical imagination, its social identity and its political future. The following chapters, by Clare Anderson and Vishvajit Pandya, explore how the contentious ramifications of these 'mainland' projects are reflected in the myriad material and symbolic inscriptions on the Island landscape. Clare Anderson begins the discussion by looking at the aftermath of the Second World War and the period of the Japanese occupation to show how mainland histories and local identities collided and configured one another.

3   Entangled struggles, contested histories: the Second World War and after

Clare Anderson

Introduction

In 1972, two elderly ex-convicts, Shri B. S. Arunachalam and Shri P. S. Kandaswamy, petitioned the Chief Commissioner of the Andamans. During 1937 to 1938, the men claimed, they had been working as compounders in the Port Blair hospital. There they had acquired the materials necessary to make explosives, with which they had intended to blow up the Cellular Jail and release its political prisoners. The British discovered their plot, however, and tried, convicted and sentenced each man to ten years imprisonment. In their petition, presented to the Chief Commissioner more than two decades after they had been released, the men wrote that they were 'freedom fighters' and entitled to the issue of government pensions, as was the norm for people granted that status. However, they needed records of the 1938 court judgement in order to progress their claim with the authorities in New Delhi. As the records had been destroyed during the Second World War, to date they had been unable to prove their case. In a short reply, the commissioner's assistant secretary noted that he could find no local records of the men's conviction or incarceration, and so he was unable to help them.[1]

In this petition and brief, dismissive note we find repeated, recurring themes in the post-war history of the Andamans: the claims of ex-convicts and local born to 'freedom fighter' status, and their rejection by government. In this chapter, I will describe how, through the local destruction of archives and particularly in the absence of individualized penal colony records, local-born people have been able and continue to make sense of their convict lineage through an appeal to often-generalized histories of anti-colonial rebellion, or by laying stress on the honourable roots of the crimes for which their forebears had been transported. The absence of a

---

[1] Petitions of Shri B. S. Arunachalam and Shri P. S. Kandaswamy to Chief Commissioner Andamans, 14 August 1972; K. K. Warriar, assistant secretary to Chief Commissioner, to Arunachalam and Kandaswamy, 19 August 1972, Acc. No. 985, A&N Archives.

paper trail that can link convict descendants to previous generations means that historical identities are up for grabs. As we will see, these include those of mutineer, patriot, rebel and victim. What will concern me most in this chapter is how the destruction of other colonial-era archives has opened up another space for the making – and contestation – of local-born identity: 'freedom fighting.'

My aim in this chapter is twofold. I seek to add a layer of complexity to the history of freedom fighting in the Islands, and to incorporate it into larger histories of the struggle for Independence in colonial India. I will inject local-born anti-colonialism into what is a quite established historical narrative of freedom fighting in the Islands: that the Andaman Islands was a colonial space for the transportation and confinement of mainland rebels and nationalists, and an occupied wartime space for Indian National Army (INA) operations in support of the Japanese. I want to suggest that from the very moment of the permanent colonization of the islands in 1858 through to the Second World War, the Andamans were significant in these respects, but that they were also a place of *locally generated* resistance. The history of that resistance is complex, for not only could it include criminal convict alliances with nationalist prisoners, including the case with which I opened this chapter, but it could also underpin support for *and* against the British during the war. Indeed, after the British abandoned the Andamans in 1942, at least during the early months of occupation, many Japanese-liberated convicts and local-born Islanders joined the INA in unity with Japan and its larger anti-Western imperialism campaign to establish a Greater East Asia Co-Prosperity Sphere. But as land was seized and Islanders put to forced labour, as food shortages gripped the Islands and as the occupying army became ever more violent and ruthless, many people switched their allegiance to support the British in their war against Japan. Freedom fighting in the Islands could, then, mean different things at different times: support for mainland agitation for Independence, support for the Japanese against the British *and* support for the British against the Japanese.

In redrawing the lines of association between the Islands and the mainland in relation to the history of freedom fighting, I propose that the Andamans were far from peripheral to the creation of the shared history of the struggle for Independence that was so vital for the creation of the Indian nation in 1947. Rather, they were positioned at its very heart. This shift in cartographic gaze of where the nation lies connects also to my effort to position the Andamans in the regional history of the war. As the only part of what is now the Indian nation to endure prolonged Japanese occupation, I wish to centre the Andaman Islands in larger histories of the Second World War in Southeast Asia too, for astonishingly the Islands are almost entirely absent from even the most recent, rigorous historiography.[2]

The effects of occupation in the Andamans were many; and the atrocities of the 'black days' of the war are well remembered and known in the Islands today. Indeed, perhaps as many as one quarter of the population died. Though I do not wish to downplay the real sufferings of the Islands' population, I will focus not on the hardships of the war, but on the previously untold stories of the effects of the occupation on Islanders' political status and identity. For those who fought against the British, those who joined the INA in support of Japan *and* those who fought against the Japanese have each claimed subsequently that they were freedom fighters, and repeatedly and with only limited success tried to secure compensation or special government pensions from the mainland authorities. The Indian government has never accepted their claims, reserving that privilege solely for those political prisoners who were shipped to the Islands from various mainland cities and imprisoned in the Cellular Jail. This breach in political categorization has opened up wide, deep and bitter lines of fracture between Port Blair and New Delhi; local campaigns for recognition of the important role of the Andamans in the Second World War are fading only with the death of those Islanders who were alive at the time. But in order to elaborate the issues surrounding war and compensation, I first turn to a brief history of the occupation.

From occupation to Independence

In December 1941, following Japan's attacks on Malaya, Singapore and Hong Kong, Britain declared war on Japan. Chief Commissioner N. K. Paterson began to make plans to evacuate the Andamans and to repatriate the 5,000 convicts then in the Islands. However, he was quickly overtaken by events. On 15 February 1942, Japanese troops took Singapore and started to make their way into Burma. The British knew that once the Japanese had secured Rangoon, the fall of Port Blair – a short boat trip from the port – was almost inevitable. With Japanese submarines active in the Bay of Bengal, and after three aerial bombardments, the planned rescue ships could not be dispatched from Calcutta. On 1 March, Paterson took the decision to abandon the Islands. The British establishment, Gurkha regiment, and all but a handful of British fled.

---

[2] Christopher Bayly and Tim Harper, *Forgotten Armies: The Fall of British Asia 1941–5* (London: Penguin, 2004); Christopher Bayly and Tim Harper, *Forgotten Wars: The End of Britain's Asian Empire* (London: Allen Lane, 2007).

Only Chief Commissioner Charles Waterfall and his assistant Major A. G. Bird remained from the colonial establishment. Brigadier Francis of the Salvation Army, in charge of the Bhantu settlement, also remained. The convicts, Moplahs, Bhantus, Ranchis, Burmese Karen, local-born people and other settlers had no choice but to stay behind, left to an uncertain fate. Though Anglo-Indian women and children were largely evacuated, the British also left many Anglo-Indian men in the Islands, formerly employees in the wireless, telegraph, forest, and jail departments.

Southeast Asia swiftly fell to Japanese troops. Less than a month after they overran Singapore, on 7 March the Japanese took Rangoon. Meantime, the situation in the Andamans had begun to deteriorate. Supplies were running low, and on 17 March there was civil unrest and petty looting. As the British had predicted, it was not long before the Japanese landed: on 23 March 1941. They faced no resistance, though according to well-laid British plans, officer in charge Ooty blew up the wireless and telegraph departments. The Japanese freed the convicts in the Cellular Jail, and imprisoned Waterfall and his assistant Bird. The new Japanese governor, Colonel Bucho, set up a Peace Committee, and appointed local doctor Diwan Singh to its chair. Singh gave a public speech three days after the occupation began:

The Japanese, like us, are Asians. The British were Firungees [foreigners] ... The Japanese now assure us that they will help us attain freedom from the British. They give us that pledge and therefore, they want us to co-operate with them everyway. In the light of what they say, they deserve our co-operation.'[3]

The Peace Committee set to work for the invading power, appointing more than twenty local-born people to convince Islanders to accept the occupation, and to work with local Japanese officers in running the civil administration, including the forest, police, medical and education departments.[4]

The INA, newly invigorated by Japanese successes in Southeast Asia, and under the leadership of Netaji Subhas Chandra Bose, quickly moved to enlist support in the Andamans. Japanese officer H. Eguchii spoke of Japan's commitment to Indian Independence, and of the need for Islanders' trust.[5] In November, the Japanese ceded the islands to the INA's provisional government (*Azad Hind*, or Free India), taking over the Local

---

[3] Cited in Rabin Roychowdhury, *Black Days in Andaman and Nicobar Islands* (New Delhi: Manas Publications, 2004), 123.

[4] B. B. Lall, *A Regime of Fears and Tears: History of the Japanese Occupation of the Andaman Islands* (New Delhi: Farsight Publishers, 2000 [1992]), 30–2.

[5] Lall, *A Regime of Fears and Tears*, 43–4.

Born Association (LBA) clubhouse in the centre of the bazar and turning it into the headquarters of the Indian Independence League (IIL). This was a regional nationalist organization associated with the INA.[6] They also set up the school for interpreters, across the water from Port Blair in Bamboo Flat. As local-born resident Hari Kishen told me, a few dozen young men were sent to board, and to be immersed in the Japanese language, with a view to facilitating communication between Islanders and the occupying power.[7] At the same time, *A Guide Book to Japanese Language – with Hindustani* was published for use in the Islands.[8]

In December 1942, shortly after signing a pan-Asian treaty with Japan, Netaji himself undertook a three-day visit to the Islands. At a large gathering on the Gymkhana ground in Port Blair, the Andaman branch of the IIL gave him a welcome address, and its chairman, Ramakrishna, presented him with a purse of donations totalling Rs 10,000. The LBA organised a further meeting with Netaji at the Browning Club in Aberdeen Bazar, where a further sum of Rs 5,000 was donated, and patriotic songs were sung. Later on, he spoke of the 'unforgettable event' of standing in what he described as Free India, and seeing the Indian tricolour flag for the first time. The Browning Club was even renamed 'Netaji Club' in his honour.[9]

But despite Netaji's enthusiasm for the Islands' freedom from British colonial rule, in reality this island archipelago was neither Indian nor free, and the IIL had little power. The transfer of power in the Andamans was symbolic, and largely designed for its propaganda value, for the Japanese Navy retained control throughout the occupation.[10] In the months before Netaji's visit, the Japanese had carried out numerous atrocities. Islanders were rounded up, thrown into prison, tortured as British spies or shot; others were conscripted into labour gangs to build fortifications, or forced to turn their land over to food production. Women were raped; property was looted. Forced labourers from Indonesia augmented the local workforce. Koreans were imported as garrison 'comfort women'. Meantime, local people had destroyed anything that might associate them with the British and lay them open to charges of

[6] Rama Krishna, *The Andaman Islands under Japanese Occupation, 1942–1945*, unpublished manuscript, 43, CJML.
[7] Interview with Hari Kishen, 11 December 2011.
[8] Lall, *A Regime of Fears and Tears*, 38–42.
[9] Roychowdhury, *Black Days*, 152. See also Priten Roy and Swapnesh Choudhary, *The Lost Horizon: A Tale of Ross: The Deserted Island's Citadel* (New Delhi: Farsight Publishers, 2002), 93–4.
[10] Joyce C. Lebra, *Japanese-Trained Armies in Southeast Asia* (New York: Columbia University Press, 1977), 13, 30.

spying, in effect any family papers in their possession. Whether Bose knew about the extent of Japanese violence remains a matter of great contention in the Islands today. Some contemporaries have claimed that the Japanese kept him away from local people and so he remained ignorant of the real state of affairs in the Andamans.

In one notorious incident, in May 1942, Japanese Chief Commissioner Colonel Bucho dragged the locally popular Major Bird down the Aberdeen Bazar and publicly beheaded him on trumped-up charges of spying. The elderly residents of Port Blair vividly remember the execution today, for the Japanese forced them to turn out and watch. Unsolicited, Hari Kishen reenacted the scene for my benefit, telling me that when Bird had begged for water, Colonel Bucho had sprinkled water over the sword before the execution.[11] Introduced to another respondent's elderly sister-in-law, who was told that I had a number of 'old photographs' in my possession, she asked spontaneously and again with any prompting from me about whether I had any pictures of Mr Bird.[12] Former development commissioner of the Islands Kiran Dhingra has written that the execution of Bird 'mellowed for ever afterwards the townmen's [sic] attitude to their British administrators'.[13]

After his official visit to the Islands, Bose appointed Colonel A. D. Loganathan to the post of governor, but he failed to acquire political influence. Indeed, Japanese violence escalated within hours of Bose's departure, including even the arrest of IIL chairman Ramakrishna. Continuing allied bombing raids had convinced the Japanese that British spies were at work in the Islands. On 14 January 1944, Dr Diwan Singh, chair of the Peace Committee, was found dead in the Cellular Jail after many weeks of torture as a supposed British spy. The following year, as food shortages gripped the Islands, the Japanese took out to sea and dumped over two hundred men near Havelock Island. Just twelve survived; the others drowned, were eaten by sharks or if they made it to Havelock starved to death.

The Islands' remaining Anglo-Indian population spent ten months interned on Ross Island during this period. The only woman was Dorothy Deakes, who was put to work with her husband and son. She later described their beatings, as well as their daily labour: ripping up the walls and floors of the houses on Ross to supply firewood.[14] In December 1942,

---

[11] Interview with Hari Kishen, 11 December 2011.
[12] Interview with M. Abdul Qadir, 7 December 2011. See also Lall, *A Regime of Fears and Tears*, 33–5.
[13] Kiran Dhingra, *The Andaman and Nicobar Islands in the Twentieth Century, A Gazetteer* (New Delhi: Oxford University Press, 2005), 49.
[14] Mrs D. M. Deakes, age 65, 'I was there', 1960, PCKW.

the Japanese removed the family to Changi prison camp in Singapore.[15] Other Anglo-Indians were sent to Tavoy in Burma. In May 1944 the Deakes were transferred to a camp called Syme Road. Just a month before the Japanese surrender, the emaciated seventy-four-year-old George Deakes died there in a dreadful accident.[16]

Japan surrendered to the Allies on 2 September 1945, but it was not until February 1946 that the British returned to the Andamans and resumed the administration.[17] Shortly beforehand, the Japanese had burnt all the records associated with the penal colony, including those of the jail and revenue departments. The British took the Japanese prisoners of war, after a formal ceremony of surrender at the Gymkhana Ground,[18] and arrested those locals who had sat on the Peace Committee. They released them within a fortnight, however, after the farce of the transfer of power to the IIL in the Islands became clear.[19]

The British ordered several Japanese officers to Singapore where they were tried for war crimes. Their interpreters were some of the locals who had learned to speak Japanese, including Hari Kishen. Transcripts of the trials make for harrowing reading. Nine Burmese executed for attempting to escape from Stewart Sound. The beating of an Anglo-Indian couple called Mr and Mrs Meyers. Extreme violence on local-born men and women – ordinary road labourers, professionals and merchants: a 'coolie' known only as Ovran, Dr Diwan Singh and Nawab Ali.[20] On 18 June 1946, eight Japanese were hanged at Changi Jail for Andaman atrocities. They included Vice Admiral Teizo Hara, the naval commandant, who though acquitted of the execution of the Burmese men described above, was found guilty of causing the death of the 236 people dumped at sea near Havelock.[21]

That same year, on British instructions, there were also local trials in Port Blair. These were initially presided over in the magistrate's court, and then heard by the Andaman court of sessions. A dozen Indian defendants were awarded between two and six years of imprisonment for crimes of torture, abduction and murder.[22] They included at least two policemen, who were tried and convicted under Section 330 of the Indian

---

[15] Deakes, 'I was there', PCKW.
[16] D. M. Deakes to Chief Commissioner Andamans, 18 March 1949, PCKW.
[17] Calcutta Special Report No. D.H.C. 28 (Secret), 11 February 1949, DO133/39 TNA.
[18] A remarkable twelve-minute film showing the reoccupation and ceremony surrender is held in London's Imperial War Museum, at shelf mark JFU416.
[19] Lall, *A Regime of Fears and Tears*, 73–4.
[20] Synopses of these cases can be found at War Crimes Studies Center, University of California Berkeley, http://wcsc.berkeley.edu/world-war-ii-document-archive/pacific-theater-document-archive/ (accessed 21 May 2013).
[21] *The Times of India*, 19 June 1946.   [22] *The Times of India*, 18 October 1948.

penal code, which legislated against the use of torture to extort confessions.[23] Andaman penal colony regulations were still in force in 1946, and there was no right of appeal, except in cases of murder. Thus following Independence, in 1948 the government of India agreed to hear sixteen appeals. As *The Times of India* reported, the government believed that 'these misguided men had acted under fear of their Japanese masters':

They proved over-loyal and allowed themselves to be tools of their conquerors in terrorising the local population. Employed as interpreters and police officials, they extorted confessions from people suspected of pro-British sympathies by barbarous methods and even aided the Japanese troops to abduct women for nefarious purposes.[24]

In this description of events, we find an early expression of the debates that were played out for many years after the occupation: whether and to what extent local people assisted (or resisted) the Japanese, voluntarily or under duress. And, in so doing, did their loyalty lie with a free India? I will return to how IIL allegiances were used by locals seeking the political status of 'freedom fighter' later in the chapter. But in order to understand the historical roots of these claims, first I would like to continue with the story of the Andamans in the months and years following the Japanese surrender.

The abolition of the penal colony: repatriation, Andaman Indians and Andamanians

With the British reoccupation of the Andamans at the end of the war in 1945, the penal colony was abolished, the mainland provinces were asked to agree to the remission of the balance of all sentences, and convicts and ex-convicts were given the opportunity of repatriation. Almost 4,000 took up the offer. While awaiting their return to India, many meantime joined the Andaman and Nicobar Development Force, which also included a free, civil pioneer force from the mainland.[25] Convicts who had been under sentence or self-supporting as ticket-of-leave holders in March 1942 were *compelled* to join this unit; those who would have been released between March 1942 and reoccupation were not offered any form of government support and so were *encouraged* to 'volunteer'. The Development Force was organized in the same way as convict work gangs had been formerly, with N. K. Paterson believing that it was easier

---

[23] Brij Lal, government pensioner Aberdeen village, to Chief Commissioner Inamul Majid, 17 November 1947, Acc. No. 992, A&N Archives.

[24] *The Times of India*, 18 October 1948.

[25] Abdul Gafoor, no. 10524 certificate of release, 7 May 194[?], A&N Archives.

to 'adopt a system already understood and worked by all concerned', with 'discipline and supervision ... enforced as in the pre-occupation system'. This included the use of non-commissioned officer (NCO) overseers from among the men. There were two key differences though: discipline and punishment were brought into line with the civil pioneer regime, and that the volunteer force was paid.[26] There was a series of eventual repatriations, with the former convict ship the S. S. Maharaja returning ex-convicts to the mainland during 1946 and 1947.[27] Detailed lists of the men, women and children on board accompanied them, and on arrival in Calcutta they were handed over to the commissioner of police. He was charged with arranging the issue of rail warrants and subsistence allowances to the ex-convicts and their families, and with seeing them onto trains back to their home districts.[28]

In other cases, mainland families petitioned Chief Commissioner Paterson requesting the repatriation of their surviving relatives. One man, Hassan, wrote that his father had been transported to the Andamans in 1926; his mother and two siblings had followed him in 1934. During the occupation, his parents had died, but his brothers and sister were still alive. He wrote that he wanted to go to the Islands to bring them home. Paterson ordered their repatriation by the next boat. A second man, Hachan Howaldar, petitioned that his cousin and wife had died, and asked for the repatriation of their six children. Though two girls had married fishermen, the Chief Commissioner agreed to the request.[29] At this time, about 8,500 local-born people remained in the Andamans. Many were the descendants of the nineteenth-century transportation convicts, and unlike more recent arrivals they had lost all connection to the mainland provinces. Also remaining in the Islands were the five hundred or so Bhantus who had, in Paterson's words, become 'mixed up with the general population' and so were also treated as free.[30]

---

[26] Rates of pay for Andaman 'Pioneers', Acc. No. 333, A&N Archives; Treatment of Convicts on Reoccupation and Formation of Andaman's development: Notes of N. K. Paterson, 5 August 1945, Acc. No. 339, A&N Archives.

[27] Repatriation lists of ex-convicts, n.d., Acc. Nos 8, 16, A&N Archives.

[28] Repatriation and release of convicts: arrangements to their homes along with their families in India: Memorandum of N. K. Paterson, 13 December 1945, Acc. No. 14, A&N Archives.

[29] Repatriation and release of convicts: arrangements to their homes along with their families in India: Hassan, resident of Dargahi Shah district Jhang Punjab, to Chief Commissioner Paterson, 29 January 1946; petition of Hachan Howaldar, cousin of late life convict Iman Khan, to inspector general of prisons Bengal, 1 February 1946; enquiry by Tahsildar Aberdeen, 16 April 1946, Home, Acc. No. 14, A&N Archives.

[30] Future of the Bhantu settlement: Notes of N. K. Paterson, 23 May 1945, and B. L. Pandey, 15 June 1945, Acc. No. 203, A&N Archives.

Meantime, as the repatriations were in progress, rumours abounded about the fate of the Islands. There were tentative plans to give over the Andamans to the Anglo-Indians, as a homeland called 'Britasia.' Given their strategic location in the Bay of Bengal, and proximity to East Pakistan, the authorities in what was to become the new nation of Pakistan staked a claim on them too. In June 1947 it was further reported in the Indian press that the Islands would be ceded to Britain, and converted into a naval base, a rumour that government quickly moved to deny.[31] After all this national posturing, ultimately the Islands became part of India. However, at least as far as the local population was concerned it was on far from equal terms. The LBA claimed that because of the Islands' history as a penal colony, mainland administrators looked down on the Andaman population, viewing locals as politically backward and incapable of self-government. It pointed out that government had given the Islands one seat in parliament, but for a nominated rather than an elected representative, as was the norm in other parts of India. The LBA also noted that it was the only province in the union that had no representative in India's Constituent Assembly, which had been set up in 1946 to draft the Indian Constitution.[32] The LBA was to complain repeatedly over the years that followed of this kind of discrimination, with respect to lack of consultation with the Islands over political change, denial of Islander access to mainland politics, employment and other resources.

In April 1947, LBA member Mohamed Abdas Sabhan, seeking a break with the Islands' penal past, asked the association to consider a change of name to the Andamanian Association. He cited the customary use of the words Malayan, Tavoyan, Merguian, Korian, Iranian and Indian, to describe the people of various regions and nations, arguing that 'Andamanian' would serve the population of the islands well. 'We cannot find a suitable word in the old vocabularies', he argued.[33] Subsequent to his suggestion, the LBA underwent two name changes, first becoming the Andaman Indian Association (AIA) and later taking the title Sabhan had suggested: the Andamanian Association (AA). These shifts in appellation went further than an attempt to find a new vocabulary of convict descent, and beyond an effort to distance the association from the Islands' history as a penal colony. They were indicative also of the concern that local people felt about being able to distinguish themselves from the short-stay

---

[31] *The Times of India*, 9 June 1947; 19 June 1947.

[32] The other provinces with representatives were Ajmer-Merwara, Baluchistan, Coorg and the NWFP.

[33] M. Abdas Sabhan to secretary Local Born Association, 2 April 1947, MLPC.

mainland Indians who had begun to arrive as administrators and in other official capacities. Further, the association's name changing might also be read as an early expression and invocation of a language of domicile and even claims of indigeneity.[34] Both were to become more pronounced after 1949, following the resettlement and rehabilitation of Bengali refugees in the Islands, when many pre-1942 settlers sought to establish themselves as the 'real' inhabitants of the Andamans.

After 1947, the LBA (then AIA and AA) met repeatedly with government of India ministers, calling attention to local grievances and making political demands. Of especial importance after the three-and-a-half-year occupation was education, for schools had not operated normally from 1942 to 1945 and many children had received no instruction at all. Locals also repeatedly pressed their claims for political representation – at local and central levels – and access to government employment, for at the time routinely government appointed civil servants from the mainland to Andaman postings.

Although many people's convict parents and grandparents were long since dead, the penal colony had of course only recently been abolished, and it was becoming clear that transportation had left significant political legacies. LBA secretary Sri Ratnam wrote to Mahatma Gandhi in January 1947, pressing the association's desire to have a stake in Andaman affairs:

During the British time Anglo Indians and Europeans were bossing and now with our own Government we find that Indians from the mainland are doing the same. This is where it pinches us ... Probably the Government of India are misrepresented facts by some men who do not wish us any good.

As proof of local-born people's capacity for office, which seemed to be in question due to the stigma of their convict descent, Ratnam drew attention to the important role that they had played in running the civil administration during the Japanese occupation. Appealing to the Andamans' similarity to the British Empire's other great penal colonies, he wrote:

[T]here are men among us who can be an asset to the Administration ... We are tied to the soil and the Islands are our home. In due course a social status has grown up among us. We have become permanently settled here with no other home and taken to all walks of life that can be imagined in any colony. Our case, in other words, on a small scale is similar to Australia.[35]

---

[34] For example, Sri Ratman, Secretary LBA, to Rajendra Prasad, President Indian Constituent Assembly, New Delhi, 8 July 1947, MLPC.

[35] Sri Ratnam, secretary LBA, to Mahatma Gandhi, 2 January 1947, MLPC.

The LBA, AIA and AA did not affiliate to any political party, and it was perhaps partly for this reason that, incredibly, by the early 1950s there had still been no democratic reforms in the Islands. Andaman governance remained foregrounded in the rules and regulations of the penal colony. Thus there was no elected advisory or administrative council. There was no municipal board in Port Blair. And, there were no village *panchayats* (assemblies). The judiciary was not independent from the executive, and many penal colony–era laws remained in force. These included colonial labour laws, which meant that there were no industrial tribunals or social insurance schemes. Land tenure regulations remained unchanged from those drawn up in the 1870s following the recommendations of J. S. Campbell and H. W. Norman's important 1874 report.[36] However, there was one significant change in administration. In 1951, after Chief Commissioner A. K. Ghosh wrote that 'local born' had 'a rather humiliating connotation', the 1951 Census created a new, more incorporative category of 'Andaman Indian', which included all permanent residents of the islands. This shift in categorization had profound and lasting effects, for it included all but mainland workers on Andaman postings, in Ghosh's words, 'be he a new settler from East Bengal, a naturalized Karen from Burma or a person born here out of convict ancestry'. The Chief Commissioner added: 'all non-tribal peoples in the Andamans are settlers – the difference is only in the point of time of settlement'.[37] Not all Islanders agreed, as evidenced in the later creation of the political category 'pre-42'. This marked a point of distinction between convicts and others who had been forcibly shipped to the Islands during the British colonial period – and who had intermarried with each other – and those who had arrived in the years following Indian Independence.

In 1954, Sri K. R. Ganesh assumed the presidency of the AA, and oversaw the publication of the bimonthly *Hamari Awaz (Our Voice)* – the first ever non-government newspaper or magazine produced in the Andamans. That same year, the first elected President of the new Indian republic, Rajendra Prasad, visited the Islands. The AA called upon him to institute reform. By this time, Bengali refugee settlers had begun to arrive, and fearing the prospect of political union with (East) Pakistan,

---

[36] Deputation of the Honourable Sir H. W. Norman KCB, to visit Port Blair: Report on the requirements of the Penal Settlement of Port Blair, P/528 Home (Port Blair), August 1874, nos. 51–84, IOR.

[37] A. K. Ghosh, *Census of India, 1951, Vol. XVII, The Andaman and Nicobar Islands, Appendix I* (Calcutta: Government of India Press, 1955), p. xliv.

locals asked government to ensure that in future settlers be brought to the Islands from all parts of India.[38]

In 1956, the AA sent a six-member deputation to India, visiting Calcutta, Madras and Delhi, to press for the representation of the Islands' interests in India's second five-year plan (1956–61). It was of the view that even the Chief Commissioner of the Andamans had 'the attitude of ... veiled hostility to the old settlers'. At the time, the AA was the only mass organization in the Andamans. It had a base in almost every village, and had a membership of 2,500 (about 7 per cent of the total population of the Islands), a sixty-member general council, and a working committee of fifteen. Included in the delegation were President Ratnam; Sri Bharath, an elderly man who claimed descent from an 1857 convict, and who travelled as a representative of the Islands' Hindustani speaking *kisans* (peasants); Francis Lobo, who had worked for over forty years as a welder in the marine department, travelling on behalf of the Islands' industrial workers; two Moplahs, Kunji Moideen Kutty and Aly Ahmad; and the editor of *Hamari Awaz*, Mr Ganesh. The AA claimed that the delegation represented the 'cultural and economic composition of the Andaman Islands'.[39]

The delegation represented to the Indian government that despite the resettlement of Bengali refugees, the first five-year plan (1951–6) had promoted little other development in the Islands. It pushed for the expansion and modernization of agriculture, the distribution and con-solidation of land holdings (ten acres per family), as well as innovation in irrigation, the expansion of rural credit and guaranteed minimum prices for agricultural produce. It also called for the development of timber and other commercial crops; the establishment of housing schemes; and the expansion of educational, medical and cultural facilities. Finally, it asked that residents of the Islands get priority in government employment, as well as the one-third extra pay allowance that was granted to mainland government employees in recognition of the high cost of living in the Islands. I would also like to note that at this time the AA also supported various demands of the Bengali settlers, regarding land allocation, employment, education and entitlement to the preservation of cultural distinction.[40]

In more recent years, under the presidency of John Lobo (1979–90), the AA became even more active, demanding the allocation of house

---

[38] Citizens of Andamans to Rajendra Prasad, President of the Republic of India, n.d., MLPC.
[39] Deputation to India, Andamanian Association, statement to the press, n.d., MLPC.
[40] Deputation to India, MLPC.

plots, the prevention of settler encroachment on local-born landholdings, the restriction of in-migration, and the reservation of places for local-born students in medicine, dentistry, engineering and agriculture.[41] The association also became known as the LBA once again, as in the context of in-migration from all over India following Bengali resettlement in the 1940s and 1950s, it sought to differentiate what it saw as acceptable privileges of access to government resources by pre-42s *and* Bengali refugees, in contradistinction to those who had followed both settler groups. Part of this disassociation was bound up with what the LBA saw as entitlement to government aid in the aftermath of the shared experiences of forced relocation. It also related more specifically to local-born sufferings during the Second World War. With this in view, I now turn to a discussion of local-born claims to wartime compensation, relief and government pensions, and come back to the underpinning theme with which I opened this chapter: the contentious landscape of political claims to 'freedom fighting' status.

Wartime compensation, relief and pensions

As part of a larger policy of Indian non-alignment, believing that it imposed too many restrictions on Japan compared to the allies, India's first Prime Minister Jawaharlal Nehru refused to sign the Treaty of San Francisco, which came into force to end the war on 28 April 1952. Instead, on 9 June 1952, India and Japan signed their own Treaty of Peace. The Treaty of San Francisco had directed Japan to pay compensation for any war damages it had inflicted on occupied territories. This included Burma, which was a signatory. However, though India's Treaty of Peace with Japan restored diplomatic relations between the two powers, it made no provisions for compensation at all. Rather, the treaty stated clearly:

India waives all reparation claims against Japan ... India waives all claims of India and Indian nationals arising out of action taken by Japan and her nationals in the course of the prosecution of the war.[42]

This meant that at the time, Japan was not under any legal obligation to compensate India or Indians for war damages, or to pay any form of reparations. This included Indian soldiers killed in action while serving

---

[41] Rabin Roychowdhury, *Andaman and Nicobar: The Untold Islands* (New Delhi: Manas Publications, 2011), 329–30.

[42] Article 6, Treaty of Peace between Japan and India, ratified and signed into force, 27 August 1952, www.gwu.edu/~memory/data/treaties/India.pdf (accessed 19 March 2012).

in the British armed forces, as well as those living in the Islands during the Japanese occupation.

Before the Treaty of Peace of 1952, the government of India had put in place its own War Injuries Scheme. In the Andamans, it typically granted widows' pensions of 10 rupees per month.[43] But the scheme proved difficult to administer. First, the deputy commissioner had to gather information and then compile lists of those who had died during the occupation. He did this by writing to each government office, and asking for relevant details. The lists are distressing: Munia Gounda, peon in the shipping office, killed by Japanese. Velu Kutty, a store tally clerk, died in British Bombing.[44] Wuzir Ali, serang in the engineer and harbour master's office, 'rounded up and presumably killed by Japanese'. Md Yusoof, a tindal, 'ditto'. Abdul Jabbar, 'ditto ditto'.[45] The lists of names go on – the home, forest, posts and telegraphs, education, public works, medical departments. The jail, police and supply offices. Warders, clerks, compounders, orderlies, bakers, foremen, mechanics, carpenters – local people 'rounded up', 'killed', 'murdered', 'died as the result of tortures', or simply 'presumed dead'.

The deputy commissioner relied on local information about who had died – and whether they had died at the hands of the Japanese or of 'natural' causes – for there were no surviving records. And, of course, there were many who fell in between the cracks of the scheme's categories, notably labourers killed in accidents, the elderly, and those who died after succumbing to illness while malnourished. A key question for the administration was whether these were 'war' or 'natural' deaths.[46] To complicate matters further, some of those who had survived the war had been left debilitated by the occupation, and applied for pensions on the grounds of disability. In 1947, for instance, Brij Lal petitioned the Chief Commissioner about his incarceration in the Cellular Jail on a charge of spying for the British. He had undergone such torture and violent beatings that subsequently the medical board had invalided him. He had been unable to complete his pensionable service, but asked that he be issued with a pension in recognition of his wartime experiences.[47] Abdul Rahman, wrote in 1948 that the Japanese had beaten him and a man named Ahmed

---

[43] Memorandum of Deputy Commissioner, 27 December 1947, A&N Archives.

[44] Office of the Shipping Offices, 12 November 1946, A&N Archives.

[45] Office of the Engineer and Harbour Master, 19 November 1946, A&N Archives.

[46] War injuries scheme: Rai Sahib K. C. Banerjea, secretary to Chief Commissioner, to *inter alia* secretary to government Bihar, judicial department Bihar, 1 December 1948, Acc. No. 41, A&N Archives.

[47] Brij Lal, government pensioner Aberdeen village, to Chief Commissioner Inamul Majid, 17 November 1947, A&N Archives.

Khadim so badly that Khadim had died, and his (Rahman's) left hand had been left so injured that he had been permanently incapacitated.[48]

A couple of days before Rahman's petition landed on his desk, deputy commissioner Kishan Singh had complained that he was receiving applications for relief every single day. He contended that in the absence of any paper records of Japanese occupation, after their initial petitions were rejected individuals changed their names and 'procured tutored evidence' to make further applications. Thus he recommended the institution of a three-month limit for persons resident in the Islands during the occupation to lodge their claims, unless family members had died.[49] By May, the government of India had decided to accept his position, arguing that the individuals concerned had already had ample time to put in applications.[50]

There was a local uproar, for the Andamans had been left so devastated by wartime occupation – let us not forget that perhaps a quarter of the population died – that many people had missed the deadline. To some extent, the government subsequently reviewed its position, deciding to introduce a local system of relief loans. It allocated Rs 10 lakhs (Rs 1,000,000) for this purpose. However, this was a very limited response to the Islands' huge losses. The scheme offered loans, as distinct from compensation or relief. Illustrative of its limitations was the Chief Commissioner's failure to respond to the AIA's call for a year's pay for all those village headmen, watchmen and labourers who had been in employment but had not been paid during the Japanese occupation. The AIA was well aware that free grants were being given to residents of Burma, Malaya and Singapore, which had all been occupied by the Japanese, and it even knew about the issue of relief in the Channel Islands, the only part of the British Isles that had been overrun by Germany. 'This was the only part of India to suffer the full force of the war, loss of life, property and natural resources,' AIA secretary Ratnam urged the Chief Commissioner in 1950, 'which has left a permanent impress on the economic life of the people and as every where else the people have not yet recovered from the [e]ffects of the ... Japanese ... administration.'[51]

---

[48] Petition of Abdul Rahman, 28 January 1948, A&N Archives.
[49] Memorandum of deputy commissioner Kishan Singh, 26 January 1948, A&N Archives.
[50] War injuries scheme: Rai Sahib K. C. Banerjea, secretary to Chief Commissioner, to *inter alia* secretary to government Bihar, judicial department Bihar, 1 December 1948, Acc. No. 41, A&N Archives.
[51] Reorganization of system of village officials: Sri Ratnam, secretary Andaman Indians Association, to Chief Commissioner, 19 April 1950; Memorandum of Secretary to Chief Commissioner K. C. Banerjee, 26 July 1952; note of A. K. Ghosh, 15 April 1950, J&R Acc. No. 31, A&N Archives.

The twin issues of compensation and relief were raised repeatedly during the years that followed: for instance, in 1953, when the government of India decided to take over Ross Island, where previous to the war local people had owned houses and shops. During the occupation, the Japanese had used Ross as their headquarters, occupying buildings, looting supplies and dismantling unwanted structures for their stone and timber. Many locals had had property and business interests there, usually following the issue of colonial government licenses decades earlier. During the war, they lost everything. Afterwards, with the Chief Commissioner keen to explore new uses for the island, the government decided that they would neither be compensated for the destruction of their property nor be allowed to rebuild their former homes and businesses.[52]

In June 1957, over a decade after the end of the war, and with no indication that Islanders saw the issue of compensation as in any way settled, the Chief Commissioner set up an advisory committee for the 'grant of relief to persons who suffered losses during the Japanese occupation'. Its goal was to enable locals to 'restart their life and to get them on their own feet'. Government made clear that the grants were to be issued in the form of loans or *ex-gratia* payments, and that they did not indicate acceptance of any liability for wartime losses. Only those in financial difficulties were eligible to apply, and even then for a maximum grant of just Rs 3,000. Over the coming months the committee met more than three dozen times, and by 1961 it had spent the large majority of its Rs 660 lakhs (Rs 66 million) budget. Full records of just one of these gatherings survive in the Andaman and Nicobar Archives – the sixty-eight petitioners to the 34th committee meeting – giving extraordinary insights into wartime losses and post-war grievances. For that reason, I would like to explore in some detail the records of that meeting here.

As mentioned above, legally speaking, this was a programme of *relief*, not *compensation*. However, my sense from reading the extensive correspondence of and petitions presented to the committee is that individual applicants did not perceive it as such. They were looking for compensation, or at least explicit government recognition of their losses. In their submissions, the often elderly applicants – about half of whom were widows – detail the material devastation wrought by the Japanese:

---

[52] Ross Island, policy regarding Petition of Sri Venkat Raj Appalswamy, 2 January 1953; Chief Commissioner's memorandum, 24 January 1953, J&R Acc. No. 141, A&N Archives.

the theft of buffaloes, cattle, goats, poultry, boats, gold, ornaments and money; and the destruction of brick-built (*pukka*) and thatched (*kachcha*) houses, paddy fields, sugar plantations and shops. Mainly, they requested money for the purchase of livestock, or for house construction or repair. And, almost all the applications were successful, though most applicants received either loans or *ex-gratia* payments of between Rs 300 and Rs 500, typically about half the amount that they had applied for. Nevertheless, given that at the time the annual income of a peasant cultivator in the islands was around Rs 900, a widow's monthly pension was Rs 12, and a family's Rs 35, these were not insubstantial sums, particularly for those elderly men and women who were not expected to pay the money back.[53]

Some applications were rejected, though: well-off men, widows who had remarried and, curiously, paupers, perhaps because government saw them as 'undeserving poor' or unlikely to repay the loans. But those men and women of means who were filtered out of the process felt greatly disadvantaged, because though they were not poor, still, they had lost a great deal. Further, for reasons that are not entirely clear, at the 34th committee meeting the administration decided to bar government employees from making further claims. This was not well received by Islanders, many of whom were working in government posts. Consider the following petition, presented by Mohamed Hanif, an orderly in the deputy commissioner's office:

That he is a sufferer from the Japanese atrocities and have applied for reparations, and approached the general section of the Secretariat to know the fate of his application and was given a bleak reply that Government servants are debarred from having any such losses made good ...

That during the occupation he has lost 4 Singer [sewing] Machines, 8 animals, all the fruit bearing trees in his Garden, a good house as also ready cash to the tune of about 11,000/-.

That the order for stopping payment was passed in the 34th meeting, whereas there [are] lot[s] of other Government servants in better and higher positions than himself who have been lucky to get such reparations, and at the same time being in Government service.

He is aggrieved in pin pointing him and separating his case for not entitling to be helped by Government.[54]

---

[53] Grant of relief to persons who suffered losses during the Japanese occupation, meeting of the relief advisory committee held on 30 August 1961, enc. Statement showing the persons of the category as specified in item no. IV of the Chief Commissioner's memorandum, dated 6 June 1957, Acc. No. 140, A&N Archives.

[54] Mohamed Hanif to Chief Commissioner B. N. Maheshwari, 26 March 1962, Public Acc. No. 140, A&N Archives.

I do not know what became of his 'prayer for personal interview and representation'.[55]

The position of the independent Indian government was a sharp contrast to that adopted by the British at the height of the war. As part of a larger commitment to compensation, a British memorandum of November 1942 had ordered that central government servants were entitled to the following compensation, albeit limited:

one month's pay, or R1,000/-, whichever is less, for the loss of their personal kit due to evacuation from any territory, since occupied by the enemy ... In addition the Government of India are prepared in deserving cases to grant special advances of pay up to three month's [sic] pay ... recoverable in ... monthly instalments ... such advances will be interest free.[56]

Subsequently, during 1942 and 1943 the British government processed a stream of petitions for compensation from abandoned Indians and from Anglo-Indians who had been evacuated to the mainland.[57] Petitioners put in claims for the furniture, cars, bicycles, clothing and household effects that they had been forced to leave behind in Port Blair – including even framed photographs, gramophones, records, meat safes and second-hand Singer sewing machines.[58] Even Mrs Francis, evacuated wife of Brigadier Francis, in charge of the Bhantu villages, who had stayed behind in the Andamans as a prisoner of war, made enquiries about the compensation scheme. Her petition was only rejected because with her husband still in the Japanese occupied Islands, government could not assume that her property had been lost. 'I am therefore to express regret that we are unable to entertain your claim for compensation at present', the secretary to the government in the home department wrote to Mrs Francis, in July 1943.[59]

---

[55] Mohamed Hanif to Chief Commissioner B. N. Maheshwari, 26 March 1962, Public Acc. No. 140, A&N Archives.

[56] Compensation to Central Government servants for personal kit lost in enemy occupied territory in which they were on duty, government of India finance department memorandum, 3 November 1942, Acc. No. 19, A&N Archives.

[57] List of Andaman evacuees, Acc. No. 127, A&N Archives.

[58] Grant of compensation to Mr N. H. Young, formerly deputy jailor, Port Blair, for property lost in the Andamans, due to enemy occupation on the Island: N. H. Young, Japanese internment camp, Purana Qila, New Delhi, to joint secretary to government of India home department, 27 September 1942, and N. N. Banerji to deputy secretary government of India home department, 25 September 1942, Acc. No. 17, A&N Archives; A. A. Khan to secretary government of India home department, 16 September 1942, Acc. No. 23, A&N Archives; Grant of compensation for loss of property in the Andamans, by Mr W. Lockwood: W. Lockwood to secretary to government of India, 17 July 1943, Acc. No. 80, A&N Archives.

[59] Mrs Francis to Evacuee Department, Government of India, New Delhi, 5 May 1943; A. W. Lovatt, government of India home department (jails), to Mrs Francis, 13 July 1943, Acc. No. 79, A&N Archives.

The government learned later on that the Japanese had employed the brigadier in that most humiliating of labours: the cleaning out of the Islands' drains.[60]

The Indian government's distribution of war relief in the Andamans perhaps formed part of the backdrop to a further treaty with Japan, signed in December 1963. For reasons that I have been unable to decipher, and despite the denial of financial claims in their 1952 peace treaty, Japan agreed to pay India ¥9 million – Rs 119 crore (million) – in compensation, in final settlement of Indian war claims. Responsibility for its distribution lay with the government of India.[61] None of the money ever made it to the Andamans, despite protests by Islanders when evidence of a transfer of funds came into public view in the year 2008. The matter, one suspects, is far from settled.

Also of importance in the Islands were contemporary events on the mainland. In 1969, the ministry for home affairs decided that 173 mainland nationalists, who had served more than five years imprisonment under the British, were 'freedom fighters' and so would be given a pension of Rs 200 per month each. This decision gave a further boost to Islanders seeking compensation for their wartime losses. Of further significance was the government of India's August 1972 announcement, marking the twenty-fifth anniversary of Independence, to grant pensions to people who had taken part in the Khilafat non-cooperation movement in Malabar, also as 'freedom fighters'. At this time, however, the government was clear that it was not willing to consider claims from those who had participated in the Malabar rebellion of 1921, some of whom had been transported to the Andamans *en masse*. The Andaman widow of a man called Lachmiah, for example, petitioned in 1973 for a pension on the basis that he had taken 'active part in RAMPA rebellion/freedom fight' during 1922 to 1924. It was rejected.[62] In other cases where locals claimed that they had been transported for revolt, they could not produce documentation to support their petitions. In 1975, for instance, an inspector general of police reported with respect to some of the old

---

[60] Noel Paterson, *Experiences of a District Officer: Andaman and Nicobar Islands, The Reoccupation 1945–47*, transcription of taped records, courtesy of Selma Chalabi.

[61] Arrangement between the government of Japan and the government of India regarding settlement of certain Indian claims, 14 December 1963, www.gwu.edu/~memory/data/treaties/India.pdf (accessed 11 September 2012). The agreement specified a conversation rate of ¥75.60 : Rs 1.

[62] Central scheme for the grant of pension to freedom fighters and their families: petition of Smti Govindamma, widow of late Lachmiah, Aberdeen Bazar, to Chief Commissioner, 7 April 1975, Acc. No. 1152, A&N Archives.

Madras Presidency claims that all the central prison records had been eaten by white ants, and so he could not verify what the petitioners had said about the crime for which they had been transported.[63]

In 1975, the home minister visited the Andamans and agreed to meet with community representatives to discuss this general issue. They put forward 199 Moplah rebels for pensions, alongside the names of sixteen men who had participated in the non-cooperation movement. 'We firmly believe that most of us were sentenced and deported to these Islands on charges of revolt against the crown', their petition asserted, 'and that we are eligible for the pension under the scheme for grant of pension to freedom fighters sanctioned by the Government of India.'[64] Not long afterwards, the government made the decision to recognize the Moplahs in the Andamans as 'freedom fighters', and to grant them the same pension as their compatriots who had remained in Kerala.[65]

Despite the Moplah decision, which aligned the fate of those imprisoned on the mainland or sent to the Andamans, there remained a fundamental incompatibility between the mainland definition of freedom fighting and island-centred understandings of it. Government argued that only mainland incarceration or transportation to the Cellular Jail of the Andamans counted. Local-born people and repatriated ex-convicts urged them to consider the importance of joining the INA and supporting the Japanese for the freedom struggle. In 1971, one Asharfilal Sheonarayan petitioned that he had been deported from Lucknow jail to the Andamans in 1940, and at the time of Japanese occupation he had offered his services to Netaji for, as he put it, 'the liberation of India from the British domination'. He had, he wrote, supervised the construction of army barracks in the jungle; supervised and assisted with the growing of food; and worked as a police interpreter in Hindustani, Japanese and Malay. The Japanese had paid him the equivalent wartime currency of Rs 12,000 for his services, but after reoccupation this currency had been declared worthless. He had since received no compensation or relief, and after he was repatriated to mainland India in 1947 he found that his property had been 'misappropriated by others'. He asked

---

[63] Central scheme for the grant of pension to freedom fighters and their families: inspector-general of police Madras to deputy secretary to government Madras, 14 March 1975, Acc. No. 1152, A&N Archives.

[64] Central scheme for the grant of pension to freedom fighters and their families: Moplah petition to K. Brahmananda Reddy, home minister, government of India, n.d. [1975], Acc. No. 1152, A&N Archives.

[65] Central scheme for the grant of pension to freedom fighters and their families: Warrior to secretary to government of India, ministry of home affairs, 7 April 1975, Acc. No. 1152, A&N Archives; *National Herald* news clipping, 22 May 1975.

that 'the assurances given by Netaji Subhas Chandra Bose at the time of
enlisting for the freedom fight be substantially given effect to.'[66]

Asharfilal elaborated further in a second petition to the Chief
Commissioner:

I am preparing a historical book with my own pen wherein a great deal of what
I saw *while taking part in the freedom struggle in the Andamans* how Japan came
challenging the British rule; how the Britishers who came across were done away
with … how Japan succeeded in taking over and handing over the Andamans …
it will prove an immortal story.[67]

He added: 'Japan gave me an assignment of taking work from 500 labourers on account of the very work I was doing, in the Freedom Struggle'.[68]
But government never agreed to his position; advising Asharfilal: 'the
scheme for pension formulated by the Government of India is meant only
for those freedom fighters who had suffered imprisonment in Andaman
Cellular Jail.'[69] The Andaman administration did make enquiries on his
behalf, in an attempt to strengthen his case, interviewing ex-convicts
known to him. However, this was not because they were sympathetic to
his pro-Japanese alliance. Rather, the investigation was centred on finding out whether he had ever been imprisoned in the Cellular Jail.[70]

Islanders continued to submit petitions on the basis of their INA
membership, however, often through the local Ex-INA Men Association
of Port Blair, which liaised with the All-India INA Committee in the
issue of certificates of membership. But the assistant secretary to the
Chief Commissioner continued to hold that 'there was no freedom
movement as such in this territory and none in this territory has so far
been recognised as a freedom fighter.' Ultimately, only three Andaman
pension claims were ever accepted by the mainland – Bejoy Lall Banerjee, of Haddo, and Nihar Chandra Dutta, of Dundas Point (Rs 200 per
month each); and Smt Susma Rani Sain, the widow of Siddheswara Sain

---

[66] Freedom fighters incarcerated in Cellular Jail, Port Blair: petition of Asharfilal
   Sheonarayan, aged 50, residing at Dataram Shahu-ka-Makan, … Lashkar, Gwalior,
   MP, to Chief Commissioner of the Andaman and Nicobar Islands, n.d. [1971], Acc.
   No. 985, A&N Archives; Asharfi Lal alias Malind to Warrior, assistant secretary to Chief
   Commissioner, 17 February 1971, Acc. No. 985, A&N Archives.
[67] Freedom fighters incarcerated in Cellular Jail: Asharfi Lal, alias Malind, to Warrior,
   17 February 1971 (my emphasis), Acc. No. 985, A&N Archives.
[68] Freedom fighters incarcerated in Cellular Jail: Lal to Warrior, Acc. No. 985, A&N
   Archives.
[69] Freedom fighters incarcerated in Cellular Jail: N. B. Kumar, deputy secretary to
   government of India, to Shri Ashrafi Lal Tewari, 30 October 1971, Acc. No. 985,
   A&N Archives.
[70] Freedom fighters incarcerated in Cellular Jail: Warrior to Chief Commissioner, 19 July
   1972, Acc. No. 985, A&N Archives.

of the department of lighthouses and lightships, who received Rs 70 per month. Two more were issued to residents of Campbell Bay in the Nicobars: Bansi Sharma and Gulzara Singh.[71] Into the 1970s, Islanders continued to protest about what they saw as mainland discrimination against them. The Andaman and Nicobar youth congress committee recorded in 1975: 'Freedom Fighters all over India (except these Islands) have been sanctioned pensions under the Govt. of India's instructions.'[72]

Histories of commemoration and memorialization

As this chapter has shown, there have been deep fractures between the mainland and the Andamans in the politics of identity, most especially claims about identity, in the decades since the end of the Second World War. There have been divergent views about the appropriate reward for loyalty to the Indian Independence movement, and in particular about who was engaged in freedom fighting. Compensation for wartime losses was never agreed; rather, Andaman residents were offered loans, and the issue of Japanese compensation remains unresolved. The LBA underwent name changes that were connected to the drawing of boundaries of social, cultural and economic inclusion and exclusion, and in turn to efforts to change aspects of the islands' political relationship with the mainland. The articulation of the history of this complex landscape of belonging sets the stage for an appreciation of the history of the commemoration and memorialization of freedom fighting. This history will be the focus of the final part of this chapter.

The development of state-sanctioned commemoration in the Andamans might best be viewed as an elaboration of the working through over time of these local political identities and mainland–island relationships. After 1947 local-born people engaged with official agendas of memorialisation – but firmly on their own terms. Independence Day, the penal colony and the war: all these things were and are still remembered in the Andamans. But I contend here that in order to secure an integrated understanding of what is remembered, where and how, it is imperative to show that commemoration has a history of its own. In the next chapter, Vishvajit Pandya will take forward this integrative approach, and at the same time shift our gaze to everyday *practices* of memorialisation in the

[71] Central scheme for the grant of pension to freedom fighters and their families: Warriar to secretary to government of India, ministry of home affairs, 3 May 1974, Acc. No. 1152, A&N Archives.

[72] Central scheme for the grant of pension to freedom fighters and their families: Andaman and Nicobar youth congress committee, n.d. [1975], Home, Acc. No. 1152, A&N Archives.

Andamans. His intervention turns on Deleuze and Guattari's idea of the rhizome, and he invokes the concept of rhizomatic landscapes to show that locals give variegated meanings to official sites associated with the penal colony and with the Japanese occupation. In some cases, everyday engagements with particular memorials or other meaningful sites have a quite different character to that intended or marked by the Indian nation state. In this chapter, my focus is on debates between government and Islanders, Islands and mainland in the *production* of monuments and memorials. The layered relationship between officials and ordinary people, and between the centre and periphery of the nation, as seen through the commemoration of history in the Andamans, is complicated and at times, at least on the surface, appears to be contradictory. Here, I seek to foreground and to historicize the state-managed creation of various celebrations, official monuments and the Cellular Jail National Memorial, and local responses to them. I will return to their connection with local-born identity formation in Chapter 5.

My history of history-making begins with the Independence Day celebrations of 15 August 1947, when the LBA organized a five-day programme which included musical entertainment, a flag hoisting ceremony, distribution of sweets in the villages, 'feeding by merchants' at the Netaji Club, an exhibition hockey match and a fancy dress show.[73] Elements of this programme were repeated annually in the years afterwards. The twenty-fifth anniversary of Independence was marked in 1972 with a series of events. It included a flag hoisting ceremony at the Gymkhana Ground; a 'ceremony in commemoration of martyrs' at the central tower of the Cellular Jail; a special cultural evening in Port Blair, presided over by Chief Commissioner Sri Har Mander Singh; and prizes for the three best decorated shops in Aberdeen Bazar. Those present at the events were instructed to make a pledge:

At this solemn moment when the people of India celebrate the 25th Anniversary of Independence won through suffering and sacrifice, I do dedicate myself in humility to the service of India and her people to the end that this ancient land attain her rightful place in the world and make her full and willing contribution to the promotion of world peace and the welfare of mankind.[74]

The deputy commissioner further noted: 'All shop keepers are requested to cooperate and to participate in the Celebrations.'[75]

---

[73] Local Born Association Independence Day Celebrations Programme, 14–7 August 1947, MLPC.
[74] 'Pledge', 14 August 1972, A&N Archives.
[75] Cultural evening invitation; ceremony in commemoration of martyrs invitation; 'Appeal', deputy commissioner Andaman and Nicobar Islands, 14 August 1972, A&N Archives.

In 1957, ten years after Independence, the government of India ordered the erection of plaques to the leaders of India's freedom movement imprisoned by the British, including in the Andamans but not exclusively so.[76] But with no surviving records in the Islands, and no firm information beyond what it described at the time as 'hearsay from a few old warders still living', the Island administration could not propose any locals for inscription on such a memorial, and so it did not mount a plaque.[77] In 1960, the Island administration received a letter from the Calcutta-based Ex-Political Sufferers' Association, which included men incarcerated in the Cellular Jail, asking that they host a 'Martyrs Memorial Conference'. Associated requests received at about the same time were to hang a portrait of the famous Andaman nationalist prisoner V. D. Savarkar in his former cell, to erect a memorial, to put up commemorative stone tablets or marble plaques and to preserve the Cellular Jail as a national memorial. A member of the Hindu Mahasabha, a nationalist political party, even compared the jail to the French Bastille, with all the symbolism to the cause of republicanism that the comparison implied.

The Islands' administration was rather less enthusiastic than these mainland groups about such memorialisation. It noted that the Japanese had destroyed two of the wings of the jail for bricks, and partially a third, which was so unstable that the Indian government had since demolished it. It had ideological objections too, premised on the fact that the nationalist prisoners incarcerated in the Cellular Jail were a small number of the total that passed through its gates. The Chief Commissioner wrote: 'A kind of sentiment is being woven on the mainland around the Cellular Jail, irrespective of the fact that it had harboured several thousand hardened criminals ... It does not deserve the honour which the sentimental persons ... would like to bestow on it.'[78] But nevertheless the Lok Sabha (lower parliament) in New Delhi passed a resolution: that the central government take immediate action to put up a plaque in the jail, and so commemorate all the political prisoners transported to the

---

[76] Proposal to set up suitable plaque in jails and cells as memorials to leaders of freedom movements: Gajinder Singh, under secretary to government of India, to all state governments, 19 July 1957, Acc. No. 169, A&N Archives.

[77] Placing suitable plaques in jails and cells in which martyrs and important leaders were imprisoned – suggestion regarding: memorandum, Superintendent Cellular Jail, 30 June 1957, Acc. No. 382, A&N Archives.

[78] Martyrs Memorial Conference to be held in October-November 1960: Statement of Sri Haridas Shaha, Bengal provincial Hindu Mahasabha, 6 January 1961; Note of Chief Commissioner Sri M. V. Rajwade, n.d., Acc. No. 126, A&N Archives.

Islands.[79] This was the context in which the local government decided to erect a masonry column in Marina Park, just down the hill from the Cellular Jail, in memory of the 'heroes' of the 'national revolution of 1858'. It did not incorporate the names of any particular individuals.[80]

Compiling the mainland-direct list was no easy task, for not only had the Japanese destroyed the jail records, but some of the men came from areas that were in newly partitioned East and West Pakistan. There was much discussion about whether (and if so, how) they could be appropriated as *Indian* patriots. As a result, it took several years to draw up the required list, eventually including their names also. It was only completed through the assistance (and persistence) of the Ex-Political Sufferers' Association, by then called the Ex-Andaman Political Prisoners' Fraternity Association, which was based in Calcutta. In 1969, after the list of names was submitted for inscription, the Fraternity Circle reminded the Chief Commissioner of its desire that the Cellular Jail become a national memorial. After much prevarication, the Ministry of Home Affairs in Delhi finally agreed to what it called a matter of 'national importance'. At the same time that it opened the way for the transformation of the Cellular Jail into a national memorial, it commissioned the publication of an Andamans *Who's Who of Martyrs*, an alphabetized, biographical account of the principal mainland actors incarcerated in the Islands during the freedom struggle.[81] A year later, a commemorative postage stamp was issued in honour of Savarkar.[82]

In the late 1960s, the Fraternity Circle of Andaman Freedom Fighters began to make annual visits to the Islands. Members of the Circle and their families called these trips *Mukti Tirtha*, or 'pilgrimages of salvation'. They were elaborate affairs that incorporated all the symbolism of the sea voyage, for a key element of the punishment of transportation was the journey over the black water, or *kala pani*. The pilgrims stayed in government bungalows, participated in official ceremonies, watched the

[79] Setting up of a plaque in the Cellular Jail to commemorate the sacrifices made by the leaders of freedom struggle: resolution of Lok Sabha, 10 June 1960, Public Acc. No. 131, A&N Archives.

[80] War memorial, Netaji Subhas Chandra Bose and Indian National Army, Secretary to Chief Commissioner Port Blair, to the Home Department, New Delhi, 1 June 1967, Public Acc. No. 397, A&N Archives.

[81] Freedom Fighters incarcerated in the Cellular Jail, Port Blair: Ministry of Home Affairs to Shri Bhargava, Chief Secretary Andaman and Nicobar Islands, 22 October 1969, Home Acc. No. 985, A&N Archives.

[82] Release of special postage stamps in honour of late Shri V. D. Savarkar, G. V. Subba Rao, office of the postmaster general Calcutta, to S. L. Bhargava, chief secretary to government Andaman and Nicobar Administration, 16 May 1970, Public Acc. No. 520, A&N Archives.

unveiling of new statues and were invited to state receptions and formal dinners. These trips often coincided with the August celebrations of Republic Day. In the Chief Commissioner's speech of 1974, which marked the Indian nation's twenty-fifth anniversary and was made before a group of pilgrims, we see how the history of freedom fighting and patriotism was represented as rooted in a shared attachment to the land (*Bharat*) – across mainland and Islands. I cite his words at length:

> [India's] difficulties can be overcome only by a united, dedicated, disciplined and hardworking nation. Our ancient country has seen many ups and downs. The Himalayas have been a witness to this nation rising to the peak of its glory and then dissipating that glory in fratricidal conflicts. This has occurred over and over again. Our nation has the capacity to rise afresh to new peaks of glory from deep depths. Whether this will happen again is dependent entirely on us, the citizens of Bharat [India].
>
> I am gratified that on this occasion we have a contingent of nearly 400 freedom fighters among us. They come from all parts of India and represent the many thousands who actively fought and struggled for our freedom so that we may have the privilege of living as a free people. These three hundred people and many more were incarcerated in the Cellular Jail at Port Blair and bore untold sufferings. It is difficult to express in words the debt we owe to these dedicated patriots …
>
> My fellow countrymen, I would like to extend to you warm greetings on behalf of my Administration and on my own behalf for your health, happiness and prosperity. May you all find happiness in the coming year and may you dedicate yourselves afresh in the services of one motherland!
>
> Jai Hind [Victory to India]![83]

In this way, the central government elevated mainland 'martyrs' incarcerated in the Andamans to national posterity, as the creators of a free India. Simultaneously, it sought to commemorate regional nationalism in pre-Independence India, requesting lists of freedom fighters from the districts. In its response to Delhi, the Port Blair administration altogether denied that any Islanders had played such a role. This had the effect of hiding from official view convict resistance to Empire, and ex-convict and local-born allegiance to the anti-imperial, pan-Asian political agenda of the Japanese and their Indian allies. The many convicts who intended to form anti-British forces in Burma after escaping in 1858, and were executed, were forgotten. The attempt on first Superintendent J. P. Walker's life in 1859 was silenced. Even Shere Ali's extraordinary assassination of the Viceroy, the Earl of Mayo, in 1872 did not count. Neither did criminal convict support for mainland nationalists in

---

[83] Republic Day celebrations: Chief Commissioner's speech, 15 August 1974, Public Acc. No. 1542, A&N Archives.

the Cellular Jail or the convict-supported IIL activities during 1942 to 1945 described above. None of these were mentioned as worthy of consideration. 'There were no reportable patriotic activities in this Union Territory', the deputy commissioner wrote in 1973, 'and the question of considering [the] erection of suitable monuments does not arise.'[84]

Despite its refusal to acknowledge Islanders' roles in either resisting transportation to the penal colony, or in the larger struggle for Independence, the mainland was keen to celebrate the heroic importance of INA leader Netaji Subhas Chandra Bose. In the mid 1970s, the administration commissioned and erected a huge bronze statue of him in Marina Park, looking out to sea, just beneath the Cellular Jail. The cost of the statue was a staggering Rs 36,266.[85] Shortly beforehand, the local government had refused a request for the allotment of land at Homfray Gunj, where as Vishvajit Pandya elaborates in Chapter 4, the Japanese had taken Islanders to dig their own graves, and then shot them dead. Their refusal came despite Islanders having raised Rs 5,000 privately for that purpose.[86] In the 1970s, when the Bose statue was erected, other than the 1957 column to the 'national revolution', the only other statues in the Islands were of Gandhi-ji and the great Bengali poet Rabindranath Tagore, and both had been funded privately. There is some evidence of Islanders' unease at the development of this commemorative agenda, gleaned from the records of the local administration. It can be seen not only in Port Blair's initial distaste for the idea of transforming the Cellular Jail into a national memorial, but in other areas of political concern. In 1976, for instance, the chief secretary's advisory committee unanimously advised against a proposed name change of the islands, to either *Swaraj Dweep* (Self-ruled Islands) or *Shaheed Dweep* (Martyr Islands), or after famous nationalists. It rejected the possible alternatives of Subhas, Netaji, Savarakar and Bhai Parmanand Islands. The chief secretary noted that renaming the Andamans 'would hurt the sentiments of the local people', though he did not elaborate on how or why.[87]

---

[84] Celebration of 25th anniversary of India's Independence: deputy commissioner Port Blair to assistant secretary Andaman and Nicobar Administration, 6 July 1973, Public Acc. No. 628, A&N Archives.

[85] War memorial, Netaji Subhas Chandra Bose and Indian National Army: secretary to Chief Commissioner Port Blair to Home Department, Delhi, 1 June 1967, Public Acc. No. 397, A&N Archives.

[86] Allotment of land for raising a memorial with the object of 44 persons killed at Homfray Gunj during Japanese occupation of this territory, note of development commissioner, 8 December 1970, J&R Acc. No. 1036, A&N Archives.

[87] Naming of villages, creeks, roads, etc. in the Andaman and Nicobar Islands, correspondence regarding: chief secretary's note, 16 July 1976, Acc. No. 846, A&N Archives.

In 1985, a further structure was put up within the Cellular Jail, this time to the 'heroes of the first war of independence – 1857 – and all those brave sons of India who were incarcerated in these islands during their ceaseless struggle for freedom of our beloved motherland.' This was significant, because it centred a monument to pre-nationalist transportations in the principal commemorative site of national struggle for the first time. I will explore further the discursive transformation of the 1857 convicts into freedom fighters in my later examination of how local-born people make sense of their convict ancestry. Here I would like to note that in 1999, marking fifty years of Independence, Indian President N. K. Narayanan visited Port Blair, and several new government-sponsored anniversary publications appeared. They included works on Ross Island, which had been the headquarters of the British penal colony; Viper Island, the site of secondary punishment and execution; and the Cellular Jail. Commemorative stamps and one-rupee coins were also released, together with a commemoration pamphlet to accompany the unveiling of six life-size statues of freedom fighters who had died in the Cellular Jail: Indu Bhushan Roy, Baba Bhan Singh, Pandit Ram Rakha, Mahavir Singh, Mohan Kishore Namadas and Mohit Moitra. The minister of state was present at the opening function.

Until recently, the political and symbolic importance that is attached to 15 August, Republic Day, has overshadowed the local importance of 10 March as the date the first transportation convicts arrived in the Islands in 1858. However, the local administration built a new memorial to commemorate the 150th anniversary of the arrival of the 1857 mutineers and rebels on Chatham Island, in 2008, marking the first 'pioneer freedom fighters'. Since then, each year there has been a small ceremony at the site. Though dignitaries from the mainland regularly visit the Andamans, to pay tribute to Indian nationalists at the Cellular Jail, the introduction of this monument to nineteenth-century transportation is an entirely local affair, with foundation stones laid and inaugurations usually performed in the presence of the Andaman and Nicobar administration only.[88]

The archival records do not allow us to say with any certainty that this date has had any ongoing significance for local-born people in the second half of the nineteenth and twentieth centuries, before Independence. But we do know that in 1982, marking 125 years of permanent colonization of the Andamans, under the presidency of John Lobo, the newly renamed LBA scripted and published an anniversary pamphlet. The pamphlet

---

[88] See, e.g., *Andaman Sheekha*, 10 March 2012.

celebrated the accomplishments of local borns, detailing their struggles and achievements, and wrote them firmly into the history of colonization. The pamphlet recounted that in the nineteenth century: 'The Local Born people declared themselves the real inhabitants of the territory. They were right because they had developed the forest land of Andamans into a greenery.'[89] Again we see the importance of a landscape of belonging and entitlement.

The pamphlet is also significant for centring local borns in the history of anti-imperialism, in the context of the development of an agenda of the commemoration of martyrdom that I have described above. It elaborated how, during the war, local borns had been active in the IIL, joining the INA and supporting Bose and his *Azad Hind* government, despite terrible suffering under Japanese occupation. It drew explicit parallels between local-born wartime activity and the first convict transportees of 1858, who had been shipped to the Islands in the aftermath of the 1857 Revolt. It surmised of the association's role in the INA: 'We were fighting for the cause which our forefathers had fought about a century ago in the sub-continent.'[90]

The text of the document is interesting because since Indian Independence in 1947, just as early twentieth-century nationalists have been elevated to 'martyrdom', the history of the 1857 Revolt has been rewritten not as a military mutiny or peasant rebellion, but as the 'First War of Independence'. Of particular note in this respect is Andaman nationalist prisoner V. D. Savarkar's *The Indian War of Independence, 1857*. Savarkar had first written the book in Marathi in 1909, seeking to historicize contemporary nationalist campaigns. The British promptly banned it. It was only published, in English, with Independence in 1947.[91] Since then, Indian government-generated history writing continued with the collation and publication of national and state archives on the Revolt for the voluminous one hundredth anniversary volume *Freedom Struggle in Uttar Pradesh*.[92] Many officially sponsored volumes on freedom fighting appeared subsequently, both on the mainland and in the Andamans.[93]

---

[89] Local Born Association Celebration of Indian Settlement, 125th Anniversary, 10 March 1982, MLPC.

[90] Local Born Association Celebration of Indian Settlement, MLPC.

[91] V. D. Savarkar, *The Indian War of Independence, 1857* (Bombay: Phoenix Publications, 1947).

[92] S. A. A. Rizvi and Moti Lal Bhargava, *Freedom Struggle in Uttar Pradesh: Source-Material* [five volumes] (Lucknow: Publications Bureau, Information Department, 1957–61).

[93] For example, see Rashida Iqbal (ed.), *Unsung Heroes of Freedom Struggle in Andamans: Who's Who* (Port Blair: Directorate of Youth Affairs, Sports and Culture, Andaman and Nicobar Administration, 1998); Ratanlal Joshi (ed.), *The Martyrs* (Bombay: Udbodhak Granthmala, 1994); Shrikrishan Saral, *Indian Revolutionaries: A Comprehensive Study,*

The LBA pamphlet might be read as a component of this production of a history for all-India. It positioned the Union Territory of the Andamans centrally within the history of the nation state, arguing for a clear, uninterrupted, continuous line of nationalist progression between a supposedly 'national', anti-colonial 'movement' of 1857; Indian 'freedom fighting' in the early twentieth century; and Independence. But furthermore, it associated the 1857 rebels with the *ordinary* convicts shipped to the Andamans, as well as the INA. It transformed rebels and criminal convicts alike into nationalist martyrs; or 'freedom fighters'. In this way, it refused any distinction between Islanders and mainland 'martyrs'.

Since the work of Benedict Anderson, Ernest Gellner and Eric Hobsbawm we understand that nations are in part constructed from 'imagined communities', and that the tracing, crafting and even the *invention* of shared histories that connect people and communities together is a vital part of national formation.[94] And, following the intellectual currents of what we might call the spatial turn, and which is so vital to the theoretical thrust of this book, we understand that 'place' is constituted through social practice; and that there is a close relationship between place, social practice and social identity. It is not difficult to see the relevance of this idea of 'imagined communities' and 'invented or shared histories', to ideas of place and identity in and about the Andamans. Over time in the Andamans the descendants of convicts have created shared histories. Further, these *locally*-generated histories have emerged both in congruence with and in divergence from *mainland*-generated 'national history'.

Returning to the LBA pamphlet, it made a series of explicitly political points, too, in the context of the issue of compensation and pensions that I discussed above. These included, first, that new, post-war settlers were advantaged in having reserved education in their home states, unlike the pre-42s in the Andamans who had lost contact with the mainland and so had no connections and no such rights. Second, that the introduction of 'scheduled caste' categories in the Islands would disturb their unique social makeup, because of Andaman 'castelessness'. And, third, that following extensive sub-division over time, as land passed down the generations, local-born people were especially vulnerable to the government's decision to seize landholdings of under three acres for its various

1757–1961 (New Delhi: Ocean Books Pvt. Lts., 1999); M. P. Srivastava, *Freedom Fighters of Indian Mutiny 1857* (Allahabad: Chugh, 1997).

[94] Benedict Anderson, *Imagined Communities* (London: Verso, 1983); Ernest Gellner, *Nations and Nationalism* (Ithaca NY: Cornell University Press, 1983); Eric Hobsbawm, *Nations and Nationalism Since 1780: Programme, Myth, Reality* (Cambridge: Cambridge University Press, 1990).

development schemes.[95] And so we see in the 1980s how the legacies of the penal colony continue to manifest themselves in political life. I will return to these themes in Chapter 5.

Meantime, I close this section with an observation of the way in which mainland Indian tourists move around, participate in and talk about this commemorative agenda. The officially sanctioned narrative of the Andamans as an important symbolic space within the larger nation seems to have wide appeal to many of the Indians who visit Port Blair from outside the Islands. Some tourists lay flowers at the Cellular Jail's gallows; some stand in silence at the end of the evening's Sound and Light show, which ends with the projection of the colours of the Indian flag onto one of the wings of the Cellular Jail. They punch the air and shout 'Jai Hind!' on boat trips to Viper Island, where there was another set of gallows. One young man from Delhi with whom I spent time at Chennai airport on the way home to Britain told me that his father had remarked during a visit to the Cellular Jail, 'Why do we go and pay our respects to the gods in the temple? These men [the freedom fighters] are our true gods.' Exploring tourists' experiences in the Andamans would make for a fascinating study.

Conclusion

In this chapter, I have shown that there were profound differences in understandings of the meaning of freedom fighting in the Andamans, and that these had their origins in divergent mainland and Island-centred views of the character of the penal colony, and Islanders' role as resistors or collaborators during Japan's wartime occupation. Attitudes to social distinction were central to mainland views, for they accorded the elite class of intellectuals who were incarcerated in the Cellular Jail greater status in Indian national history than the descendants of ordinary labouring convicts, whatever their role in resisting the British had been. In this respect, mainland administrators also refused to recognize the history of the Islands during the Japanese occupation, by which time all the elite political prisoners had left, as a history of anti-colonialism: whether or not Islanders had joined the INA or resisted Japanese imperialism. These attitudes were clearly displayed in government policy on compensation in the years following the war. Islanders received only small amounts of relief, mainly in the form of loans, and few if any were granted the kind of government pensions issued to freedom fighters living on the mainland.

---

[95] Local Born Association Celebration of Indian Settlement, MLPC.

The LBA and other local associations have made multiple claims over the decades that due to the Islands' history as a penal colony, mainland administrators have seen their population as politically backward. Thus it did not consult them, denied them adequate representation in parliament and blocked access to mainland jobs and education. It was in this context that after Independence, the LBA continued to organise Islanders, calling meetings, writing pamphlets and visiting officials on the mainland, to plead for their interests. In this drive for recognition, the post-colonial association has shown remarkable continuity with its colonial-era activities, particularly with respect to the boosting of community esteem and morale. I have reflected here on some of the ways in which these issues and controversies have played out in state-sponsored efforts to remember the colonial history of the islands during the 1950s to 1980s: through Republic Day celebrations; the transformation of the Cellular Jail into a national memorial; and annual freedom fighter pilgrimages from the mainland. Next, the book explores other sets of mainland–island connections, imagined and otherwise, in Vishvajit Pandya's analysis of landscapes of everyday practice and social identity.

4 The making of a 'rhizomatic' landscape: place, space and the politics of memory in the Andamanese Islands

Vishvajit Pandya

Introduction: embodied and rhizomatic landscapes

As the flight from Calcutta comes to a halt at Port Blair, many settlers returning from mainland India as well as Indian tourists, particularly from Bengal, step on the tarmac, quietly and quickly touch the ground and then gently touch their forehead. This is a typical Indian salutation (*pranam*) normally a gesture of touching and seeking the blessings of an elder, but in this case a gesture of reverence to a 'sacred land' (*punya bhoomi*). This is perhaps no different from sentiments that are invested in visits to war memorials or pilgrimage sites in different cultures. They can invoke identical feelings for visitors who are motivated to establish a social relation or to fulfil an obligation by going to a specific place to connect something from the past with something for the future. Consequently people leave gifts and offerings at various memorials and shrines and set up their own relationships to the embodied places across the landscape. Landscape here is conceptualized as an assemblage of socially produced material forms, constituting cultural records arranged through time and space that may be interrogated as symbolically loaded signifiers of meanings.

Many Indians also regard the Andamans as *muktitirtha* (a pilgrimage of salvation), a place made sacred by the blood, toil and tears of many who languished and died in the infamous Cellular Jail. The Islands were also the place where during the Japanese occupation Indian nationalist leader Subhas Chandra Bose came and hoisted the Indian national flag. For the returning settlers or local born, however, the *muktitirtha* was made by their blood and sweat as much as it was by the nationalist leaders who served their sentences on the Islands. It was on this land that their ancestors toiled relentlessly to clear the 'menacing' forests, to plant crops and to make homes, and live in constant fear of death. Yet for them there are also memories of a homeland (a *muluk* or *desh*) left behind, a place somewhere on the mainland to which they return when they can. Some of them, on reaching the Islands, would explain to me that this journey from the mainland was a journey from one's *desh* (country) to one's *zameen* (soil) or, in Bengali, *maati*. I often wondered what this meant: was it *maati* or *desh* that took precedence in their narratives of identity and belonging? I wondered what the gesture of *pranam* meant in this context: was it just a gesture of thanking God and the ancestral spirits for facilitating the journey from the *desh* to the *maati*, or was it one of staking claim to the land as its original inhabitants? If it was, then what did this mean for the Islands' indigenous communities? Where was their position in this *maati*, or where was their position in this *desh*?

Simply put, we see that different people relate to the Andaman Islands in different ways. They approach the Islands with different meanings, dividing its landscape into places through historical experience and cultural practice, both of which relate to land as a structure. Gestures, memories, meanings inherited and meanings made, as well as the potentiality of interpretation, make the land in the Andamans an embodied object of diverse subjects.

Erodode Tewar is a convict descendant, or local born, who makes a hard living on a plot of land in Mithakhari, on the outskirts of Port Blair.[1] His father, Periyarswamy Tewar, bought it in late 1911 for a sum of Rs 240. Today, Erodode, at age seventy-eight, refuses to sell or lease out his inherited plot of land knowing full well that there is not much life left in the soil. The soil had begun to show signs of degeneration with rapidly falling yields, and it was only left for brackish waters to trail into the field following the 2004 tsunami and suck out what life remained. The steadily dwindling income from the land has compelled his son to leave for Port Blair and make a life there. However, the living patriarch finds a 'healing' quality in the soil because his father had toiled on it. Erodode explained his refusal to leave the family holding: 'my father's sweat is still deep in this plot of land. I cannot let go of it ... even if it doesn't get me any returns'.

Human attachment to particular places requires understanding of peoples' traditional knowledge, cultural practice, forms of communication and conventions for imagining the past. That is, world-building, place-making and constructing places constitute basic tools of historical imagination through multiple acts of remembering, conjecture and

---

[1] Mithakhari (sweet swamp) is known for its watermelon crop. It was dredged and reclaimed by Colonel M. L. Ferrar (Chapter 2) who undertook this tedious task involving both heavy financial investment and the massive use of convict labour. It was badly affected by the 2004 tsunami. Today, son Erodode Tewar has a difficult time staying on in the area but told me that he cannot leave the soil here and live with his son in the city of Port Blair. As he put it poignantly, 'because the soil here makes me breathe alive – it has my father's sweat infused in it!' Field notes, October 2010.

speculation. Keith Basso argues that self-knowledge cannot be reconstructed without place-worlds: 'If place-making is a way of constructing the past, a venerable means of doing human history, it is also a way of constructing social traditions and, in the process, personal and social identities. We are, in a sense, the place-worlds we imagine.'[2] How can we understand and analyze a place like the Andaman Islands that generates the urge to perform *pranam*? How does one make sense of the Andaman Islanders' understanding of how culture, society, space and historical relations coalesce together?

Erodode Tewar's piece of land is more than just a place or materiality. While his land functions as a setting for social and economic reproduction, the landscape is a theatrical stage-like space where group identity is acted out in relation to other groups and other institutions, including government. It is the cultivator's daily toil – and death – in a particular place that transforms abstract space into a social and psychic geography. Both a cognitively derived *knowing* about place and an intuitive *sense* of place are profoundly integrated into peoples' identity. As Allan Pred has it, 'historically contingent processes' contribute to 'specific biographies of places'.[3] Places, like people, have their own biographies in as much as they too are formed, used and transformed in relation to cultural practice. Stories acquire part of their mythic value and historical relevance if they are rooted in the concrete details of locales in the landscape, acquiring material reference points that can be visited, seen and touched.

Home to a diverse population of migrants, descendants of convicts and refugees the Andaman Islands, situated 1,260 km from the Indian mainland, became the site of a complex process of landscaping both for the Indian state and the communities who came to stay there. The multiple subjectivities and practices that defined the projects of landscaping are best understood as both state-making and place-making processes, that emphasize mediation between subjects and the world where meanings are articulated through collective activities. In these processes both state and community invest the land with cultural meanings in order to reinforce its centrality as a site constitutive of both state authority and social identity.

Scores of descendants of settlers on the Islands on visiting their ancestral homes in 'mainland' India are known to bring a bit of soil and mix it

---

[2] Keith Basso, *Wisdom Sits in Places: Landscape and Language Among the Western Apache* (Albuquerque, NM: University of New Mexico Press, 1996), 7; Steven Field and Keith Basso (eds.), *Senses of Place* (Santa Fe, CA: School of American Research Press [Seattle], Distributed by the University of Washington Press, 1996).

[3] Allan Pred, *Even in Sweden: Racism, Racialized Spaces, and the Popular Geographical Imagination* (Oakland, CA: University of California Press, 2000).

in the land allotted to them on the Islands. Individual families that trace their homes to contemporary Bangladesh or Myanmar also mark the connection to the Andamans as their 'homeland' by mixing soil from the lands they were compelled to leave. Some Hindu families also keep a small container of soil at the family shrine along with a sealed container of water from the river Ganga, both forming a ritual requirement for sacralizing the dead as bodies are readied for cremation on the soil of the Andamans. All these acts constitute in many ways ritual engagements with the ancestral landscape from where they were once historically displaced and the land that they now have made their own. Exploring these practices, the 'making of one's own land', in the context of the larger narratives of state-making on the Islands offers possibilities of understanding ways in which landscape is thought, experienced, imagined and narrated on the Andamans.[4]

Observing the range of ideas expressed and ritual activities conducted at five memorial sites, this chapter explores contending memorializing practices around the theme of sacrifice,[5] heroism and martyrdom, and the ways these play out in state-making and place-making projects in the Andamans. It seeks to address the shaping of a dialogical relationship between the statist discourse of 'nation-making' on the Island and the peoples' discourse of 'place-making'. These discourses, it is argued, are different yet interconnected by negotiations and compromise. In sum, the chapter unravels the political and cultural logic mediating place-making and nation-making projects on the Andamans and tries to understand how multiple regimes of memorializing coexist and interface to constitute the Island landscape as an inherently rhizomatic space.

---

[4] Essentialist views of collective identities have been challenged by those arguing for the importance of invented traditions and imagined or constructed identity. From this perspective, national identities are historical constructions that are constantly being reconstituted according to a presentist agenda. Rather than being primordial entities, national identities are generated by 'symbolic processes that emerge and dissolve in particular contexts of action'. See Richard Handler, *Critics Against Culture: Anthropological Observers of Mass Society* (Madison, WI: University of Wisconsin Press, 2005). It follows from this that we need to understand the ways in which nationalizing states are continually reimagining themselves as homogeneous units, and ask ourselves if this is appropriate for a contemporary society in its local and global contexts. See Benedict Anderson, *Imagined Communities: Reflections on the Origin and Spread of Nationalism*, 2nd Revised edn. (London: Verso, 1991). Clare Anderson explores nation-making further in Chapter 5.

[5] My definition of sacrifice is derived from the classical writings of Robertson Smith, Emile Durkheim and Marcel Mauss. I conceptualize the ritual of sacrifice as a way in which Andaman Islanders – both indigenous people and settlers/ migrants – integrate past historical experiences to create a desired form of history to be experienced for the future.

Deleuze and Guattari, in proposing a model of nomad thought, challenged the modality of 'arborescent' thought that they conceptualized as a process of thinking inherently structured like a tree. A thought structure that is firmly grounded and represented by a vertical axis of development confined to a domain, going deeper as a root and expanding its branches above the ground but remaining disconnected to contexts other than where it is planted or located. Challenging this model of knowing and organization of ideas, Deleuze and Guattari proposed a new operational metaphor: that of the rhizome. For Deleuze and Guattari, the rhizome is a network, 'an endless pattern in which everything is linked to everything else'. The rhizome itself assumes diverse forms, from ramified surface extension in all directions to concretion into bulbs and tubers. Principles of rhizomes include cartographical connectivity, heterogeneity and a multiplicity sustained by regenerative capacity that is anti-genealogical. For Deleuze and Guattari, the most important characteristic of this network as embodied in the 'rhizome' implies that there are always multiple entranceways. Having no subject or object, the rhizome is composed of 'directions in motion' and grows from the middle, extending its 'lines of flight': 'The rhizome operates by variation, expansion, conquest, capture, and offshoots.'[6]

This chapter argues that the metaphor of the rhizome offers a useful imagistic and conceptual tool to comprehend the complex practices of state-making and place-making in the Andaman Islands. Philosophically, the state's discourse on nation-making and memorializing history is focused on a linear structure, with specific points of origination, and clear lines of movement, that are representable as an arborescent model. In contrast, Islander discourse about place-making forges linkages that are not formal, clear-cut pathways between discrete units; rather, they traverse domains of reality as 'lines of flight' coming and going, arriving and departing in relation to history. Memorialized sites for the people are rhizomatic, operating according to principles of connection, heterogeneity and multiplicity. Like the growing form of a rhizome, the people on the Andaman Islands make connections of different times on to different places both within the land and beyond.

Front yards and back yards

Land, as a 'given natural', is culturally and historically transformed through organized ideas infusing it with certain values. Structures that make the landscape may be common but the processes of landscaping are

---

[6] Gilles Deleuze and Felix Guattari, *A Thousand Plateaus: Capitalism and Schizophrenia*, trans. Brian Massumi (Minneapolis, MN: University of Minnesota Press, 1987), 14, 23.

culture specific. So a Japanese garden is distinguishable from a Victorian garden by the way it is conceptualized and by the statements it makes by what is installed and grown in it. At a more general social level, we distinguish our front yard from the back yard by flowers and ornamental plants in the front as opposed to vegetables or just plain grass at the back. The front yard makes an orderly, neat statement of achievement, but the back yard often remains a site of disorderly production.[7] In some ways the more visible front landscape is apparently a frozen moment of domestication and control. The back yard is visible only by the mediation of a residential structure, and is a place of wilderness and disorderliness waiting to be transformed. Colonial and post-colonial landscaping on the Andamans involved both a conceptual and physical division of the island landscape, reflecting implanted and cultivated ideological, gardening-like practices.

Colonial landscaping of the Andaman Islands began in earnest in 1857 through 1858, with the setting up of 'front yards' in Port Blair and Ross Island. These made up the administrative seats of the penal settlement. Just a few miles west of Ross Island was the 'mainland' Andamans; until the 1860s, the area remained the unexplored, wild back yard. Colonial landscaping in the Andamans saw the front yard as a space governed by the civilizing ethos of the rule of law and the ethic of labour, while the back yard was marked by the rule of might and an inaccessible and unproductive wilderness. For the British, the inaccessibility of the back yard both by virtue of its terrain and resistance by indigenous communities marked the limits of its presence and authority in the Andaman Islands. This consisted of wide stretches of mangrove, dark malarial swamps and miles of deep impenetrable forest. Although the colonizers deployed all their might to enter the forest and expand their control over its resources, the task remained extremely daunting because of a flawed assumption that the interior forest was the domain of 'savages' who could be pacified and contained. The immediate area around Port Blair and South Andaman Island was thus cleared along with some parts of the north, but the area beyond the immediate vicinity of Port Blair remained the unwieldy back yard, marked by the treacherous depths of the forest and the site of chaotic, hostile and often violent encounters between the Andamanese tribes and the colonial administration. In the clearings, the stumps of trees were burnt to nourish the soil and prepare it for cultivation so that crops could be raised to sustain the penal population. In course of time the front yard was ordered and inscribed with an iconography of colonial power and authority in the form of wooden buildings and gardens.

---

[7] Read for a related conceptualization, U.R. Ananthamurthy's essay "*Literature in the Indian Bhashas: Frontyards and Backyards*", in Paranjpye Makarand and G.J.V Prasad (eds) Indian English and Vernacular India, Delhi, Chennai, Hyderabad, Pearson, 2002, pp 149–52.

Figure 4.1 'The Cellular Jail (under construction)',
photographer unknown, c. 1900. Photographs of the Andaman
Islands (308 (541.9) TUS). Courtesy Horniman Museum
and Gardens.

The reappropriation of the Island landscape by the Indian state in the
wake of Independence marked the beginnings of a new project of
landscaping that sought to both build upon and reverse the conceptual
and spatial practices of the colonial authorities. Landscape was now to be
inscribed with the history of the anti-colonial struggle on the Andamans,
foregrounding the fact of suffering and martyrdom as the constitutive
connections between the Islands and mainland Indian histories of anti-
colonial resistance. The nationalizing of the Island space, or reinscription,
meant that the colonial back yard denoted by the Port Blair Cellular Jail
became the post-colonial front yard. From 1950, when the Andamans
became a Union Territory of India, Port Blair became a place to project
the Indian nation state's ideology through memorials and monuments.
Landscape was inscribed with installations to denote progress and to
connect the Andaman Islands with a larger nationalist history. Old memories were given new meanings within discourses of sacrifice and a
nationalist meta-discourse. Port Blair was no more solely a place for
disciplining colonial convicts, or a place that demanded hard labour and
strict surveillance. It was rapidly made into the displayed front yard of the
Republic of India. Port Blair's sea front was covered with manicured

Figure 4.2 Cellular Jail as national monument declared
in 1969. Photograph: Clare Anderson.

gardens and statues of national leaders. Installations of military tanks and
airplanes made two important statements. First, citizens should never
forget the sacrifice made by their national leaders:[8] it was their martyrdom

---

[8] It is interesting to note that in the colonial period no significant monuments were left on
the Islands, but British authority was inscribed in other ways. Notably, they named places
in honour of individuals who had explored or altered the history of the Islands, or the
Indian subcontinent as a whole. These included: J. G. S. Neil, Henry Havelock, Henry
Lawrence, M. L. Ferrar and F. J. Mouat. Considering Port Blair as the centre of the
settlement, as one radiates away, the nomenclatural reference to British officers declines
and what is invoked is in favour of naming after either geographical features, botanical
markers or names taken from the language and culture of Burmese coolies and guides,
Ranchi labourers or the Andamanese indigenous peoples who were in contact with British
forest exploration and clearing operations. Examples of these include: Jhau Nallah,
Mahua Tekree, Fall Bay, Shoal Bay, Flat Island, Baratang, Potattang and Porlob Jig.
Places of refugee settlement frequently recapitulate the names of places associated with
eastern parts of the subcontinent, like Kadamtalla, Phooltalla, Bakultalla, Ramakrishana
Puram, Brindaban and Mathura. Interestingly, different communities that have settled on
different parts of the same landscape reflect in their terms of reference for places names
that have come from their observed and experienced history. For example, Land Fall
Island was a British name, but during the Second World War American Gis, as part of the
allied force, had landed there in amphibious crafts, so the Karens call it *American JeeHai
tapu* (a possible distortion of the American 'GI' and '*tapu*,' meaning island). Port

that gave freedom to a nation that was once colonized. Second, that India is a democratic republic that is well secured and unified through national patriotism.

The Cellular Jail, an icon of penal authority in a colonial back yard, is now the mnemonic icon of nationalism in the Islands' post-colonial front yard. An extreme colonial margin has now became a central sacred site marked by nationalist iconography and state rituals. The old back yard has been effectively reappropriated and reconfigured as a new front yard for the whole of the Andamans Islands, and symbolically steeped in its narratives of sacrifice.[9] The Cellular Jail in other words, exemplifies a paradigmatic relationship to the whole of the Islands, generating a constructed and consecrated topography at large, sustained by ritual commemorative practices at places beyond Port Blair. Outside the frames of the nationalist narrative, however, and further away from Port Blair, in the depths of the island back yard new narratives of heroism and sacrifice were being inscribed on the landscape as part of a more tenuous yet symbolically laden project of place-making. It is through an exploration of these projects, nation-making and place-making, that we can we see a particular ordering of the material, social and semiotic flows that make the island landscape a transformational multiplicity of assemblages.[10] These 'assemblages' have made the land 'rhizomatic' in its propensity to make new meanings, memories and histories. Land remains not a mere object of reproduction by 'clearing and planting', but the site of the production of historical knowledge. It is through an understanding of the seemingly disparate historical connections made on the land by the people that we can understand the politics of time and place that define the multiple dimensions of the island landscape.[11] The Andamanese landscape is marked not merely by statist

Campbell is today known to Karens as *Loka Mati Joung Karuw* (Loka's Headman of the Great Andamanese – Loka's first wife was killed by Jarawa here), for in the context of Karens, the Great Andamanese were long-time collaborators with the British against Jarawas in the forest. Similarly, the *Ranchiwallas* and Karens call Petrice Island *Hiran Tekree* (meaning, 'mound to kill deer at'). I am indebted here to discussions with my fellow researcher on the Islands, Manish Chandi.

[9] It must be noted that the British administration had also named places for individual military gallantry or fatal expeditions. During Subhas Bose's Second World War visit it was proposed that the Andaman Islands be renamed Shaheed Dweep and Azad Dweep (Martyrs Islands and Free Islands, respectively). From time to time the political party Forward Block of India associated with Bose resurrects this demand, most recently in 2009.

[10] Deleuze and Guattari, *A Thousand Plateaus*, 23, 503.

[11] According to Deleuze and Guattari, a rhizome has no beginning or end; it is always in the middle, between things, inter-being, *intermezzo*. The tree, on the other hand, has filiations, but the rhizome is alliance, uniquely alliance: 'The tree imposes the verb "to be," but the fabric of the rhizome is conjunction'. This conjunction carries enough force to shake and uproot the verb 'to be'. As a consequence, 'Where are you going? Where are

inscriptions of colonial and nationalist trails but by the complex social and political relations generated in the Islands between its indigenous communities and the ceaseless flows of migrants, settlers and refugees. In the following sections of this chapter I deploy an ethnographic reading of five memorial sites, and try to show how individuals and communities invoke the notion of sacrifice and martyrdom and interpret specific historical encounters within the structures of their quotidian social practices.

The ironies of Aberdeen

Since 17 May 2007, every year at Port Blair's Marina Park celebrations are held to mark the anniversary of the 1859 Battle of Aberdeen. This is not the actual site of the battle, as the ground where the battle was fought and the hill overlooking it have been transformed into a municipality managed sports complex, and the area behind it has become the Aberdeen Bazar. It is not clear why, 148 years since the incident, the government of India felt the urge to commission the construction of a new war memorial. Nonetheless, at the Marina Park, on the new 'front yard' of the Island administration, a twenty-foot high cement and marble structure was installed. The Marina Beach front is a beautifully tiled and landscaped area with a few shops, facing the sea. It is an area frequented by tourists and locals who stroll there in the evening or catch boat rides to nearby Ross Island. A display of cannons and tanks from the Indian Army, and gigantic statues of Subhas Chandra Bose, Mahatma Gandhi and Rajiv Gandhi stand on high platforms, surrounding the commemorative structure.

Common to all the statues is a characteristic frozen movement urging the viewer to 'move ahead'! This location suggestively makes the ideological statement that the Andaman Islands are an integral part of the Indian nation and a place built upon sacrifices made by national heroes. The logic of the new front yard contextualized in nationalist discourse becomes explicit in the text inscribed at the monument for the Battle of Aberdeen. It reads:

This monument is built in the memory of those Andamanese aborigines who bravely fought the Battle of Aberdeen in May 1859 against the oppressive and retaliatory policy of the British regime.

Much as Indians have interpreted the Revolt of 1857 as the first national struggle for freedom, British colonial records presented the Battle of Aberdeen as a 'tribal insurgency', which was put down by the determinate

you coming from? What are you heading for?' become totally redundant questions. Deleuze and Guattari, *A Thousand Plateaus*, 24–5.

valour of British servicemen.[12] The Indian state, on the other hand, now commemorates it as a patriotic uprising against British colonialism.

At the inaugural public event of 17 May 2007, the Indian state insisted that the 'Battle of Aberdeen', fought on 17 May 1859, was an integral part of the Indian freedom struggle, wherein Andamanese indigenous aboriginal people put up a concerted resistance to the might of British colonial authority. But the irony in this acknowledgement of 'tribal' heroism was the overtly statist interpretation of that history and the complete exclusion of the community from the commemorative celebrations. The Andaman administration's press release on the occasion made a point of stating that this was to 'immortalize a decisive battle fought against the British by an ancient tribe of India, the Andamanese; a race of near-naked aborigines that has existed in the archipelago for centuries'. At the official ceremony, the Lieutenant Governor was quick to note the enigmatic role of Dudhnath Tewari (an Indian convict) in the battle. The invocation of Tewari's name by the head of the administration was a tacit acknowledgement of the significant presence of settlers on the island who see Tewari as a hero, who led the battle of Aberdeen, much like the Indian nationalists who fought against the British authorities.[13] Many settlers have perpetuated the image of Tewari as a freedom fighter, along with other national leaders, and as a person who 'sacrificed' his life for the nation. At Port Bair, a local radio station and a drama club have together produced a play to project Tewari as the leader of a struggle against colonial rule. School children put his name on charts that display the individuals who resisted colonial power and fought for a free India. Yet what was Tewari's role in the Battle of Aberdeen?

Tewari was convicted of manslaughter in a family feud in Eastern India. In 1857, the Jhelum Commission of Enquiry sentenced Tewari to life imprisonment on Andamans. On 23 April 1858, Tewari and nine other convicts managed to escape into the forest, of which they had

---

[12] Interpretations of the incident differ. Some regard it as an insignificant attack of the type often undertaken for the sake of plunder. However, the scale on which the assault was planned pointed to the involvement of an escaped convict, Dudhnath Tewari. The Reverend H. Corbyn, chaplain at the settlement, termed the clash a 'ludicrous skirmish', but M. V. Portman, a member of the administration, later described it as a 'most desperate and determined attack' undertaken with the intention of exterminating the settlers on the Islands. M. V. Portman, *A History of our Relations with the Andamanese, Vol. 1* (Calcutta: Superintendent Government Printing India, 1899), pp. 279, 288, 422. Cf. R. F. Lowis, *Census of India, 1911, Volume II: The Andaman and Nicobar Islands* (Calcutta: Superintendent of Government Printing, 1912), p. 54.

[13] See Vishvajit Pandya, 'Sacrifice and Escape as Counter-Hegemonic Rituals: A Structural Essay on an Aspect of Andamanese History', *Journal of Social Analysis*, 41, 2 (1997), 66–98.

Figure 4.3 Monument built in memory of the Battle of Aberdeen at Port Blair. Photograph: Vishvajit Pandya.

practically no knowledge. In the course of his journey into Middle Andamans, Tewari was confronted by a band of Jarawa tribals. Wounded and
scared, Tewari followed the tribal band around and after about a year in
their presence he found himself accepted within the tribal community
and was even allowed to marry.[14]

It was known later from his own accounts that Tewari started organizing the Andamese for an attack on the British who he so resented. But his
planning and role fell apart as he lost Jarawa goodwill. Apparently, Tewari
was unaware of the Andamanese tradition of giving away one's own child
for adoption. As a consequence he had negotiated marriage with his first
wife's child from a previous marriage who had been adopted into another
family. Tewari's ignorance angered the Andamanese and they ostracized
him. Feeling uncertain about whether he would be allowed to participate
in the attack, Tewari decided to escape back to Port Blair. He came out
from the forest, returned to Port Blair, and on 14 May 1859 informed the
colonial authorities about the impending attack and asked for pardon.
What we see here is that Tewari, who was a hero in escaping from the
penal settlement and playing a role in organizing the Andamanese attack,
gave up the cause, reverted back to the British authorities and became
instrumental in dealing with the counter attack on the Andamanese.[15] It
is questionable whether the sacrifices made by Tewari were consistent
with any ideology or cause except with that of sheer selfish motivation.
The 'Battle of Aberdeen', as the 'attack' was subsequently dubbed, was
forestalled because of Tewari's warning to the British for which he was
commended by the colonial administration. His name was recommended
to a special court in England and Tewari was pardoned and honourably
discharged from the penal settlement.[16]

---

[14] Government of India (Home Department, Judicial Branch) Official Consultation
No. 39, 5 October 1860, NAI. See also Lowis, *Census of India, 1911*, 54.
[15] Immediately on receiving the warning, Superintendent J. P. Walker instructed
Lieutenant Col. Hellard, Commander of the Naval Guard, to anchor the ship *Charlotte*
between Ross Island and Atlanta Point. Lieutenant Ward landed a party of naval forces
and marched them to the top of Aberdeen Hill. All convicts working in the area were
instructed to bury their spare implements and to retreat towards the rear of the hill close
to the coast. Before the plans could be completed, in the early morning hours of 17 May
1859 the Naval Guards spotted the Andamanese. In order to check their movement,
bursts of gunfire were fired. They fired on them, but this had no effect on a second
group, which continued on towards the convict workstation and occupied it. Only the
arrival of reinforcements brought an end to half an hour of fighting, during which several
of the Andamanese were killed, wounded or taken prisoner. This was the first large-scale
attack organized by the indigenous Andamanese on the convicts, and their British guards
called it the Battle of Aberdeen. See Portman, *A History of our Relations with the
Andamanese*, 279–87, 279, 288, 422.
[16] Pandya, 'Sacrifice and Escape as Counter-Hegemonic Rituals'.

The Andaman administration publicly commemorates tribal resistance as patriotic heroism, but it also restrains the very same communities from participating in the public life of the nation. The Indian state's declared policy of 'non-interference' with the culture of primitive tribal groups, sits uneasily in the context of 'reserve territories' created for the 'primitive tribal groups' in Andaman Islands. The Andamanese indigenous communities are expected to remain restricted within the confines of the Tribal Reserve Territories, allow the perpetuation of an interventionist welfare structure but remain out of public view. It is this ambivalent positioning of the Andamanese indigenous communities within the Indian state that makes the commemoration of the Battle of Aberdeen so problematic. The Andamanese remain the patriotic heroes of the Battle of Aberdeen – but not quite. The glorification of the sacrifices of Dudhnath Tewari on the same occasion, and the simultaneous exclusion of the members of the indigenous community from the commemorations are ironic reminders of the ambivalence of the historical narrative of Aberdeen and the place of the Andamanese in it.

On the day after the inauguration of the Aberdeen memorial, Reuters carried a report entitled 'India shuns last survivors of Andaman tribe'. The reporter, Sanjib Kumar Roy, after having interviewed the last of the fifty-four Great Andamanese, of Strait Island (reserve territory),[17] concluded: 'the community of the Great Andamanese had expressed outrage on Friday at their treatment by India, after not being invited to a function to mark the 148th anniversary of a battle against the British'. They claimed that the Great Andamanese were nearly all 'wiped out' in the battle they fought with British forces'. The community of Great Andamanese felt concerned that as the administration paid 'floral tributes and made speeches' to honour their deceased ancestors, it was all done in the absence of their descendants. Surmai, the acknowledged 'Queen' of the community (not a traditional title but an administrative construct), told Reuters: 'We are neglected by everyone, the authorities did not

---

[17] The Great Andamanese, who are descendants of groups like Aka-a-Bia, were always in conflict with the Jarawas, and were in close contact with the British, so the possibility of them being involved in the scene of Battle of Aberdeen is questionable. However, it must be noted that of all the Islands' indigenous peoples, they are the most assimilated and 'integrated' with mainstream society, mainly through the dole provided by the welfare organization of AAJVS. See Dilip K. Chakraborty, *The Great Andamanese, Struggling for Survival* (Calcutta: Seagull Books on behalf of the Anthropological Survey of India, 1990). Non-tribal settlers are very critical of the Great Andamanese, now settled on the Strait Island Tribal Reserve. They look upon them as the 'state's sons-in-law', parasites who fritter away their money on alcohol and other substances. They also argue that as none of the Strait Islanders are of 'pure' tribal descent, they are ineligible for state welfare and other benefits.

invite us and we also do not care about them. We could have gone on our own, but our pride came in the way and we were hurt'.[18] Since the 2007 inauguration celebrations, the Andamanese have been actively inducted into the nationalist narrative of the freedom struggle in the state's projection of the history of nation-making on the Islands. Yet the similar induction of Dudhnath Tewari as an icon of local sacrifice has made this inclusion both ambivalent and suspect.

Years after the first commemorative event of the Battle of Aberdeen, in December 2013 I took Lecho, a young Great Andamanese woman, her mother and her daughter to the Aberdeen Memorial site in Port Blair. Lecho ran up the stairs of the monument, pointed proudly to the plaque and said that it noted something about an important battle where many of their community died. She said she had known about this battle from her father and grandfather. Her mother, however, looked at the monument but did not bother to accompany her daughter to view the plaque. She looked rather tired. Lecho's young daughter, who went to a local school with settler children, was incompletely indifferent. Her school had taught her a different story of the nationalist movement, where the real heroes were those who served their terms in the Cellular Jail. The Battle of Aberdeen in the school history textbooks she read was a mere footnote in that larger and perhaps more glorious history of the nation in the Andaman Islands. She remained visibly unmoved when her mother, the only one from amongst the three, recalled the memory of that struggle with a faint sense of pride.

Contentious memories: the Japanese occupation

As different communities came to settle in the Andaman Islands, they signified their identities through diverse architectural forms. Bengalis, Moplahs, Ranchiwallahs, Karens and Bhantus, for instance, maintained distinctions through house facades and layouts, in what has been described as the Islands' back yard space beyond the confines of Port Blair. Many of these communities have also constructed shrines, temples, *mazars* (Islamic shrines made at burial sites) and other minor memorials to commemorate the struggles and sacrifices made by their members in making their lives and homes on the Islands.

Installations of a plaque, an image or a structure operate as inscriptions on a landscape that commemorate through everyday practices and rituals

---

[18] Sanjib K. Roy, 'India Shuns Last Survivors of Andaman Tribe', *Reuters*, Port Blair (18 May 2007).

a value for a specific event, (in the past), at a place for the future and across space as a whole. Instances of death represented as sacrifice and ritually memorialized, is seen to radically transform the landscape. When body fluids like blood, sweat and tears are lost through the wounds of war, conflict and labour, and infused into the soil of these sites, the land becomes sacred, trans-substantiated and alive. It is these narratives of sacrifice that transform a mere physical location into a site of emotional belonging. The soil of the island as a whole becomes an object that imbibes new forms of subjectivity. Subject and object in a way get fused at memorial sites, and rituals sustain them through myriad beliefs and practices. In this respect, place-making for the settler populations of the Andaman Islands could be seen as the elaboration of a specific forms of rhizomatic thinking, marked by unexpected connections of thought, transferred onto the landscape where geographical points and historical periods become intermeshed. It is this rhizomatic thinking that inscribes innumerable memoryscapes onto the island landscape, sometimes amicably and sometimes contentiously.[19]

For all these diverse groups who have been on the historic landscape of the Islands, the deepest marks of contention remain inscribed in memories of the Japanese occupation. Local-born people (convict descendants) in particular, remember, represent and ritualize the Japanese regime which they resisted and under which they and endured extreme forms of torture and exploitation. In the vicinity of Port Blair there still stand a Japanese temple and bunkers, occasionally visited by Japanese tourists who come to pay homage. Just as the Japanese temple commemorates the loss of Japanese imperial forces, the local borns remember the spots where their forefathers were tortured and killed. Remembering death and killings at particular locations forms a trope for the ritualized commemoration of the anti-colonial movement on the Islands. Today local-born discourse frames the Japanese as the worst on the Islands. Yet there is

---

[19] Communities seek to root themselves in the landscape through collaborations on the landscape in order to construct their own meanings. In *A Thousand Plateaus*, Deleuze and Guattari invite us to think of subjectivity in a rhizomatic fashion. Subjectivity is not cemented or fixed – it is fluid and shifting – because it is constantly under construction. Subjectivity is to be understood as a heterogeneous assemblage of processes which society has imposed on itself. Rhizomatic sites are marked by a multiplicity of lines and connections – plural, heterogeneous and constantly transcending boundaries and stereotypes, open and constantly inventive. Any point of a rhizome can be connected to any other and must cut across boundaries imposed by hierarchies and order in connecting any point to other point. It trails not necessarily to link traits of the same nature, but plays upon different regimes of signs. See Deleuze and Guattari, *A Thousand Plateaus*.

resentment against the fact that this story gets underplayed in a statist discourse that predominantly communicates India as a nation built on sacrifice and struggle against the *British* as the occupying force.[20] A recent visit to a museum dedicated to the memory of the Japanese occupation seemed to underscore this point more compellingly than I expected.

In late 2013 the Police and Tourism Department of the Andaman and Nicobar Administration collaborated to create a war museum at Port Blair in the area known as the Police Lines. This is the part of the city that primarily houses various police departments. One of the old wooden colonial-style buildings has been refurbished, with a mounted gun in the front yard, and is now popularly known as the Japanese or Subhas Bose Museum. In the front porch, resembling the old-fashioned barracks, stands a policeman dressed as a 'Japanese' soldier complete with a replica of a period rifle, under a Japanese flag. Needless to mention, it is always a member from Nicobarese community who is recruited for this role, perhaps in the misplaced belief that he may be passed off as an authentic Japanese! Although not yet very popular among tourists, the few pages in the visitors' book make it clear that the museum has touched the right chords and visitors have been moved by the stories of Japanese oppression. The centre of the gallery is dominated by a huge Indian flag with a spinning wheel at its centre, placed together quite ironically with a contemporary Japanese flag. The four walls of the gallery display old black-and-white reproductions of photographs from Japanese newspapers, war publicity pamphlets and some orders that were passed by the Japanese administration, along with clippings from the *Andaman Shinbum* (newspaper). In a way the thrust is to emphasize the order and system set up by the occupying Japanese forces on the island. What is also portrayed, in a somewhat understated manner, is the sacrifice of Indians who resisted the occupation and lost their lives. The memories of Subhas Chandra Bose's landing on the Islands are invoked as in any other narrative of the Japanese occupation, but there is little in the museum of the local reactions to it. Nor is there anything in the museum

[20] It should be noted that the Cellular Jail is now a national monument and transformed into a museum. It displays reconstructed models and figures to convey the pain and sacrifices that the Jail inmates experienced on a daily basis. Their sufferings are well documented and have become part of nationalist lore. What is less known, documented or memorialized are the horrific tales of torture and suffering inflicted on the Andaman Islanders by the Japanese occupying forces. See Jayant Dasgupta, *Japanese in the Andaman and Nicobar Islands* (New Delhi: Manas Publications, 2000); Rabin Roychowdhury, *Black Days in Andaman and Nicobar Islands* (New Delhi: Manas Publications, 2003); Tilak Raj Sareen, *Japanese Occupation of the Andaman and Nicobar Islands 1942–5* (New Delhi: Pragun Publications, 2012).

Figure 4.4 A local policeman dressed as Japanese soldier standing in front of the war museum. Photograph: Vishvajit Pandya.

to suggest that Subhas's alliance with the Japanese forces of occupation created a context for the deliberate erasure of one of the most tragic phases in the lives of the local Islanders.

The state's deliberate blurring of the history of the Japanese occupation generates a sense of ambivalence among the local borns in particular, especially towards the positioning of Netaji Subhas Chandra Bose who came to the Islands during the Japanese occupation. In a sort of parallel way, what the exalted positioning of Dudhnath Tewari does to the commemoration of the Battle of Aberdeen, the effusive commemoration of Subhas does in the commemoration of the Japanese occupation. If Tewari had 'betrayed' the Great Andamanese insurgents by turning informer, Subhas had mistakenly befriended an enemy who inflicted the worst kinds of pain on the people of the Islands. In the state commemoration of the Battle of Aberdeen and in the representation of 'tribal' heroism, the character of Dudhnath Tewari appears constantly, erasing any idea about his ambivalence from collective memory. Similarly the logic of memorializing the Japanese occupation is reversed by the state that purportedly seeks to downplay the ambiguity of Bose's involvement with the Japanese. In statist discourse, the historical fact of Subhas's alliance with the Nippon military force is underplayed and his figure as Netaji (or revered leader) is recontextualized as a nationalist figure who sought to singlehandedly liberate the Islands from British rule. In the process, the role of the 'tyrannical and ruthless' Japanese force in the Andamans is erased from public memory on the Indian mainland. Among the descendants of the sufferers of the Japanese occupation, however, this story is remembered differently.[21]

On 30 January 1944, forty-four Islanders who were suspected as British spies were brutally tortured to the point that they could no longer express any pain. They were put in two trucks and driven 18 kilometres away from Port Blair to an isolated location in Homfray Gunj. They were drenched with buckets of cold dirty water to revive them in the scorching midday sun and ordered to dig a 15-foot long trench. The Japanese soldiers ordered the victims to stand along the trench and all were shot dead, one by one, with the bodies falling in the burial trench that they had dug for themselves.[22] It is believed that the news of the brutal death at the site leaked out in the city after a week as the relatives went around frantically looking for individuals who had not returned home.

---

[21] At the level of popular local born consciousness, Subhas was deceived by the Japanese. As a result, despite the unfurling of the national flag, he had no control over the Islands and could not or did not make much effort to address the conditions of the Islanders during his visit. Much to their dismay, Subhas was not allowed (or was simply restrained by the Japanese) to interact with distressed Indians. This ambiguity about Subhas's role in the Andamans is hardly known or discussed in mainland Indian nationalist discourse. His image on the Indian mainland is very different from that in the Andamans, particularly among descendants of the local born. For them, the mainland celebration of Subhas's heroism serves to erase their own stories of sacrifice and heroism in the face of a tyrannical and brutal occupying force.

[22] The elderly residents of Port Blair who frequently visit and socialize in the Settlers Association and among themselves provided me with this description. An identical eyewitness account of the incident is also published in B. B. Lall, *A Regime of Fears and Tears: History of the Japanese Occupation of the Andaman Islands* (New Delhi: Farsight, 2001 [1992]), 58–9. Many of the frequent visitors to the Association's new building, rebuilt after its destruction in a recent fire (located near Sunny's grave), think about the Andamans as 'our homeland' and regard India's subcontinent as a 'mainland' that exports employees (Andaman government officials) who have no sensitivity to the Islands' particular culture and needs.

The Japanese authorities did not allow anyone to visit the place, and the pile of forty-four dead bodies was left behind without proper burial.

In Chapter 3, Clare Anderson noted the refusal of the local administration to support a local born request to build a memorial at this place in 1970. Four years later, in 1974, Gauri Shanker Pandey, son of Prem Shanker Pandey who was killed by the Japanese at Homfray Gunj, approached Mohammad Amin Khan (a prominent trader of Port Blair) and proposed that something should be done to mark the place of sacrifice. Amin Khan, who had few financial resources at the time due to a devastating fire that had recently broken out in the Aberdeen Bazar and destroyed his business, promised help. He started to slowly contribute resources for clearing the area and making a compound and a permanent platform at the site of the trenches. Meanwhile, through the Local Born Association small contributions were regularly made to continue the work at the site, though easy access to the location nearly 8 kilometres from the main road was a major obstacle.[23]

By 1987 the Local Born Association along with the Andaman Nicobar Pradesh Council completed a memorial structure and installed a stone slab at the site, with a list of the individuals who were killed there. For the first time the local people of the Islands had made their own statement about themselves and their link to India's struggle for Independence by reinforcing their role in the struggle against the Japanese on the Island. It was in the Andaman Nicobar Pradesh Council session of 9 August 1987, to mark the celebrations of the fortieth anniversary of India's Independence, that the Council declared:

This session of the Pradesh Council pays its respectful homage to all those heroic patriots who were killed by the Japanese during the Second World War in these Islands and those who laid their lives in the Cellular Jail.[24]

The declaration made by the Pradesh Council led to the completion of the Homfray Gunj site, including the construction of a connecting road, and a garden, much like the other landscaping done by the administration in the front yard of Port Blair. The Homfray Gunj site was also given a new official name, *Balidan Vedi*, or Sacrificial Altar. The signage at the location made the point that it was the Union Territory of Andaman and Nicobar Martyrs' Memorial and not a National Memorial as is the case and representation of the Cellular Jail at Port Blair.

Since 1987, the local administration of the Island has maintained the place. Every year in the last week of January labourers are brought in

---

[23] Lall, *A Regime of Fears and Tears*.
[24] Records of Pradesh Council (local body), 1987, A&N Archives.

from Port Blair to spruce up the place by the morning of 30 January, which happens to be India's national day for the commemoration of martyrs. A moment of silence is maintained all over the nation to remember Mohandas K. Gandhi, who was assassinated in Delhi on that day in 1948.[25] Administrative heads and politicians participate in solemn ceremonies all over the country, and pay homage to the 'Father of the nation'. Because of this prescribed ritual on the national calendar, the representative of the Indian state, the Lieutenant Governor, comes from Port Blair to Homfray Gunj and celebrates 30 January as the local 'Martyrs' day at *Balidan Vedi*. Although the dates of the Homfray Gunj massacre and that of the assassination of Mahatma Gandhi were coincidentally the same, the Indian state sought to draw a deeper connection between the two. Since 1988, the customary practice has been to remember the martyrdom of both the local Islanders and the Mahatma in the same breath and therefore to blur the largely different contexts of the tragic end of both.[26]

The *Balidan Vedi* as a memorial site reveals how the state uses a place of 'killing' as a spot to invoke memories of local martyrdom annually, in synchronization with the mainland national calendar. But what happens to the *Balidan Vedi* for the rest of the year? What does the *Vedi* mean to the local population on days when it remains outside the bounds of state ceremony?

According to locals, villagers in the vicinity of Homfray Gunj visit the site with their families or on their own and often perform a peculiar ritual of prayer and offering. This is performed with a great degree of discretion and care. They bring along with them an egg, a bunch of incense sticks and a sheet of written paper along with some flowers. At the site the flowers are laid, the incense is lit, the sheet of paper is burnt and finally

---

[25] At the location in Birla Bhavan on Tees January Marg, New Delhi, where Gandhi was assassinated on his way to a morning prayer assembly, a National Monument and a modern multimedia interactive museum have been built. Each year on 30 January a prayer meeting (*sarva dharma*)-is held, where leaders and members from all religious communities participate to commemorate the martyrdom of the Mahatma. This ceremony signifies the constitutionally enshrined idea of secularism as well as the notion of sacrifice that underpinned the birth of independent India.

[26] It is interesting to note that at the *Balidan Vedi*, the inscription on the stone peculiarly signifies that the freedom struggle in the Andamans was pro-British. It reads: 'Dedicated in gallant memory of the martyrs of Indian Independence League shot dead and buried by the Japanese forces on January 30 1944, in British counter espionage, to eliminate anti-British during World War II.' The awkward syntax of the inscription leaves the impression that the British were not the colonizers, and only freedom from Japanese was the important issue. There are parallels in this play of ambivalence in the invocation of the name Dudhnath Tewari in the context of the 1859 Battle of Aberdeen, for Tewari was also a colonial collaborator with the colonizers who played a key role in the massacre of indigenous Islanders.

Figure 4.5 Balidan Vedi at Homfray Gunj. Photograph: Vishvajit
Pandya.

the egg is cracked on the ground as an offering. There is no specified day for this ritual, but on most occasions there is a context that motivates this ritual visit. If a conflict or a dispute with a fellow villager continues and the problem remains unsolved among neighbours, particularly if it cannot be resolved by a mediator or any legal or administrative channel, the frustrated family writes down the name of the 'offending' individual on the paper and burns it.[27] The cracking of the egg is seen as the sacrifice made to the spirits (*atma*) of the forty-four Indians killed by the Japanese. The villagers regard these men as having tried to resolve the conflict and eliminate the pain caused by the exploitative Japanese regime, but who were ruthlessly done away with. Their spirits reside at the site of the *Balidan Vedi*, and come to help the Islanders and lead them to the path of 'good thinking'. It is believed that the spirits compel the people whose names are burnt to give up the contentious issue and thus facilitate the return of peace and harmony in the village. For the villagers who are largely latter-day settlers on the Islands, the *Balidan Vedi* has little significance in terms of the larger history of the Islands. The knowledge that this was a site of killing and sacrifice of innocent lives is enough to make it sacred. The spirits of the martyred represent for them kindred souls who understand the pain of suffering and who, therefore, are also keen to end it. The offerings made to them are in recognition of their benevolent presence on the Islands. For these settlers, the hardships of life on the Islands, the struggle to build new homes and to forge new relations with people compel them to seek the mediation of Gods and spirits. They believe, however, that offerings made to the spirits at the *Balidan Vedi* will get them the best results as the spirits there 'know the pain of being on this land!'[28]

For descendants of the local-born population of the Islands, memories of the Japanese presence on the island has taken on new forms and become imbricated in new struggles for identity and justice. It is worth reiterating Anderson's earlier point (Chapter 3) that as late as 2008 an Association of Andaman Islanders made claims on the compensation paid by the Japanese Government for the war damages suffered by their families, and vociferously argued that what was owed to them had been

---

[27] Frequently villagers from areas near the *Balidan Vedi* in Homfray Gunj describe the situation by using the English term 'tension': that 'happens, is taken by oneself or is given by another' (*tenshan hona, tenshan lena* or *tenshan dena*).

[28] The settlers' ritual at *Balidan Vedi* is identical to the signification, representation and recapitulation of sacrifice as represented and signified by the nation state. In the ritual process of burning a sheet of written paper to communicate with the spirit world and cause an action in this world, Islanders retrace the Burmese ritual of Nat worship. (the Burmese were a significant community in the Andamans during the colonial period).

appropriated by greedy politicians.[29] Among those who did not join the campaign for compensation or political justice demanded by the formal organization of the local born, the injustices of the Indian government towards them are expressed in more discreet but powerful ways. Interestingly, most of these local narratives of the Japanese occupation begin with the history of the brutality unleashed by the Japanese occupying forces in the time immediately preceding or following the visit of Subhas Chandra Bose to the Islands.

In March 1942, after the Japanese occupied the Andaman Islands, South Andaman was fortified with bunkers to hold Japanese troops and frequently forests were bombed randomly to ensure that no British sympathizers, including the indigenous Andamanese, were in hiding. By August 1943 the Japanese forces intended to partly hand the Island's control to INA commander Subhas Chandra Bose. Soon after his arrival on the Islands, Bose, on 30 December 1943, unfurled the Indian tricolour at Port Blair and declared in a strong nationalist fervour:

Comrades, Officers and Men, with your unstinted supported and unflinching loyalty, *Azad Hind Fauj* [The Indian National Army], will become the instrument of India's liberation With the slogan – 'Delhi Chalo' [onwards to Delhi] on our

---

[29] CNN-IBN reported on Friday, 15 August 2008, in an article entitled, 'War Damages Lost? India, Japan in Denial Mode', that the Government of India had denied the descendants of war victims (nearly 1,000) compensation that had been paid by the Japanese government forty-four years previously. Japan had paid ¥9 million, then valued at more than Rs 150 crore (million) if it had been kept untouched in a bank, to the Indian Government to be paid to the war victims. Descendants of the Japanese war victims had formed the Homfray Martyr's Memorial Committee in Port Blair in the late 1980s, when they came to know about the Japanese compensation. The Committee had written letters to Indian prime ministers and presidents for the previous twenty years and received nothing until 2002. The CNN-IBN article clarified further the issue: 'During the NDA [National Democratic Alliance] regime, the Home Ministry officially accepted that the Indian and Japanese governments had signed a treaty way back in 1963. The documents clearly show that 9 million Yen was paid to the Government of India. "Government of India is the trustee of the money. But now they say they don't know where the money has gone," lawyer for Humphrey [*sic*] Gunj Martyr's Memorial Committee, Bhupender Yadav, said ruefully. However, the UPA [United Progressive Alliance] Government decided to contest that claim. They opposed the petition in the High Court in Andaman Islands terming it vexatious, malafide and motivated. But the Government forgot to tell their lawyer not to include one particular document as annexure in this petition, which was from the East Asia Division of the Ministry of External Affairs and which was marked confidential. Sent in 2007, it clearly stated that the compensation money was kept in Bank of Tokyo accounts in Bombay and Calcutta and the Mitsui Bank in Mumbai. Interestingly, successive governments have claimed that they have no record of any actual payment of this amount to the Government of India. The Japanese embassy, too, has refused to respond. Now no one apparently knows where the money has vanished even as the next generation of the war victims await the compensation that has been due to them for decades now.' 'War Damages Lost? India, Japan in Denial Mode', CNN-IBN, 15 August 2008.

lips let us continue to fight until our national flag waves over the Viceroy's house in New Delhi and *Azad Hind Fauj* [The Indian National Army] holds the victory parade inside the ancient Red Fort of the Indian Metropolis.[30]

In memory of this historic occasion, the Andaman Nicobar Island Administration celebrates every 30 December as National Flag Day, at the historic site of 1943, now known as Netaji Stadium. Once again, the Indian state invokes the spirit of patriotism of a person who hazarded and eventually sacrificed his life for the nation. Among a section of the local born, the celebration of Subhas's visit, though never openly criticized or challenged, is silently resented. The resentment is not necessarily directed at Subhas himself, but to an administration that seems to consider that one occasion of his visit as a high point of patriotic fervour in the Islands, when there were so many other acts of heroic resistance against the Japanese that had gone unnoticed. This was a feeling one got when I visited a small memorial site dedicated to a young twenty-four-year-old Punjabi Muslim boy, Zulfikar Ali, popularly known in his neighbourhood as Sunny.[31]

Sunny's *mazar* seemed to me to be a classic site that counter-asserts the glorification of Subhas particularly when seen in context of the Japanese occupation. The memorial site is located in the old courtyard of his family home that was originally surrounded by the open ground that housed the original Gymkhana Club in Port Blair's Aberdeen Bazaar.[32] On 25 March 1942, Sunny was shot dead at the corner of this ground. Today a narrow by-lane from the Aberdeen Bazaar leads to this old neighbourhood. It has quite a few shops of wholesale suppliers, some old family homes and drinking bars that open along with the bazaar in the early morning. As I walked up the lane towards the *mazar*, a small group of elderly men volunteered to direct me up to the point. One of them began to tell me the story of Sunny and his neighbourhood. 'Those were the dark days', he said, 'when we were forced to stay locked in our homes most days. The Japanese troops would enter any neighbourhood at whatever time of the day and bully any male member of the house they entered or misbehave with their women.' Recounting one such incident, he said that in the early evening of 21 March 1942, Japanese troops walked in and forced open some of the doors and dragged out the women

---

[30] Japanese Museum display, Police Lines, Port Blair.

[31] The fieldwork and group discussions with the residents were held during the last week of December 2010.

[32] After the original wooden structure was destroyed in a blaze, the Andaman and Nicobar Administration funded the reconstruction of a building at this place for the office of First Settlers' Association. In 2010, the Association announced that a museum on Subhas Chandra Bose will be built there.

from the house and started publicly humiliating them. Just when they were about to molest them, the situation took a dramatic turn. Sunny could not take this insult and walked out of his house and fired into the air, signalling the Japanese troops to retreat. The next day, the troops came back in greater strength and demanded Sunny be handed over to them. As the community did not respond to the demand, the troops declared that in the next two days they would return, and if the community did not hand over Sunny, they would set their homes ablaze and burn the whole neighbourhood. Over next two days, the community collectively decided that they would face the consequences but not surrender Sunny. However, Sunny was insistent that he face the troops again. On 25 March 1942, when the Japanese came back for him, he bravely stepped out to face them and allowed himself to be tied and dragged outside his house. He was then taken to the centre of the neighbourhood and brutally lynched in the presence of his family and relatives. Soon after, a firing squad surrounded him, and he was ruthlessly gunned down. His relatives were not allowed to move his bleeding body for days. Much later the community was able to bury Sunny in front of his house in a courtyard. On the headstone of his mazar, an epitaph in Urdu states:

Phool to do din baharey jaan fiza dikha gaye. Hairaan to un guchcho pe jo bina khiley hee murjha gaye!
Flowers bloom and enthrall us with their beauty even for the two fleeting days they do! Tormented is one by those tender buds that wither away even before they can bloom.

Sunny's tomb is not frequently visited by outsiders, but on my first visit many of the retired elders in the neighbourhood, and a few distant relatives of Sunny's family, gathered around to talk to me about the memorial. About five generations ago the core of this area was made up of families who were originally Punjabi Hindus, who had converted to Islam and became scribes in the colonial administrative offices. One man said, 'our ancestors on the mainland have never been Hindus or Muslims in any strict sense of the term. We were raised and educated in the culture of Urdu. It was only after the Mutiny that some line of divisions emerged. In recent times there has been a greater sense of urgency in redefining our identity. After the destruction of Babri Masjid incident of 2002 in Ayodhya, the residents of this area raised money and decided to upgrade the tomb dedicated to Sunny.'

Several elders emphasized that they were perfectly 'secular' in their outlook, but resented the fact that the administration, on every 30 December, proudly invoked Subhas Bose's historic achievements but failed to recognize the heroism of this young man. They argued that

Figure 4.6 Sunny's Tomb in Port Blair. Photograph: Vishvajit Pandya.

the Indian State should remind the nation that the Japanese kept Subhas ignorant about all that their forefathers had to endure. The historical pathos for residents of Sunny's neighbourhood is underscored by the fact that in 1943, when Bose unfurled the Indian flag in the grounds of Port Blair, he never bothered to know what happened in that adjacent corner where Sunny had been killed in 1942.

Henceforward, the discussion took a new turn. So what if the state ignored Sunny's martyrdom? There was no denying that it was an act of enormous sacrifice and patriotism. Sunny's blood had sacralised the soil of the Islands in ways more powerful than the unfurling of the national flag by Subhas. It gave them a new sense of belonging to the Islands and the belief that it was the soil (*zameen*) of the Islands that nurtured them from their births to their deaths. But what about the soil of the mainland? How did it matter to them here? Would the Islands be able to take the place of the original motherland? One amongst the elderly group of the elderly answered poetically:

Our ancestors brought back the soil of the Punjab and mixed it into the soil of Port Blair to make it a true home for their descendants. One's land (*apnee zameen*) is not just something you inherit (*jaydaad*), it has to have one's inherited essence (*ruuh*) in it to be remembered. It is this spirit of the soil that has the capacity to support our roots, sustain our self-respect, and protect for women; and it is these comprise our treasured possessions (*jaydad*, *izzat*, and *zenanna*). Remember how the Emperor Bahadur Shah a few miles from here in Rangoon yearned for a little clump of soil for his own burial![33]

The notion of *apnee zameen* translated both as 'one's land' and 'one's soil' brought back memories of a conversation I had with the old local-born cultivator in the outskirts of Mithakhari, whose lands had been destroyed by the brackish deluge in the aftermath of the tsunami of 2004. For Erodode Tewar, notwithstanding the dwindling returns from the land formerly cultivated by his father, it was something he could never give up. That piece of land, that stretch of soil he said, was infused with their sweat, tears and blood; it was sacred. Like Tewar, for the descendants of Sunny's family too, what made a 'place' their own was when it was marked by an act of sacrifice that could be collectively memorialized and ritualized. A fist of soil, in this context, was not an inert object. It was perceived as having a deeply subjective essence, a spirit.

It is these connections made between locations, values and subjects and the meanings of history and memory invested in the land, that dissuaded the living descendants of Sunny to ever think of giving up and moving away from the plots that they'd owned for generations. As Sunny's 'twice-removed' paternal nephew stated: 'the administration said that it would pay us a hefty sum of money and we could even return to the mainland if we wished, but we declined. How could we leave the place where Sunny lay? If we go from here they will remove him and his memory. Sunny belongs here and we belong to Sunny and this is his place.'

---

[33] In 1857, Bahadur Shah Zafar, the last Mughal Emperor of Delhi, was arrested by the British and exiled to Rangoon. Zafar was an accomplished Urdu poet and calligrapher. While he was denied paper and pen in captivity, he wrote on the walls of his room with a burnt stick, including the following *ghazal* as his epitaph. It is in this famous writing that Zafar expressed his deep sorrow for not having even two yards of his own land to be buried in. The English translation of the Urdu composition reads as:

My heart has no repose in this despoiled land / Who has ever felt fulfilled in this futile world? The nightingale complains about neither the sentinel nor the hunter / Fate had decreed imprisonment as the harvest of spring / Tell these longings to go dwell elsewhere / What space is there for them in this besmirched heart? Sitting on a branch of flowers, the nightingale rejoices I have strewn thorns in the garden of my heart / I asked for a long life, I received four days / Two passed in desire, two in waiting / The days of life are over, evening has fallen / I shall sleep, legs outstretched, and in my tomb / How unlucky is Zafar! for his burial / Not even two yards of land were to be had, in the land of his beloved.

'Bahadur Shah Zafar's Ghazal', www.bestghazals.net/2007/06/bahadur-shah-zafars-ghazal.html (accessed 14 September 2014).

For the community, Sunny is not just a historical subject but also a valued substance that is imbued in the soil of the neighbourhood. It was by walking, touching and breathing the vapours that arose from the soil that the community sustained its life and nurtured its future generations. One man said, 'It is a feeling that grows within; it is in the soil ... our boys and girls will all be always like Sunny irrelevant of whether they are in Andaman, or India.' Sunny's descendants connect intensely to the neighbourhood and to the Islands. They also forge their own connections to the mainland. But these are links that seldom connect to state discourses or rituals. Commenting on the state ceremony conducted every year on the 30 December, one of the younger men in the group said:

We do not need ceremonial dramas and shows organized by the state and the Lieutenant Governor visiting us on some pre-fixed day and reminding us that this is a land that has been free because of the sacrifice made by a single individual. We know that this land was freed because of the many sacrifices made by lesser known people who have lived on this soil for decades and called it their home.

The memorialisation of Sunny's martyrdom remains a poignant link to the three sites that mark the ambiguities of state-organized events and rituals connected to memories of sacrifice and heroism in the context of the British colonial and Japanese presence on the Andamans. I will now discuss two sites that have no explicit or implicit reference to the historical narratives of colonialism or occupation. They belong to what I would call the lesser-known narratives of the Island back yard – of places of historical encounters between the settlers and the Islands' indigenous communities. These are places where notions of sacrifice and martyrdom take on different meanings. Here, rituals of commemoration are performed not to strengthen or glorify local settler or national identities but to heal fractured ties between communities. These sites lie outside tourist circuits and the state ceremonial calendar but are testimony to the many histories of settlement and place-making that mark the complex relationships between the Islands' settler communities and the indigenous 'other'.

Mazar at Sona Pahad

Driving northwest from Port Blair towards Tushnabad, off the main road and surrounded by forest is a 100-feet-high mound known as Sona Pahad. At the foot of the mound is a meandering freshwater stream that gushes forth with seasonal supplies of prawns and small fish. On top of the mound is a well-maintained *mazar* surrounded by a small compound and covered with metal sheet roof. The *mazar* is decorated with flowers and incense, and the whole place is swept and cleaned every day by a small group of workers. This is one of the oldest *mazars* on the Islands and is attributed to Peer Yaskeen. But there is controversy here. The local *waqf* (an Islamic endowment of property to be held in trust and used for a charitable or religious purpose) board is not willing to recognize the Yaskeen as a *peer*, or mystic, or as a religious man. Thus, the land around the *mazar* remains disputed. But for the locals in Tushnabad, it is not important who Yaskeen really was and if he was ever a *peer* at all. There are several local stories about the *mazar*, but the one most commonly known is that this man called Yaskeen was an old convict serving his sentence in the Islands. One day he escaped from the forest labour camp managed by the British prison authorities and found refuge near a stream at the foot of the mound. Fatigued and famished, he sought to rest, have a drink of water and move on. But sheer exhaustion made it impossible for him to walk any further and he fell asleep. At this point, a group of Jarawa men found him and took him into their forest camp. They kept him for quite some time and nursed him back to health. The Jarawas built a shelter for him near their own hutments (*chaddhas*). One night, after spotting fire at this location, British sepoys hunted down Yaskeen and tried to recapture him. But while he was surrounded, the Jarawas counter-attacked the British troops. In the ambush, the Jarawas succeeded in driving out the British forces. In a fit of rage, Yaskeen cursed the soldiers that they would eventually die of severe skin wounds. It was rumoured that many of the soldiers did indeed suffer from fatal infections and perished. Some of those who survived came back to Yaskeen seeking help and forgiveness. Yaskeen was said to have relented and offered to heal the afflicted. He would prepare medicinal balms from the soil on the mound and local herbs that the Jarawas taught him to use. Yaskeen would also meditate at Sona Pahad for several days at a stretch. He soon came to be revered as a mystic. Over the years, both settlers and Jarawas would visit Peer Yaskeen's *mazar* and seek his blessings for protection against the Jarawa attacks that escalated with the rapid clearing of forests at the turn of the century. Peer Yaskeen would use his healing powers not only to help the suffering but also to spread the message that the Jarawas were not to be feared. They were not inherently hostile. If they did attack the forest workers they did so in self-defence. Yaskeen insisted that the forest workers not insult the Jarawas or see them as savages.

After Peer Yaskeen passed away it was believed that the Jarawas did not allow his body to be removed from the site. They buried him on the spot where he meditated. Later, over a period of time the burial spot was given the semblance of a *mazar*. Villagers in the vicinity of the *mazar* continue to believe that through his death Peer Yaskeen became one with both Allah and the Jarawas with whom he spent much of his life. Today, the Sona Pahad *mazar* has become a site for thanksgiving and celebration for one and all irrespective of class, community or ethnicity. An old tree at the *mazar* site is covered with little red threads bearing prayers and wishes to Peer Yaskeen. Once their wishes are fulfilled people visit the *mazar* with their friends and family and organize a feast.

On such occasions of feasting and festivity many locals believe that Jarawas come and hide behind the forest nearby, to make sure that their Yaskeen is not mistreated in any way. The local settlers of Tushnabad regard the area to be relatively safe from Jarawa hostility. There have been no incidents of Jarawa hostility or attacks and the enduring peace in the area is attributed to the blessings of the old Peer Yaskeen. As a Tushnabad resident explained:

As travellers on the road approach the mazar, they see traffic slow down. The mazar reminds them of the ephemerality of life, of misfortune, of death, of accidents. They look upon Sona Pahad as a speed breaker on the road, and seek a quiet blessing from Peer Yaskeen to keep them safe.[34]

Unlike the local settlers of Tushnabad, however, who seemed to have made peace with the Jarawas through the mediation of Peer Yaskeen, there are swathes of settlements in the vicinity of the Jarawa Tribal Reserve (JTR) in the Middle Andaman Islands where the history and present reality of Jarawa hostility clouds the lives of many. These were the areas that were rapidly deforested in the mid 1970s, making way for a deep expansion of settlements and the building of the Andaman Trunk Road (ATR). Until 2000, Jarawas of the forest in these parts were known to have been the cause of much misery both to settlers and forest labourers. There were frequent incidents of Jarawa attacks, and life for the settler seemed to be beset with perennial fear of death (*khatarnak zindagi*). It seemed as if danger always lurked in a forest that was violently reconfigured by routine incidents of brutal and bloody encounters with the 'Junglees'.[35] In the context of this relentless violence, settlers were

[34] Discussion with Krishna Gopal Singh and locals of Tushnabad, 16 November 2010.
[35] In the settler narrative, the tribals (indigenous peoples) are *junglee* (wild and hostile) – their violence makes them essentially different from civilized settlers. These are notions that continue to be propagated thus making the forests an ideologically embattled zone. The settlers' image of 'the tribal' as 'Other' is sustained also by the fact that they 'don't understand how to grow things' and that they 'don't wear clothes'. See Madhusree Mukherjee, *The Land of Naked People: Encounters with Stone Age Islanders* (Boston, MA: Houghton Mifflin, 2003), 138. However, the irony lies in the fact that the Indian state has always tried to 'protect' the forest and the indigenous communities within it. Individual attacks either on settlers or on indigenous people are seen as an attack on the entire community, and produce a discourse of enmity sustained by the memory of previous acts of violence and disfigurement. A popular theory among settlers is that the

seen to mark out places where encounters with Jarawas were more frequent and where lives were lost in some of the more gruesome attacks. Villagers often got together to put up their collective might against such attacks but on most occasions failed to mount any determined resistance. As many in the vicinity of the Jarawa Tribal Reserve (JTR) in Middle Andaman recounted, 'our young men lost their lives in these encounters – this soil is reddened with their blood'.

At Jirkatang check post number 7, the north–south road, known as the Andaman Trunk Road (ATR), enters the Jarawa Reserve Forest. At the check post, the police processes permits to travel through the reserve area and provide escorts to the convoys. Just about a hundred feet away from the road is a temple (*mandir*) built by one Kalimuttu Swamy. After all the paperwork is done, commuters on the road often go up to the temple and place an offering. Upon their return from the temple, the gates are opened and the traffic convoy starts moving. Descendants of forest workers and public works department (PWD) labourers as well as early settlers are some of the more regular visitors to the shrine, which is dedicated to the mother goddess Mariamman (*Durga*). Mariamman's blessings are particularly sought by residents of the South Andaman Islands who believe they are in 'the zone of death and danger' the moment they enter the Middle Andaman region.

violence of indigenous communities derives directly from their dependence on killing animals to survive. A life-taking activity, hunting is declared less worthy than other activities such as the cultivation of the soil. Prasenjeet Haldar, head of a Bengali settler family, explained: 'As workers in fields, in small shops and offices, we nurture life for the living.' 'Jarawas hunt outsiders' has become an easy phrase used to sum up the disposition of a whole people. Such labels are not just invocations of colonial-era conflicts, but a reflection of how 'hunting' is singled out as a way of life based on violence. Settlers are far from learning how to unpack the idea of the 'Other' by distinguishing different historical occasions for violence. On the contrary, the idea is rigidified by their arguments about the extreme savagery of the actions of these 'ruthless', 'habitual' killers of animals and humans. Contemporary incidents sustain the belief that Jarawa hunt 'outsiders'. Rarely do settlers see these acts of hostility as expressions of protest registered by the Jarawa against the loss of their autonomy. Popular wisdom lacks the sense of history that would entail this recognition, though ethnographic accounts observe that these killings must be understood in terms of Jarawa beliefs, including notions that intruders must be sacrificed and territorial boundaries must be respected. See A. R. Radcliffe-Brown, *The Andaman Islanders: A Study in Social Anthropology* (Cambridge: Cambridge University Press, 1922), 86; R. C. Temple, *Census of India, 1901, Volume III: The Andaman and Nicobar Islands* (Calcutta: Superintendent of Government Printing, 1903), 69–90. In Miletilak and Aniket, dismembered settler bodies recovered from the forest are seen as sacrifices to Jarawa *jungleepan* (wildness) and their notions of revenge, a perception that leads bereaved relatives to lose sight of their own acts of transgression that led to their deaths. The disfigurations stir both awe and revulsion, as mutilation is seen as exacerbating the humiliation of the victims, and are read as a signal that any community provoking Jarawa anger will be similarly humiliated.

Figure 4.7 Kalimuttu's Mandir at Jirkatang. Photograph: Vishvajit
Pandya.

Kalimuttu came to the Andamans from Tamil Nadu around 1975,
and was recruited by the Public Works Department (PWD) of the
island administration. Like many others who made up the PWD labour
force, he was posted at the Jirkatang forest camp where workers were
engaged in clearing tracts of forests to construct the ATR. On 25 August
1986, at around 4:30 PM, Kalimuttu along with two other workers were
returning from work to their base camps. They carried with them a
couple of axes, machetes and a load of cane and firewood. All of a
sudden, they found themselves face to face with eight armed Jarawamen.
'We had no idea where they were hiding; they are so dark that they
blended into the thick forest. Since they had no clothes you couldn't
see them at all; our dogs too couldn't smell them and warn us! Kalimuttu
narrated this story to me almost a decade ago.[36] Two of his companions
were killed on the spot, as the Jarawa arrows were shot from close range.
Armed with little else other than his implements and an empty basket,
Kalimuttu started throwing these at the Jarawa to create confusion in
their ranks. The one item he held onto was his machete, which served to

---

[36] Interview with Kalimuttu Swamy, December 1998. Swamy passed away in Winter 2001.
Today his distant relatives come from mainland India to look after the temple.

inflict some serious injuries on his enemies as he whirled it round and round.[37] He himself was hit in the limbs by twenty arrows that the doctors in the hospital at Port Blair were able to remove with much difficulty. His left foot however had to be amputated as his ankle developed gangrene. In 1998, while showing me his scars, he had proudly declared that these were the marks of grace he had received from Mariamman! He used the land and money he was given as compensation to build a temple to Mariamman on a small hill at Jirkatang, close to the place of the bloody encounter, and declared that it was the goddess who protected him thereafter. Kalimuttu became a renouncer and was there- after known as Kalimuttu Swamy. Until his death in 2001, as chief priest of the temple, he performed rites to ensure the safety of those working near the forest. People visited him to seek his blessings in the form of amulets. These amulets were made by twining black and red thread with consecrated grass, to protect people in their 'life in the forest', particularly during exigencies such as childbirth, snake bites, chronic illness and above all in the event of an ambush Jarawas. Many visit the temple to take a pinch of ash from its altar and keep it in protective amulets.[38] Others bring in new metal implements to the temple to be blessed and empowered. Such ritual practices and the larger narrative of sacrifice that frames these, configure a sacred geography on the fringes of the forest, imbued with historical consciousness and sustained by a 'home-grown' theology.

The *mazar* at Sona Pahad and the temple of Kalimuttu Swamy now stand as repackaged memory structures on the peripheries of the forest. These locations, serving spiritual and mystical needs, have transcend locational, community and ethnic moorings to become universal sites of healing. What is remembered, though, are the individual acts of sacrifice and pain that become the sources of the healing powers that the sites later acquired. While ritual offerings are made and new acts of faith invoked through tying sacred threads with prayers, the memory of the event of sacrifice is not eroded. Among many settlers, an act of sacrifice (*balidan kar na*) is a commonly repeated trope in narratives of quotidian life in the Andaman Islands. The notion of sacrifice entails a conscious act of giving something in order to acquire something either

---

[37] Settlers believe that at this particular moment Kalimuttu became possessed, goddess Durga (in southern Indian Hindu mythology also known as Mariamman), who was chosen by the gods and bestowed with wisdom, power and weapons to fight the elusive and powerful demon Mahishasur. Durga was able to kill the demon and save the world from chaos and disorder.

[38] This has strong parallels with practices at Sona Pahad.

for one's own self or a larger collective. Upon successful acquisition or accomplishment, rituals of continuous gratitude and remembrance are conducted in order to secure the prospect of further gains. Sacrifice thus becomes a constitutive moment that sets up a relation of exchange, a historical process that symbolically re-enacts the original giving for future gains and benefit. In doing so, what people seek through ritual is the memorialization of history embodied in a peculiarly Andamanese culture of land.[39] Kalimuttu, in fighting back against the Jarawa attack, was mutilated. Yet he survived (by either 'divine intervention' or presence of mind), and this is what made him a revered hero who risked his life and 'sacrificed' a part of his body. Kalimuttu, in articulating his own theological point of view, saw the Jarawas' 'act of hunting' animals and their 'killing of poachers and intruders as bearing a logic of 'sacrifice', similar to the ritual slaughtering of animals at his temple. He told me:

If you take something from God you need to give something to God too. If you take what belongs to the Jarawa and their forest, they too will take you and your material possessions. All I do is to pray for the life of those who enter the forest to secure their livelihoods.[40]

In Kalimuttu's statement we see a projected phenomenon, whereby notions peculiar to his faith were grafted onto his explanation of Jarawa behaviour, leading to a shift of meanings that provided a distinctively new 'texture' to the landscape.[41]

---

[39] This is similar to agrarian cultures, that practice fertility rituals, where the tiller of the soil returns fertility to the soil through ritual and symbolic acts. It affects the radical asymmetry between sacrificer (tiller) and what they had sacrificed (fertility). See Ralph W. Nicholas, *Rites of Spring: Gajan in Village Bengal* (New Delhi: Chronicle Books, 2008). Headhunters do a similar practice to sustain slash-and-burn cultivation. See Renato I. Rosaldo, *Ilongot Headhunting 1883–1974: A Study in Society and History* (Stanford, CA: Stanford University Press, 1980); Paolo Sponz, Chui Sponz and Shanchulla Sponz, *Tangkhul: Head Hunting Nagas* (New Delhi: India Research Press, 2007). In the case of the Andamans, the settlers, being largely agriculturists, were compelled to destroy the forests that were the domain of hunter-gatherers. The violent confrontations between them and the indigenous communities that often followed as a result of this has created an asymmetrical relation of power between the two, where the values of the 'field' prevail over the values of the 'forest', and every act of violation or transgression is remembered and marked with rituals and symbolic affect.

[40] Interview with Kalimuttu Swamy, December 1998.

[41] See Paul C. Adams, Steven D. Hoelscher and Karen E. Till, *Textures of Place: Exploring Humanist Geographies* (Minneapolis, MN: University of Minnesota Press, 2001); Yi-fu Tuan, *Space and Place: The Perspective of Experience* (Minneapolis, MN: University of Minnesota Press, 1977). Violence, bloodshed and killing, as ways of taking or giving life, and as foundations to the notion of sacrifice, have resonance in the way that land is textured to create a landscape. The work of Tim Ingold directs attention to hunter-gatherer societies as distinctive in subverting 'the very foundations upon which the

Conclusion

Although it is tempting to look at the diverse practices of memorializing as potentially inconsistent, and draw battle lines between local community and nationalizing forms, it is far more instructive to understand the ways in which these practices are articulated and mediate with one another in Andamanese island culture. While the state appropriates the relics of the colonial state and redefines the material and symbolic order of the Islands' landscape, most of its settler communities carve out their own places within it by translating and renegotiating the nationalist narrative in terms of their own memory practices. The trope of sacrifice and martyrdom may be common, but the intent of memorialization remains different but not overtly conflicting.

If nation-making through memorializing is premised upon the idea of recapitulating the roots of the nationalist struggle and consolidating its branches on the Islands, the place-making projects of the people are premised upon the memorialization of the gaps, silences and ambivalences within the nationalist narrative. Thus while Subhas Chandra Bose acquires iconic status within the nationalist history of the Islands, Sunny, the young boy shot to death by Japanese aggressors, goes unnoticed. The community that memorializes Sunny's martyrdom does not articulate a counter-discourse; it merely creates a space for connecting with the nationalist narrative on its own terms. Similarly, while the statist history of the Battle of Aberdeen commemorates the role of 'tribal' fighters, the Islanders begin to wonder why a ceremony to honour their ancestors is conducted in the absence of their descendants. In other words, they counter pose the state's rhetorical inclusion of the tribal within the nationalist narrative with the fact of the lived reality of their exclusion from the nation state.

---

concept of society ... in any of its modern senses' is built: *The Appropriation of Nature: Essays on Human Ecology and Social Relations* (Iowa City, IA: University of Iowa Press, 1987), 399. It requires us to rethink our definition both of social being and of violence. Relations are constituted by the sharing of food and company rather than by formal obligations (Ingold, *The Appropriation of Nature*, 406), and in some cultures, a hunt consummated with a kill is seen as proof that the animal has 'willingly allowed itself to be taken', making the hunt an attempt to 'establish a working basis for mutuality and coexistence'; also see Tim Ingold, *The Perception of the Environment: Essays on Livelihood, Dwelling and Skill* (London: Routledge, 2011), 69. The broad lines of Ingold's argument support my contention that the manner in which the Jarawa take life, though grotesque to outsiders, follows a prescribed sequence of actions meant to transform a being foreign to the community into something that can be incorporated into their world. Actions of cutting and bloodletting turn animals belonging to the domain of nature into meat that can be brought into the campsite.

In the state's narrative of the nationalist struggle the British remain the constant 'other', while in that of the community, the Japanese acquire a similar position. The ambivalence of the nationalist narrative vis-à-vis the ravages wrought by the Japanese occupation become clearer in the commemorative discourse around the *Balidan Vedi*, where the invocation of martyrdom moves out of its historical specificity in the Islands to the more familiar event of the Mahatma's martyrdom on the mainland. What stands out in this entire commemorative exercise is the quiet quotidian rituals performed out around the *Vedi* by those for whom the historically recorded event of martyrdom acquires far less importance than the belief in the healing powers of the spirit embodied in the martyr's memorial. A site of nationalist remembrance thus becomes a site of ritual healing.

The ambivalence surrounding the narratives of sacrifice and heroism around the *mazar* of Sona Pahad and the temple of Kalimuttu Swamy also points to the centrality yet marginality of the 'tribal' presence in the Islands as both neighbours and 'others'. In the commemorative discourse at Sona Pahad, the Jarawas come across as friends but at the temple of Kalimuttu Swamy, they remain the oft misunderstood 'other'. At Sona Pahad, both the Jarawas and the settlers commemorate Yaskeen but at the temple of Kalimuttu Swamy the memories of such goodwill are ritually forgotten.[42] It is in this complex web of practices of commemorating and forgetting that the projects of nation-making and place-making play out on the Islands, charting out multiple paths for both the state and communities to integrate their histories onto the landscape. Such integration is never straightforward or easy; it is contingent upon multiple mnemonic negotiations. It has to be remembered that community identities on the Islands are defined by a long history of flux – everyone has complex cultural origins. In a context of ceaseless movement and change, the search for roots makes for difficulties. What acquires greater significance is the constant forging of new connections.

---

[42] Within the mutual discourse constructed by the contact between non-tribals as intruders and Jarawas as the residents of the forest, there is a dominant reference to the violence as a way of life among the Jarawas as *junglee shikaree* (wild hunters). What is implicit is that for the inhabitants of the forest (Jarawas) there are important perceived parallels between encounters with animals while hunting and encounters with intruders (settlers who enter the forest for poaching and illegal extraction) in the forest. See Vishvajit Pandya, *In the Forest: Visual and Material Worlds of Andamanese History, 1858–2006* (Lanham, MD: University Press of America, 2009), 203–59. Both kinds of encounter take place outside domesticated space, involve the taking of life and entail situations loaded with uncertainty and danger, because both animals and intruders are defined as outside of what is tribal domesticated place within forest space.

Such connections may be spontaneous or considered but are deeply contingent upon the struggles of survival on the Islands.[43]

Conceiving the Island landscape as inherently rhizomatic allows us to explore the maze of multiple sites and practices and symbolic codes through which social and political relations as well as cultural identities are constituted, negotiated and narrated in the Andaman Islands. As assemblages of humanly produced material forms, landscapes, as has been pointed out, constitute cultural records through time and space that may be interrogated as artefacts, but landscape also constitutes a discourse through which identifiable social groups frame themselves and their relations with both the land and other human groups. In the case of the Andaman Islands, the landscape analyzed through the heuristic of the rhizome allows us to move out of linear and bounded historical frameworks and explore the potentially richer possibilities of ensuring space and legitimacy for the presence of communities and places that face the threat of forever slipping out of its frames. In the following section of the book, we turn to a deepening of this insight, through three focused studies of specific communities and their relations with each other, the mainland and history. In Chapters 6 and 7, respectively, Madhumita Mazumdar and I explore narratives of belonging among the Matua sect and Jarawa community. Meantime, Clare Anderson turns to a history and ethnography of the convict descendants living in the Islands today: the local born.

---

[43] Here is a typical report of the Republic Day celebration on the Islands on 26 January 2010: Early in the morning, the Lt Governor first visited the Cellular Jail National Memorial at Port Blair and placed a wreath at the Martyrs' column there. Then the main event moved to an impressive parade at the historic Netaji Stadium. After the unfurling of the national flag, there was a march organized by school children. Individuals were honoured by the state in front of all the citizens and administrative staff. The culmination of the ceremony was the speech made by the Lt Governor, General (Retd) Bhopinder Singh. It recapitulated all that the state had achieved and planned to do in future for the Islands. The most significant part, and typical of any speech made on such occasions, was the beginning and end. Singh first paid his obeisance to the freedom fighters for their sacrifice for the motherland. While remembering the contribution of freedom fighters who were incarcerated in the Cellular Jail during the freedom movement, he said that 'culture of unity in diversity prevailing in these islands is the contribution of the freedom fighters which is a role model for the rest of the country.' The speech ended with the following call: 'we should take a pledge to protect our Constitution at every cost and contribute our might towards the development of the country in general and these islands in particular.' See *The Daily Telegrams*, 28 January 2010.

Part II

Affective landscapes

5   The Andaman local born: history, identity and convict descent

Clare Anderson

Introduction

After the British reoccupied the Andamans following the Japanese surrender on 7 October 1945, British commissioner N. K. Paterson returned to the Bay of Bengal. He abolished the penal colony and gave the 7,000 or so convicts then in the Islands the choice of either returning to India, or of settling permanently in the Andamans, as free men and women. Just under half chose to stay.[1] They joined the convict-descended population – known as 'local born' – which totalled about 3,000 to 4,000 men, women and children, and who mainly lived in and around Port Blair.[2] A few years after the abolition of the penal colony, which was followed by Indian Independence, in 1950 the Andamans became a Union Territory of the new nation state of India. Since then, the number of local-born Islanders has continued to grow.

During the penal era, convicts came from all over the Indian Empire, including Burma, and from the very first years of transportation, men and women from diverse social, cultural and religious backgrounds were forced to journey, work and live together. Convicts and ex-convicts married each other, as did their descendants, and, after the importation of Moplahs, Bhantus, Karens and other labourers in the early twentieth century, they wed other colonial settlers. Distinguishing themselves from the post-Independence Bengali refugee settlers described by Madhumita Mazumdar in Chapter 2, and more recent migrations, today *all* colonially descended people in the Andamans – including local born but not exclusively so – constitute the political category 'pre-42' (1942 marks the year of Japanese occupation). They claim for themselves a distinct culture in which religious, caste and other forms of social distinction are largely absent. Until recently, the pre-42s comprised the only 'Other Backward

---

[1] Report on a tour to the Andamans by Mr A. J. Brown from 22 to 29 July 1950 (secret), DO133/39, TNA. Three thousand ex-convicts chose to stay in the islands.
[2] A. K. Ghosh, *Census of India, 1951, Volume XVII: The Andaman and Nicobar Islands* (Calcutta: Government of India Press), 1955, x.

135

Castes' (OBCs) of the Islands. OBC is an official government of India classification given to castes that are socially and educationally disadvantaged, and OBCs are granted 27 per cent reservations in public sector work and higher education. In 2011, Bengali settlers petitioned successfully for inclusion on the Andaman list.[3] Since then, other more recent migrants from places like Andhra Pradesh have made claims for OBC status too, as yet unsuccessfully.[4] The penal colony and its associated and subsequent coerced and assisted migrations have, it would seem, left tangible postcolonial legacies on the Andaman social and cultural landscape.

This chapter will explore the historical evolution of the locally born, convict-descended community in the Andamans, in order to make sense of some of the social and economic claims of Islanders today. I will examine what colonial archives reveal about how ex-convicts and their descendants were able to establish and consolidate their grip on land to the 1920s, and on how during this period transportation and coeval punishment and labour regimes effected transformations in practices of everyday life, had particular cultural outcomes and produced new social norms. I will show that, over time, the process of colonization and settlement, and its associated social reproductions and reinventions, created forms of desocialization and resocialization, and had profound effects on labour practices, gender relationships, and religious practices and affiliations. As we will see, the cultural effects of transportation were often encouraged, if unintentionally, by the British administration, though the growing number of freeborn Islanders presented it with profound economic, penal and social dilemmas.

I will also bring my research in colonial archives into dialogue with my ethnographic work amongst local-born people in the Andamans. My aim here is not to use oral history as a means of 'filling in' archival gaps. Rather, the chapter will explore how local-born people understand their history and represent their identity, and how these understandings and representations coalesce and conflict with mainland views of the Islands. I will show that since Independence, despite mainland refusal to accept Islanders' role in the nationalist struggle, and the long road to political incorporation, as discussed in Chapter 3, both Islands and mainland have celebrated the cultural legacies of the penal colony, in particular their apparent erasure of many forms of social distinction and differentiation.[5]

---

[3] National Commission for Backward Classes, A&N Bench, Advice No. 2/A&N/2009, http://ncbc.nic.in/Pdf/Andaman%20&%20Nicobar%20Islands/2.pdf (accessed 16 May 2013); *Andaman Sheekha*, 13 February 2012.

[4] *Andaman Sheekha*, 27 August 2012.

[5] For a somewhat different, anthropological perspective on some of these issues, see: Philipp Zehmisch, 'Freedom Fighters or Criminals? Postcolonial Subjectivities in the

Land and labour

During the colonial period, most Andaman convicts returned to India when they were released or pardoned, but from the very first years of transportation in the nineteenth century a small proportion of ex-convicts remained, often marrying convict women and having children, or sending for their left-behind wives under various family settlement schemes. Given that several thousand convicts arrived each year, this population quickly grew in size. By the mid-1870s, colonial officials were writing of the presence of several hundred children in the settlement.[6] According to decadal censuses, in 1881 there were 754 'locally born' people in the Andamans; in 1891 there were 1,499; in 1901 2,030; and in 1921 2,745.[7] In 1929, Chief Commissioner Colonel M. L. Ferrar wrote that in the six years since he had taken up his post the number of children alone had risen to perhaps as many as 4,000.[8] Born free, the administration was often exorcised about the correct treatment of these children. Uniquely in the Indian Empire, in the Andamans hospitals were free to everybody, not just convicts; education was compulsory; and so-called industrial training was strongly encouraged. Convicts' children were so well cared for, Commissioner R. C. Temple claimed in 1901, that it was quite normal for the whole of a young family to survive into adulthood.[9]

The first school for convicts' children was set up on Ross Island in 1876, following the recommendations of the wide-ranging report of J. S. Campbell and H. Norman. Just one year later, there were 224 boys and 68 girls enrolled in 13 schools, initially staffed mainly by convicts and self-supporters. The colonial administration faced no difficulty in enforcing attendance, even at a cost of R2 per child per month. It complained, however, that the convict teachers could not speak English and were otherwise incompetent. The 'narrow horizon' of local-born

Andaman Islands, South-East India', in Paula Pannu (ed.), *Kontur Nr. 22 'Colonial and Post-Colonial Subjectivities'*, (2011), 4–16.

[6] Report on the requirements of the penal settlement of Port Blair, 13 June 1874, P/528 Home (Port Blair proceedings), August 1874, nos 51–84, IOR.

[7] *Statistics of the Population Enumerated in the Andamans, 17 February 1881* (Calcutta: Superintendent of Government Printing, 1883), Form X; R. C. Temple, *Census of India, 1901, Volume III: The Andaman and Nicobar Islands* (Calcutta: Superintendent of Government Printing, 1903), 295–6; R. F. Lowis, *Census of India, 1921, Volume II: The Andaman and Nicobar Islands* (Calcutta: Superintendent of Government Printing, 1923), 10.

[8] M. L. Ferrar to his mother, 26 September 1927, Ferrar Papers, CSAS.

[9] Temple, *Census of India, 1901*, 295–6.

teachers remained a common refrain into the 1920s.[10] Nevertheless, large numbers of ex-convicts and self-supporters took advantage of access to education and sent their children to school, too. In the 1910s and 1920s, the Local Born Association played a pivotal role in encouraging attendance, especially of girls.[11]

The numerical growth of a convict-descended population was underpinned by convicts' remarkable success in acquiring land and property. Up to the 1870s convicts were routinely given tickets-of-leave (conditional pardons), and were allowed to bid at auction for five-year rent-free licenses on cleared land in the districts, in order to become 'self-supporters'. Whilst they could be remanded to the convict barracks for any misconduct, as long as they did not commit offences against discipline they were permitted to take employment, grow crops and vegetables, and keep cattle and poultry. Under the land allocation system, those ticket-of-leave convicts who had arrived soon after 1858 were able to get licenses for the best quality acreage. This led to their claim to quite extraordinary economic power, for they did not always cultivate that land but instead sublet it to make considerable profits as absentee landlords. Campbell and Norman's 1874 report criticised that this had come to pass, calling for the regulation of tickets-of-leave, and lamenting that self-supporters were able to make large profits from renting land or selling produce to the government commissariat at inflated prices. Speaking of their 'rise to considerable influence' and near-aristocratic status (some, it claimed, even had convict servants), Campbell and Norman recommended that land be assessed and appropriate rents paid.[12] Subsequently, government decided that convicts could not become self-supporters until they had served ten years of their sentence, and that they would not be freed for another ten to fifteen years more – to return to India, or to settle in the Islands. By 1879 government had introduced a formal land settlement, based on the system of revenue

[10] Government of India Home (Port Blair) proceedings, June 1876, nos. 19–22, CJML; P/1006 Home (Port Blair), February 1877, nos. 43–4: Educational arrangements at Port Blair: C. A. Barwell, officiating Chief Commissioner, to officiating secretary to the government of India, 16 November 1876, IOR; *Report on the Administration of the Andaman and Nicobar Islands and the Penal Settlement of Port Blair for 1921–2* (Calcutta: Superintendent of Government Printing, 1922), 3.

[11] Opening of a girls' school in the settlement of Port Blair, as an experimental measure for a period of five years: R. F. Lowis, officiating superintendent to secretary to the government of India, 21 July 1919, enc. Copy of minute of the female education committee, Held Browning Club, 7.30 PM, 19 October 1918, P/10592 Home (Port Blair) August 1919, IOR.

[12] Deputation of the Honourable Sir H. W. Norman KCB, to visit Port Blair: Report on the requirements of the Penal Settlement of Port Blair (henceforth Campbell and Norman Report), P/528 Home (Port Blair), August 1874, nos. 51–84, IOR.

collection in India's North West Provinces. Self-supporters, including traders and shopkeepers, were required to pay tax; to pay rent on their land; and to pay other fees and cesses, for instance, for grazing rights and the provision of schools.[13]

In the grossly gender-imbalanced penal colony, furthermore, unusually gendered patterns of land occupation developed. This was exacerbated in particular by the mass release of convicts in 1877, when Queen Victoria assumed the title Empress of India. All at once the British granted free pardons to a large number of convicts: more than 350 men and women. Government established new villages in the northern districts for those who wished to settle. Some men chose to return to India, though, and left property behind with self-supporting wives, who stayed on their former landholdings.[14] One convict of means who was released in 1877 and returned to India, for instance, noted later on that he had left his wife Jan Bibee with a 'hut house', 10 cows, 2 chests, 2 charpoys, 2 copper handis (bowls) and '1 iron pot to boil things'.[15] Additionally, the small number of self-supporting women in the Andamans were able to consolidate land holdings through the *de facto* transfer of licenses after their husbands died, often followed by swift remarriages to other ticket-of-leave landholders. Indeed, in one of the settlement's largest villages and districts, Aberdeen, in 1915 self-supporting women held 32 out of 67 licenses; and local-born women 221 out of 654. Given that they comprised only 14 per cent of the Islands' total settler population in 1911, and just 12 per cent in 1921, these figures are quite astonishing.[16] 'Many of these women are ruthless money lenders and haunt the civil courts in the recovery of their loans,' Superintendent M. W. Douglas reported.[17]

---

[13] Land revenue of the Andamans: Superintendent C. A. Barwell to C. Bernard, officiating secretary to government of India, 21 August 1878, P/1006 Home (Port Blair), October 1878, nos. 14–5, IOR.

[14] Releases and other indulgences granted to convicts in Port Blair and the Nicobars on the occasion of the assumption of the title of Empress of India by Her Majesty, Inc. settlement order no. 21–991, 1 January 1877, P/1006 Home (Port Blair), February 1877 A, nos. 58–68, IOR. Question of the release of male and female convicts who have been left in the Settlement after the return to India of their absolutely released consorts: the humble petition of SYED ASHRUF ALI late prisoner No. 7225 of Port Blair, present residence No. 15, Wellesley Street, in the Town of Calcutta, 30 May 1877, P/1006 Home (Port Blair), August 1877 A, nos. 14–21, IOR.

[15] Humble petition of SYED ASHRUF ALI late prisoner No. 7225.

[16] Lowis, *Census of India, 1921*, 8.

[17] System by which convicts are permitted to support themselves at Port Blair: Superintendent M. W. Douglas to secretary to government of India, 10 May 1915, P/9716 Home (Port Blair), September 1915, no. 37, IOR.

As the number of self-supporters and convict children grew, officials in the Andamans began to express concerns about the management of the increasingly complex settlement, which was no longer straightforwardly or solely a penal colony. For instance, government wavered on what to do about marriages between self-supporting men and the (free) daughters of convicts. They fretted that the former seemed able to escape discipline once they were married, and that the latter risked the prospect of abandonment if their husbands were stripped of their ticket-of-leave for committing misdemeanours and returned to the convict barracks.[18] For this reason, officials worked against the development of 'mixed' villages, in which self-supporters and free inhabitants lived side-by-side, and towards a policy of separating them from each other.[19] After another 1891 Andamans report (C. J. Lyall and A. S. Lethbridge), which was critical of the failure of the penal colony to become either self-supporting or economically productive, government actively tried to encourage ex-convicts to stay permanently. However, few did, in large measure because they were not allowed to live where they wanted. Government concentrated released convicts in the southern district and self-supporters in the northern district. After their release, those living on the wrong side of the line were forced to move.[20] For obvious reasons, this was hugely unpopular amongst self-supporters. Compounding this detrimental policy was the fact that government continued to auction off occupancy rights to land every five years. As early ex-convict arrivals had long since settled in the Islands and made money in agriculture or through other kinds of work, new self-supporters found it difficult to compete. With only marginal land left at licence prices that they could afford, and that concentrated in outlying, isolated villages, by the early 1900s freed convicts were not inclined to settle in the Islands, and to the administration's disappointment they

---

[18] Regarding marriages of convicts with free persons. Officiating Commissioner Protheroe to Mackenzie, 14 November 1881, P/1670 Home (Port Blair), March 1882, nos 45–51, IOR.

[19] Proposed rules and conditions to be observed by persons desirous of landing and residing in South Andaman: Protheroe to Mackenzie, 16 March 1882, P/1670 Home (Port Blair), September 1882, nos. 62–7, IOR.

[20] Report on the working of the penal settlement of Port Blair by Mr C. J. Lyall and Surgeon-Major A. S. Lethbridge, 26 April 1890, P/3658, June 1890, IOR; Draft rules having reference to the settlement in the Andamans of released convicts, P/3887 1891, December 1891, nos. 36–8, IOR; Separation of the free-convict population: R. C. Temple to secretary to government of India, 27 September 1895, Home (Port Blair), January 1896, nos. 111–6, NAI.

often returned to the mainland, confounding its long-term goal of self-sufficiency.[21]

By this time, the convict-descended local-born population largely lived either in the Aberdeen Bazar area of Port Blair, or in the eastern districts of the colony in villages set apart from convict stations and the villages of convict self-supporters.[22] Though their status was quite different and they lived apart, broadly speaking, self-supporters and locally born people followed similar occupations. About half were agriculturalists, one-third were employed in government service and the remainder as traders, shopkeepers or in private service.[23] They worked as clerks, boatmen, foresters, rangers, gunners, drivers, goldsmiths, tailors, blacksmiths, carpenters, fishermen, graziers, sawyers, vegetable and milk sellers, *dhobis* (washer men), petition writers, servants, draftsmen, and shopkeepers.[24] Moreover, despite government intentions, the self-supporting and free populations were interdependent – in trade and work, as well as marriage and other areas of life – with released convicts and their descendants even on occasion money-lending to their self-supporting neighbours.[25]

I write in detail of the local born acquisition of land, because it has been so important to the creation of the economic landscape of the Islands today. I noted in Chapter 3 that in the 1970s the Local Born Association claimed to have *created* the 'greenery' of the Andamans. In the previous section of the book, Madhumita Mazumdar discussed the colonial landscaping of Ferrargunj; and Vishvajit Pandya conceptualized everyday practices of commemoration by Islanders in the 'front yard' and 'back yard' of the Islands. Understanding the history of local-born attachment to land is key to the identity claims that I will return to later in this chapter. It adds also further depth to my earlier articulation of local born claims of national belonging, as evinced in the contentious debates about who has been accorded the political status (and privileges) associated with 'freedom fighting'.

---

[21] Suspension for the present of the grant of permission to released convicts to remain in the settlement, Douglas to secretary to the government of India, 25 February 1915, P/ 9716 1915, July 1915 no. 1, IOR.

[22] Temple, *Census of India, 1901*, 352. The free districts were Ross, Aberdeen, Haddo and Garacherma, and the convict districts were Viper and Wimberlygunj.

[23] R. C. Temple's 1908 Andaman Gazetteer, draft typescript, 103, CJML.

[24] M. C. C. Bonington, *Census of India, 1931, Volume II: The Andaman and Nicobar Islands* (Calcutta: Government of India Central Publication Branch, 1932), 'Occupations of Local-Born Population returned at the Census of 1931', 30–1.

[25] Separation of the free-convict population: R. C. Temple to secretary to government of India, 27 September 1895, January 1896, nos 111–6, NAI; Suspension for the present of the grant of permission to release convicts to remain in the settlement: Superintendent M. W. Douglas to secretary to the government of India, 25 February 1915, P/9716, July 1915, no. 1, IOR.

Culture, religion, society and sexuality

The British viewed transportation as an important punishment, because in shipping convicts across the *kala pani* (black water, or sea) it was supposed to cut ties of family and kin, and place convicts from all communities in close contact with each other, so rendering Hindus outcaste. Convict responses to transportation were rather more complex than government appreciated; for instance, men of resources could largely wipe out its effects through offerings, prayers and feasts. But it is the case that many convicts never saw their homes or families again, and that government deliberately organized the penal colony in culturally unfamiliar ways. When convicts arrived in the colony, they were employed in manual labour, and as Census Commissioner R. F. Lowis put it in 1911, they were 'forced to associate and form friendships with men they would not willingly associate with in their own country'.[26] The British employed a few low-caste sweepers (*mehtars*) and high-caste Brahmin cooks, but otherwise they refused to respect caste in allocating convicts to work. Similarly, they refused to permit the building of religious buildings or institutions or the operation of caste *panchyats* (councils) in self-supporter villages.

Nevertheless, for Hindus caste did not disappear entirely, but rather transportation offered some remarkable opportunities for social mobility. In 1901, Chief Commissioner R. C. Temple gave many examples of a process historians and anthropologists now call 'Sanskritisation', including the 'masquerade' of low-caste convicts claiming that they were high-caste; ex-convict settlers adopting 'a mode of dress and life, which would be quite inadmissible if they were to return to their native villages in India'; and low-caste Hindus' conversion to (casteless) Islam. But religion and caste were clearly not convicts' sole concerns in this social manoeuvring. Temple also noted that men sometimes volunteered to become *mehtars*, 'debasing their social status in order to adopt what they have regarded as a less arduous mode of life than daily cooly labour'. For these reasons, according to Temple's farsighted analysis, the locally born population (which he called 'indigenous') would eventually and inevitably become '*sui generis*', and differentiated from equivalent communities on the mainland.[27] Indeed, Lowis had earlier

---

[26] R. F. Lowis, *Census of India, 1911, Volume II: The Andaman and Nicobar Islands* (Calcutta: Superintendent of Government Printing, 1912), Appendix B.

[27] R. C. Temple, *Census of India, 1901*, 295, 369; [R. C. Temple], *Imperial Gazetteer of India, Provincial Series: Andaman and Nicobar Islands* (Calcutta: Superintendent of Government Printing, 1909), 66–7.

noted: 'there are young men calling themselves Hindus who are unable to give the name of the caste to which they claim to belong.'[28] Meantime, new kinds of specifically penal rather than cultural solidarities began to emerge. Senior Medical Officer J. M. Woolley wrote in 1912 that convicts 'constitute a very firm amalgamated society. This becomes evident directly one begins to make enquiries into cases. They will not tell about each other. Punishment is willingly undergone rather than do that.'[29]

Temple further claimed that Andaman-born Hindus possessed a distinct caste feeling, but that it was distinct from that felt in India. No doubt, this difference was in part the product of the British approach to convict marriage. Given that convicts came from all over the Indian Empire, it was impossible for the local administration to work out whether an individual's choice of spouse – as represented to government in applications for marriage licenses – conformed to established cultural practice in their home communities. Before 1881, the British allowed same-religion marriage generally, but subsequently for Hindus decided to recognize the four main caste *varna* (Brahmins, Kshattriyas, Vaisyas and Sudras) and to permit endogamous marriage within those categories. Temple himself was interested in how the children of what would have been mixed-caste marriages on the mainland went on to reproduce caste in the specific context of the Andamans. In an ethnographic report on the issue, he noted that they followed the paternal line, constituted through the four broad *varna*, and by ignoring their mother's caste attempted marriage within them. He reported that the groom's means of support was more significant to family agreements to marry than was caste; that the bride's parents did not give wedding gifts (dowry) to the groom's family; and, that it was the groom's family that paid the wedding expenses unless they did not have the means to do so. 'Thus is a full caste system like that of India being developed among the descendants of the convicts', Temple concluded.[30] Though the caste names were familiar, they had 'a fundamental difference in sense'.[31]

---

[28] Lowis, *Census of India, 1911*, 71–2. There are interesting parallels here with the cultural outcomes of indentured Indian migration in sugar colonies like Mauritius, Fiji and Trinidad.

[29] R. F. Lowis, *Census of India, 1911*, Appendix B: J. M. Woolley, 'Convict marriages in the Andamans', reprinted from the *Indian Medical Gazette* 47, 3 (1912).

[30] [Temple], *Imperial Gazetteer of India*, 68, 398–400; R. C. Temple's 1908 Andaman Gazetteer, draft typescript, 105–6, CJML. Appendix D of the 1901 census is a detailed list of the caste and district provenance of convict fathers and mothers, and the stated caste of their local-born children: 'Results of enquiry into the caste history of local-born men and women in the penal settlement of Port Blair'.

[31] Temple, *Census of India, 1901*, 297.

Language was another important area of social transformation and distinction in the Andamans. Campbell and Norman had recommended in 1874 that the common practice of schooling the children of convicts in the language of their fathers come to an end, and that one single language be taught and used in the settlement. This was partly because convicts' children were unlikely to ever return to their father's home place. But they also had longer-term goals; a perhaps remarkable foresight in recognising that these children would come to 'form a community of which the members should stand by and help one another ... and be associated in the management of the convicts.'[32]

After Campbell and Norman's report, the penal colony's daily records and returns were kept in Urdu, a language which became the vernacular of all convicts – whether they had previously spoken Bhojpuri, Bengali, Hindustani, Oriya, Malayalam, Tamil, Burmese or any other language. But this was no ordinary Urdu; as Temple put it in 1901, it was a partly creolized tongue that was peppered with English and 'specialised applications to new uses of pure or corrupted Urdu words'. It was peculiar to 'local conditions and the special requirements of convict life';[33] 'spoken in every possible variety of corruption and with every variety of accent'.[34] To be sure, the colonial administration encouraged the development of this new language. They wanted convicts to converse with each other in a shared Hindustani creole, for language was seen as an important safeguard against secret plots.[35]

Temple noted several examples of Andamans Urdu, with English words transformed through customary pronunciation. To give a flavour of its local and penal specificity, I reproduce and annotate extracts from his quite extensive list here:

> *Bijan*, Urdu version of the English word division (b-j-an): convict barrack.
>
> *Tapu*, island (Hindustani): convict station – originating from the time when convicts were concentrated on small islands in Port Blair harbour.
>
> *Peti afsar*, derived from 'belt' (peti), and the English word 'officer': petty officer.
>
> *Total.* Temple writes 'In common use among the convicts, who are being constantly counted for all sorts of reasons.'
>
> *Kilas*: class.

---

[32] Campbell and Norman Report, 47.   [33] Temple, *Census of India, 1901*, 362.

[34] Temple, *Census of India, 1901*, 362; [Temple], *Imperial Gazetteer of India*, 64.

[35] Temple, *Census of India, 1901*, 362; R. C. Temple's 1908 Andaman Gazetteer, draft typescript, 95, CJML.

Sher sahib, derived from 'tiger' (sher), to mean European overseer.

Sikāman: sick man or convict in hospital.

Rashan: ration.

Messcott, from the English word 'mess' and 'kot' (house): mess house.

Tikatliv: ticket-of-leave; *tikatwallah*: self-supporter.[36]

I will return to the issue of language, and how it relates to claims of local-born community cohesion, later on in the chapter.

I noted earlier that colonial administrators were keen to separate convicts and self-supporting ticket-of-leave holders from ex-convicts and their descendants. Beyond the desire to keep men and women of different penal status apart, in this government was also concerned about the preservation of sexual 'morality' – or rather what it described as the prevention of 'immorality'. Its intervention in the sexual life of the colony was part of larger efforts to improve 'discipline' and to safeguard what Temple described as children's 'moral welfare and education'.[37] Colonial officials were concerned that the constant change in land holdings under the license system worked against the formation of 'natural' village communities, and against what in 1915 Superintendent Douglas described as a shared moral code.[38] Indeed, from the last quarter of the nineteenth century, the colonial administration had been making frequent complaints about what might be described as social chaos amongst convicts and ex-convicts. Chief Commissioner Temple expressed the view that locally born children of convict parents – boys and girls – were at best 'of loose character'. Furthermore, it was partly to avoid sexual relations and more especially sexual exploitation that successive administrations stressed the need to separate self-supporters, convicts and the free population from each other, as described above.[39]

---

[36] Temple, *Census of India, 1901*, 362–4.

[37] Report on the working of the penal settlement of Port Blair by Mr C. J. Lyall and Surgeon-Major A. S. Lethbridge, 26 April 1890, P/3658, June 1890, IOR; Draft rules having reference to the settlement in the Andamans of released convicts, P/3887 1891, December 1891 nos. 36–8, IOR; Separation of the free-convict population: R. C. Temple to secretary to government of India, 27 September 1895, January 1896, nos. 111–116, NAI.

[38] Suspension for the present of the grant of permission to released convicts to remain in the settlement: Douglas to secretary to the government of India, 25 February 1915, P/9716, July 1915, no. 1, IOR.

[39] Measures for the prevention of immorality among free persons at Port Blair. Temple to secretary to the government of India, 30 April 1895, P/4755 July 1895, IOR; J. P. Hewett, deputy secretary to the government of India, to Temple, 26 July 1895, P/4755, July 1895, nos. 79–81, IOR.

Census Commissioner Lowis wrote in 1911 that the shortage of girls in the Andamans encouraged prostitution among self-supporters, because every girl was 'a source of revenue to unscrupulous parents; a valuable asset, not to be lightly parted with, as long as she can be kept in a state of dependence.'[40] Senior Medical Officer Woolley added a further layer to our understanding of sexual relationships in the penal colony. Self-supporter villages were quite affluent, he claimed, because male convicts were paid small gratuities after five years of service, and if they saved their money they were able to accumulate goods like silks and gold ornaments. It was this relative wealth – and more especially the lack of restraining influences from family and kin as would have been the case outside the penal colony, in free society – that led to 'loose living.' The sexual liberation of men in this respect was compounded by the fact that convicts had access to women and girls because their barracks were so close to self-supporter villages.[41]

Lowis further reported that, during the early years of transportation, convicts commonly married only those who they could have married in their communities in India. But as their cultural expectations and self-imposed strictures gradually relaxed over the period of their sentence, and in the absence of sanctions from left-behind kin networks, when convicts became self-supporters they took what he described as a 'most chaotic' approach to their choice of partners. In stark contrast to the mainland, men and women of different castes – even widows – commonly married. They also divorced and remarried. Accompanying these considerable cultural transitions, compared to the mainland, and under-scored by the grossly unequal sex ratio, came considerable benefits to women. The British did not allow girls to marry until they had reached the age of sixteen, which meant that there were very few young, or child, widows.[42] Purdah (female seclusion) was almost unknown and, despite (or perhaps because of) claims about their sexual licentiousness, female children were highly prized and infanticide was non-existent. It is debatable whether all women in the Islands were in a better social position than they would have been on the mainland, particularly given the sex trade that was such a focus of colonial concern. But because of their grip on land, as discussed earlier, overall, at least some women enjoyed a higher status than they would have done on the mainland, and this was certainly the view of contemporary British officials.[43]

---

[40] Lowis, *Census of India, 1911*, 67.

[41] Lowis, *Census of India, 1911*, Appendix B: J. M. Woolley, 'Convict Marriages in the Andamans', reprinted from the *Indian Medical Gazette* 47, 3 (1912).

[42] Temple, *Census of India, 1901*, 291.   [43] Lowis, *Census of India, 1911*, 65–7.

A sentence of transportation was clearly socially and culturally trans-
formative, then, but the colonial regime's support for the breakdown
and reformation of religion and caste, including through intermarriage,
and its discouragement of religious worship, had some unintended
effects, particularly given the homosocial character of the penal colony.
By the turn of the twentieth century, the colonial administration began to
express concern at the absence of social sanctions in the Islands. One
1914 report complained that self-supporting convicts had become 'opu-
lent and lazy, unrestrained and sexually licentious':

There must be moral restraints, religious restraints and social restraints. These do
not exist at present and never can exist among large bodies of men deprived of
female society, without caste influences, with no village opinion, and without any
religion; these very influences which keep men in respectability in an ordinary
Indian village or town are more than ever required in the task of leading a man to
regain lost respectability.[44]

Superintendent Douglas added in 1915 that perhaps the British had been
mistaken in their previously secular policy: 'The only bond common to
all is that of the convict fraternity ... morality without religion, in some
form or other, is an impossible conception in an oriental community.'[45]
Calling for the re-establishment of religious customs, his conclusions
about the long-term effects of the penal colony on everyday life were
remarkably circumspect. He went on:

It is perhaps unreasonable ... to expect a normal standard of morals or
development from the ex-convict colony ... but there can be no question
that the environment of a convict Settlement administered on current lines
must permanently exercise a demoralising and depressing influence on any
independent community residing within its limits.[46]

In a further report of 1919, he called for Indian priests to visit the Andamans, and to make 'exhortations to right conduct' in convict villages.[47]

---

[44] Report of a visit to the penal settlement at Port Blair by the Hon'ble Sir Reginald
Craddock in November 1913, P/9949, April 1914, no. 34, 91, 93, IOR.
[45] Suspension for the present of the grant of permission to released convicts to remain in
the settlement: Douglas to secretary to the government of India, 25 February 1915,
P/9716, July 1915, no. 1, IOR.
[46] System by which convicts are permitted to support themselves at Port Blair: Douglas
to secretary to the government of India, 10 May 1915, P/9716, September 1915,
no. 37, IOR.
[47] 'Report on the Reform of the Andaman Penal Settlement' by Lieut.-Col. M. W.
Douglas, C.I.E., I.A., Superintendent, Port Blair and Chief Commissioner, Andaman
and Nicobar Islands (New Delhi: Superintendent Government Printing, 1919),
P/10592, August 1919, IOR (henceforth Douglas Report).

Douglas also drew attention to the possibility of the sectarian consti-tution of villages by calling on the example of the new canal colonies that had been established along these lines in the Punjab.[48] There is an interesting contemporary parallel here, for the government of India was concerned that the lack of binding ties of custom rendered the canal colonies especially susceptible to 'immorality'. Therefore, they looked to articulate moral principles through the creation of particular kinds of material settings that could mould behaviour and create orderly habits.[49] Besides helping us to place sexuality in the Andamans within a larger cultural context of subaltern mobility and displacement, this is a useful way to understand some of the motives behind village and urban planning there. I have already mentioned the forced relocation of ex-convicts and their families to separate villages. Of further interest is a 1931 government order, declaring Aberdeen a municipal area and ordering that houses be built according to a standard pattern of construction. As a consequence, many local-born people had to pull down and rebuild their homes.

Douglas' comments on the unhappy coexistence of a penal colony with a freeborn society reflected the development of larger concerns about local born self-esteem and morale at the time.[50] The penal colony forged new lines of social and cultural association and distinction, to be sure, but it also impacted on everyday attitudes to colonial forms of labour and governmentality. In the early 1900s, convict descendants were keenly aware of their free status, and it seems that they commonly refused to do the kinds of work associated with penal labour.[51] The government made repeated efforts to engage them in agriculture, engineering and manufacture, but they prized office-based government employment.[52] Commissioner Temple wrote that though convict children were bright and intelligent, the boys in particular:

[E]xhibit much defiant pride of position, in being free as opposed to the convict, combined with a certain mental smartness, idleness, dislike of manual labour, and disrespect for age and authority that stand much in their way in life. Their defiant attitude is probably due to the indeterminate nature of their social status, as has been observed of classes unhappily situated socially elsewhere.[53]

---

[48] Constitution of self-supporting villages on a racial or sectarian basis: Douglas to secretary to government of India, 30 October 1915, P/9716, December 1915, nos. 15–6, IOR. See also Douglas Report.

[49] William J. Glover, 'Objects, Models, and Exemplary Works: Educating Sentiment in Colonial India', *Journal of Asian Studies*, 64, 3 (2005), 539–66.

[50] *Report on the Administration of the Andaman and Nicobar Islands and the Penal Settlement of Port Blair for 1929–30* (Calcutta: Government of India Press, 1931), 2.

[51] [Temple], *Imperial Gazetteer of India*, 63.   [52] Lowis, *Census of India, 1911*, 69.

[53] [Temple], *Imperial Gazetteer of India*, 63.

Moreover, quite understandably growing up in a penal colony gave convict descendants a particular outlook. They were acculturated to what Commissioner Temple referred to as 'minute supervision' and 'excessive governing', and though he understood their reasoning, he lamented that they had become so heavily reliant on government support.[54]

The creation of the penal colony, and its associated settlement by ex-convicts and their descendants, brought new kinds of social formations into being. Culture, language, religion, marriage, sexuality: all seem to have undergone profound transformations, or reinventions, creating distinct kinds of gender relationships and religious practices and affiliations. The cultural effects of transportation were deep, then; and as for the importance of penal colonization for land acquisition and distribution, its history allows us to add depth to our understanding of contention and belonging in the Andamans today. I will explore that theme in the second part of this chapter. First, my final section on the history of the penal colony: debates about ex-convict self-sufficiency and 'morale'.

Colonial self-sufficiency and community morale

After broad-ranging enquiries during 1919 and 1920, the Indian Jails Committee recommended the abolition of transportation, and its replacement with a sentence of rigorous imprisonment on the mainland. It added that the Cellular Jail at Port Blair – by then associated with the incarceration of mainland nationalists – should be reserved for 'really dangerous criminals' only. Recognizing that Indian jails lacked the capacity to underpin its recommendations, the committee was pragmatic enough to recognize that the end of transportation to the Andamans would come gradually. Meantime, it proposed the accommodation of convicts already in the colony in properly guarded jails or stations.[55]

As we saw in Chapter 2, during his tenure as Chief Commissioner (1923–31), M. L. Ferrar subsequently oversaw a period of rapid change. He took charge of a new scheme through which mainland prisoners volunteered for Andaman transportation, revolutionizing the penal regime. The previous ten-year period of probation from convict to self-supporter gave way to a transition from prisoner to *talabdar* after just three

---

[54] [Temple] *Imperial Gazetteer of India*, 63; R. C. Temple's 1908 Andaman Gazetteer, draft typescript, 96, CJML.

[55] *East India (Jails) Committee: Report of the Indian Jails Committee, 1919–20* (London: H.M.'s Stationery Office, 1921), 308.

months, with volunteers moved into barracks and employed by government. After one year of service, they could become self-supporting.[56] Volunteer prisoners as well as those transportation convicts already in the Andamans were permitted to send for their families, and for the first time in the colony, the free population began to outnumber the convicts, and the number of women and children rapidly rose.[57]

During this period the British began to ship a small number of other settlers to the Andamans too, adding a further layer of social and cultural complexity to the Islands and their population of convicts, self-supporters, convict descendants and volunteer *talabdars*. Following the Malabar Rebellion of 1921–2, arguably the biggest threat to colonial authority since the 1857 Revolt, the British deported about 2,000 Moplahs (Kerala Muslims) to special villages in the Andamans. Though some were considered dangerous enough for incarceration in the Cellular Jail, most were encouraged to become cultivators in a district called Wimberleygunj. They had self-supporting status, they were not segregated from the convicts and they were allowed to call for their families at government expense.[58] Between 1926 and 1928, the British also sponsored the Salvation Army to 'rehabilitate' about 300 Bhantus in the Andamans, releasing them from mainland jails on the condition that they went to live in the island district of Ferrarganj. The peripatetic Bhantu community had been classified as one of hereditary criminals under the Criminal Tribes Acts (1872–1924), since when they had been forced to live in reservations in India's Central Provinces. Salvation Army captain Edwin Sheard (later held prisoner of war by the Japanese) accompanied dozens of families to the Andamans in 1926, taking charge of the building of houses and other structures, the planting of fruit trees and other agricultural enterprises, the employment of his charges in saw-mills, and the setting up of a handloom weaving factory. This was a disciplinary regime of rehabilitation through useful labour and Christian proselytization.[59] Finally, government also shipped to the Islands a few hundred agricultural contract labourers (north Indian Ranchi and Burmese Karen) to

---

[56] Notes on the Andamans for the Information of Volunteer Convicts, 1938. I thank Taylor C. Sherman for this reference. For a fuller account of this scheme, see her article, 'From Hell to Paradise? Voluntary Transfer of Convicts to the Andaman Islands, 1921–1940', *Modern Asian Studies* 43, 2 (2009), 367–88.

[57] Bonington, *Census of India, 1931*, 7–8.

[58] British House of Commons debates, 18 February 1924, volume 169, c1282: Moplah rebellion (prisoners) http://hansard.millbanksystems.com/commons/1924/feb/18/moplah-rebellion-prisoners (accessed 13 April 2012).

[59] Bonington, *Andaman Census 1931*, 41–3; Edwin H. Sheard, *Sergeant-Major in the Andamans: Kanhaiya Gariba* (St Albans: Campfield Press, 1957), 11–2.

work in the development of forestry; a migration directly related to the Islands' labour requirements.[60]

The colonial government made explicit efforts to encourage economic self-sufficiency in the colony at this time, particularly among the established, convict-descended free population. It leased coconut plantations to them on favourable terms, granted them shares in timber exports and encouraged them in setting up a Co-operative Land Syndicate.[61] However, the British repeatedly drew attention to the stigmatization and lack of self-respect of convict descendants,[62] and engaged in a series of efforts to raise community 'morale'. One was the promotion of Robert Baden Powell's Boy Scout movement among ex-convicts' and their descendants' children, initiated in the Andamans in 1921. Though on the mainland there was some ambivalence about allowing Indians to join the Scouts (Baden Powell himself supported their exclusion), Scouting was viewed as a route to developing 'character' through the encouragement of physical fitness, honour, manliness and loyalty to Empire.[63] In the Andamans, many local-born children joined the Wolf Cubs, Scouts or Girl Guides. The packs were headed by Ferrar and his wife, and supported by a prominent and wealthy Andaman born merchant called Khan Sahib.

Andamans Scouting developed in parallel with the Local Born Association. Colonel Cecil Beadon, Chief Commissioner of the Andamans, 1920–3, oversaw its establishment. Initially, it operated under the presidency of a gazetted (i.e. British) officer with the stated aim of fostering self-esteem, through sport and other social activities, and creating a forum through which the freeborn could represent their interests to government.[64] They gathered together for meetings and discussions, and to read newspapers and magazines. Government fully supported their efforts, and in 1921 agreed to allow them free use of an empty building in the bazar.[65] Under Ferrar's watch, the members came to elect their own president. They raised 20,000 rupees for a large community building – the Browning Club – which, centred in the bazar, became a

---

[60] Bonington, *Census of India, 1931*, 29–30. On these points, see also F. A. M. Dass, *The Andaman Islands* (Bangalore: Good Shepherd Convent Press, 1937), 70–1.

[61] *Report on the Administration of the Andaman and Nicobar Islands and the Penal Settlement of Port Blair for 1927–28* (Calcutta: Government of India Press, 1929), 54.

[62] *Report on the Administration of the Andaman and Nicobar Islands, 1929–30*, 2.

[63] Carey A. Watt, 'The Promise of "Character" and the Spectre of Sedition: The Boy Scout Movement and Colonial Consternation in India, 1908–21', *South Asia: Journal of South Asian Studies* 22, 2 (1999), 41–6, 53–4.

[64] Bonington, *Census of India, 1931*, 29.

[65] Conversion of a government building in Aberdeen Bazar Port Blair into a Club House for local-born youths of convict descent, July 1921, P/11048, nos 4–10, IOR.

Figure 5.1 'Local-born guiding', Ferrar Collection, Courtesy Centre of South Asian Studies, University of Cambridge.

focal point for activities including Scouting, and also amateur dramatics, hockey cricket and an agricultural show.[66] Ferrar wrote in 1926 that the success of the latter was 'a great index ... of the wonderful improvement in morale of the convict population.'[67] Association members were appointed to the schools management committee.[68] The community grew in number, and during this period, seems to have developed a more cohesive identity, which subsequently underpinned its post-war advocacy for the Islands, including that described in Chapter 3, around political representation on the mainland and wartime compensation.[69]

Simultaneously, the colonial administration began to sponsor the professional training of convict-descended youths. One young man was sent to Calcutta to train to be a vet; and three men went to Rangoon – two to

[66] Dass, *The Andaman Islands*, 71–2.
[67] Ferrar to his mother, 28 September 1926, Ferrar Papers, CSAS.
[68] *Report on the Administration of the Andaman and Nicobar Islands, 1929–30*, 43, 53.
[69] Bonington, *Census of India, 1931*, 29.

train as surgeons and one as a sanitary inspector.[70] By the 1930s, the British were recruiting locally born police constables, sponsoring the education of one man in the Phillaur police training school in the Punjab, and shipping another to Calcutta to train in anti-communist censorship and work. Other local-born men were sent to Calcutta University to take teaching qualifications.[71]

Despite efforts to encourage community pride and self-sufficiency, and though some convict descendants like Farzand Ali (the scoutmaster) rose to be described as 'one of the leading merchants of the place',[72] colonial officers repeatedly lamented the largely negative mainland view of the locally born. As early as 1908, Temple maintained that though they were sympathetic towards convicts under sentence, non-convict settlers regarded marriage into families with what he called 'the taint of convict blood' as 'degrading'.[73] It was commonly said that they looked down on them not because of their convict origins *per se*, but because of their fluidity with respect to matters of religion and caste, particularly their marriage practices.[74] It was partly for this reason that Ferrar applauded the 1929 official visit to the islands by Lord Birdwood, Commander-in-Chief of the British Indian army, writing that it was good for Islander respect to have such 'a great man here who is all civility to them and moves with safety among them'.[75]

The view from the mainland was also related to sexuality in the Islands. Later administrators drew attention away from Temple and Craddock's earlier criticisms of immorality; pointing out that sexual propriety had improved with the birth of the second generation, in particular with respect to the increasingly balanced gender ratio. M. C. Bonington wrote in the 1931 census that at the time local-born people held high-grade positions in the local administration, and through strong public opinion had effected 'distinct improvement' in morality.[76] Indeed, the 1931 census reveals 695 local borns earning a wage. A significant proportion – about 100 – was employed as clerks, mainly in the forestry department. Over one-third of them were cultivating owners, tenants or labourers. The next largest group – forty-four – worked on the

[70] *Report on the Administration of the Andaman and Nicobar Islands, 1929–30*, 36.
[71] *Report on the Administration of the Andaman and Nicobar Islands and the Penal Settlement of Port Blair for 1935–6* (New Delhi: Government of India Press, 1936), 4; *Report on the Administration of the Andaman and Nicobar Islands and the Penal Settlement of Port Blair for 1937–8* (New Delhi: Government of India Press, 1936), 4, 21.
[72] Dass, *The Andaman Islands*, 63; Khan Sahib to Ferrar, 12 September 1932, CSAS.
[73] [Temple], *Imperial Gazetteer of India*, 67.   [74] Bonington, *Census of India, 1931*, 29.
[75] Ferrar to his mother, 22 December 1929, Ferrar Papers, CSAS.
[76] Bonington, *Census of India, 1931*, 29.

settlement boats. The list of occupations is long, and includes *inter alia* foresters and rangers; *patwari* (village accountants); gunners; drivers; goldsmiths; tailors; blacksmiths; carpenters; fishermen; graziers; sawyers; toddy, vegetable and milk sellers; *dhobis* (washer men); firemen; petition writers; servants; draftsmen and shopkeepers.[77] As one Indian visitor, F. A. M. Dass, put it in 1937, the locally born had suffered a great deal, including social boycotts. In his view, the very classification local born was 'not only unsuitable but also rather contemptuous'.[78]

In the post-colony: 'unity in diversity'

When the Andamans became a Union Territory of India in 1950, the newly independent mainland Indian administration decided that the term local born was 'humiliating', and decided upon a broader category to describe *all* Islanders – 'Andaman Indian'. For the purpose of education, social assistance and employment, this category was, in turn, included on a larger list of 'backward communities' that also included the 'deno-tified' (previously 'criminal') castes and tribes, as defined during the British period. The deputy commissioner and superintendent of the 1951 census, S. K. Gupta, wrote:

> The artificial creation and nurturing of a special community as 'Local Borns' were obviously due to the social disabilities to which the early convict settlers were subjected to in those days. But it certainly has created a fissiparous tendency which is very undesirable in the present political context of the country. A feeling of separateness attended with an inferiority complex has crept in, retarding the progress and development of the people. As one young graduate very aptly put it the other day 'the people here are suffering from "backward-phobia"'.[79]

What Gupta did not understand was that local-born claims possessed the same kind of 'firm amalgamated society' that the British had attributed to the convicts fifty years before. In this respect, his belief that local born claims to the Islands, in the face of Bengali refugee settlement, were 'gradually dying out' was quite mistaken.[80] The granting of special rights to local borns and the descendants of other forced settlers who arrived before 1942 (the 'pre-42s'), as OBCs, has set the stage for disputes about

---

[77] Bonington, *Census of India, 1931*, 'Occupations of Local-Born Population Returned at the Census of 1931', 30–1.

[78] Dass, *The Andaman Islands*, 68.

[79] A. K. Ghosh, *Census of India, 1951, Volume XVII: The Andaman and Nicobar Islands* (Calcutta: Government of India Press, 1955), Appendix I, Notes of S. K. Gupta, Deputy chief commissioner and superintendent of census operations, 21 March 1951 (henceforth Notes of S. K. Gupta), xliv.

[80] Notes of S. K. Gupta, xliv.

land and privilege that endure to the present day, as later migrant settlers from the mainland strive for the same classification.

And yet at the same time, in the aftermath of millions dead or displaced through the violence and bloodshed of the Partition of India – when 'Hindu' India and 'Muslim' Pakistan were created – the new government of India found much to praise in the afterlife of the penal colony. In 1951, Deputy Commissioner Gupta also wrote of the Islands as 'a sociological experiment of tremendous national importance'. Community life, he claimed, was entirely secular, and religion was a 'completely personal matter'.[81] The Secretary to the Ministry of Home Affairs, H. V. R. Iengar, had visited the Andamans a couple of years earlier, in late 1949. It is worth quoting at length an extract from his later broadcast on All India Radio, for it reveals a great deal about his belief that penal transportation had forged a new kind of 'model' society, lacking in distinctions of language and religion, and about how this was appreciated by mainland visitors:

[W]hen I was in Port Blair, I happened to run into a young man who seemed a typical member of a community with whom I had come into much contact in Bombay and Gujrat. His facial cut, his beard and his personality seemed characteristic of this enterprising commercial community. I thought I would introduce a homely touch into our conversation by talking to him in Gujarati. But after a while it became clear to me that he did not know a word of that language. The conversation then turned into Hindustani of which his knowledge, unlike mine, was excellent. He told me he had never been to India, had only vaguely heard that his ancestors came from Surat and that he spoke no other language than Hindustani. A little while later, I met a young woman who seemed absolutely typical of the class of South Indian women who work in the factories in Coimbatore. It would have been ludicrous to talk to her in any language other than Tamil or so I thought half unconsciously, and I spoke to her in Tamil accordingly. But she did not understand a word of it; the only language she knew was also Hindustani and that she spoke excellently.

It soon became clear to me that the Indians in Port Blair have solved a problem which is still being debated on the mainland ... The mother tongue of every Indian there, whether his people originally came from the Punjab or Bengal or Madras is Hindustani.... Religion ... is regarded as an entirely personal matter – so personal indeed that it does not affect even family relations. There are families in Port Blair some of whom are Muslims and some Hindus and they see no incongruity in this whatsoever. In fact the people do not understand why religion should be regarded in India as a barrier between human beings.[82]

---

[81] Notes of S. K. Gupta, xliv.
[82] Andaman and Nicobar Islands 'A Paradise on Earth', Mr H. V. R. Iengar's broadcast talk, All India Radio, 3 January 1949, 9.40 PM, DO142/373, TNA (henceforth 'A Paradise on Earth').

Inegar concluded that he was 'astonished' at this 'remarkably practical and sensible attitude to religion,' and to their solution to the 'problem of a common language'.[83] Twenty years later, in 1966, a visiting journalist from the *Indian and Foreign Review* agreed, writing that the islands were 'a source of inspiration to the people of the mainland'.[84]

Today, Islanders often claim that the Andamans are a space of tolerance and 'unity in diversity', a cultural model for all India, or as they describe it, 'mini India'. The Islands, it is said, are a place where settlers from different places, speaking different languages and practising different religions have come together to live harmoniously. Society in the islands is inevitably more complex than this simplistic representation implies, but the claim suggests – albeit indirectly – the cultural profundity and enduring effects of the experience of penal transportation that I have discussed in the chapter so far. The pages that follow will investigate this proposition further, taking an ethnographic turn to suggest the importance of connecting history to the present. This section of the chapter looks at the past as manifested in society today, particularly in how local-born people represent their convict origins and the social and cultural outcomes of penal transportation. My goal here is not to present local-born testimonies as oral histories that chime with or challenge what we can learn from colonial archives. Rather, I seek to unpack some of the ways in which people in the Islands understand the significance of colonial history in the post-colonial social formations – and landscapes of affect – that they now construct and experience in their everyday lives.[85]

I first met Mr John Lobo in February 2011. I had known of him, of course, for some time – I say of course because everybody who lives in or works on the Andamans knows John Lobo – for he is ex-president of the Andamans Local Born Association, and still a prominent and active member. One of the people I had been discussing the project with, the British radio producer Selma Chalabi, had debriefed me when we met just before I had left England for the Islands – my first visit for almost a decade. She told me that I would have no difficulty in finding him, for he spent most evenings sitting with friends by the fountain at the bottom of the Aberdeen Bazar in Port Blair. Selma had met Mr Lobo when she was making a programme on BBC Radio 4, *Kala Pani: A Forgotten History*, in

---

[83] 'A Paradise on Earth'.

[84] 'The Little India out in the Sea', *Indian and Foreign Review*, 15 May 1966, 9–10.

[85] In this, I acknowledge but take a different approach to Shahid Amin, in his celebrated account of popular memory and national remembering of an anti-police riot in colonial India: *Event, Metaphor, Memory: Chauri Chaura 1922–1992* (New Delhi: Oxford University Press, 1995).

which she had explored aspects of the history of the Andamans penal colony.[86] Selma's grandfather N. K. Paterson was the last British Chief Commissioner of the Islands. As we saw in Chapter 3, he had been evacuated shortly before the Japanese occupation of the Second World War, but had returned to Port Blair to oversee reconstruction work after the Japanese surrender. Selma and her mother – who lived in the Andamans as a young child – have in different ways been trying to make sense of their family connection to the penal colony. They are especially perplexed by their grandfather's role in the violent repression of Indian nationalism, and *kala pani* in many ways represented Selma's journey into her family's past. During my time in the Islands, at the start of 2011, local historian, former speech writer to the governor and head of J. N. R. Mahavidyalaya (College) Port Blair, Dr Francis Xavier Neelam, took me to Mr Lobo's residence in the Aberdeen Bazar: a recently built concrete block constructed after a fire destroyed the family home in 1996. With his wife, Mr Lobo greeted me with great hospitality and warmth. They produced Fanta and biscuits, and we sat, chatted and laughed. Three floors up, the flat was bright and airy, and a welcome breeze offered respite from the humidity of the bazar below. A clock ticked on the wall, beating time to a European-style painted landscape, while a fan whirred softly in the background. Theirs was a good-looking family, evidently comfortably off, and full of opinion and good humour. It was obvious that Mr Lobo much lamented that with his age his previously regular evening walks had come to a somewhat abrupt end – and unable to manage the stairs to take some outside air in genial company I could see why.

I was by no means the first researcher to meet Mr Lobo, and our first meeting gave fascinating insights into his family and community history. He was proud of his office in the Local Born Association, he said, telling me that his great-great-great grandmother had come to the Andamans from Burma in the 1870s, and his great-great-great grandfather had come from India as personal staff to the Chief Commissioner. Mr Lobo now sits at the head of a large family. He has been married for fifty years, and is proud that he is a Christian and his wife is a Muslim. The couple have two sons and a daughter, and many grandchildren, one of whom, Lester Lobo, I later met and corresponded with after he joined the merchant navy. Mr Lobo's daughter was at home when we first called, and she told me about her work as an English teacher in a local school. One of Mr Lobo's daughters-in-law came by, too. She was from a Bengali settler family,

---

[86] 'Kala Pani: A Forgotten History', BBC Radio 4, 21 April 2010.

and has taken advantage of a recent boom in backpacker tourism to open a guesthouse in the bazar. Business was brisk, no doubt in large part as word of mouth spread about her generous and playful spirit. Her guests came from all over the world, and she had learned to speak a little of many languages.

Mr Lobo himself cut a handsome figure. He spoke of life under the British Raj and since, reminiscing in the way that reminded me of the elderly in my own family. Like many Anglo-Burmese in the last years of the British Raj, he had forged his career in the forestry department, and had worked with Ranchi labourers from North India, as well as other Indians and Burmese. His face lit up as he described his work with elephants. He had childhood memories of talking to the ticket-of-leave convicts as they worked in the bazar, too, though he was unable to say what the topic of conversation had been. They wore badges on their upper arms, he said, pointing to the spot on his own shirtsleeve. I asked him if they had wooden tickets round their necks. 'No, no', he said, 'not at that time'. I asked if this young boy had been frightened of them. Emphatically, he replied: 'no'.

It was not long before talk turned to the present. The whole family joined Mr Lobo in lamenting the passing of what they called the 'old' Andamans. They spoke much of recent settlers' land encroachments, but most of all they complained about changes to the traditional way of life. The family was especially proud of its multi-faith make-up, of the non-conversion of either Mr or Mrs Lobo when they married – but was firmly of the opinion that such arrangements would come to an end within a generation. During this and subsequent research trips, I was to discover that laments about changing ways of life are common amongst the locally born. Many of them regret not mainland migration *per se*, but what they perceive as the failure of those migrants to recognize and to respect the cultural distinctiveness of the Islands. It is this, they fear, that will bring to an end what they see as their unique 'castelessness' and religious harmony.

As Mr Lobo spoke of his nostalgia for the old days, I thought of all the atrocities that have marked the lives of Islanders in almost unfathomable ways: the many deaths at the hands of the Japanese. Here, I pick up one such narrative from the notes of Selma Chalabi. Two hundred or so locals were taken by the Japanese out to sea in 1945 and dumped near Havelock Island. Only a handful of men escaped drowning or the sharks, and according to local legend one man who made it to an outlying island had survived by eating the flesh of those who had starved to death. To be sure, the benevolence of the British colonizers against the cruelty of the Japanese

Figure 5.2 Photograph of Mr John Lobo and family. Photograph: Clare Anderson.

occupiers had proved a common refrain during my entire research trip, and had been mentioned by everybody that I interviewed. Perhaps as many as one quarter of Islanders had died during the occupation; the Japanese had engaged in widespread looting, abuse and torture, and imported 'comfort women' to service the 20,000-strong garrison. In this context it should perhaps have surprised me less than it did that the local-born people I met were effusive in their praise of the British, describing the horrors of the occupation against a harmonious life under the Raj. After all, even if it was true that the British had abandoned the Islands to their fate as Japanese ships made their way across the Bay of Bengal, in 1942, this had been forgotten when they had come back to rescue the surviving Islanders from devastation and near-starvation in 1945. In this way, during my interviews, local-born people brought together the penal colony and the Japanese occupation as interrelated and significant markers of the past. This finding in part coincides with Ann Laura Stoler and Karen Strassler's anthropological 'memory work' in Java, which was also occupied by the Japanese during the Second World War. Stoler and Strassler heard repeatedly that the Dutch were 'good' and that the Japanese were 'bad'. But, they also found that in modern Indonesia, colonialism was not 'a discrete domain of experience of telling', for empire and occupation were often 'mnemonically fused to such an extent that they cannot be accessed independently'.[87] In this respect, the Andamans are quite different, for the penal colony and its legacies are entirely separated from the Japanese occupation, and are central to historical memory and representation.

During this and subsequent meetings, I showed the Lobo family what I first described as 'some old photographs'. They were enthusiastic, for there had been no commercial photography in the Andamans until well after the Second World War, and so even without the destruction of family papers over the years, photographs were rare. As we will see in my chapter on visual representations of the penal colony (Chapter 8), the pictures in my collection capture and represent visually what we might loosely call landscape and landscaping, and convicts and the penal colony. I began by showing the family some late-nineteenth century images of Port Blair and its surrounds, digitally stored on my laptop from many archive collections, and there were whoops of joy as they began to point out places, buildings and vistas – mapping space and place in the Islands as they discussed days gone by and located landscapes of material and social change. Though the photographs were old, their detailed local knowledge was incredible, and it added volumes to my captions and catalogues.

On this first meeting, I asked the Lobos if they would like to see another album that had belonged to Chief Commissioner M. L. Ferrar during his Andaman tenure (1923–31). Ferrar was and is still known as 'the father of the local born' and his album accompanies an important collection of papers in the South Asia collections of the University of Cambridge. Both are greatly concerned with ex-convicts and their descendants. The album includes an image of the Local Born Association clubhouse – burned to the ground in the Aberdeen Bazar fire in 1996 along with the Lobo family home – photographs of prominent members of the community, and pictures of Girl Guides, Wolf Cubs and Boy Scouts – drumming, playing the triangle, learning morse code and even learning a Jarawa (tribal) dance. If the family had been delighted with old pictures of Port Blair, it was thrilled with this set of photographs.

Mr Lobo lost no time in identifying the adults in the pictures, mapping genealogies of descent as he described the fate of their children and

[87] Ann Laura Stoler and Karen Strassler, 'Castings for the Colonial: Memory Work in "New Order" Java', *Comparative Studies in Society and History* 42, 1 (2000), 4–48, 11.

Figure 5.3 'Local Born Association', Ferrar Collection. Courtesy Centre of South Asian Studies, University of Cambridge.

grandchildren: where they lived and worked, their health, departure from and return to the Andamans, and other concerns. The photographs stimulated further discussion of the depth and pace of change in the Islands. Mr Lobo's Bengali daughter-in-law, whose parents had arrived in the Islands many years after the picture was taken, and newly married into the Lobo family, seized immediately on the image of one man, laying claim to him as her grandfather on the basis of a strong family resemblance. In this way, as I interpret it, she sought to use the picture as evidence of her *affective belonging*, and she asked repeatedly that I send copies for her to frame and hang at home. That evening, as I sat on the hotel veranda, I wrote my field notes for the day: 'Showed old photos of places that they remembered very well. The family became v. v. animated when showing photos of Local Born Association. Recognising people, and mapping connections ... They enjoyed it v. v. much. It was lovely to watch ... an elderly man looking at old times, while living in a fast moving world.'[88]

As the months turned into years, I have thought much about this encounter – of people, words and photographs. It is clear that the images 'set the context' for our discussion of both social change and the contemporary politics of association and engagement, as well as the Lobo family's projections about the future. Though we talked together many times over the following year-and-a-half I am certain that they lubricated our discussion at our first encounter, and led to further invitations to meet. In this, I was related to the family not just in the present moment, but through our ongoing relationship to the images. We read and placed them together, to our mutual pleasure and with reciprocity.[89] As sociologists D. Byrne and A. Doyle have argued in their analysis of visual research methods: 'images seemed to enable words. It would be false to pose a dichotomy between images and words – between the visual and the logocentric. The one enabled the other.'[90] And yet, that first evening in Aberdeen Bazar was about more than methodological innovation in the use of photo elicitation in working together of words and pictures in researching the relationship between history and contemporary society. It was to do with that, to be sure, as the photographs stimulated talk of days gone by as well as present economic, social and political concerns. But it also captured some of the post-colonial ambivalences that characterize the meshing together of historical, anthropological and sociological fields. As I thought of Mr Lobo and his family's sighs of nostalgia and lamentation of social change, it opened out to view not a new kind of history *of*, but the complexities of history *in* the Islands, and what it means to be mainlander, Islander and local born at the start of the twenty-first century.

There are many other well-known local-born residents in Port Blair, and here I will describe my meetings with two of them: Dr Rashida Iqbal and Mr Ahmad Mujtaba, who is affectionately known locally as Mustafa Sir. Dr Iqbal is the curator of the Cellular Jail Museum, the huge memorial to the central place of the Andamans in the sacrifices of the Indian martyrs in the great nationalist struggle against the British Raj. The brutalities of their incarceration in the Cellular Jail are well known, and for this reason, in the popular Indian imagination the Andamans are

---

[88] Clare Anderson's research diary, December 2011.

[89] I thank Emma Battell Lowman for this important insight.

[90] David Byrne and Aidan Doyle, 'The Visual and the Verbal: The Interaction of Images and Discussion in Exploring Cultural Change', in Caroline Knowles and Paul Sweetman (eds.), *Picturing The Social Landscape: Visual Methods and the Sociological Imagination* (London: Routledge, 2004), 169, 174.

closely connected with 'freedom fighting'. Dr Iqbal's position is an enormously important symbolic one in the Islands, for she receives a near-constant stream of official visitors from the mainland, including the families of freedom fighters (Ex-Andaman Political Prisoners Fraternity Association). Presidents and prime ministers also visit to pay their respects. Dr Iqbal started her career as a teacher in the mid 1980s, moving to the Jail in 1996, and rising to the position of curator within a decade. She recently completed a PhD at Hyderabad's Osmania University that reflects her professional position in the grand narrative of Andaman history: 'Role of the Cellular Jail in the Indian Freedom Struggle'. On our first meeting, we drank sweet milk tea and I made arrangements to take advantage of the Museum's (excellent) historical collections. Dr Iqbal pressed a folded sheet of paper into my hand. 'Read it later', she said. 'Not now'. She had already mentioned that until she started work in the jail, she had no interest in her family history, though her father and eldest brother had sometimes spoken of it at home.

I was intrigued, and as soon as I got back to my hotel I made more tea, extracted the paper from my bag, and settled down to look at what turned out to be a photocopy of a newspaper article written by Dr Iqbal, titled 'Back to the Roots'. It had been published in the Islands' newspaper, *Light of Andaman*, a few years before. The article added further details to Dr Iqbal's account of her family history, as Selma Chalabi had recorded for the BBC. Her Peshwari father Ainullah Khan had been transported to the Andamans for a revenge murder, or 'honour crime', characteristic, she wrote, of Pathan 'short temper'. Her maternal grandfather had been a convict from Kerala. The newspaper article ended with the words: 'Like many others, I too have this proud identity – daughter of a convict'. Her sentiments in this respect were echoed in her interview with Selma, when she had reiterated that she was part of a local-born *community*, 'people like me who have convict parents ... They consider themselves that they are the actual people of the islands. Their forefathers have contributed a lot for the development of the islands.' Echoing the Lobo family pride at their mixed marriage, she also claimed the Andamans as a new kind of society that developed without caste or religion. 'It gives a message to the whole world of unity and diversity', she said.[91] In this we see claims to a collective identity for the descendants of convicts living in the Islands today.

---

[91] Rashida Iqbal, 'Back To My Roots', *Light of Andaman*, n.d.; transcript of interview between Selma Chalabi and Rashida Iqbal, n.d. I thank Selma Chalabi for sharing her radio transcripts with me.

Like Mr Lobo, Dr Iqbal is part of an educated and accomplished social element of the local-born community that dates back to the early years of the twentieth century. I called in at the Museum again the following day, and Dr Iqbal started to speak more freely about her genealogy. 'My father was a murderer', she told me, 'I have no hesitation saying this.' On the surface, this seems to sit uneasily against mainland Indian views of the Andamans as a space of anti-colonial struggle, rather than a penal colony as such, as discussed in my and Vishvajit Pandya's chapters in Part I of this book. And yet the mainland agenda has offered much to the local born. Indeed, in an early speech on convict origins, in 1932, the president of the Local Born Association Khan Sahib (Dr Nawab Ali) said that the majority of convicts were not from the criminal classes, but were from well-to-do families, including the *zamindari*:

Misfortune, temporary insanity, and agitation, combined with misunderstandings, were the chief causes of the misfortune of our ancestors, so that they suffered throughout the rest of their lives.[92]

In my interviewing work, I have found four ways in which local-born people make sense of their convict origins. Some are unable to lay claim to particular or specific genealogies (in the sense of western-style 'family history'), but speak of their descent from brave heroes and patriots of 1857. This is contradicted by the archives, which reveal that the majority of the first transportation convicts were sentenced for crimes committed during the Revolt, rather than for 'political' offences *per se*. Other local born are able to name their ancestors, and claim that what were often rather ordinary criminal offences were in fact acts of rebellion against the British. In this way, they draw lines of association between their forebears and the famous, mainland 'freedom fighters' who were temporarily incarcerated in the Islands. Like Dr Iqbal, a third group frame transportation offences as 'honour' crimes, viewing murder, infanticide and similar acts of violence (in one case, even witchcraft) as culturally justifiable within the particularities of their originating communities. Fourthly, in only one case did the head of a local-born family tell me that he was descended from what he called (in English) 'ordinary criminals'. I speculate that many other Islanders hold this view, at least privately, but it is not something that they wish to share with outsiders. The politics of what in the Australian context might be called the 'convict stain' are, in the Andamans, quite complex.

---

[92] Speech by Khan Sahib on the occasion of the opening ceremony of the new club house of the Local Born Association, 3 December 1932, Ferrar Papers, CSAS.

Mr Mujtaba falls into the second of these categories – a man who can trace his specific family descent. He told me that he is descended from a convict who was a high-caste scholar, Pandit Ayodiya Rai Sharma. He had been transported from Shahjahanpur to Port Blair in 1871 'as a rebel of [the] British Empire'. He was freed in 1891, when he converted to Islam and took the name Nazir Mohamed. Nazir Mohamed married twice; after his first wife Fata-bibi died, he married a woman from Malabar, Chan-bibi. They had six sons; Mr Mujtaba was born of the youngest, on the eve of the Second World War. He told me that he grew up listening to stories of the penal colony and the occupation. During the war, the Japanese imprisoned and tortured his mother and father in the Cellular Jail, but they survived and his father worked later as an interpreter during the ensuing war trials in Singapore. As a young man, Mr Mujtaba qualified in Geography and worked as a teacher and lecturer, rising to headmaster, principal and education officer and inspector.[93] Now retired, he and his family are scattered across Port Blair, and like Dr Iqbal and many other convict descendants, the majority of his relatives are employed in government service. One brother, who I met later on, runs the entire electricity department.

In the years after his transportation, Mr Mujtaba told me, his grandfather kept in touch with his relatives in Shahjahanpur, and though their written correspondence has not survived, the connection between the families endured for more than eighty years. Some ten years after Indian Independence, in 1956 or 1957 when Mr Mujtaba was a young man, his father returned to the family's hometown with Mr Mujtaba's sister. Mr Mujtaba remembers descriptions of the trip very clearly, for the visitors reported on their return that the pandit had served their food on separate plates, and father and daughter had realized that they had been outcaste. The offence was enormous – the snub irreparable – and subsequently the family cut off all contact with the mainland. Mr Mujtaba himself drew a sharp line of distinction with the mainland, too, when he told me that Islanders never spoke of 'freedom fighters' for the ordinary convicts, but used the Hindi word *khaidi* (prisoners). 'That was a mainland thing', he added.

Like most of the local-born people that I met, Mr Mujtaba remembered the British with enormous affection. He and others were the descendants of convicts, three, four or five times generations. They had not been convicts in the penal colony, and suffered the degradation and hard graft of the chain gangs, but they had experienced the horrors of the

[93] Ahmad Mujtaba, *The Silent Past of Andamans: Few Freedom Fighters of 1857*, pamphlet, 2004.

Japanese occupation as well as the joy of British reoccupation. A frequent refrain was 'fairness'. Like Mr Lobo and another local-born man, called Mr Ram Sing, Mr Mujtaba spoke of British religious tolerance. Earnestly, he told me: 'even their places of worship were painted together, Muslims, Hindus and Sikhs'. It is difficult not to interpret these claims within the context of present-day contests around who deserves OBC status, as well as ideas about the desirability of equality of access to political, social and economic life.

The one exception was Mr Hari Kishen, and I close this section with an account of our first meeting in December 2011. I had learned about Mr Kishen from Philipp Zehmisch, a German graduate student in anthropology who was at the same time carrying out fieldwork on aspects of history, society and social transformation in the Andamans. He told me that Mr Kishen had worked as a Japanese interpreter during the Second World War. I was especially keen to meet him because at the time I was grappling with the meaning of 'freedom fighting' in the Islands. Previous to my work in the Andaman and Nicobar Archives, I had taken for granted the mainland definition of 'freedom fighting', that it referred to the anti-colonial nationalists who were transported to the Cellular Jail for 'terrorist' activities after its completion in 1906. But as I worked through voluminous sets of Islander petitions for government pensions, dating from the 1950s and 1960s, I came to realize that in the Andaman Islands Islanders perceived 'freedom fighting' as support for Subhas Chandra Bose and the Indian National Army (INA), or *Azad Hind* (Free India), which set up a provisional government in the Andamans during the Japanese occupation. The government of India did not agree, and drew a clear line of distinction between them, as I elaborated in Chapter 3. I wanted to find out what Mr Kishen thought about this and other wartime issues.

And so one Sunday morning in December 2011, I jumped in a rickshaw and gave the driver instructions to head for a small parade of shops on one of the roads out of Port Blair, where Philipp told me Mr Kishen lived.

Philipp had told me that Mr Kishen was proud of the work that he had done for the Japanese and for the Indian nationalist cause. I eased my way into what I thought would be a difficult conversation about the British regime in the Andamans, initially by steering talk in other directions. I told him that I had spent a year living in Japan, in a small *inaka* (middle-of-nowhere) town on the Noto-hanto peninsula of Ishikawa prefecture. Much to our mutual amusement, we spoke a little Japanese together. After these and other pleasantries, I became a little more serious, and said that I was sorry about all the horrors of the penal colony, which was a source of great shame for many people in Britain. 'I worked as a Japanese interpreter', he quickly replied.

After a little prompting, Mr Kishen told me all about his work for the Japanese. He had been little more than a child at the time of his recruitment for interpreting service. The Japanese occupiers, it seems, had picked out some bright-looking boys and sent them to a boarding school at Bamboo Flat where they were only allowed to speak in Japanese. Under headmaster Saito-sensei, discipline was strict, though Mr Kishen said that the boys were not mistreated. He told me little about his actual work, excepting his graphic description of the Japanese execution of Mr Bird, which he had witnessed, and which he stood up and re-enacted for my benefit. I have already discussed in some detail the issue of 'freedom fighting' and Islanders' struggles for recognition as 'freedom fighters' in Chapter 3. I close this one with the argument that an appreciation of local-born histories *of and in* the Islands are equally important for understanding the formation and contemporary articulation of the postcolonial relationship between the Islands and the mainland.[94]

Conclusion: the afterlife of empire and the essence of India

Journalist Suresh Vaidya, who travelled to the Andamans in the late 1950s, was told: 'we do not know who is an old convict and who is not. You will have to find out for yourself'. It was bad form to ask convicts why they were transported, with crime considered old history.[95] Vaidya wrote that he had been astonished at the openness with which locally born people revealed the circumstances of their birth. He found this openness 'touching'.[96] Vaidya's lengthiest meeting was with Dadoo Lal, an ex-convict who had been released in 1919 for saving the assistant commissioner's life, and as a reward had been given a coconut plantation in Panighat, near Bamboo Flat. A high-caste Hindu, Dadoo Lal had sent for his wife from India. He set up as a cultivator, and began selling coconuts in Rangoon. He made a little money during those early years, and had since accumulated forty acres of land, sixty head of cattle and an orchard. He grew bananas, papayas and lemons, and had plans to plant a mango grove. A few years earlier, he told Vaidya, the first President of

---

[94] Benedict Anderson, *Imagined Communities: Reflections on the Origin and Spread of Nationalism*, new edn. (London: Verso, 2006), 9–36.

[95] Suresh Vaidya, *Islands of the Marigold Sun* (London: The Travel Book Club, 1960), 36.

[96] Vaidya, *Islands of the Marigold Sun*, 33.

India, Dr Rajendra Prasad, had toured the Andamans. Dr Prasad had visited his farm, congratulated him and given him a certificate of merit for his labours.[97]

Fifty years later, we see a striking visual elaboration of this erasure of the 'criminal' past, and concentration on the distinctive cultural present, in the closing film of the 2011 Indian Panorama Film Fest, which was held for the first time in Port Blair. The film in question was made by local-born director Naresh Chander Lal, and is called *Gandhi: The Mahatma*. The movie presents a dreamlike account of Gandhi's travels through the Andamans as he watches people from all over India living together, greeting each other in a shared language and carrying out random acts of kindness. For Gandhi, the Andamans are *bharat* (the essence of India), a place where his legacy of non-violence and peaceful coexistence lives on.[98] This is the model of 'mini India' and 'unity in diversity' that the Islands present to their mainland audience today.

The British Empire has left deep post-colonial legacies in the Bay of Bengal. Penal transportation underpinned large-scale population movements and provoked important social transformations, and their effects endure to the present day. But the Islands are far from static or unchanging, and the grooves of colonialism are gradually being worn. Following the great fire of Aberdeen in 1996, the site of the old Local Born Association clubhouse stands empty, and all that is left is a Victorian, copper-roofed bandstand. Though the Local Born Association remains active in the Islands' community and public life, particularly around issues relating to other communities' OBC claims, it might be said that the imaginative erasure of the islands' specifically *criminal* past points to the ultimate success of the colonial project of reformation and rehabilitation through penal labour. The education of convicts and other coerced settlers to supposedly useful citizenship was accomplished so completely that as officers from R. C. Temple to M. L. Ferrar ultimately desired, and as local-born people have recast the meaning of their convict origins, at least in public life, convicts have almost vanished – right in front of our eyes. And yet for those who know where to look, the material legacies of forced labour are everywhere. They can be found in the roads that cling to the shoreline as they cut around the Andaman coast from Corbyn's Cove to Port Blair and beyond; in the pukka (brick-built)

---

[97] Vaidya, *Islands of the Marigold Sun*, 57–63.
[98] Preview available at www.youtube.com/watch?v=3yQKgRRUsfw (accessed 28 June 2012).

structures that dot the town, the villages and the ruins of the British headquarters at Ross Island; in each pickaxe mark heft into the stones of now collapsed jetties; in reclaimed land and cleared jungle; and in neatly constructed bunds, bridges and barracks. Whether their cultural legacies will remain so enduring is another matter.

6   Dwelling in fluid spaces: the Matuas of the Andaman Islands

Madhumita Mazumdar

Introduction

Narratives of belonging and identity constitute some of the richest archives of the social and political history of the Andaman Islands. Clare Anderson's account of the local-born community (Chapter 5) and Vishvajit Pandya's account of Jarawa lives in the forest reserves (Chapter 7) reaffirm the argument that although these narratives lie outside the bounds of the official archive and often remain an elusive source for the historian, there is little doubt about their significance in understanding the complex relationships between settler societies and indigenous people in the Islands. As Alessandro Portelli argues, oral accounts help us understand how individual biographies and historical processes are imperceptibly woven into each other.[1] It is these stories of individuals and communities in the Andaman Islands that offer new ways of engaging history, memory and identity as they play out in the lives of those who were displaced from mainland India under varying historical circumstances. This chapter brings together stories of belonging among the Bengali settlers of the Andaman Islands and tries to understand how bonds of faith, affect and community mediated their memories of displacement from the Indian mainland and framed new ways of experiencing and living in the Islands. It also tries to show how any ready assumptions about ethnic or caste identities in the Andaman Islands are constantly undermined the moment we move away from the archives and engage the field. This chapter that begins with a chance encounter with the religious sect of Matuas takes us deep into the lives of the Bengali settlers of the Andaman Islands and compels us to rethink the 'mainland' frames through which we see them.

---

[1] An argument that runs through his several reflections on oral history including 'History-Telling and Time: An Example from Kentucky', *Oral History Review*, 20, 1 (1992), 51–66.

Every year on the last Wednesday of the Bengali month of Agrahayan, hundreds of Matuas, or members of an anti-caste Hindu sect among Bengali settlers in the Andaman Islands, congregate at one of their largest temples in Pahargaon, Port Blair for a festival.[2] This three-day celebration is organized to mark the inauguration of the temple in the early years of the settlement. Large groups of men and women pitch tents around the temple to participate in daylong communal singing and dancing in praise of their founder Harichand Thakur. Vishvajit Pandya and I who were researching the Bengali settler community in the Andaman Islands at this time, reached the Pahargaon temple on the first day of the festival on the 11 December 2011, we saw a small group of men and women dancing and singing at the small canopied centre of a colourful tarpaulin tent constructed on the temple grounds. The rest of the area still looked a bit empty. We got to know about the Pahargaon Matua Mandir festival from Bengali settlers in the Kadamtalla region of the Middle Andaman Island who we interviewed only a few days before we came back to Port Blair.[3]

After waiting for a few minutes we were greeted by the priest of the temple, Bhabesh Sil, who told us that the festivities had just begun and that a large group of the 'inter-Island Matuas' was yet to arrive. The men and women who had begun the proceedings belonged to Port Blair alone. The ceremonies, he said, would reach their best moment when Matuas from the furthest limits in Middle and North Andaman would gather together and take the *kirtans* to another level.[4] He requested that we return the next day. While we spoke, the dancing and singing acquired more verve and within minutes we saw some of the women among the small group of singers swirling around in circles and swaying in trance-like movements to the frenzied beats of the drums and cymbals that were slowly reaching a crescendo. Some of the dancers moved towards the seated audience, touched their feet and then hugged one another with great passion. The young touched the feet of the old and the old reciprocated by touching the feet of the young – a gesture unusual in the context of conventional Hindu custom. Bhabesh Sil told us that both Harichand Thakur and his son Guruchand defied Hindu caste society to

---

[2] In the Bengali calendar, the month of *Agrahayan* roughly coincides with the time between mid-November to mid-December of the Gregorian calendar. All religious rituals or festivities in Bengal follow this calendar.

[3] The visit to Kadamtalla in the Middle Andamans was part of our research on Bengali settlers who came to the Islands as refugees from East Pakistan in the years between 1949 and 1971.

[4] *Kirtans* are devotional songs largely associated with various *Vaishnava* (devotees of Vishnu or Krishna) sects in Bengal.

Figure 6.1 The Matua Mahotsav, Pahargaon Temple, December 2011.
Photograph: Madhumita Mazumdar.

found a community of believers who believed in a philosophy of egalitar-
ianism and brotherhood.

On the next day, the scene of the temple grounds had changed
dramatically, large groups of men and women with small bundles
huddled in groups filling up the large extent of the tent waiting for their
turn to perform at centre stage. A few local journalists and some government officials stood at the fringes of the tent, guiding and explaining
things to a couple of tourists and onlookers who had come to watch the
proceedings. Among them stood Manmohan Mistry, a gentleman who
worked for the Central Agricultural Research Institute (CARI) in Port
Blair, and who introduced himself as a prominent member of the local
Matua sect and someone second only in importance to the organizer of
the event, Bhabesh Sil. Mr Mistry told us that the festival had grown
much larger than it had been when it was begun almost fourteen
years ago.

Of late there had been a lot of support and interest in the Port Blair
festivals from Matuas from the mainland. The long years of isolation of
the Islands' Matuas had ended and new connections were made with the
mainland. For Mr Mistry, it marked a dramatic shift in the lives of those
Matuas who came to the Islands as refugees from East Pakistan under

the Government of India's rehabilitation programme way back in 1949. Mr Mistry was evidently proud of his community and the ties of solidarity its members enjoyed both within the islands and with members of the sect in West Bengal. He told me how the newly elected Trinamul Congress Party in Bengal was supportive of the Matuas and how the Chief Minister herself had visited the Matua headquarters at Thakurnagar to assure the community of her cooperation.[5] But he added rather ruefully that one would not hear much about the community in discussions of Bengali settlers at large. I was not quite sure what he meant by Bengali settlers at large, because as I came to know, the Matuas themselves constituted about 80 to 85 per cent of the Bengali settlers in the Andaman Islands.

I realized the purport of Mr Mistry's comment, however, when I began research on the Bengali community in the Andaman Islands. I was struck by the fact that books devoted to the study of the history and everyday lives of the Bengali community in the Andaman Islands had little to say about the community of the Matuas. The Bengali settler community, it seemed, represented a homogenous community of settlers who may have come in separate batches and from different areas of Bengal but who shared a common ethnic/religious identity. Swapan Kumar Biswas's meticulously researched book *Colonization and Rehabilitation in the Andaman Islands*, with its specific focus on the Bengali settlers, for instance, mentions the Matuas only once in the course of a description of Bengali festivals. Here, after an enumeration of the Bengali Hindu festivals celebrated in the Andaman Islands, Biswas writes: 'Apart from this Bengali settlers are influenced by various Vaishnava sects, Gobindo, Matua Sangha and Satsangi.'[6]

There is no further elaboration of these sects or their systems of belief and practice. Another author from the Islands, Dr Jyotirmay Raychaudhuri, who wrote a book in Bengali titled, *Andamaner Bangali: Sanskriti Binimay* (translated as *Bengalis of the Andamans: Acculturation in the Andamans*), also discusses the Matuas as an afterthought. In his chapter on Bengali cultural festivals he makes a note of the Matua Utsav of *Baruni* celebrated in the month of March every year in commemoration of the birth of the founder of the sect Harichand Thakur. Raychaudhuri writes:

---

[5] For a report on the Chief Minister of West Bengal Ms Mamata Banerjee's support for the Matua see: Jayanta Gupta, 'Mamata gets Matua Membership', *The Times of India*, 6 December 2009, http://timesofindia.indiatimes.com/city/kolkata/Mamata-gets-Matua-membership/articleshow/5306294.cms (accessed 23 July 2014).

[6] Swapan Kumar Biswas, *Colonization and Rehabilitation in Andaman and Nicobar Islands* (New Delhi: Abhijeet Publications, 2009), 212.

The Matua festival of Baruni is celebrated in the month of Chaitra every year. It is Andamans prime 'folk festival'. It is celebrated by Namasudra communities who came from Khulna, Barishal and Faridpur districts of erstwhile East Pakistan. The founder of the Matua sect and the leader of the Namasudra community is referred to as 'Baruni'. The festivities commemorating his birth are marked by participation of all communities of the Andaman Islands, Hindus as well as Muslims. The celebrations are conducted at various Matua temples all over the Islands: some of the largest celebrations are held in the Matua temple of Pahargaon, Guptipara, and Wandoor in the Port Blair area, in Ramkrishnapur in the Little Andaman Islands, at Billyground Bazaar and Limbudera in the Middle Andaman and in Togapur in the North Andaman Islands. The celebrations draw massive crowds and include events and include days of communal singing and dancing. The Harisingkirtan in fact is at the heart of all Matua festivals.[7]

This is all there is in the entire length of the book on the Bengali settlers. When I asked Dr Raychaudhuri why this was so, he told me that the Matuas do not look upon themselves as being any different from the other Bengali Hindu settlers.[8] They, in fact, constitute the bulk of the community. Although, he added, no caste-based studies had been undertaken on the Islands after 1952, it was well known that the most of the refugees who were sent for resettlement in the Andaman Islands in the aftermath of the Partition were of lower caste origin, mostly Namasudras. He said, however, that caste identities were successfully transcended on the Islands and the phenomenon of acculturation was so widespread as to make it practically impossible to ascertain 'pure' Namasudra identities. Many Namasudras, he added, had taken on upper caste surnames and identified themselves as Bengali caste Hindus rather than as members of any sect. What all this implied was that a discussion on Matuas as a distinctive community among the larger community of Bengali settlers was redundant.

My own conversations with Bhabesh Sil, his mother, Manmohan Mistry and other members of the Matua sect at the Pahargaon temple, however, seemed to indicate that the there was a story about the Matuas in the Islands that needed to be told. This was a large community and evidently proud of its distinctive social identity. It mingled well with the caste Hindu Bengali settlers as well as with other ethnically diverse settler communities on the Islands, but was keen to sustain its own history and identity.[9]

This chapter derives from two phases of fieldwork conducted amongst first- and second-generation Bengali Matua settlers in the Andaman

---

[7] Jyotirmay Roychowdhury, *Andamaner Bangali: Sanskritir Binimay* (Kolkata: Sahitya Prakash, 2004), 152.
[8] Conversation with Dr Jyotirmay Roychowdhury, 12 December 2012.
[9] Conversation with Dr Jyotirmay Roychowdhury, 12 December 2012.

Islands in 2010 and 2011 through 2012. The first phase of research was conducted in the villages of Kadamtalla and Rangat *tehsil* (sub-division of a district) in Middle Andaman in November and December 2010, while the second phase, from November 2011 to January 2012, was conducted among local Matuas of the Port Blair region as well as those who I had interviewed earlier in Middle Andaman. The first phase of research formed part of a larger inquiry into the lives and memories of Bengali refugees who made their way into the Islands in the post-Partition years. It was in the course of this phase of research that I entered the world of the Matua and their lived experience of the Islands. What pushed my line of research to questions about Matua belief and practice in the Islands was the sense that an understanding of the experience of faith and community among Bengali settlers in the Islands seemed to offer new points of entry into studies of social identities in the Andaman Islands, something that more conventional frameworks of 'acculturation' seemed to ignore.[10] My research also pointed to new ways of engaging with the questions of 'refugee identity and experience' in the Andaman Islands, particularly how such identities and experiences differed from those in mainland India or South Asia.

Historian Uditi Sen has recently argued that the 'refugee' predicament in the Islands takes on a whole new meaning in comparison to what is recorded for the 'mainland'.[11] Sen argues that dominant themes in the prevailing historical literature on the Partition in India have centred on the victimhood of refugees and the trauma of lost homes, displacement and eternal longing. It is here that the refugee experience in the Islands offers a different perspective. Based on her research among refugee families in the South, North and Middle Andamans, she argues conclusively that refugee identities were not necessarily built upon loss and victimhood rather on active articulations of agency and selfhood.[12]

Bengali refugees in the Andamans, Sen argues, did not conform to the received wisdom on similar experiences of violence and displacement in the course of the Partition. Her respondents in the Islands had little or no interest in reminiscing about their lost homes in East Pakistan. Familiar themes of refugee memory such as displacement, violence, trauma and nostalgia were conspicuous by their absence while memories of homeland

---

[10] I refer in particular to Biswas, *Colonization and Rehabilitation,* and Roychowdhury, *Andamaner Bangali.*
[11] Uditi Sen, 'Dissident Memories: Exploring Bengali Refugee Narratives in the Andaman Islands', in Pippa Virdee and Panikos Panayi (eds.), *Refugees and the End of Empire: Imperial Collapse and Forced Migration in the Twentieth Century* (Basingstoke: Palgrave, 2011), 219–44.
[12] Sen, 'Dissident Memories', 219.

had lost their emotional charge.[13] What was significant, however, was that most respondents chose to reminisce about rebuilding their lives in the Islands. The memories of displacement had been replaced by more recent memories of 'pioneering agricultural expansion' in the Andamans leading them to form new collective identity – that of settlers or 'agricultural pioneers'. She argues that this replacement of one set of memories by another has to be seen in the context of the arrival of new settlers on the Islands, the competition for jobs and resources and the overall social and cultural marginalization of the Bengali settlers as a consequence.[14] Bengali settlers in the Andaman Islands have refused to remain confined within the stereotype of the hapless refugee and mobilized memories of early life on the settlement more as nostalgia than as trauma to project themselves as 'agricultural pioneers' with a greater sense of entitlement and belonging in the Islands, particularly in the context of threats posed by new migrants as well as earlier entrants to the Islands such as the convict-descended local-born community.[15]

Sen argues that the reminiscences of refugee settlers of the Andamans illustrate the risk of advocating a typical or representative refugee memory or identity. The act of remembering is informed not only by past experiences but also by present location. The reminiscences of the Bengali refugees settled in the Andamans illustrate one such radical reconfiguration of memory and identity.[16]

While there is much in Sen's description and analysis of refugee memory and identity in the Andamans that is valid and significant, my own research among similar groups of men and women, around the same time, brought forth a further set of questions. I agree with Sen that most first-generation Bengali settlers remained indifferent to the memories of Partition, violence, trauma and subsequent displacement; but what struck me was why unlike refugees elsewhere they chose not talk about the 'homes' or 'lands' they had left behind. Had their self-consciousness as agricultural pioneers, as Sen suggests, obliterated their earlier memories of displacement? Was this refusal to address the experience of lost homes a deliberate act of choosing to forget an oppressive past in order to forge new ties of belonging to the Islands? Or was it reflective of the ways in which Bengali refugees/settlers chose to mobilize different kinds of memories to build threatened community solidarities on the Islands? Could we identify the 'dissident' refugee voice in the Andaman Islands as a typically ethnic Bengali voice or were these voices reflective of more diverse social/cultural formations among the post-Partition settlers? And

---

[13] Sen, 'Dissident Memories', 221.   [14] Sen, 'Dissident Memories', 233–8.
[15] Sen, 'Dissident Memories', 238.   [16] Sen, 'Dissident Memories', 239–40.

finally, to what extent did Matua belief and practice structure the discourse of home, community and belonging on the Islands? How did community mobilize faith and affect to define their social identities and the terms of their relationship to the Islands?

What follows in this chapter is an exploration of some of these questions. Section 1 charts the historical context of Bengali refugee settlement in the Andaman Islands, particularly in the South and Middle Andaman region. Section 2 focuses on settler reminiscences to draw attention to the purchase of community life and the moral order of the Matua in the early days of the settlement. Finally, Section 3 explores Matua notions of home and community in the contemporary experience of living/dwelling in the Islands.

The Bengali 'settler' on the Islands

To scholars of the Islands' post-colonial history, the proposal for the colonization and development of the Andaman Islands drawn up in 1949 was in many ways a hurried job done in the context of imminent crisis. The sudden and massive influx of Bengali Hindu refugees into the relief camps of West Bengal, Assam and Tripura in the context of Noakhali-Tipperah riots of 1946, and the subsequent institution of the Radcliffe Award, compelled local governments to appeal to the Ministry of Relief and Rehabilitation to look for alternative locations for their rehabilitation.[17]

In October 1948 an exploratory party headed by the Minister in Charge of Refugee Rehabilitation visited the Andamans, with a view to examine the possibilities of resettling a few hundred displaced families from East Bengal in the Islands.[18] After a careful survey the party was unanimous in their opinion that the Islands were admirably suitable for colonization by displaced persons. Part of this favourable appraisal for colonization by East Bengali refugees was based on the fact that most of these displaced families were 'agriculturalists'. Later studies, however, suggest that the refugee resettlement scheme in places in the Andaman Islands were based on 'discriminatory caste lines'. It was observed that upper caste Hindu refugees were settled mostly in and around Calcutta, while Namasudra refugees were settled in the 'uninhabitable

---

[17] For a detailed survey of all Government of India reports exploring the possibilities of resettling Partition refugees in the Andaman Islands see Kiran Dhingra, *The Andaman and Nicobar Islands in the Twentieth Century; A Gazetteer* (New Delhi: Oxford University Press, 2005), 69–94.

[18] Dhingra, *The Andaman and Nicobar Islands*, 75.

camps in districts of 24 Parganas, Nadia, Burdwan, Midnapur or
Coochbehar – or deported to the inhospitable areas of Dandakaranya
or Andaman Islands'.[19]

The formal statement on the colonization of the Andamans, however,
was prepared by H. Shivdasani, of the department of Home Affairs,
Government of India, who along with his three-member team proposed
a plan based on 'objective' assessments of the availability of land in the
Islands and the viability of settling a new class of agriculturalists there.[20]
On the specific issue of the incentives needed for such a rehabilitation
project, the Shivdasani Report as it came to be known endorsed the view
of the local administration that the refugees who were to be brought in to
colonize the Andamans were to be given special concessions. Apart from
free passage from Calcutta, each head of family would be given ten acres
of land free of cost with remission of revenue for the first two years.
Additional incentives would be the grant of plough cattle, milch cattle,
seed paddy, agricultural implements and manure free of cost. Non-
agricultural families would be given half an acre of land for construction
of houses and financial assistance admissible to agriculturalists for a
period of three months.

Studies of the refugee rehabilitation and colonization scheme of these
years tend to suggest that the terms of resettlement and rehabilitation
changed constantly as a result of differing points of view from the Islands
and the mainland:[21] the number of families to be sent; kind of families
to be sent (agriculturalists or artisans); areas to be settled; and, more
importantly, the infrastructural and financial requirements of the
scheme. There were also fears about the reactions of the local-born
community to the new settlement schemes. As has been observed, the
community was struggling to pull their shattered economy together. It
felt that the Government of India and the local administration were too
busy with the resettlement of Bengali refugees in the Andamans to
consider the rights of old settlers or to provide them with adequate
economic means to re-establish their lives following the Japanese occupation of the Second World War.[22]

There were fears that a sudden, hasty dispatch of refugees from camps
in West Bengal might result in distress not only for these families but for
the Islands' administration at large. This was a view that was constantly

[19] Praskanva Sinharay, 'Caste, Migration, Identity', *Seminar*, 645 (May 2013), 56–7.
[20] For a detailed discussion of the Shivdasani Report, see Chapters 2 and 9.
[21] See Biswas, *Colonization and Rehabilitation*, for a broad overview of reports and correspondence on resettlement and rehabilitation, 36–94.
[22] For more details, see Dhingra, *The Andaman and Nicobar Islands*, 92.

communicated from the office of the Chief Commissioner of the Andaman and Nicobar Islands to that of the Home Ministry and the Department of Rehabilitation. Notwithstanding these initial anxieties about the refugee resettlement programme, the first two batches of Bengali refugees comprising 198 families reached Port Blair on 13 and 31 March 1949, respectively. They were first accommodated in temporary barracks at Manpur, Colinpur, Homfray Gunj, Manglutan and Nayashahar in the South Andaman district. Between 1949 and 1952, a total of 420 families were sent to the Andaman Islands. During the same period, about seventy families were repatriated to the mainland.[23]

Swapan Kumar Biswas argues that there were many reasons for the growing demands for repatriation during these years. Many families with young children or with older members could not adjust to the conditions of life in the Islands. There were few or no healthcare facilities and many succumbed to waterborne diseases or malaria. Other problems included the unavailability of immediately cultivable land, the slow arrival of equipment and cattle, and the chronic shortage of rations. There was general uncertainty of lives in the camps and many families could not cope with the pressures of everyday survival and the uncertainty of ever returning to the mainland. Repatriation, however, was allowed only when such families were able to repay their loans before leaving the Islands.[24]

The 350 families belonging to the first batch that stayed back were settled in the villages of Manpur, Colinpur, Tirrur, Chouldari, Mathura, Manglutan, Wandoor and Shoal Bay.[25] All these villages had come up during the late 1920s and 1930s when the colonization and settlement programmes of the Ferrar years were underway. These were mostly in the vicinity of Port Blair and were surrounded by older villages inhabited by local borns, many of whom continued to resent the new settlers in their midst. The new villages were also in close proximity to the forests inhabited by the Jarawas. In fact, conflict between the new Bengali settlers and the Jarawas during these years has also been cited as one of the reasons for the growing demands for repatriation.

The second phase of settlement of Bengali refugees extended from Uttar Kadamtalla to Rangat in the Middle Andamans.[26] The settlement in these areas was expanded solely through new villages established by the Bengali settlers. There were few local-born villages in this area and most

---

[23] Biswas, *Colonization and Rehabilitation*, 76–9.
[24] Biswas, *Colonization and Rehabilitation*, 77.
[25] Biswas, *Colonization and Rehabilitation*, 79.
[26] Biswas, *Colonization and Rehabilitation*, 79.

of the forested areas were inhabited by the Jarawas. The settlement was started in 1953 and the last village was developed in 1959. A total of 850 families were settled in this region over a period of six years. By 1959, twenty-nine villages had been established, pushing the population of this area to 3,453.[27] This number acquires significance in the context of the fact of that unlike the South Andamans, the Middle Andaman region was mostly forested area. The extent of cleared space was extremely limited and forest labour scarce. Most of the refugee families had to work intensely to lay claims upon their ten-acre allotments in this area. The last area to be colonized was North Andaman. Here, Bengali refugee families were settled in fourteen villages and included 350 families.[28] This area, however, was partially inhabited by local borns and old settlers including the Burmese Karens. The North Andaman *tehsil*, it must be noted, was an important area for forestry operations. The Andamanese forests had been systematically exploited since the turn of the century and forestry had received a great push during the interwar years. It was during this phase that batches of 'forest labour' were brought in from the Chhotanagpur area on the mainland and from Burma. The Karens from Burma and the 'Ranchis' from Chhotanagpur inhabited these areas in what were called 'forest villages'. The new Bengali villages were established around the older settlements of Mayabunder, Webi, Lucknow, Pokadera, Basantipur, Latow and Deopur.[29]

Following this initial phase of settlement in the central chain of the Andaman Islands, later Bengali families were settled in the islands of Little Andaman, Neil and Havelock in the years between 1959 and 1976.[30] It is important to remember this periodization and geography of Bengali refugee resettlement in the Andaman Islands as issues of identity, memory and belonging tend to acquire different textures in accordance with the specific experiences in these different regions and in particular through the different relations the Bengali settlers developed with the Island's local-born community, older settlers and indigenous communities. The experiences of Bengali refugees in Neil or Havelock islands, for instance, would be completely different from those settled in the South, Middle or North Andaman islands. Similarly Bengali families settled in the South Andaman islands would have different memories of their early lives in the camps and villages with those settled in uninhabited islands of Neil and Havelock. In other words, Bengali settlement and

[27] Biswas, *Colonization and Rehabilitation*, 79–80.
[28] Biswas, *Colonization and Rehabilitation*, 79–80.
[29] Biswas, *Colonization and Rehabilitation*, 80.
[30] Biswas, *Colonization and Rehabilitation*, 81–4.

life in the Andaman Islands followed different trajectories and were told through different stories.

In 1952, anthropologist Surajit Sinha conducted one of the earliest studies of the condition of Bengali refugees in the Andaman Islands.[31] The Refugee Rehabilitation Department of the Government of West Bengal commissioned Sinha's work and the objective of the study was not only to understand the socioeconomic composition of the Bengali settlers on the Islands, but also to assess further possibilities of Bengali refugee resettlement in the Islands.[32] Sinha concentrated his study mostly on settlers who came into the Islands between 1949 and 1952 and who were settled in the South Andaman region: 392 families in twenty-four settlements.[33] The first major finding of the survey was the origins of these families, more specifically that these refugees came from ten districts of East Pakistan. The largest number came from Barishal (50 per cent) followed by Faridpur, Dhaka, Khulna, Tipperah and Noakhali. Most of these families were offered the opportunity to come to the Andaman Islands in the years between 1948 and 1949.[34] Sinha's study suggested that among the communities that came in from these districts, most of them (almost 66.5 per cent) belonged to the Namasudra caste, while others belonged to various other sub-caste groups including those of Napit, Tanti, Saha, Karmakar, Pal, Halua Das and Gandharba Banik.[35] The upper-caste Brahmins constituted 9.2 per cent of the families, while Kayasthas were among the remaining 10 per cent.[36] Most of the families including the upper-caste Brahmins were agriculturalists but often had no land. They were either sharecroppers or landless labourers. The Namasudra community, in particular, was economically the most backward, and according to the survey was most affected by the communal riots of 1948 to 1949. The massive spate of killings in the villages they came from forced them to give up whatever little that belonged to them and flee their homes to other side of the just-declared borders.

While Sinha's study was focused mostly on the refugee families settled in the South Andaman Islands, his broad findings on the

---

[31] Surajit Sinha (1926–2003): Anthropologist who published widely on tribal politics, state systems, thought and culture, and also pioneered the methods of historical sociology.

[32] Surajit Sinha, 'Resettlement of East Pakistan Refugees in Andaman Islands: Report on Survey of Further Possibilities of Resettlement: January–May 1952' (Alipore: Superintendant of Government Printing, West Bengal Government Press, 1953), A&N Archives.

[33] For a detailed list, see Sinha, 'Resettlement of East Pakistan Refugees', 6.

[34] See table 'Cast distribution in different refugee settlements', in Sinha, 'Resettlement of East Pakistan Refugees', 6.

[35] Sinha, 'Resettlement of East Pakistan Refugees', 6.

[36] Sinha, 'Resettlement of East Pakistan Refugees', 6.

socioeconomic backgrounds of those who came to the Islands in general, and of the caste composition of the Bengali refugee community as a whole, remains largely the same for settlers in the Middle and North Andaman Islands. Although specific studies of caste have not been undertaken since, nor have any caste censuses been taken in the Islands since Independence, the fact of the dominance of the Namasudra caste among Bengali settlers remains largely undisputed.[37] While this fact has little relevance in understanding caste dynamics or social stratification, since the terms of such stratification seldom hold in the Islands, the large presence of the Namasudras indicates the possibilities of studying a different social dynamic centred around the complex configurations of settler identity and 'belonging' in the Islands. In Chapter 5, Clare Anderson charted the intricate trajectories of local-born history and identity on the Islands, pointing to the numerous ways in which the community has sought to carve out a distinctive political and cultural niche. Studies of the Bengali settlers too have pointed to the growing political presence of the community and the ways it has registered its dominance in the Islands' social formation. But what often remains untold is the early history of the Bengali settlers on the Islands, of those refugee families who struggled to make their lives in an alien terrain and for whom the hope of possessing a piece of land remained the only incentive to stay on.

Meeting the Matuas

I visited the Bengali settler villages of Uttara and Phooltala in the Kadamtalla *tehsil* and later Billyground in Rangat *tehsil* in the Middle Andaman region in December 2011.[38] Most of my interviews were conducted in Uttara and Phooltala where the settlers I spoke to brought in their friends from Billyground. These were seldom interviews with a single individual, but rather conversations that spilled over a week at

---

[37] A study conducted by the Union Ministry of Social Justice in response to demands made by the Bengali settlers to be included in the OBC category revealed that most of the post-1949 category of Bengali settlers, who came to the Islands under various government resettlement schemes during the years 1949 to 1973, belonged to lower castes. Based on findings about their socioeconomic status, levels of literacy and other markers of social backwardness, they were notified as OBC on 26 December 2011. They now form a specific category along with local borns, Karens, Moplahs and Bhatus and receive special entitlements in the form of reservation in government jobs and institutions of higher education. See Soma Basu, 'OBC Status for Bengali Settlers in A&N' (blog), http://deshlai.wordpress.com/2011/12/26/obc-status-for-bengali-settlers-in-an/ (accessed 25 June 2014).

[38] Field visit, 6–14 December 2010.

various people's houses and at the Kadamtalla Guest House where
we stayed. Vishvajit Pandya, who was keen to understand the growing
complexities of Jarawa–settler relations in this area, accompanied me.
The Kadamtalla region was significant in this context because it was from
here that the story of the first friendly 'contact' between Jarawas and
settlers had begun in 1997–8.[39] A decade later relations between the
Bengali settlers living on the edges of the Jarawa Tribal Reserve had taken
a new and disturbing turn. Pandya focused his interests around this
issue, while I searched for some of the older residents of the area to get
to know more of their early history of arrival and settlement in the region.
The local *pradhan* of Kadamtalla, known affectionately as Pagol Mondal
(the 'mad' Mondol), arranged for us to meet some of the oldest living
residents of the village of Phooltala.[40] These were first-generation
Bengali refugee settlers. We travelled with him deep into the village along
narrow *als* or pathways along large swathes of paddy fields into a decrepit
hovel. In the middle of the courtyard, four elderly men sat on a *charpoy*
(daybed) waiting for us. As we entered the courtyard, I asked Mr Mondal
if this family had been given the promised ten acres of land on his arrival
in the Islands. Pagol Mondal pointed his fingers to paddy fields in front
of the house and the betel groves at the rear end of the courtyard to tell
me that that owner of the property was indeed the oldest man sitting on
the *charpoy*, and introduced him as Mr Keshub Rai. It seemed a bit odd
to me that despite the apparent wealth in land the household looked so
stark. I was later to find out that the present circumstances of Mr Rai
were a bit uncertain because he had lost his son and there were not too
many hands to help out in the fields. This was the cause of their steadily
declining income. Yet, he would later add, 'life never moved in predict-
able ways, there were good times as there were bad. And all that one
could do in the circumstances was to remember the blessings of the
Lord'.[41]

We sat around the *charpoy* on red plastic chairs, while Keshub Rai's
widowed daughter-in-law brought us tea in small earthen cups. The rest
of the men included Satis Pramanik, Sukanto Pramanik, Kalinath
Mondol, Ananta Das, Gurupada Barui and Harinath Mondol.[42] All
of them were in their late seventies and eighties and seemed eager to

---

[39] For a critical comment on the changing relations between Jarawas and settlers in this
region see Vishvajit Pandya, *In the Forest: Visual and Material Worlds of Andamanese
History, 1858–2006* (Lanham, MD: University Press of America, 2009), 268–96.
[40] *Pradhan* refers to the elected village head.
[41] Conversation with Keshub Rai, 6 December 2010.
[42] Gurupada Barui and Harinath Mondol belonged to the neighbouring village of Uttara.
They were all friends who came to the Andaman Islands between 1953–5.

reminisce about their past. It was evident that most of them chose to begin their stories in the Andaman Islands from the moment of their arrival in the islands. The earlier part of the story, that is, the time spent in refugee camps in Bengal, was recounted somewhat hurriedly. In all of this, however, one important fact stood out. When I asked them why they agreed to come to these Islands once known as the dreaded *kala pani* (black waters) most of them said that there were several government officers who came to them and told them that the old jail had been destroyed and the convicts freed. The Islands were now a free place and the new Government of India wanted young men and women to make their homes there. Keshub Rai had faint memories of Raha Babu, who showed them a film on the Andaman Islands one evening in the camp. It showed cleared lands and small stretches of paddy fields surrounded by miles and miles of coconut groves. 'I was reminded of my home in Barishal', he said. Others agreed that the settlement officers who visited their camps held out promises of a new life where they would be owners of land.[43]

Following this trail of the narrative of their arrival in the Islands, I was soon led into more darker stories of their early life in the barracks, that were often built on the outskirts of forests inhabited by the Jarawas. Until the time they arrived in the Andamans, many of them knew little about the Jarawas or the other indigenous communities of the Islands. What they did hear was that there were some *junglees* who had inhabited the islands during the period of British rule but that most of them had died. The forests of the Andaman Islands, they were told, were free of wild animals or any other sources of danger. When they arrived on the Islands however, they encountered a different reality. It was at this point that all the elderly men began to reminisce their lives of struggle, steeped in hardships, struggle and fear.

It was Satis Pramanik, I remember, who pushed the conversation onto a different track. Satis Babu came to the Islands in 1954 as a refugee from the Khulna district of East Pakistan.[44] Satis Babu's claim to distinction in the village of Kadamtalla, apart from his being one of the oldest and most respected members of the Bengali community, was his feat of single-handedly warding off a Jarawa attack in his village in 1971. In the course of narrating this story to me, Satisbabu invoked the name of Guruchand, almost by accident, for it did not feature in his earlier reminiscences. Yet, when the name of Guruchand was invoked, it was with a sense of compelling conviction and reverence. The Jarawa incident, it seemed, acquired new meaning in the context of his *Guru* and his *samaj*. It urged

---

[43] For a similar reference to Sadhan Raha see Sen, *Dissident Memories*, 227.
[44] Satis Pramanik is now a resident of Uttara village.

me to ask him more about the 'community' or *samaj* he referred to and the presence of Guruchand in their lives in the Andaman Islands.[45]

Mr Pramanik asserted that the decision to come to the Andamans was theirs alone and was not forced on them by rehabilitation authorities. Refugee families like his were taken in batches to the Islands from various camps all over northern, central and eastern India, and their selection as suitable candidates for the Andaman scheme was determined by their own abilities to cultivate land and by the availability of cleared land for cultivation.[46] The first area to be colonized was predictably the South Andaman region because of the ready availability of cleared tracts and because of its proximity to the administrative headquarters in Port Blair. Soon Middle Andamans, according to early survey reports, became one of the most important centres of the colonization scheme.

The settlement project in Middle Andaman, initiated in 1952–3, came to be known as the Rangat Valley scheme. One early account of the Middle Andaman colonization, by P. K. Sen, suggests that the colonization of the Rangat Valley proved to be one of the more successful projects in the Islands.[47] The success of adaptation in the Middle Andaman was attributed to the following: the selection of people was good and they were all agriculturalists; the people who settled in the Middle Andaman were thoroughly informed about their land by both the government and the early settlers; and finally there was no intrusion of people from other communities. This helped them focus all their energies on re-building their own hearths and homes.[48]

In drawing a comparison with other settlements in the South Andamans, this early account went on to observe that the settlers in the Middle Andaman were found to develop into a 'peaceful gregarious unit with little trouble from inside and [sic] well as outside'.[49] Under such circumstances the development of the land as well as the adaptation of the people there depended on their 'human quality'. The settlers of the Middle Andaman, it was suggested, were morally well prepared to cope with the challenges of adapting to a new environment.

When I put forth this observation to my respondents, they looked pleased. Mr Pramanik, however, found it to be a most inadequate description of their early lives in the Islands or a plausible explanation

---

[45] Conversation with Satis Pramanik, 7 December 2010.
[46] Conversation with Satis Pramanik, 7 December 2010.
[47] Probhat Kumar Sen, *Land and People of the Andamans* (Calcutta: The Post-Graduate Book Mart, 1958).
[48] Sen, *Land and People of the Andamans*, 38.
[49] Sen, *Land and People of the Andamans*, 38.

for their eventual adaptation to it. The Middle Andaman, he argued, may have had a favourable geographical location in terms of fresh water supply and proximity to forest headquarters, but vast tracts were still covered with dense jungle when their families were brought in.[50] Pramanik's complaints about the challenges presented by the topography of the region finds resonance in P. K. Sen's description of the problems faced by the settlers in the Middle Andaman region. He writes:

The topographical problems arise out of the nature of the soil, forest clearance and other factors. The undulating nature of the land in the Andamans exposed to soil erosion as the lands for settlement have been cleared and heavy rainfall is accelerating the problem. The refugees are not accustomed to terrace cultivation and the undertaking of such a type of cultivation cannot be practiced without training. The lands after forest clearance are studded all over by stumps of the trees ... The thorough cultivation of the land is hampered due to this. Bunds should be built all over the agricultural plot to check the creep of the soil.[51]

Life in Middle Andaman, in short, was perpetually arduous and insecure. There were other problems too. Satis Pramanik and his friends were a little hesitant to talk about these at first. One elderly respondent (later identified as Sukanto Pramanik) who came with his wife and extended family suddenly spoke up. He said there had been persistent fear of attacks on their women, their wives and daughters.[52] There were several cases of abduction and sexual assaults by settlers who came in as bachelors or who had left their families in the mainland refugee camps. The predatory logic used by the offenders to justify these attacks on women was *bal jar, bou tar* or the assertion that the 'whoever had the strength to take a wife by force could do so'.[53] The physical hardship of clearing forests, tilling the land, warding off stray animals and finally securing the life and liberty of women in the settlement often proved to be deeply overwhelming. Sustaining a moral order within the settlement in these circumstances was a particularly compelling problem. Gurupada Barui chose to remind us that it was at these times that the teachings of Guruchand and his son Harichand Thakur were invoked. They came to believe that the only way in which lives and homes could be rebuilt on the islands was through strengthening and extending the bonds of the Matua *samaj* or community.[54]

[50] Conversation with Satis Pramanik, 7 December 2010.
[51] Sen, *Land and People of the Andamans*, 39.
[52] Conversation with Sukanto Pramanik, 8 December 2010.
[53] Conversation with Sukanto Pramanik, 8 December 2010.
[54] Conversation with Gurupada Barui, 8 December 2010.

In his pioneering study of the beginnings of the Matua sect in the late nineteenth century, Sekhar Bandopadhyay wrote that it achieved its cohesion and visibility when it came to be associated with the Namasudra social protest movement started in 1872.[55] The Matua sect had been founded by Harichand Thakur (1811/12–78) who was born to a Vaishnavite peasant family of Namasudras in the Gopalgunj subdivision of Faridpur. Bandopadhyay describes the Namasudras as an 'amphibious' *dalit* (untouchable) group that was emerging as a settled peasant community, colonizing the marshy lands of Southern Faridpur, North-Western Bakhargunj and the adjoining regions of Jessore and Khulna.[56] In analyzing the growing centrality of the Matua sect in the social and political life of the Namasudras, Bandopdhay argues that the sect offered a new locus of Namasudra identity as it came to acquire a certain cohesiveness in the late nineteenth century. This cohesiveness was born out of three conditions: Firstly, through the radical transformation in patterns of livelihood, from boating and fishing to settled agriculture in the wake of the reclamation of the deltaic marshlands of Bengal; secondly, through the fact that caste subordination coincided with class subordination in the sense that most of its members remained share croppers and agricultural labourers rather than rent receivers; and, finally, notwithstanding the limited social mobility acquired by some of its members through trade or money-lending, the Namasudras as a whole remained confined within the lower rungs of the Brahminical ritual hierarchy. The persistence of social discrimination and prejudice spurred them to collective mobilization against the hegemonic ritual order. They felt a genuine need for an effective social organization that helped them in their pursuit of self-respect. It is at this point that Harichand Thakur's new sect offered new promise.[57]

The early Matua community acquired its strength and growing numbers under the leadership of Harichand Thakur's son, Guruchand Thakur. It had an eclectic theological core that derived from a host of social reformist influences in Bengal. Commenting on its specific theological sources, Bandopadhyay notes that though claimed as a new religion, Matua texts were carefully drawn from both orthodox Hinduism as well as various popular religious or *bhakti* traditions. In terms of its core beliefs, the Matuas rejected all Hindu Brahminical

---

[55] Sekhar Bandopadhyay, *Caste, Protest and Identity in Colonial India: The Namasudras of Bengal, 1872–1947* (Richmond: Curzon Press, 1997).

[56] Sekhar Bandopdhyay, *Caste, Culture and Hegemony: Social Dominance in Colonial Bengal* (New Delhi: Sage Publications, 2004), 98.

[57] Sekhar Bandopadhyay, 'Social Mobility in Colonial Bengal: The Namsudras', in Ishita Banerjee-Dube (ed.), *Caste in India* (New Delhi: Oxford University Press, 2008), 182–3.

rituals along with the religious and social hegemony enjoyed by Brahmins. It was meant to be a religion of pure personal devotion with no mediation of the guru. Guruchand's son, Harichand, believed that no rituals except devotion to God and faith in mankind and love for all living creatures were acceptable to the Matuas. His father had made it clear that neither mantras nor initiation rites were needed to chant Harinam or to express devotion to the Supreme Being.[58]

In terms of their social outlook, the Matuas firmly rejected the caste order of Hindu society. 'Matuas were all one, there were no divides', Bandopadhyay wrote.[59] Extending the same logic, the Matuas also said that there could be no differentiation in terms of gender, as women were to participate as equal partners in the congregational singing, or *kirtan*, the only ritual that the sect insisted upon. This remains as true now as it may have been in the early days of the community. My ethnographic research among the Matuas during the festival at the Pahargaon temple in Port Blair confirmed both the significance of the *kirtan* or congregational singing as the heart of the Matua ritual and the equal participation of women in it. Bandopdhayay notes that since the sect was integrally related to the Namasudra movement, collective singing served other social and political purposes too. It was, he argues, 'a ritual to assert political will, boost self-confidence and fight marginality through expressions of solidarity'.[60]

The Matua moral order

Among the Matuas who came as settlers to the Andaman Islands, it was the sect's teachings in the realm of personal ethics and morality that seemed to be most compelling. Matua teachings encouraged their followers to lead disciplined married lives and to refrain from all adulterous practices. The ideal Matua, in some senses, had to live out the role of the ideal householder, devoted to his wife and family. Harinath Mondol, who was amongst the group that reminisced about their lives of struggle and deprivation in their early days in the Middle Andamans, categorically stated that had it not been for the weekly *kirtans* in the small Matua temple that was constructed in the premises of the barracks, life would have been truly hard to sustain. The temple became the critical site wherein the trauma of violence, the pain of losing homes and the physical

[58] Bandopdhayay, *Caste, Culture and Hegemony*, 96.
[59] Bandopdhayay, *Caste, Culture and Hegemony*, 96.
[60] Bandopadhyay, *Caste, Culture and Hegemony*, 98.

Figure 6.2 Women as equal participants in the Matua congregational
singing or *kirtan*. Photograph: Madhumita Mazumdar.

hardships endured in a place with chronic food and water shortages came
to be shared and eventually healed.[61]

Keshub Rai, who came in with one of the refugee families from Khulna,
recounted how many a time he felt like running back to East Pakistan, but
was dissuaded by fellow Matuas who held him back with the promise that
life would get better with the Guru's blessings. The Matuas were able
collectively to work to improve their conditions in the area. They were
strongly inspired by the ethic of work and believed quite literally in the
saying *haathe kaam, mukhe naam* – a lifelong commitment to work and
devotion to the name of Hari. Although they were agriculturalists living
on the edges of swamps and marshes, their new lives in the Islands
demanded new forms of hard labour in the forests. This was particularly
true for the settlement areas of the Middle Andamans, where large areas
were uncleared and where forest operations proceeded at a slower pace
than that of the South or the North Andamans. As Keshub Rai ruefully
recounted the backbreaking work he had to put in to rake, beat and
pulverize the clods of earth to prepare it for sowing, he asked who could
have helped him during that time but the Lord?[62]

[61] Conversation with Harinath Mondol, 9 December 2010.
[62] Conversation with Keshub Rai, 9 December 2010.

Bengali Matua families in the area had to send endless petitions to the island administration for more regular rations, for the extension of electricity in the villages and for more ready sources of water. Keshub Rai hated the smell of saltwater fish and the taste of vegetables that grew on a soil that was never irrigated with the sweet waters of streams and rivulets, yet he had to survive. He put his ability to cope with it all to the many evenings he spent at the Matua mandir participating in the weekly *namkirtans* or congregational singing.[63]

The Wednesday 'Harisabhas' were also devoted to discourses on Harichand Thakur's 'Twelve Commands' or the *Dvadosh Ajna*. These commands embodied the core beliefs of Matua theology and ethics. They included instructions to always speak the truth, respect parents like Gods, treat women with respect, love all creatures of the world, remain tolerant of all religions, never discriminate on caste or other counts, try to establish Harimandir (temple of the Lord) wherever one dwells, sit in prayer every day, be ready to sacrifice oneself for God, but not practice asceticism, hold the six cardinal vices in check and chant the name of the Lord while working with one's hands.[64]

All these constituted a set of practical instructions meant for structuring individual and collective life around a core set of principles. For Satis Pramanik, Gurupada Barui, Harinath Mondol or Keshub Rai of the Middle Andamans, the twelve commandments of Harichand Thakur, reminded them of their identity as a people endowed with a philosophy of life and a guide to everyday living whose mandate transcended the bounds of region and nation. The Matuas were not merely East Bengali refugees, but part of a larger community 'that could grow bloom like a garden even in the midst of the wildest jungles'.[65]

The soul of community life, however, resided in the weekly congregational singing or *kirtan* that was performed in every Matua temple. These small weekly affairs at the local Matua temple gradually acquired the scale of week-long festivals held at various other temples that were established all over the Islands. Often such annual festivities were held to commemorate the inauguration of a Matua temple in a particular location. Festivities and congregational singing in the early days of the

---

[63] Conversation with Keshub Rai, 9 December 2010.

[64] Conversation with Keshub Rai, 9 December 2010. For more details and a critical comment on how Matua teachings were integrally related to issues of social mobility and self-respect, see Bandopadhyay, *Caste, Culture and Hegemony*, 96–7. Also Sekhar Bandopdhyay, 'Popular Religion and Social Mobility in Colonial Bengal: The Matua Sect and the Namasudras', in Rajat Kanta Ray (ed.), *Mind, Body and Society: Life and Mentality in Colonial Bengal* (Calcutta: Oxford University Press, 1995), 155–92.

[65] Conversation with Harinath Mondol, 9 December 2010.

settlement offered the Matuas the experience of an intense feeling of community and a kind of immersive solidarity in times when the life conditions of physical hardship and isolation became unbearably oppressive.

Bhavani Biswas, Police Sub-Inspector at Kadamtalla police station and among the group of Matua families we spoke to days after the Pahargaon festival in Port Blair, pointed out that notwithstanding the growing popularity of the *harisangkirtans*, the structured normative principles of community life were hard to sustain.[66] It seemed as if he was referring to the argument that the Matuas often to found it difficult to develop an appropriate relationship between the normative community and the spontaneous existential community. 'When all were together at the *harisangkirtans* it seemed that the teachings of Guruchand and Harichand were alive yet in the everyday lives of the Matua the moral standards and norms of the community seemed to be under threat', he told us.[67] The tenets of Matua worship or the moral order it demanded was were far more difficult to uphold than encouraging members to join in community festivities or the practices of devotional singing.

Yet, he believed that Hari Thakur's twelve commands were more relevant now than ever before as members of the community grew, diversified and moved out of the Islands to places far away. Many of them, he said, did not know how to create homes in these new lands. Using a somewhat unusual but interesting metaphor, he said that settling in a new place is about growing roots in a new soil:

To grow strong roots however the tree needs to offer shade and nurturance to others, or else it might be felled prematurely. A good tree can grow and survive only if it can offer its fruit and spread the fragrance of its flowers all around ... Harichand Thakur's commands tell us how to make homes and grow new roots in new lands by living a life of piety and by strengthening the bonds of community.[68]

At this point, Biswas gestured to a young boy who had come to sit and watch us talk and asked to him to quickly get me a copy of the Matua songbook or the compilation of *kirtans* that were normally sung by the congregation. He said I had to read some of the verses in order to understand better what home and dwelling meant for the Matua. A few minutes later the young boy handed over a worn songbook with frayed covers and a faintly visible printed text. Biswas took the book and rapidly flicked the pages to come to a song he thought best explained what he

---

[66] Conversation with Bhabani Biswas, 14 December 2011.
[67] Conversation with Bhabani Biswas, 14 December 2011.
[68] Conversation with Bhabani Biswas, 14 December 2011.

meant. He said there were many among the first generation Matuas who longed to leave the Islands and go back to what they considered to be their 'real' homes, while there were others who could not take the isolation and petitioned the administration to give them the opportunity to visit the pilgrim sites of Navadwip and Vrindavan at least once before they died.[69] Financial and logistical constraints of travel to mainland India, however, meant that many of these wishes remain unfulfilled. It was at these times, Biswas continued, that they turned to Harichand for comfort. He read out two songs from the book that, roughly translated, read:

> Who needs to go to Nabadwip or Nadia?
> Who needs to go to Gaya, Kashi or Vrindavan?
> Our pilgrim souls are blessed at the feet of Harichand!

The second song was about 'home and belonging', and Mr Biswas was convinced that I would find all my questions answered in it. He read aloud:

> What is this sense of belonging?
> When the tidal waves of *Harinam* (the word of the Lord) beckon?
> Whoever thinks of *desh* or *kul*? (land or lineage)
> Whoever thinks of *poribaar*? (family)
> Whoever of pride?
> The *bhakt* (devotee) is drunk in the name of the Lord,
> The *bhakt* revels in the sea of love,
> All that was sacred and precious have lost their sheen,
> All that matters is the presence of Hari!
> All that matters is his name![70]

The question of home and rootedness, however, seemed to be more complex than Mr Biswas had implied, for the others who sat around him and even he himself invoked more nuanced metaphors to qualify what he had initially said. What then did the Matuas really feel about home and dwelling now and how did the younger generation relate to these ideas?

---

[69] Vrindavan, an important Hindu pilgrimage site, is located in the Mathura district of the Indian state of Uttar Pradesh. It is said to be the site of an ancient forest where, according to the Hindu epic the Mahabharata, Lord Krishna was supposed to have spent his childhood days. Nabawip in the Nadia district of West Bengal is associated with the life and times of Chaitanya Mahaprabhu (1486–1534), a medieval saint who was a proponent of the Vaishnava school of Bhakti. Kashi refers to Benares or present day Varanasi in Uttar Pradesh, while Gaya in Bihar is a sacred pilgrim site for Hindus, Jain and Buddhists. For Hindus, it is a place where special rituals are performed for the spiritual salvation of departed souls.

[70] Conversation with Bhabani Biswas, 14 December 2011.

The Matua sense of home

For the second generation of Matuas who were born and raised in the Andaman Islands, questions relating to original homes, or roots, evoked either lukewarm or no responses at all. Manmohan Mistry, who guided us through the festival proceedings at the Matua Mandir in Pahargaon, Port Blair, told me that apart from his ninety-year-old mother, few in the family cared to talk about their homes in erstwhile East Bengal.[71] Some elderly members of the community he said did go to Bangladesh in what he described as search for their roots, but this was not a general trend. Younger Matuas are more keen to visit the 'mainland' to go to what has now become the main pilgrim point for Matuas everywhere, Thakurnagar, in the North 24 Pargana district of present-day West Bengal. This was where Guruchand's grandson P. R. Thakur had set up home following Partition.[72] It is their descendants who are now the focal point of the Matua community all over India.

Mr Mistry went on to suggest that if the Guru's own family could leave their ancestral homes in East Bengal, and re-establish the community in a different place, why couldn't the same be replicated by Matuas everywhere? The Matuas of the Andaman Islands, for instance, seldom regretted their loss of ancestral homes, because they believed that their homes were really where their Guru resided. To explain what this meant, Mr Mistry told us that Bengali settlers who came from Barishal to the Andamans in the 1950s brought along with them their precious icons known as *vigrahas*. For them, the possession of the *vigraha* was to remind them both of the pain of displacement as well as of the promise of a new future in the Islands. The *vigraha* or icon at their homes in the Andamans reminded them of the early formation of the community in Bangladesh and gave them the belief that home was wherever the Guru resided.

In his book on the lives and journeys of Tamil labour in the Malay Peninsula in the late eighteenth and nineteenth centuries, historian Sunil Amrith writes insightfully on the ways in which migrants and more significantly the coastal spiritual traditions that took shape through their travels gave new meanings to 'history and geography'. In his words:

[71] Conversation with Manmohan Mistry, 11 December 2011.
[72] P. R. Thakur was elected to the Bengal Legislative Assembly as a Congress candidate in 1946. After Partition he came to West Bengal and settled in a village in the North 24 Parganas district of West Bengal, which later came to be known as Thakurnagar. It is from here that in 1949 he tried to revive the Matua Mahasangha. The Sangha has since then acquired new strength and life and is regarded as the principal site of pilgrimage for all Matuas.

[P]roximity was measured by spiritual intensity rather than physical distance, time was cyclical rather than linear. Every migrant in a new place seeks to recreate some trace of home – arrival becomes a kind of return. Building replicas of the shrines they had known, migrants made new landscapes familiar. Sharing rituals they made intimates of strangers. Seeing their journeys in the footsteps of holy men they overcame their fears of the unknown.[73]

For the Matuas, the icons of the Guru they installed in their new homes on the Islands were a link as much as a protective shield. The recreated Matua *mandirs* would also instruct them about what Mr Mistry interestingly proposed, of how one could be a good 'Matua and a good citizen' in any place – not just in Orakandi or Thakur Nagar, places associated with Harithakur's original home and that of his descendants in present-day West Bengal.[74]

When they came to the Andaman Islands, Matua families that came from Barishal or Faridpur could easily relate to those from Khulna and Noakhali. They saw themselves as part of a large family of Namasudra settlers. Things began to change, however, when refugees from Dhaka came in at the tail end of the Rehabilitation programme, and were allotted lands in the vicinity of Matua settlements in the North, South and Middle Andaman. The Dhaka group, which was mostly non-Matua, was prone to look down on the other Bengali settlers as 'low caste scavengers'. This negative stereotyping of the Matuas, by other Bengali settlers, unfortunately found resonance in settlement policies. Although there would not be any official documentation on this, Mr Mistry continued, that settlement officers who came from Kolkata were pressurized to put the Matua in separate *padas* or neighbourhoods and told not to forge relations with the other Bengali Matua settlers.[75]

The Matua community's response to attempts at this kind of social segregation in the Andaman Islands was resolute. It steadfastly held on to the belief that the soil they had tilled in the Andamans was theirs and the homes that they built therein were blessed by their Gurus. These homes were open to all irrespective of caste or gender. Mr.Mistry went on to elaborate a compelling philosophy of Matua hospitality that he believed, worked as a moral counter-offensive to the attempts to reintroduce old style caste prejudices among Bengali settlers. The effort paid off and as Mr Mistry said, Bengali Matua settlers did not succumb to the invidious practices of settlement politics of the early years.

---

[73] Sunil Amrith, *Crossing the Bay of Bengal: The Furies of Nature, the Fortunes of Migrants* (Cambridge, MA: Harvard University Press, 2013), 88–9.
[74] Conversation with Manmohan Mistry, 11 December 2011.
[75] This was the first time I heard any of the Bengali settlers speak of differences between them. In most cases the voices were ones of solidarity.

These observations spurred new questions about the role of community life in mediating the experience of living in what is generally
perceived as the 'isolating' space of the Islands. Back in Kadamtalla,
I had asked Mr Biswas and his friends, what did living on an 'island'
mean to Matuas? Did it really generate a sense of isolation? Or did the
Matuas believe they were always connected by the ties of faith to other
Matuas everywhere? How were such networks of faith sustained over
the years?

There was a bit of initial silence to this question. But a few minutes
later and after some looks were exchanged between the members of the
group, one elderly gentleman, Guripada Barui, said:

We have been displaced many times so too was Guruthakur's own family! We
have been planted and transplanted. Now after all these years we have finally
settled and grown our roots here. We never feel isolated or disconnected even if
these islands are far removed from the rest of India. We all are connected to each
other like the beads in our rosary. As we chant the name of our Gurus, we feel
connected to all who believe in him. We also feel connected to our earlier lives in
East Bengal. There the river waters rose and fell with rains and tides, so too in the
Andamans! What was dismantled in Bengal was patiently put together here in the
Andamans. All this has been possible because we have had Hari Thakur with us –
we do not need associations like the Tamil Sangam, or the Atul Smriti Sadan or
Ayyapan temples, we have Hari Thakur in each of our hearts and in our homes.[76]

I turned next to Mr Sukanto Pramanik, Mr Biswas's friend, who sat
quietly next to him for most of the time. I asked him if Matuas on the
Andamans ever felt the need to break out of their isolation from the
mainland? Or did they think their relative isolation from the mainland
helped them sustain their community better? He said thoughtfully:

We do not feel isolated as we are together and yet when we are together we never
feel constrained. Our *bhakti* makes us all attached to the values that are with us
and therefore there is no longing for other places. We can always go to Bengal on
the mainland or even to Bangladesh and then come back to our homes here. But
to the question as to where my real home is, I can only say that the *bash* (dwelling)
we all know is the *bash* of Hari and all those in whom He resides. It is this sense of
bash that reinforces our bonds and spares us from feeling isolated.[77]

As the evening plunged into the darkness of the night, Pagol Mondal,
who was rather tired of my questions, finally spoke up to give a deeper
philosophical take on community life on the Islands:

---

[76] Conversation with Gurupada Barui, 14 December 2011. The *Atul Smriti Sadan* and the
Tamil Sangam are the cultural associations formed by Bengali and Tamil settlers
respectively in Port Blair.
[77] Conversation with Sukanto Pramanik, 14 December 2011.

Our faith in our gurus are like pools of life-giving water. Whenever anyone needs our help we channel ourselves like the irrigation ducts to flood and nourish a barren tract or a cultivable plot. Our community is like a water body that is filled with *bhakti*. The water in this pool rises up to the brim when more and more immerse themselves in the Matua faith. The *utsav* is one such occasion when the pools of faith (*bhakti-r pukur*) are filled to the brim and when every Matua immerses his/herself in its waters that connect to the world of the Gurus and the realms of *paramananda* (or eternal bliss).[78]

There seemed to be no direct references to 'lost homes' or 'abandoned villages', but there was a distinct notion of what 'home' meant for a Matua and how they were to live out their lives within it. This was a sense of home that was grounded solidly in spiritual terms. No Matua could articulate a sense of home and belonging without reference to the Matua Mandirs, the day long communal singing or *kirtan* and the everyday ties of community life. The experience of home or dwelling, in other words, meant more than an attachment to a land; it meant a place that allowed the re-creation of an immersive space of community life.

As many of my respondents argued, the Matua faith encouraged the construction of multiple homes in the inner spaces of one's physical home and more significantly in the fluid spaces of community or wherever it came alive through *bhakti* or devotion. The home for the Matua was one which was blessed by the aura of the Guru, one that was found through immersing oneself in community, and one that was housed in a place that embraced all with respect. The Andaman Islands were indeed a place where the Matuas were able to dwell in all three.

Conclusion

It was clear from our many conversations with Matua families between 2010 and 2013 that Matua notions of home, homeland and memories of displacement remain complex. Although it is tempting to argue that the possession of land and the role of agricultural pioneers that was thrust upon them gave the Matuas a more rooted sense of 'home' in the Islands, it was evident from our many discussions that the concepts of home and identity were more complex and nuanced than I had imagined previously. The notion of fluidity is key here. My findings support the conclusions of earlier studies of Bengali Matua by scholars like Sekhar Bandopadhyay. On the specific issue of caste protest identities and political mobilization, Bandopadhyay pointed out the necessity of looking at

---

[78] Conversation with Pagol Mondal, 14 December 2011.

the 'conjunctural' and 'transient' articulations of caste identities and the complex trajectories of caste movements rather than 'their assumed homogeneity or unilinear progress'.[79]

On the specific issue of caste identity and mobilization among Namasudra refugees in Bengal, Bandopadhyay argues that 'in post-colonial West Bengal the Partition violence and refugee influx has led to rephrasing the idioms of victimhood and resistance, placing less emphasis on caste and focusing more on the predicament of migration and the struggles of the refugees and hence in spite of the perpetuation of caste based discrimination "caste" as an idiom of protest disappeared from the public space'.[80] On the face of it, this argument holds for the Andaman Islands, too, but for slightly different reasons. None of the Matua respondents I spoke talked either about 'caste' issues *per se* or of histories of Matua politics in undivided Bengal. The oppositional/combative rhetoric characteristic of anti-caste sects was, as many agreed, completely irrelevant. One of my respondents, a relatively well-to-do member of the Matua community in Uttara, told me that to them Andaman was a 'caste-free' society, hence there was no need for them to sustain any politicized rhetoric against social hierarchies.[81] However, he added the contemporary situation on the Islands demanded that 'caste' identities be reinvoked. He told me that the Andaman and Nicobar Backward Class Commission (est. 1995) had submitted its recommendations for the inclusion of post-1949 Bengali settlers in the Other Backward Classes Category, along with the Local Born, Moplahs, Bhantus and Karens. While some of the Bengali settlers welcomed this move, there were others who believed that the entitlements to jobs and reservations in institutions of higher learning would be served better if the Bengali settlers were included in the Scheduled Caste category. He said:

In the Andamans we have no caste, our leaders taught us unity ... but now caste is an important social marker – we need it to secure jobs for our children who would otherwise have to compete in a general category.[82]

---

[79] Bandopadhyay, *Caste, Culture and Hegemony*, 33.
[80] Bandhopadhyay, *Caste, Protest and Identity*, 248.
[81] Conversation with Manik Das, 12 December 2010.
[82] Das was trying to argue that the inclusion of the post-49 Bengali settlers along with pre-42 settlers meant they would have to compete with four other groups. Had the post-49 settlers been recognized as Scheduled Castes they would have had a monopoly over this category as they would have been the only Scheduled Castes within the group who migrated via settlement schemes. See also Shamik Bag, 'OBC Job Quota Move Casts Shadow Over "Casteless" Andamans', *The Indian Express*, 20 June 2006, http://archive.indianexpress.com/news/obc-job-quota-move-casts-shadow-over–casteless–andamans—/6887/0 (accessed 31 July 2014).

This was December 2010, a time when Matuas in mainland West Bengal too were demanding the repeal of the Citizenship Amendment Act of 2003 that debarred citizen status to those refugees who had crossed the border and come to India in the aftermath of the Indo-Pakistan war of 1971. Many of those who came in belonged to the Namasudra caste and were members of the Matua sect. It was in this context that the Matua Mahasangha, until then a relatively quiet association of Matuas, acquired a distinctive political colour. From 2010 onwards they organized agitations, hunger strikes and street demonstrations, and called for unified Matua opposition to an Act that deprived fellow Matuas from Bangladesh of Indian citizenship.[83]

Far away in his village in the Middle Andamans, Manik Das was following these developments on his little black and white television set perched precariously atop a narrow wooden table in his sitting room. He believed that the time had come when old caste solidarities needed to be asserted for political purposes. But he lamented that the Matuas in the Andaman Islands were largely apolitical. In December 2010, when I spoke to him, he said that the 'die had already been cast' and the Scheduled Caste status that many Bengali Matuas demanded would not be realized. They would have to remain content with whatever the administration granted them. He said that Matuas in the Andaman Islands might be looking to consolidate ties with their community on the mainland but they refused to get embroiled in the 'politics' of Bengal. 'People,' he said in conclusion, 'like the Islands, because they were peaceful and not politicized like mainland India'.[84]

The Matua perception of the island space, of rootedness and dwelling, complicates our understanding of Bengali refugee memory and identity in the Andaman Islands. Although no official figures are available, local observers on the Islands believe that the Matuas constitute over 80 per cent of the Bengali settler population on the Islands. The retrieval of their voices and an engagement with their narratives of displacement and settlement, compel new understandings of not only refugee memory and identity but of larger settler identities that have been forged on the Islands.

The complex articulations of caste identity among Bengali settlers in the Andamans is an important point of entry into the question of whether refugees may be looked upon as spatial and temporal extensions of *a priori* natural identities rooted in locality or ethnicity, or whether such identities are contextual and contingent. Members of the Matua

[83] For details, see Sinharay, 'Caste, Migration, Identity', 55–9.
[84] Conversation with Manik Das, 12 December, 2010.

community with whom we spoke in Bengali confessed that most of their children had begun to take to Hindi as their first language. They talked about themselves as being Bengali in distinction to other non-Bengali 'settlers', but refused to identify with those they considered to be upper-caste custodians of Bengali culture. Their children hardly read Tagore or knew much about Bengali *sahitya* (literature) or *sanskriti* (culture). They had little or no interest in the established literary or cultural canon of Bengal. Their strongest link to its social and cultural milieu was their knowledge and understanding of the Matua movement and the philosophical teachings of their Guru. Their identities as Matua/Bengali were both inclusive and strategic. In the presence of their upper-caste brethren, many Matuas were happy to downplay their sectarian identity. They were happy to participate in mainstream Hindu festivals such as Durga Puja and Diwali, in spite of their Guru's commands not to do so. They understood the importance of maintaining strategic alliances with the deemed 'upper' caste Hindu Bengali settlers of the Islands while sustaining their own community solidarities.

But what about the indigenous communities or the Jarawas who lived on the edges of the Bengali villages in which Satis Pramanik or Keshub Rai made their homes? In all the Matua renditions of 'home' and belonging in the Islands, the Jarawas and indigenous communities remain an intractable 'other'. They surfaced in Matua memories of the past as fearsome and hostile and in contemporary contexts as undeserving parasites of the state. Nowhere in these narratives were any concessions made to the fact that the forests that many Bengali settlers claimed as their own were 'home' to these people, too. Some of my Matua respondents avoided a discussion on the issue while others argued that the government took care of them and therefore there was no need for debate. When I asked them if they ever thought that their settlements were made on the land that belonged to Jarawas, they remained silent. They said they never wanted to come here on their own, their circumstances had brought them here and they accepted whatever their Guru wanted of them.[85]

In the ordered worldview of the Matua, the Jarawas remain a shadowy and troublesome presence. They remain integral to their narrative of home in the Andaman Islands; yet continue to remain 'outside' its inclusive possibilities. Satis Pramanik's heroic feat of staving off a Jarawa attack remains an inspiring story in the locality, yet in all the Matua stories of home there is little interest or understanding of the argument

---

[85] Conversation with Keshub Rai, 8 December 2010.

that such attacks were symptomatic of the traumas of displacement felt by Jarawas. Even while poachers enter the Jarawa Tribal Reserve to steal forest resources, or as encroachers move into parts of the reserve forest to set up hutments, the Bengali Matua response is muted. It is in this context the boundaries between the villages and the Jarawa reserve remain tense. This is particularly ironic for the settlement of Uttara where the first story of friendly contact with the Jarawas was scripted. As Vishvajit Pandya argues, repeated contact but lack of a shared discourse marks the uneasy relationship between the Bengali settlers and the Jarawas in this region.[86]

The Matua notions of home, homeland and of belonging bring out the complex trajectories of place-making and identity formation in the Andaman Islands. They show how received notions of refugee identity of displacement and stories of belonging are repeatedly subverted or questioned in the context of the island. They show how the materiality of place and home can be articulated in the complex terms of spiritual belonging and devotion. They also show how one narrative of home in the Islands can be scripted at the expense of another. It is these entangled narratives of space, place and identity that configure the Islands, forest and fields as complex landscapes of affect. In the next chapter, Vishvajit Pandya looks at 'narratives of dwelling' from inside the forest, where the Jarawas live out their precarious lives under the watchful and often deeply resentful eyes of their Bengali neighbours.

[86] Pandya, *In the Forest*, 319–21.

7 In pursuit of fireflies: the poetics and politics of 'lightscapes' in the Jarawa forests

Vishvajit Pandya

Prelude

In 1770, Captain John Ritchie, Marine Surveyor to the English East India Company, conducted the first survey of the Andaman Islands.[1] His report also contains the 'first' description of an encounter with the Islands' indigenous inhabitants. These encounters, dated 20 January 1771, were recorded in a farcical description of a group of Andamanese trying to set fire to the crew who attempted to bring them on board their ship. The cautiously curious Andamanese, who finally did embark, were most interested in grabbing as much iron as possible from the deck. Though they were provided with boiled rice, clothes and coconuts, what made them happiest was the gift of iron nails. The rest was all unacceptable. Ritchie throughout his account stated how hard pressed he was for time. His priority was to find suitable anchorage points and landmarks, and to update existing hydrological maps. In his report he interestingly notes, that he was struck by the fact that throughout his day time explorations of the coast he seldom spotted the Andamanese in large groups. It was only at night that the shores seemed to come alive.

During all this time we saw no boats, nor was there the least appearance of houses, or cultivation, any where upon the land about the place; in the nights indeed, the shore was lighted up with hundreds of torches, which made an

[1] In 1901, Chief Commissioner R. C. Temple rediscovered and published Ritchie's account under the heading 'An Unpublished 18th Century Document about the Andamans', *The Indian Antiquary*, 30 (1901), 232–8. Temple wrote: 'Since communicating Capt. John Ritchie's remarks on the Nicobars to this Journal under the title of "An Unpublished Document about the Nicobars", Vol. XXIX. p. 341, forming part of a MS. in the India Office entitled "Remarks upon the Coast and Bay, of Bengal, The outlets of the Ganges and interfacing rivers, according to Surveys by John Ritchie, Hydrographical Surveyor to the Honorable the United India Company". This manuscript, now numbered C.10, is endorsed on the cover as follows: 'Captain Ritchie's Nautical Remarks for which I have given a Receipt to the Secretary the 25th March 1820. Jas. Horsburgh.' It relates to the work done by Ritchie in 1771: John Ritchie, An unpublished eighteenth century document about the Andamans, *The Indian Antiquary*, 30 (1901).

appearance, as if we were in the middle of a great Lake; surrounded by houses lighted up.

Introduction

Ritchie was evidently excited by what he saw. The quivering beams of light in the midst of the engulfing darkness confirmed to him the presence of human habitation. There was no way to make sense, however, what these sources of light were or could be. Ritchie imagined them to be small fires, but they could also have been the thousands of fireflies that lit up the forest every night. Could these be what the Jarawas later explained to me as part of the complex 'lightscape' that sustained their lives in the forest, illuminating their trails, guiding them in their wanderings, securing for them their belief in the patterns of the universe and convincing them of their need to stay within it no matter what the temptations of the outside may be?

This chapter follows the trail of these thoughts and addresses the problem of space and affect as it figures in the larger questions of state-indigenous relations in the Andaman Islands. It seeks to draw attention to the ways in which concepts of space are framed in contemporary debates on indigenous futures in the Andaman Islands as they are elsewhere. Where should the Jarawas be living in the years to come? Should they continue to stay within the confines of the reserves or should they be mainstreamed and brought to live outside the forests in concrete houses and ordered settlements? What about their titles to their territory? Would their claims to these rights weaken if they chose to live in the settlements? In sum, how would these 'spatial' issues determine the chances of their survival or ensure for them their identity and dignity?

Debates around the community of the Jarawas of the Andaman Islands are often placed within polarized positions on their future either in the forest or in the settlement. Proponents of both positions seem to assume that the Jarawas have a clear either/or position in their preference for a life in a forest insulated from the settlements or for a life in the settlement outside the confines of the forest.

One of the overriding concerns of the Indian administration has been to keep the 'primitive tribal groups' in the Andaman Islands 'protected' within designated spaces termed 'reserves'. The state assumes that the reserves remain the best possible way of keeping the Jarawas and the other hunter-gathering communities of the Islands both protected *and* free to carry on with their traditional cultural and livelihood practices. The Jarawa Tribal Reserve (JTR) it may be noted was formed in 1957 under the provisions of the Andaman and Nicobar Protection of Aboriginal Tribes Regulation, 1956.[2] The Jarawas, who today number only 440, continue to live in the original 742 square kilometre reserve allotted to them in the South and Middle Andaman Islands.[3] The JTR area was increased in 2004 and is now a little more than 1,000 square kilometres. Situated in between two interconnected regions in the Middle and South Andamans, the JTR stands as a dense dark forest surrounded by cleared area consisting of clusters of small village settlements. Lying in close proximity, therefore, are two distinct places, one designated as the 'primitive' space of the Jarawa and the other the 'civilized' space of the agricultural settler. A notional Buffer Zone is meant to police the bounds of these two spaces by monitoring and apprehending intruders on either side.

In the late 1990s, with the end of Jarawa hostility towards 'outsiders', relations between the community and the settled villagers have acquired a new complexity. Apart from the evidently corrupting and eventually fatal consequences of contact that are feared to threaten the survival of these people, the state welfare structure has also had to contend with the changing conditions of the reserve territory itself. Since 2004, the state has been trying to argue that the Jarawas are finding it difficult to sustain their traditional cultural practice of hunting and gathering within the designated reserve forest. It has observed that in the context of increasing welfare dole, dependence on hunted pig, gathered fish, tubers and fruit had declined. The rice, spices and biscuits provided by the settlers had become new items of desire that made the Jarawas keen to forage out of the forest. Meanwhile the declining hostility of Jarawas increased illegal poaching and encroachment by non-tribal settler communities into the reserve forest area.

By 2006 the Andaman and Nicobar Administration and its social welfare agency (*Andaman Adim Janjati Vikas Samiti* or AAJVS) was finding it hard to police the bounds of the JTR forest and the surrounding village settlements. Welfare workers complained that Jarawas, who even a few years earlier had been reluctant to leave their forest dwellings, were increasingly drawn to the villages in search of small items for barter. This proved to be the starting point of an exploitative exchange relationship. Despite several persuasive strategies employed by welfare staff, interaction and movements between the forest and the settlement could

---

[2] For details of the Jarawa Tribal Reserve see Pankaj Sekhsaria and Vishvajit Pandya (eds.), *The Jarawa Tribal Reserve Dossier: Cultural and Biological Diversity in the Andaman Islands* (Paris: UNESCO, 2010).

[3] Sekhsaria and Pandya (eds.), *The Jarawa Tribal Reserve Dossier*.

not be controlled. The Jarawas were particularly keen to procure rice, chewing tobacco, matchboxes, fancy clothes, cosmetics and small trinkets. The failure to regulate Jarawa visits to the settlement generated a sudden debate on the logic and practice of tribal welfare and more critically on the future of the Jarawas. The focus of the debate centred on contending interpretations of the Jarawas' 'coming out' into the settlement and their increasing demand for articles of settler consumption.

However, the state and its policy-makers held on to the view that the Jarawas as an indigenous people of the Islands were rooted in their territory and needed to be protected and preserved within its confines. Arguments about mainstreaming could be made only if the Jarawa displayed a certain cultural preparedness. The settlers, however, had a different point of view. They argued that their villages, now frequently visited by the Jarawas, indicated that the settlements were indeed a 'place of desire' for the tribals, and a place where they would eventually want to 'belong'. Settlers around the Jarawa Reserve in fact had begun questioning the very rationality of what was, to them an extravagant welfare system for a people who no longer seemed to be helpless 'primitives' in need of continuous state protection. As the deputy revenue office representative (*tehsildar*) of Middle Andaman commented:

I simply cannot understand why Jarawas move from place to building different shelters in different parts of the forest! Why can we not make them clear a plot of land and give them proper housing and they stay put in it and cultivate crops or raise plantations. [The] state has to teach them civilization and make them give up wilderness. We have to think of their future, as they being primitive cannot wonder about future! They live only day-to-day![4]

The administrative authorities however, remained cautious in their response to the demands of settled villagers. After a series of conversations that former Chief Secretary to the Andaman and Nicobar administration, Vivek Rae and his staff had with different Jarawa groups, it was argued that the Jarawa practice of coming out of the forest and occasionally foraging in the village settlements, or their increasing propensity to go to the local hospital to receive medical attention, were 'good' signs for the future. But as of now they were clearly keen to remain in the forest along with their children.[5] Curiously enough, the Jarawa also demanded that the administration should facilitate their movement along the

---

[4] The *tehsildar* of the area, an elected official, was a young graduate of social work who had been educated in mainland India but went back to work on the Islands as he had been born and raised in Tirrur. The extract is from author's interview with the *tehsildar* Mr Pal on 23 September 2010.

[5] *The Light of Andamans* 34, 16 (13 November 2009).

Andaman Trunk Road in motor vehicles, when and if they wanted to visit settlements. The vehicles should also bring them back to the forest when the objective of their visit had been accomplished. What was clear from both these conversations and the nature of the demands from the settlements was the evidently ambivalent relationship of the Jarawa not only with settlers, but with the idea of the settlement more broadly. Many among the younger generation of the Jarawas have come to know of the outside world selectively, based on what they want to incorporate and use. If by doing so they were articulating new terms of engagement with the state and settlers, how do we make sense of those in their own terms?

The aim of this chapter is to explore and understand the structures of cultural practice and the terms of affect that mark the ambivalent spatial relations between the Jarawa Reserve territory and the surrounding settlements. This ambivalence, I argue, indicates the criticality of the problem of space that informs the social and political relations between the Jarawas, the state and the settlers. The attempt in this chapter is not to explicate the problem as framed by the settlers in the Andaman Islands. Instead of a mere translation of an 'indigenous' response to a settler question, I wish to develop an ethnographic approach to the problem of space as it is articulated by the Jarawa in the context of the terms of *their* engagement with the settlement and the forest. What is it that defines the limits of their engagement with the settlement and what is it that draws them back to the forest as their eventual place of dwelling?

I took these questions to two groups of Jarawa men and women during two phases of fieldwork from 2011 to 2013. The two groups belonged to two different regions of South and Middle Andaman, Tirrur and Kadamtalla. It is instructive to note that settler-Jarawa relations in both areas have been complex. In the Kadamtalla region in Middle Andaman, Jarawa relations with the settlers have not been overtly hostile. Jarawa visitations to the settlement and accompanying perpetuation of instances of petty theft and harassment, however, have goaded local villagers to approach the tribal welfare officers and propose projects of education, reform and settlement.[6] Earlier in 2005, the local MP for the Andaman and Nicobar Islands, Shri Manoranjan Bhakta, took cues from these settler sentiments and threatened to go on a hunger strike if his demands for 'settling the Jarawas' were not met.[7] He argued that there were several indications that Jarawas had shown a keen interest in the settlement and that the government should prepare them for life within it. Bhakta's

---

[6] See Vishvajit Pandya, *In the Forest: Visual and Material Worlds of Andamanese History, 1858–2006* (Lanham, MD: University Press of America, 2009), 260–316.
[7] Pandya, *In the Forest*, 287–91.

demands were met with an official inquiry into the Jarawa predicament and a slew of angry protests from activists. The matter seemed to have been resolved for some time only to be raised periodically by anxious settlers who see in tribal welfare policy a drain of public wealth and the perpetuation of an undeservedly 'primitive life' in the forests. Settlers in Tirrur, on the outskirts of Port Blair, have been even more vociferous in their demands to bring the Jarawa to 'settled life'. Here relations between the Jarawas and the settlers have been both hostile and collusive. While events of Jarawa attacks have been reported by settlers, welfare workers have also apprehended settlers/poachers who routinely enter Jarawa territory and steal resources. In many instances, poachers have lured Jarawas into procuring shells, venison, fish and other forest and sea produce in exchange for small portions of rice and other items of food and clothing. Outbreaks of hostility have been frequent whenever the relations of exchange/exploitation have come under strain. Settlers who have resented the Jarawa-poacher nexus have argued that the only way to circumvent this situation is to plan out a roadmap to lead the Jarawas out of the forest into the ways of civilized cultivation. In this way, the unused in the land in the forest too could be put to productive use and the Jarawas would have a new life outside its confines.

In all these arguments for and against settled life, predictably the Jarawas have had little to say. There has been hardly any interest in listening to them either. Yet on my talking to them it appeared that the settlements in the vicinities of the Jarawa Reserves of Tirrur and Kadamtalla remain both 'integral' and 'alien' to the Jarawa worldview. The settlement possessed a duality that was hard to fathom in simple terms. Initially, there were no ready answers to the questions I posed in both Tirrur and Kadamtalla. However, the sudden appearance of a whole host of fireflies in the vicinity of a Jarawa medical centre in Kadamtalla one evening, and my questions to a group of Jarawa elders about the names they had for them, opened up a conversation on the forest and the settlement in completely surprising ways.

What follows here are ethnographic vignettes that derive from these conversations. They focus on the Jarawas' understanding of space in relation to light and luminosity as revealed in myths, in the construction of residential spaces, in practices of movement within the forest, and finally in the long-standing resistance to the tools and techniques of state illumination. It is here that I attempt to deploy anthropological perspectives on the role of light in its relationship with space, people and things, and hence affect the experiences and materiality of these, in culture-specific ways. The Jarawas' metaphoric pursuit of the firefly as a defining condition of dwelling in the forest reveals the complex contours of a politics of spatiality that mark the tense and ambivalent relations between the Reserve forest and the settlement and complicate any easy understanding of the choices they would make for their futures.

The order of light in the forest

Just as we convey an understanding of space through dimensions such as length, breadth, height or depth, Jarawas see space as a container of brightness and darkness that produces the related experiential aspects of temperature and moisture. Light within Jarawa culture is a way to measure three-dimensional space, which includes the natural (world around humans), supernatural (domain of natural elements and forces, heavenly bodies and ancestral spirits), as well as cultural places (residential structures and resource territories). Each of the three worlds is contained one within the other separated by a *wilpo*, a shelter or a roof that serves as a container.

According to Jarawa mythology, which is akin to what colonial anthropologist A. R. Radcliffe-Brown noted in his conversations with the Great Andamanese, in the world above the forest is the home of the moon and his wife the sun. The moon and sun, however, were never seen together. In Jarawa mythology, the moon, after marriage with the sun, wanted to consummate their conjugal relationship but never could because the disruptive presence of blinking stars would never allow them a single moment of togetherness.[8] The twinkling stars seemed to laugh and embarrass the couple making it impossible for them to ever 'embrace one another'. But in their seemingly disruptive roles as irritants, the stars ensured the rhythm of day and night. The myth goes on to suggest that if the sun and moon came too close and stopped following their alternating motions, the order of the cosmos would end and disorder set in. This notion of the sun and moon as a married couple structures Jarawa ideas about light or luminosity, informs their social and translocatory movements under the forest canopy and helps them design their residential structures. As soon as the husband and wife come close to each other in the sky, Jarawas experience the liminal moments of dawn and dusk. It is at these times that the husband and wife can be close but not together. These are times, therefore, that are neither completely bright nor totally dark.

The Jarawa myths also suggest that these are times of anticipation or even anxiety. The birds in the trees get restless and there is a change in

---

[8] See A. R. Radcliffe-Brown, *The Andaman Islanders: A Study in Social Anthropology* (Cambridge: Cambridge University Press, 1922), 140 and 340–1 on the Andamanese legend of the sun, moon and stars.

the chorus of insects. These are times when the fireflies start glowing, reminding the Jarawas, just like stars reminded the sun and moon, to heed the rules of order and keep apart husbands and wives. These are not times for conjugality. Moral standards within the community require that an ideal Jarawa couple must not remain together all the time. Instead, they must maintain and sustain individual bonds and connections with each of their age and gender sets including relatives by birth, by marriage and by band connections. Married couples are to maintain this rule as they follow each other in their periodic visits to different campsites.

In more recent times, as one Jarawa man from Tirrur told me with a mischievous twinkle in his eye, in the sleeping area designated for a married couple a piece of smouldering wood is kept to generate smoke and ward off the fireflies so that they do not disturb them. He also pointed out that when it rained heavily and the skies remained cloudy till late morning, the sun and moon could also enjoy a little more time together without being bullied by the stars that remained hidden from view by dark thunder clouds.[9]

When dawn broke and when the fireflies would stopped blinking, the forest would be filled with the noise of the cicadas. In the Jarawa cultural conception of the world, the forest and the sky both provide a *wilpo* (shelter) that contains the light from the *waye-dama* (stars) when it gets dark and cold. The *waye-dama* in the sky are the stars, but under the 'roof' of the forest canopy they are the fireflies, the embodiments of the stars above. The sky is the sheltered home for the moon and sun who follow each other in a rhythm strictly orchestrated by the stars. It is the stars that coordinate the light from the moon and sun and bring in day and night. This symbolic connection from the natural world is recapitulated and mapped on to the cultural world by seeing the stars in the sky to be homologous to fireflies in the forest.

In Jarawa language, both stars in the faraway sky and the fireflies (*Lampridae photuris petroptyx*) closer to their homes in the forest are referred to as *waye-dama*, for they share a common characteristic. Both stars and fireflies blink, or alternatively glow and fade out in regular sequences. In the term *waye-dama*, the suffix *dama* is a collective reference to light and fire that are potentially present in all things but suffer the possibility of depletion due to the contending presence of wind and rain. It is *dama*'s capacity to mediate atmospheric conditions that makes the sky a thatch or a container much like the forest canopy that holds the fireflies. The blinking movement of both the fireflies and stars are

[9] Conversation with Tahapahad, 25 December 2011.

mnemonic indicators of orderly change and movements in the sky above as well as in the forest below.

As we talked about this order of light in the forest and critical role of the fireflies and stars that maintain it, a Jarawa elder commented all of a sudden about the conditions of light in the settlement. 'There are no trees there', he said, 'whatever remains of the forest cannot contain the *dama*'. 'Look at the electric lights', he added, 'would we be able to see the fireflies in such blinding light?... Being in a place without the shade of a forest *wilpo* is like being in fire that dries up all that is under or on it.'[10]

From these sudden expressions of anxiety it was clear that the Jarawas feared both intense heat and intense light. There had to be something that choreographed and ordered the experience of both. In their mythologies, nature mediated the experience of both through stars in the skies and fireflies in the forests, and the Jarawas took cues from them and also elaborated their own culture specific rules of the use of heat and light. For instance the fire lit for cooking is regarded as an embodiment of the sun in the forest. Such fires could be made only during the day. Cooking on the fire after sunset is strictly forbidden. Other forms of fire, particularly those without intense heat or flames, are perceived by Jarawas as *bonee*, a mere light that is produced by burning resin and set on a smouldering piece of wood. Jarawa elders near Tirrur explained the significance of *bonee* to me. In their own words:

Resinous wood produces illumination like daylight in the dark forest, but not enough heat that can dry up everything around. The light from the *bonee* illuminates our paths and the smoke rising from it keeps away the flies that try to bite us. This light is not like the one that comes from sun but is bit like moon ... it is this light that sustains our lives in the forest ... the *bonee* is our friend in the forest!

The significance of fire among Andaman Islanders is well established in their mythology and narratives.[11] Among the Jarawas, fragments of fire mythology are remembered as story before the time 'the match-box

---

[10] Conversation with Tahapaha, 25 December 2011. G. Bachelard writes about the surprising dichotomies of fire. 'Among all phenomena', he notes, 'it is really the only one to which there can be so definitely attributed the opposing values of good and evil. It shines in Paradise. It burns in hell. It is gentleness and torture. It is cookery and it is apocalypse.' Fire is also related to the process of change. Bachelard notes that the process of life defines slow change and the process of fire explains quick change. As he notes, 'Fire suggests the desire to change, to speed up the passage of time, to bring all life to its conclusion, to its hereafter. In this sense, all that changes slowly can be explained by life while all that changes quickly can be explained by fire.' As Bachelard says, 'through fire everything changes.' Bachelard reminds us that when we want everything changed, we call on fire. Gaston Bachelard, *Psychoanalysis of Fire* (Boston, MA: Beacon Press, 1968).

[11] See Radcliffe-Brown, *The Andaman Islanders* and Pandya, *Above the Forest*.

came to us' and when ancestors 'carried fire from place to place'. A contemporary version of the fire legend as remembered by a few elders in the group I spoke to in Tirrur, was pieced together from various sources. It gives an interesting insight into Jarawas' perpetual anxieties about heat and light in the forest and the peculiar role of fireflies in mediating or disrupting the order that sustains it. I was particularly intrigued by the homology of ambivalence that marked perceptions about the stars in the sky and the fireflies in the forest. This is what they said:

Once the *Ukaneley*, who are our ancestors could not sleep well in the forest, as there were lots of fireflies that were glowing and blinking all night. One of them took the branches on which fireflies had gathered to mate and mischievously hurled these into the cold mangrove pools around. Soon enough fireflies stopped glowing. They became cold and humid and lost their heat too. While our ancestors were asleep, in the cold, dark forest, some fire escaped and joined the stars above the sky. In the meantime the fireflies in the mangrove pool started dying out slowly. But the remains of their *dama* or body heat flowed into the pool of water. When crabs came out of the water to lay eggs in the mud they got covered in the flowing heat from the dying fireflies. This liquid heat was called *allamey*. Now crabs became hot and hard bodied. They could not come out of the water onto mud banks to lay eggs. They had to hold on to the eggs within their hard body and wait for a full moon night, when the forest around was cold, to deliver their young.[12]

As the fireflies from the forest were all gone, our *ukaneley* woke up from their long deep sleep. There was darkness all around and they could do nothing but grope. As they tried to get up and move they stumbled upon two hard objects that insisted to be picked up and taken along with them. These were the wild tuber (*geegi*) and a human stomach (*natanduyeh*). As the two sat in the Jarawa baskets they realized that they needed *nado* (cooked food). It was cold and dark and they were hungry too. The tuber and the stomach constantly cried while sitting inside the basket. The hard stomach wanted to be carried inside Jarawas body as it was hungry in the basket. While the tuber complained that it too wanted to be inside the stomach as it was too cold in the forest.

Our ancestors had no idea how to put hard things inside more hard things. It was at this point that a group of woodpeckers fluttering in the forest looking for hard wood came to help. They told the Jarawas how to find hard resin in the forest, how to burn it and carry it around their bodies to warm it up. Once the bodies would warm up they could put the stomach back inside it. Finally resin became part of the hard substances contained in the baskets of Jarawas. But the stomach inside the body of the Jarawas still cried out for *nado* or cooked food.

---

[12] Pregnant Jarawa women must avoid eating crabs, but a young mature man is ritually prescribed to feed on crabs as the crab contains fire and the glow (*allamey*) that comes out of the firefly. Jarawas regard crab as a special food because it changes its hard muddy-coloured body into fiery red when softened in external heat. So eating crab is ingesting interiorized hard heat (raw crab) transformed into exteriorized, visibly heated soft food. The cooked crab hence is apparently a twice-heated distinct food.

It was then that the resin took pity and sought to solve the problem. He suggested that the Jarawas needed to go back to the creek and dip their fingers and toes into the mangrove waters.

Our ancestors did as they were told. They went to the mangrove pools and dipped their toes and fingers as advised. The moment they did this however, they were bitten by crabs! They shouted in pain, little did they realize that they were being redeemed! The liquid heat that had flowed into the bodies of the crabs when the fireflies drowned in the mangrove pool now flowed back into the bodies of our ancestors! Those fireflies that had managed to escape their watery graves told the Jarawas that they were now saved. The Jarawas had at last interiorized the *allamey* (the heat and glow) of the fireflies and the order of light in the forest was soon to be restored. The crabs were happy to have the heat out of their bodies and asked the Jarawas to apologize to the fireflies for the heinous crime of attempting to kill them. So the Jarawas did and fireflies returned to the forest. They told our ancestors that if they are allowed to blink and glow every night they would ask the stars above to make sure that the moon and sun visit the forest and perpetuate the rhythms of light and darkness, heat and cold.

Our ancestors now knew how to retain the glow of the fireflies in their bodies. They knew when to light the fire for cooking and when to burn the resin for illumination. The cooking fire (*tuheney*) will burn till dusk while the smoldering resin (*dundul*) would burn till dawn. More importantly they now knew how to put *nado* (cooked food) into their stomach and stop it from crying!

The elders of Tirrur who narrated this story to me in all its detail and through its many twists and turns now said to me that their ancestors had actually structured the patterns of their daily lives in ways that still help them to cope with the changing circumstances of their lives in the Reserve.

Thus, every morning to this day, the Jarawas in either Tirrur or Kadamtalla begin their day with similar routines. They pick up a piece of smouldering wood that burns all night in their huts and blow on it with regular wood to set up the cooking fire. When the daylong cooking is done they pick up a burnt piece of wood from the hearth to light up their resin torches soon after sunset. The careful synchronization of these practices is meant to ensure that the heat and glow in their bodies imparted to them by the fireflies are retained no matter what. Even now Jarawas make every effort not to hurt fireflies or cut branches they sit on as they believe that any act of violence on them may cause them harm or make them lose their progeny.

In Jarawa language, the terms *tuheney* and *dundul* both imply heat or light that is induced or derived from *dama*. The heat and illumination generated by electric lights in the nearby settlements is collectively referred to as *huluwe* to distinguish it from *dama*. The specific light from the electric bulbs is called *boneye* and the cooking fire in the settlement is referred to as *tuhe*. These linguistic differentiations demarcate the sources of light and heat in the forest from that of the settlement and help us understand the cultural significance of *dama* as a material embodiment of light and a distinctive source of life and livelihood in the forest.

There is yet another dimension of bodily *dama*. It is believed that every Jarawa child is born with a source of *dama* in its body. As the child grows into adulthood this source of light expands and finds expression in the individual's capacity to live, move and strive in the forest. With age, however, this source of bodily *dama* wanes. This is reflected in the individual's declining capacities to hunt, gather or simply move. It is a stage when the individual enters a phase of life known as *heyolo*: a phase of declining bodily glow. Traditionally, Jarawas undergoing the phase of *heyolo* would be cared for until a certain age. But, as one elder told me, 'many older men would wish to be left to themselves and seek shelter in a place far away from the campsite where they could die in peace'. This last shelter of their lives is known as the *uppa chaddha*. Some elders, however, remained active till a very late age and were regarded as accomplished hunters and gatherers, whose internal glow remained within them without any signs of waning. These elders, even if they could not physically move around or remained asleep most of the day, were regarded as possessing some extraordinary powers.

Many of them were believed to be capable of moving while they slept. They were guided in these movements by dreams. In their dreams they were known to be travelling into other worlds of the forest down below or the skies above. They would have travelled far above in the skies into a star-lit space beyond the sun and the moon from where they could look down at the forest below. Elders who were known to be able to accomplish this dream travel were known as *elengeto*. They were highly regarded as mystics and oracles. The *elengeto*'s unique sight and predictions aided the Jarawas in foraging through the forest in times of rain and complete darkness. The *elengeto*'s special power is attributed to the fact that they had retained and stabilized the *dama* in their bodies so that it showed no signs of flickering or dying out. This special blessing from the spirits and ancestors of an ever-glowing *dama* is called *tukejaya*.[13] By taking care of such distinguished elders till the last day of life, Jarawas ensure the continuity of community.

---

[13] See Pandya, *Above the Forest* for the significance of *torale* dream travellers among the Onges of Little Andaman who share many cultural affinities with Jarawas of Middle and South Andaman. The importance of sleeping and dreaming in accordance with cultural prescriptions is of great significance among the Onges, much as it is among the Jarawas. For further comparative details, see Vishvajit Pandya, 'Forest Smells and Spider Webs: Ritualized Dream Interpretation among Andaman Islanders', *Dreaming: Journal of the Association for the Study of Dreams*, 14, 2–3 (2003), 136–50.

Even when they die, the bodies of the *elengeto* retain their significance. After the secondary burial of the *elengeto,* certain bones from his body, the *edang,* are recovered and shared among the descendants within the band.[14] Generally *edangs* are sections of finger bones or sections of the vertebral column that the male heads of an extended family tie around their waist when they go on hunting expeditions. *Edangs* used as amulets are seen as a means to enhance the hunter's own *dama* so that they do not get cold or scared in the darkness of the forest and can get back to their camps safely. In a way, the *edangs,* as bone parts, are regarded as sources of light and heat that guide and sustain the young Jarawas in the forest.[15] Jarawas believe that by retaining the *elengeto's* skull and lower jawbone inside the shelter, they can compensate for the waning *dama* among their living descendants and ensure an adequate reserve of heat and light in the forest.

In the Jarawa scheme of life in the forest, the ordered world between earth and sky is perceived as layers or shelters containing, regulating or mediating various sources of light or *dama.* This ordered mediation of light effects a transitional condition in the forest that is never completely dark nor completely bright. This symbolic connection from the natural world is recapitulated and mapped on to the cultural world by seeing the stars in the sky to be homologous to fireflies in the forest. Both the stars and the fireflies are looked upon as agents who help sustain the order of light in the forest. The order that ensures that absolute darkness or absolute light are never possible, for both conditions are symptomatic of disorder and impending chaos.

---

[14] On death, the living Jarawa becomes a spirit and resides in *uppa chaddha,* the place above the sky where the firefly and stars do not blink but constantly glow. Neither sun nor moon moves in this sky. The path going up to any living body never knows this perpetually bright sky, only fireflies can guide the dead body's residual body (*dama*) up to this place. This vertical pathway connects the 'other sky' with the Jarawa world under the sky and under the forest canopy. It is along this path that the spirits and fireflies come down to the forest, and as they are confused by the dawn and dusk, they get entrapped in food items they try to gather from the forest. When and if a spirit or a firefly is trapped in the woman's body, and crabs are consumed around the same time, conception of a foetus is initiated. Being pregnant is thought to impart nurturance to the child growing invisibly, but with a capacity to internally glow and be warm once it becomes visible in the forest as a new child. Cutting of the umbilical cord is therefore regarded as way to increase the collective internal *dama* of a social group, and all group members are keen to take care of the newly born child. This care and concern is no different from the attitude Jarawas have for smoldering fire, except the child is transformed by the glow and heat of the parents and will be transmitted as the materialized heat and glow to their children's children.

[15] Whenever possible, the band would attempt to recover the deceased *elengeto's* lower jawbone (*petang*) and the skull (*goterangey*). The lower jawbone and skull are worn as protective ornaments signifying the chief mourners for about two weeks and then carefully tucked in the rafters of the shelters built in the forest.

In this scheme of organizing the layers of world as series of shelters the principle of light connects not by complete presence or absence but by creating transitional phases between darkness and brightness. It is the transitions that are the ordering principles. One of the elders chose to explain this order of light in the forest to me in greater detail. He said, 'in our three layered world, the centre or the forest and the sky above and sea below is connected by of heat, humidity and light. However it is light not at its brightest nor at its weakest that holds all of it together, it is light that is somewhere in between':

but what about the ways in which this order light helps us to move in the forest, help us hunt and find our way back? Do you know that these are some of the first lessons we give our children – they must follow the order of light to move in the forest, one false step and they will be forever lost.

Moving through the lightscape

For Jarawas in the forest, living and movement is quintessentially determined by shifting light conditions. The east-west cardinal points are known as *ehaley* and *bacheyagey*, respectively. These two directions form the horizontal axis traversed by the Jarawa in the course of their hunting and foraging activities. The west signals the onset of darkness while the east signals its end. The practice of movement along the east-west axis is a transposition of the movement of the moon followed by the sun. It is this direction of movement that makes possible the experience of seasons caused by the winds that move along the north-south axis of the island. Seasons are distinguished as being warm, relatively dry and uncomfortably bright. The *Etelaham-ing*, or north winds, bring in the northeast monsoon during months of September to October, causing the forest to become cold, dark and dry while the *Katiehye-ing*, or the south winds, blow in during April to May, bringing in the southeast monsoon. It is these winds from the south that make the forest reach both its wettest and hottest points.[16]

---

[16] The experienced seasonal cycle for Jarawas is not divided into 'summer time' and 'winter time' on a landscape, but expressed as the 'wet duration' (*thouwe-egamey*) and 'dry duration' (*thumey-egamey*) on a lightscape. Wet duration (June to November) is regarded as the dark *githaley* phase when clouds often block sunlight in the forest, and during night the stars are not clearly visible in the sky. But most significantly, it is the duration in the forest when the fireflies become invisible as it is their prime breeding time.

Figure 7.1 Author, Jarawa elder Tahapahad, a group of younger men and AAJVS official Anup Mondal discussing images of Jarawa shelters at the Kadamtalla Medical Centre, November 2012.

The forest, or *kuwey* as I came to know through my conversations with the Jarawa elders of Kadamtalla, is not just a landscape but a distinctive lightscape that is actualized and made meaningful through a range of quotidian practices and rituals. Young Jarawas are socialized in a culture that provides fundamental orientation to *echeley* or pathways through the forest that help them locate resources (*uhelo*) that are nature's constants in the forest. For Jarawas, it is the capacity to perceive and locate resources that necessitates the acknowledgement of fluctuations in the conditions of light. A corollary to this shift in light conditions is also the ability to sense changes in humidity and temperature.

One of the early lessons that Jarawa parents give their children is that the forest is never brightly illuminated nor completely dark. It will always envelop living things, plants and animals within its deep recesses, and children have to locate these by moving around in differing conditions of illumination. One of the Jarawa parents I spoke with told me:

Our children and grandchildren must know all the pathways in the forest as the forest experiences differ from night-time to day-time they have to adjust to locating resources that are visible and what has become invisible for a duration.

Each pathway *echeley* leads to a particular kind of resource and movements along the pathways ensure an infinite number of possibilities of finding resources through all seasons and directions in any given situation, as long as the light conditions are never constant. Jarawa children are encouraged to be inquisitive and to move around and find resources for themselves. Such qualities are curiously described as facilitating their capacity to 'absorb darkness'.

Both complete darkness and complete light constitute an anomalous or disorderly and even a dangerous situation. For the Jarawas, the sense of control in the forest originates from the fact that by manipulating the sources of light they can mediate the conditions of darkness and brightness, thereby altering the related experience of temperature and moisture. Jarawas are socialized to locate resources by following trails in the forest. As the light orients the way to perceive and locate a particular resource, it helps to create an economy of resources that is either always present or substitutable. As complete brightness is never possible in the forest, so is complete absence of resources an absolute improbability. This makes the forest not just a feature of the landscape but a distinct, actualized, meaningful *lightscape*. For us, a 'given' map guides our movement and light facilitates that movement through an ordered landscape. So we have streetlights, vehicles with lights and torchlights to negotiate movements within a space that may have otherwise been disorienting. We have two-dimensional maps that represent and index actual space, and the user of the map has to figure out their path of movement by correlating mental and actual space.

For the Jarawas, however, shifting light conditions create a map of movements but not of space. Light conditions Jarawa movement along mutable spaces that appear and disappear, making possible the visibility of what is desired and what may be expected or incidentally acquired while moving.[17] For Jarawas, the presence of shifting light conditions from dawn to dusk, and the transition through them creates a map of movements whereby different resource locations are indexed and plotted. This suits the capacity of the Jarawas as hunter-gatherers to maximize the gathering of multiple resources each time they undertake a movement, as it makes possible to get what is desired and what may be expected or what may be incidentally acquired.

This is essential, as the contours or bounds of space are never the same or a given constant, but change according to light conditions. For the

---

[17] Cf. Vishvajit Pandya, 'Movement and Space: Andamanese Cartography', *American Ethnologist*, 17, 4 (1990), 775–97.

Jarawa, whose political economy is founded on the principles of a structured lightscape and map of movements, it is seldom said 'I am going to
forest to get pig or honey'. Jarawas just say 'I am going to the forest', and
they look around for what can be located, gathered and brought back.
For Jarawas unhindered movement is a fundamental condition of life.
Movement in their forest ensures that they always find something.

The elderly Kongoney, who has earned the notoriety of leading many
Jarawa attacks and ransacking villages near Tirrur, said:

We know that pigs are found in the deep forest with dense undergrowth and
creepers all around, but in order to get to that point the forest trail takes us
through in-between spaces that may not be dark and humid but still have tall trees
that bear honeycombs to bring back even if one fails to get a pig. These trees give
both shelter and resources. But think of moving through spaces that have no trees
at all! Some times while moving around we take your roads to the settlement, to
places with no trees nor shrubs, only fields; no insects nor birds just a place that
has bright light even when all around is dark; and there's nobody to get anything
from, so we gather whatever we find.[18]

In contrast to the cultural construct of life under the dense canopy of
forest, the settlements are seen by the Jarawas as *cholob* or clearings where
there is nothing save scrubs, bushes or just grass. For Jarawas settlements
are devoid of trees and hence perpetually awash with bright light,
whether from the sun or from electric lights. This *dama*, or light, is
blinding and not enabling as it is in the forest. The light conditions of
settlements, in other words, violate the entire order of their lives and
practices as they know them in the forest. The 'blinding lights' of the
settlement are deeply anomalous in their scheme of things.

In Jarawa conceptualization, moving in the forest implies a practice
capacitated by a keen ability to negotiate shades of visibility and invisi-
bility. Movement connects clusters of points across places. But movement in a cleared, brightly lit settlement is capable of connecting only
those points in a space that is illuminated. This lessens the potentiality of
finding multiple resources in unexpected locations. The illumination
of the cleared space devoid of forest in fact limits the availability of
resources. Jarawas therefore express:

For some to eat well, implies getting everything together – pigs, fish, honey and
tubers – but none of this is ever really found together – there are seasons there are
times – you have to wait, search and then find. When we are in the hospitals or
other 'clearings' we get the same stuff everyday – rice and biscuits – you don't
have search for these, you just get them! There's no fun in getting the same things
everyday! To look for things and then get them satisfies hunger and helps us

[18] Field Notes, Tirrur, December 2012.

sleep! We know that the forest has a lot of things – we must know how to find them! To search and then to find is a way of life in our forest.

For Jarawas, to reside in the cleared settlement would be an enculturation that would impact on every aspect of their social and cultural reproduction, though a short visit to the settlement is a possible mechanics to aid stop-gap consumption.

To be in the forest is to be in a space that sustains Jarawa culture through oscillating time, light, temperature and humidity, but to be out in the settlement is only a temporal experience that is devoid of altering conditions. So the outsiders' belief that life is hard and there is a shortage of food that drives the Jarawa to become dependent on the cleared landscape is a misconception. In fact, the resource base in the forest for Jarawas is a polythetic region that overlaps and becomes visible as they move around in it. For the Jarawas the forest conditions allow their understanding of a fractal space within which they are socialized to negotiate and sustain a sense of control.[19]

Their experience of light in the forest produces the perception of light in the settlement as a hindrance to a Jarawa's sense of self, which, as I gathered, was embedded in their capacity to move at will. This capacity was sustained in the forests through their deep understanding of the conditions of light within it. The imperative to engage with the order of the light in the forest, to negotiate the pathways that were sustained by it and to know of the risks of transgressions was a source of their agency in it. For the Jarawas, the sense of control in the forest originated from the understanding that the changing conditions of light in the forest could be negotiated by altering the temperature of the body through carefully calibrated phases of movement and rest. Jarawas view light conditions in the forest landscape and cleared landscape (settlement) as radically different. In the forest, there are distinct transitory phases of light experienced as dawn and dusk, but in the settlement these transitory conditions remain blurred and uncertain. This in turn constrains their capacities to negotiate movement or maintain order.

The way Jarawas see light and the role that it plays in their lives not only governs where and how they move but also provides them with a distinctive cultural identity and an argument to resist any move to push them permanently into a settlement. The perception as well as experience of light within the forest sustains a Jarawa political economy that

---

[19] The Jarawas as a group have historically dealt with the uncertainty of resources. They have responded to uncertain times by visiting the settlements that are regarded as anomalous and irregular spaces; spaces within a fractal geometry that we would see as part of a Euclidean boundary-defined space.

anchors them within their own spaces and sustains a flow of exchange relations among themselves. For Jarawas, the experience of oscillating light conditions and movement in accordance to these becomes an essential life-practice.[20]

Dwelling in the lightscape

The *chaddha*, or the typical Jarawa hut, is a deceptively simple structure.[21] Yet when one looks closer, its complexities reveal a different story. It is an embodiment of the Jarawa appropriation of light and related conditions by their culture. Each of the three Jarawa bands has its ascribed traditional territory that they utilize for foraging and ritual practices, sustained by rights and obligations, but the strict control of remaining within a specific territory is never imposed or maintained.

[20] The significance of movement and the cultural transformation of forms of social organization have been a focus in earlier classical ethnographic accounts. For example: E. E. Evans-Pritchard's idea of 'oecology' derived from Nuer ethnography; Marcel Mauss and Henri Beuchat's Eskimo seasonal cycle; and Edmund Leach's 'Gumla and Gumsa' among the Kachins of highland Burma. See E. E. Evans-Pritchard, *The Nuer: A Description of the Modes of Livelihood and Political Institution of a Nilotic People* (Oxford: Clarendon Press, 1940); Marcel Mauss and Henri Beuchat, *Seasonal Variations of the Eskimos: A Study in Social Morphology* (London: Routledge and Kegan Paul, 1979); Edmund Leach, *Political Systems of Highland Burma* (London: LSE Monograph on Social Anthropology No. 44, 1954). One of the major concerns of these ethnographies was the colonial administration's concern with governing the cultural groups that challenged the notion of fixed locality and territory.

[21] Within the forest in different locations are clusters of shelters identified as *chaddha*. Each patrilineally related family forms a *chaddha* within a part of the forest. Each band has its traditional territory that it utilizes for foraging and ritual practices, but the strict control of remaining within a specific territory is never imposed or maintained. This is primarily because in marriage alliances, often formed in the course of preferred marriage patterns, individuals are expected to sustain the rule of *chaddha* exogamy. Nonetheless individual identification with a *chaddha* is reinforced and rights and obligations institutionalize loyalty to a subgroup and band. Every individual's umbilical cord after birth and bones after death are subject to secondary burial a and are always placed in their father's *chaddha*. This has made it possible for Jarawas to resist the outsiders in their forest since the colonization of the island started in 1858 and has continued into present times. This ideology of Jarawas as 'our forest' has its origin in the marking of shelters as nodal points in the forest that form coordinates on the landscape that facilitate exchange relations and interdependence among bands for sharing resources and maintaining porous borders between the political boundaries drawn within the forest. Within the Jarawa Tribal, two distinctive forms of residential structures are built at different specified times and in different locations. Over generations and year after year, the different groups, now associated with the Middle Strait, Tirrur and Kadamtalla, structure and practice their movements from about thirty of these locations. These traditional locations are either in the coastal areas or in the forest interiors. As the locations are fixed over the years, all the *chaddha* have distinct names and within the groups serve as indexical markers of points of origin and destination. Often individuals invoke the name of the location to identify kinship connections.

Each cluster of shelters is a nodal point in the forest that coordinates in a lightscape providing visible channels of movements (pathways under the forest canopy) and sustains interdependent relations that transcend the state-imposed, fixed political boundaries and borders such as Reserve forest and buffer zones.

The movement of the sun and moon along the east-west axis not only creates day and night light conditions but also marks the cardinal points of north-south that are associated with the movement of winds that add brightness to summer months and darkness to winter. Furthermore, the light conditions of the two basic seasonal durations are not only experienced in terms of temperature but also of moisture. Brightness implies increasing dryness, and darkness increased moisture. The movement of the moon and sun creates the photodynamic conditions whereby the forest undergoes a shift of temperature setting up a related thermodynamics. These two changing cycles further impact on the bodily experience of moisture and temperature via rains and winds around the shelters made in the forest by the Jarawas. The engagement with the forest lightscape is based on a fused cognition whereby inner living shelter, that is the huts, are constructed in accordance with the conditions of light sustained by the shelter (forest canopy) outside.

For Jarawas, every shelter and every site on which shelters are built must address regular patterns of darkness and light as well as the in-between times when usual light conditions are disturbed. One of these moments of challenge could be a sudden phase of darkness brought in by clouds blown in from different directions. It is at these moments that the stars in the sky and fireflies in the forest become invisible. Any condition of sudden darkness is also a deeply 'precarious' (*piyojeteh*) moment and laden with all kinds of danger. In the midst of this phase of disturbing darkness, Jarawas find security in their large shelters, with other group members spending days sitting around a burning fire waiting patiently for the arrival of *bonealey* or the season of bright light and warmth.

According to these experienced changes in conditions related to light, Jarawas construct two distinct *chaddha* with two different kinds of *wilpo* (or thatching). The shelter of the *chaddha* and the shelter offered by the forest canopy above it produce variable experiences of light, moisture and temperature for the Jarawa body.

In accordance with changes in the forest lightscape, large dark and dry shelters are constructed during bright and wet conditions, while smaller shelters with more slanted thatching are built during the hot and dry season. Seasonal change and variations in food resources also lead Jarawas to move and shift residence between coastline and interior forest.

Figure 7.2 Two basic architectural forms built by the Jarawas: *tohato-chaddha* and *tutiey-chaddha*. Drawing: Vishvajit Pandya.

The two basic architectural forms are, first, *tohato-chaddha*, with a circular arrangement of wooden poles that supports a very tightly intermeshed circular dome shaped roof. These *chaddhas* are relatively labour-intensive products and are seldom dismantled. They are maintained well to last a long time. In the interiors of the *tohato-chaddha*, space is managed and demarcated in keeping with the increase or decrease in the number of family members. Within the large *chaddha* smaller nuclear families who maintain their own fires can enjoy their own separate niches. The *tohato-chaddha*, in sum, is a stand-alone structure with all the nuclear families occupying smaller sectors under the circular roof. If required, the occupants would increase the circumference of the thatch to accommodate another family who might be visiting their *chaddha*. The other architectural structure is known as *tutiey-chaddha*, and it tends to be often disassembled and reinstalled or freshly made each season. The *tutiey-chaddha* is always associated with one nuclear family under each shelter and often series of them are built in close proximity within a campsite.[22] Sleeping patterns and the capacity to move are factored into

---

[22] Fundamental to Jarawa sociality are relations of *ankey-eh* created by collaborative movements to seek resources and share these with those who cannot move or see. Both the individual Jarawa body as well as the collective social body are aligned by bodily practices to *dama* and its material manifestations. Each individual body is subject to the experience of changing temperatures, variations in humidity and shifting light conditions, but as a member of the group, the orientation is to collaborate and support the collective relations of *ankhey-eh*. Relations of *ankhey-eh* also govern the organization of space under the forest canopy. The thatched structures (*wilpo*) that Jarawas make to live in are divided into three parts to structure bodily practices in relation to light. Major concerns are that when not moving one must have a specified place, or *itet* (sleeping area). The sleeping area that bears the possibility of bringing together husband and wife as the mythical sun and moon is constructed after careful consideration of shifting light conditions under the shelter. The sleeping area must accommodate a place to burn fire (*thuhaa*). A distinction is made between fire that burns to illuminate and fire that cooks food during the day. Different areas of the shelter are demarcated in accordance with the specific positioning of the fireplace. By maintaining the sleeping area and fireplace, the

the spatial arrangements made within the campsite to sustain social relations among families, bands and individuals.

In the centre of these large shelters there is a common hearth for all the occupants to share, and at the centre of the thatch, a gap is left for the billowing smoke to escape. The design principle that goes into the making of the *tohato-chaddha* structures the *wilpo* in such a way that it accommodates all the families as one congregation. The *wilpo* is meant to approximate the encompassing forest canopy itself. In the case of the *tutiey-chaddha*, each shelter holds a smaller nuclear family. Each of these families is meant to have its own sources of fire. This is often a piece of smouldering wood that is carried along from place to place. The cooking fire, however, is kept outside the lean-to within the ground enclosed by series of other lean-tos, which are arranged in a circle. A separate singular lean-to or larger circular thatch is always kept aside for the socially productive but sexually unproductive individuals. These lean-tos are separated along the lines of gender and age. These are known as *jepaleyeh* and *yawaeley* for the teenage boys and girls, respectively. With the change in seasons, Jarawas move their residential locations. Sometimes families congregate in a single location, while at others they scatter out into different locations. In every new location, however, the two forms of built shelters recapitulate the social rules of maintaining and regulating their sources of light.

The design elements in each hut are meant to regulate light, heat and moisture conditions. These are changed or modified in accordance with seasons, patterns of movement and, more importantly, with the particular kind of forest cover near their campsites. As seasonal changes are experienced within the system of changing light conditions, the residential *chaddhas* are shifted in consultation with both the families living in it and the whole band.

It is important to remember that when the Jarawas consider the shifting conditions of light, they do not consider the mere question of visibility. An optimum light condition is one in which the interior light or *dama* in each Jarawa body is kept alive. The elderly whose *dama* may be waning might

---

living area (*thula*) is actually structured with different kinds of shelters (*wilpo*) in accordance with the number of people in them. So relations of *ankhey-eh* among Jarawas orchestrate actions and modulate the light conditions that makes possible all that can be seen and done during that phase. Jarawas set up smoldering logs within the forest canopy so that fire is always accessible to translocating groups; much like petrol pumps along the roadside, a light and heat (*dama*) circuit is set up between the forest residential shelters. Bones of distinguished elders placed across the residential camps complete the flow of constant glow to make possible locating resources within the ceaselessly shifting light conditions of the forest.

seek out a different shelter while the younger ones keep together. The design and the location of the *chaddhas* are meant not merely to facilitate dwelling in the forest but dwelling within its structured lightscape.

It is this manipulation of natural conditions under the forest canopy and the sustenance of optimum body conditions under every *wilpo* that Jarawas seek, moving to different locations and creating appropriate living conditions. All these considerations of space, place, movement and design seem almost like an elaborate orchestration of light in the forest. In this landscape, the stars and fireflies are indexical of order. It is the order that sustains bodily practices, movement, social relations, knowledge of the forest and life in it at large. Each and every element in the natural and social world associated with *dama* is an encompassed lumen, within the larger presence or absence of light. The sustenance of lumen is socially structured and culturally practiced in the habits of moving and dwelling.[23] Structures built within the forest are an architectural (cultural) strategy that allows Jarawas to engage and appropriate light and heat from a range of sources like the sun, cooking fires or smouldering resin. Each source of light is subject to the shifting relationship between the place inside the residential structures and the space they are located in.

As a concluding point to this elaborate description of the principles of Jarawa dwelling, the elder Kongoney said very categorically, that settlement or the place of the *enen* (the outsider in general) could never be theirs. Its lights were threatening to the way of the life of the Jarawa:

Since our fathers and grandfathers were children even have been coming around our forest and clearing it and making fields and settling down! They continue to come in large numbers, and increase the area of the clearings – they build houses and never want to leave! We find it hard to believe that they stay in a place in spite of the changing seasons and changing lights in the sky. See, *enen* do not feel such changes as they stay in places that are devoid or darkness and moisture – they cut forests, build solid roofs, contain water, cover their body with clothes and even when it rains they carry an umbrella – The *enen* are strange people!

Conclusion

There is a long and undocumented history of Jarawa resistance to what could be described broadly as 'state lighting' that needs to be revisited at

---

[23] Lumen implies the amount of light that is contained in a place and depends on the distance from the source of light. The cultural idea of light being contained in different places is something that impacts the daily activity among Jarawas; the lumen becomes a unit to be composed and coordinated, much like the sounds and tones are combined to create an orchestra's sound.

this point. Villagers remember that in the mid 1970s Jarawas used to attempt to cut down wooden lamp posts at the fringes of the settlements and were often electrocuted. The recovery of charred Jarawa bodies was duly recorded in police files. Settlers regarded these Jarawa actions as early forms of Jarawa resistance to artificial illumination at the fringes of their forest world. Others attributed this act of the Jarawas as motivated by sheer hostility. The presence of electric lights at the approaches to the settlements impeded what was officially recorded as 'Jarawa raids' into the villages. In the 1980s, the Andaman and Nicobar administration, on the advice of the police department, had taken up the idea of mounting revolving searchlights on twenty-foot-high scaffolds at the Bush Police outposts on the periphery of Tirrur in South Andaman. These police outposts were selected for their proximity to the zones demarcating the Jarawa Reserve forest and outside settlements.

The original argument was that the frequent use of light beams would reinforce the differentiation of forest space and state-demarcated settlement space. This would check and limit Jarawa movement into the villages and therefore avoid incidents of theft or physical attacks. One week after the first trial of the prototype started, some members from the Jarawa community came to the site in the early hours of morning, climbed up the post and destroyed all the light fixtures. After the incident, the project was terminated. In the year 2000, when many Jarawas were brought to the G. B. Pant hospital in Port Blair for treatment, they would always insist on turning off the lights. Light bulbs were also the targets of stone pelting and sometimes even the tube lights at the settlement walkways were taken down and destroyed. There are individuals who have deep scars from such attempts and are often talked about as being 'brave and *not* foolish'.[24]

Nowadays, Jarawas have understood well the danger of electrocution. This awareness is partly due to the fact that during the construction of the Andaman Trunk Road in late 1980s, construction contractors would set up live electrical wires on the ground, connected to a generator to ward off Jarawas from pilfering the equipment at construction sites. These acts of resistance to state lighting regimes reinforce the Jarawa perception of the settlement as a space with anomalous light conditions

---

[24] For Jarawas, electric lights have no 'real heat', and are not affected by winds or rain. They never blink but are either on or not; light 'just is there or not there', making it non-conducive within the Jarawa worldview, where the emphasis is on looking and searching in light conditions that undergo transitions, and where shadows become taller and shorter. It is precisely for this reason that Jarawas who have incorporated into their material life many items provided to them by state and settlers have generally resisted the use of battery torchlights.

and hence one of potential disorder. The settlement's cleared landscape tends to be always in an extended, illuminated and constant stable condition. Here, movements could only facilitate bringing and taking things, but never finding or locating all that potentially could be found in the darker recesses of the space.

Jarawas believe that ordered luminosity in the forest is the result of the presence of stars and fireflies. It is their presence that makes possible the materialization of resources. In contrast with this is, the constantly illuminated settlement landscape where fireflies die out, resources remain limited to specific locations. In the settlement there are no alternatives that can be located, there are no unexpected pathways to be found. For Jarawas, to dwell in the forest lightscape is to be in a space that sustains their lives by helping them negotiate the shifting movements of time, light, temperature, and humidity and finding the right resources at the right time. To live in the settlement would be akin to plunging themselves in a space of perpetual disorder. The settlement therefore could be a place to visit and forage but not one in which the Jarawa could live.

Welfare workers of the AAJVS have often told me that Jarawas demand various things from time to time, depending on what catches their fancy at any given moment. This could be biscuits, rice, clothing and even matchboxes, but never battery-operated flashlights. The state welfare agency was once keen to provide Jarawas with cells and torchlights as a dole or gift item, but this was one thing that the Jarawas never accepted. Some of them said that electrical light bulbs, as well as battery lights, provided an un-flickering glow, that it was scary. In recent years, Jarawas have become increasingly resentful of the many intrusions into their territory by poachers and other outsiders. The poachers, they argue, enter the Reserve in the depths of the night armed with powerful flashlights. They cut through the undergrowth and branches to make place for the traps they set up in the forest. As they make their way through the forest cover with the 'un-flickering flash lights' in their hands, they kill all the fireflies that come in their way. As a younger Jarawa man said, 'if the fireflies are killed, the order of the light in the forest is destroyed and the Jarawas' life in it is threatened'.

So what could the Jarawa community argue in favour of their insistence on being in the forest lightscape as their desired space of dwelling? The settlement is a place worthy of visiting and only at early hours of dawn, when electric lights are turned off, when the stars and fireflies in the forest have stopped blinking, when light conditions are ambivalent, and when the moon is fading out and the sun is right behind. To live in the forest lightscape is to dwell in a space where conditions of light fluctuate and order can be made from a sequence of transformations, transitions and the contingent realities of the world of experience.

For the Jarawas, the light conditions in the settlement are akin to what prevails in the far reaches of the *uppa chaddha*, the place beyond the sky, where it is cold dry and inhabited by none other than spirits. The cleared settlement, perpetually bright and lit up by electricity, and with no fireflies, is a spatial embodiment of disorganization and chaos. This forms the keystone to Jarawa resistance to the settlement. For the Jarawas, the forest lightscape is conducive to the fluidity of practice and social life while the state and welfare agency's sedentarist reason takes the view that the survival of any social group is best ensured by containing and anchoring it to a place. This of course suits the imperatives of welfare and the agenda of development embedded in it. A welfare apparatus demands a population to be targeted within a mapped and bounded space rather than in a space marked by movements and shifting borders. To remain fixed in a place within a space is also conducive for the state to exercise surveillance and restraint. The Jarawas' resistance to state illumination as well as its perceptions of the settlement perhaps explain its sustained resistance to the outsiders' efforts to curb their rights to inhabit their own territory.

What Jarawas see as an important feature of their own concept of space is its capacity to sustain the dialectics of light and darkness and thereby maintain order. They understand the optimal conditions of their survival as residing in their capacity to inhabit spaces as lightscapes that order their livelihoods, their social and interpersonal relationships and above all their increasingly complex relationship with the outsider. The controversy about settling Jarawa outside the forests, however, remains alive both in Tirrur and Kadamtalla.[25] Here, Bengali Matua settlers, many of whom came into the Islands in the aftermath of Partition, continue to argue that land can only rightfully belong to those who cultivate it. In other words, labour is a critical element in the advancement of any claim to entitlement to land. They suggest that despite being displaced from East Pakistan they were able to make their homes in the Andaman Islands by tilling its soil and invoking the presence of the Lord in their hearths.[26] For them, the quotidian struggles of the Jarawas in the forest mean little. They remain unconvinced that the Jarawas have any legitimate right to forest land. Like their colonial forbears, they too believe that

---

[25] Conversations with Bengali settlers, Keshub Rai and Satis Pramanik, during fieldwork conducted with Madhumita Mazumdar in Kadamtalla, 2011.

[26] Rai reminded me of an important teaching of the Guruchand Thakur: *Haathe Kaam, mukhe Naam*, salvation for the Matua lay in a life of toil and worship. See Chapter 6.

the Jarawa ambivalence towards the settlement has little basis in reason. Madhumita Mazumdar's nuanced elaboration of the Matua sect in Chapter 6 urges us towards an appreciation of the complex knots of culture, land and affect that produce compelling narratives of belonging. For Jarawas however, it is the stories of the fireflies and the order of the light in the forest that conveys their current position towards the settlement. The settlement remains a place that is both integral and alien to their lives. It remains a place to visit but not to reside. Outsiders view this as a deep contradiction. But for the Jarawa elders I spoke to, the invocation of the forest 'lightscape' and their affective ties to it remain their best response to the reasons of the state and the 'enen' for the moment.

Part III

Imagined landscapes

8   Visual representations of the penal colony

Clare Anderson

Introduction

A few years after the East India Company first mapped the Andamans, in 1771, it established a settlement at a site it named Port Cornwallis, after Admiral William Cornwallis, brother of the Governor-General and Commander-in-Chief of India, Charles. Perhaps buoyed by the recent establishment of a penal settlement at Port Jackson in New South Wales, shortly afterwards the Company shipped about 300 Indian convicts to the Islands to bolster the free settlement.[1] Inclement weather and the ravages of malaria proved too challenging for the settlers and convicts, however, and the Company abandoned the Islands in 1796.[2] In the meantime Lieutenant Robert Hyde Colebrooke, a talented artist who had surveyed the islands alongside Captain Alexander Kyd and Lieutenant Archibald Blair during 1789 to 1790, produced a series of watercolour paintings of the settlement. They take as their subject the maritime power of the Company, as signified through prominent representations of ships, stores and flags. A picture of a fenced-in garden also claims visually the taming of wild, native space.[3]

This visual interest in the Andamans did not disappear with the abandonment of the colony, but rather gathered momentum with the decision to recolonize the Islands in 1857. Indeed, the survey party appointed for the purpose of choosing the best site for a second settlement not only had the founding president of the Bengal photographic society at its head (Inspector-General of Prisons, F. J. Mouat), but included his personal acquaintance, photographer Oscar Mallitte. Mallitte took eleven

[1] J. Duncan, Resident Benares, to G. M. Barlow, secretary to government Bengal, 10 July 1794, Bengal Judicial, 25 July 1794, P.128.12 IOR; Extracts from report of Captain Blair, 14 December 1789, JMS/18/45 1859 RGS.

[2] Copy of the first part of a report from Major Kyd relative to the Settlements at Prince of Wales Island and the Andamans with its appendix, 4 March 1795, G/34/1 ff. 379–518, IOR.

[3] The most complete set of R. H. Colebrooke's pen-and-ink watercolours can be found in the National Library of Australia, PIC T2940 NK170LOC 6102–5.

photographs of the islands during the expedition and had them printed, mounted and presented to the Government of India on the party's return to Calcutta. The subjects of Mallitte's photographs were the landscapes and peoples of the Islands, and they included images of Barren Island, Port Blair, Ross Island and 'Three Views of John Andaman (a native of one of the Islands)'. One of the latter images was subsequently circulated in European scientific circles, which at the time were debating whether the origins of mankind might be explained through theories of mono- or polygenesis.[4] The context of the production of both Colebrooke's watercolours and Mallitte's 1857 photographs was popular interest in the visual reproduction of a hitherto little-known space and its indigenous peoples.

A number of scholars have explored the photographing of the indigenous peoples of the Andamans, and its relationship to the production of global histories of race, the intimacies of colonial contact and indigenous resistance and agency. Drawing on a rich colonial archive, visual anthropologists, historians and sociologists have explored the anthropometric photography of two British officers E. H. Man and M. V. Portman, active during the second half of the nineteenth century, in most depth.[5] Images of the penal colony and convicts, in contrast, have been used only for illustrative purposes, and have never been subject to rigorous analysis in their own right. This chapter takes a new approach to these pictures. I suggest that officially produced images represented the Islands as a space ripe for colonization and 'civilization'; and then as a place of colonial orderliness, discipline and control. The images downplayed the

[4] Secretary to government of India C. Beadon to Inspector General of Jails Bengal, F. J. Mouat, 17 April 1858, P.188.52 Home (Judicial), 23 April 1858, IOR; *Selections from the Records of the Government of India (Home Department) No. XXV: The Andaman Islands, with Notes on Barren Island*, Calcutta, 1859, 28–9, V/3199, IOR; Photographic Drawings of the Andaman Islands (1857–8), Queen's Collection, Windsor Castle. The remaining images are: 'Port Cornwallis'; 'Remains of the Old Settlement, Chatham Island, Port Cornwallis'; 'Native Hut, Chatham Island, Port Cornwallis'; and 'Implements and Weapons of the Andaman Islanders'. The Royal Collection lacks two of the originals: 'Watering Cove, Blair Island' and 'Blair Harbour, North Shore'. For a more detailed account of the photographing of 'John Andaman', see Clare Anderson, 'Oscar Mallitte's Andaman Photographs, 1857–8', *History Workshop Journal* 67, 1 (2009), 152–72.

[5] Elizabeth Edwards, 'Science Visualized: E. H. Man in the Andaman Islands', in Elizabeth Edwards (ed.), *Anthropology and Photography, 1860–1920* (London: Royal Anthropological Institute, 1994), 108–21; Zita van der Beek and Marcel Vellinga, 'Man the Collector: Salvaging Andamanese and Nicobarese Culture through Objects', *Journal of the History of Collections* 17, 2 (2005), 135–53; John Falconer, 'Ethnographical Photography in India 1850–1900', *Photographic Collector* 5, 1 (1984); Vishvajit Pandya, *In the Forest: Visual and Material Worlds of Andamanese History: 1858–1906* (Lanham, MD: University Press of America, 2009); Satadru Sen, 'Savage Bodies, Civilized Pleasures: M. V. Portman and the Andamanese', *American Ethnologist* 36, 2 (2009), 364–79; Sita Venkateswar, *Development and Ethnocide: Colonial Practices in the Andaman Islands* (Copenhagen: IWGA, 2004).

forced-labour aspect of convict work and the violence of the penal colony. These representational functions were bolstered through the widespread publication of engraved copies of popular pictures. Further, I want to propose that Andaman images – including these official pictures, but also those taken privately for personal or familial consumption – were material objects with meanings beyond image *per se*.[6] This raises other, interrelated issues, including how photographs and photograph albums moved around, across space and over time; their role in forging and maintaining emotional ties between family and kin; how they compromised the desired isolation of the penal colony; their continued use many years after they were taken (and, often, mounted in albums) in the remembering of the past; and their visual communication of social and cultural aspects of colonialism that are otherwise unavailable in textual archives. Taking these themes together, I suggest that the content, form, reproduction, transformation and circulation of Andaman photographs and photographic albums constitute what Felix Driver and Luciana Martins have called in other contexts extended visual transactions rather than linear visual projections.[7]

A(n) (dis)orderly colony

The permanent colonization of the Andamans in 1858 coincided with the development of photography, a visual form that seemed to promise unprecedented opportunities to reproduce the peoples and landscapes of empire for scientific and ethnographic purposes. It has been described in the context of colonial India as 'indexical', as holding out the promise of a value-free, objective – and thus 'scientific' – form of representation.[8] As sociologists Lorraine Daston and Peter Galison have argued, photography seemed to create new boundaries of visual truth, to challenge art as a mode of visual interpretation, and to underpin an epistemological shift to what they call 'mechanical objectivity'.[9] Of course, photography

---

[6] Elizabeth Edwards and Janice Hart, 'Introduction: Photographs as Objects', in Elizabeth Edwards and Janice Hart (eds.), *Photographs Objects Histories: On the Materiality of Images* (London: Routledge, 2004), 1–16, quote on 3.

[7] Felix Driver and Luciana Martins, 'Views and Visions of the Tropical World', in Felix Driver and Luciana Martins (eds.), *Tropical Visions in an Age of Empire* (Chicago: University of Chicago Press, 2005), 3–22.

[8] Christopher Pinney, *Camera Indica: The Social Life of Indian Photographs* (London: Reaktion, 1997), 20. For the development of photography in nineteenth-century India, see also John Falconer, 'Photography in Nineteenth-Century India', in C. A. Bayly (ed.), *The Raj: India and the British 1600–1947* (London: National Portrait Gallery, 1990).

[9] Lorraine Daston and Peter Galison, 'The Image of Objectivity', *Representations* 40 (1992), 81–128.

requires human agency, in both the photographers' choice and composition of subject matter, and in the reproduction and interpretation of the images. It is this, rather than its apparent neutrality as a representational form, which interests me here.

As a visual medium, photography also has a history of coexistence with written texts, but surprisingly this association has been absent from much historical, sociological and anthropological analysis. Texts frequently associated with photographs include written descriptions of the production of individual images, as well as photographic labels, titles and inventories. Each is key to both the presentation of photographs and how they are read. Also of significance to this discussion is photography as the genesis for other visual forms, most notably engraved images. Skilled craftspeople transformed photographs into engravings by making detailed incisions on metal or more usually on cheap wooden plates, thus intervening in the reproductive process. In the years before the development of technologies of mass photographic circulation, these engravings were printed on paper, and used in newspapers, books and periodicals. The interplay between photograph, text and engraving is especially important *vis-à-vis* the reproduction of mid- to late-nineteenth-century photographs. At this time, it was derivative engravings, not original photographs, which were most widely seen beyond the purview of private collections.

In Oscar Mallitte's 1857/8 pictures, we see an interesting example of textual disruption to photographs and their derivative images. I note this with respect to the photograph 'One of the Labyrinth Islands, Burmese convicts', which recorded the presence of a convict work party assigned to the survey when it stopped in Moulmein *en route* to the Andamans.[10] This photograph was not circulated in the public domain, but its derivative engraving was. There, the Burmese were described not as 'convicts' but as '*pioneers*'. This transformation was noticed in contemporary reports, with *Chambers Journal* reporting that the 'convicts' were placed in Mouat's service *as* 'pioneers', an allusion to infantry soldier corps who carried out engineering and other public works across empire at the time.[11] But I find this textual shift significant in a different way, because as a descriptive change it was made in the context of wider contemporary silences about the use of transportation and convict-forced labour in Britain's Indian Empire after the abolition of the slave trade (1807) and

---

[10] F. J. Mouat, *Adventures and Researches among the Andaman Islanders* (London: Hurst and Blackett, 1863), 70.

[11] 'A Savage Archipelago', *Chambers' Journal*, reprinted in *The Eclectic Magazine*, November 1863, 286.

slavery (1843). Asian convict workers were rendered invisible within what I have described elsewhere as the liberal colonial fantasy of the 'abolition' of 'slavery' and its replacement with other forms of labour, whether apprenticed, criminally convicted, indentured or 'free'.[12]

Images of the Andaman landscape emerged in the British public domain from time to time in the years after colonization, and they were mainly lithographic reproductions of contemporary photographs. Their associated texts marvelled at the Islands' natural features – and also at the orderly development of colonial infrastructure. One set of representations appeared, for instance, after the completion of an iron lighthouse on Table Island (one of the Cocos Islands) in 1867.[13] The most wide-ranging set of representations came in the aftermath of the extraordinary assassination of the Viceroy of India, Richard Bourke, Earl of Mayo, by a convict 'fanatic' called Shere Ali, in 1872. The Viceroy had been visiting the Islands in an official capacity and was stabbed to death in Hope Town after climbing Mount Harriet to enjoy the view.[14] The government did not release photographs of Shere Ali afterwards, fearing their deployment in anti-colonial propaganda.[15] Indeed, of the three photographs of Shere Ali now in the British Library, just one bears his name. The others record simply that the pictures were of the (unnamed) murderer or assassin.[16] These images were not copied or lithographed, although they did appear in popular nineteenth-century publications on crime and punishment in India, including H. L. Adam's *Oriental Crime* (1909).

But lithographs of island landscapes did appear alongside reports of the Viceroy's death in British periodicals such as *The Graphic* and *Harper's Weekly*. They were copied from photographs, for instance from commercial photographer W. W. Hooper's picture of the jetty where Mayo died. I will return to photographic albums in more depth in the last section of this chapter, but I would like to note here that this image almost always appears in archive collections of photographs that include

---

[12] Clare Anderson, 'After Emancipation: Empires and Imperial Formations', in Catherine Hall, Nicholas Draper and Keith McClelland (eds.) *Emancipation and the Remaking of the British Imperial World*, (Manchester: Manchester University Press, 2014), 113–27. Cf. Indrani Chatterjee and Richard M. Eaton (eds.), *Slavery and South Asian History* (Bloomington, IN: Indiana University Press, 2006).

[13] New Iron Lighthouse, Table Island, Cocos Group, Andaman Islands, *The Illustrated London News*, 18 May 1867.

[14] Clare Anderson, *Subaltern Lives: Biographies of Colonialism in the Indian Ocean World, 1790–1920* (Cambridge: Cambridge University Press, 2012), 130–2.

[15] W. W. Hunter, *Rulers of India: The Earl of Mayo* (Oxford: Clarendon Press University, 1891), 200.

[16] 'The murderer of Lord Mayo', unknown photographer, 1871, Photo 124/2(46), IOR; 'Shere Ali (assassin of Lord Mayo)', unknown photographer, 1872, Photo 127/(96), IOR; 'Assassin of Lord Mayo', unknown photographer, 1872, Photo 127/(99), IOR.

Figure 8.1 'Burmese pioneers', in F. J. Mouat, *Adventures and Researches among the Andaman Islanders* (London: Hurst and Blackett, 1863), 315.

THE GRAPHIC

AN ILLUSTRATED WEEKLY NEWSPAPER

VOL. V.—No. 120
Rig⁴ at General Post Office as a Newspaper

SATURDAY, MARCH 16, 1872

PRICE SIXPENCE
Or by post Sixpence Halfpenny

1. NORTH END OF ROSS ISLAND—2. THE BAY, SHOWING ABERDEEN ISLAND—3. EUROPEAN MERCHANT'S HOUSE—4. SOUTH END OF ROSS ISLAND—5. A SHOP IN THE BAZAAR—6. GOVERNOR'S BUNGALOW

PORT BLAIR, ANDAMAN ISLANDS, THE SCENE OF THE LATE VICEROY'S ASSASSINATION

Figure 8.2 'Port Blair, Andaman Islands, the Scene of the Late Viceroy's Assassination. Images: North end of Ross Island, the Bay Showing Aberdeen Island, European Merchants House, South End of Ross Island, a Shop in the Bazar, the Governor's Bungalow', *The Graphic*, 16 March 1872.

Andaman prints. In a direct textual intervention, in the absence of any sort of explanatory caption, in the copy found in Hooper's own album, 'X' literally marks the spot. Taken together, these images constructed the Islands as an orderly space – stressing visually the assassination as unforeseeable and anomalous to the regular state of colonial affairs. They constituted also a sort of visual justification for their continuation as a penal colony, incorporating a mishmash of tropes of colonial discipline and civilization: army barracks; flagpoles; well-dressed, clean convicts; trade (the bazar, a merchant's house); cleared land and built structures – each framed by lush, 'tropical' foliage.

Of interest also in this respect is a mid 1870s photograph of an Andaman convict being led to the gallows. This photograph can be found in a photographic album belonging to Donald Stewart, who was appointed Chief Commissioner of the Andamans following the assassination of Mayo in 1872. It is now part of the Alkazi Photographic Collections, New Delhi, though there is no record of its purchase or donation.

Stewart's album is striking for its inclusion of this scene of public execution, and like the lithographs described above, it was perhaps meant to imply the colonial administration's successful restoration of penal order following the Viceroy's murder. It shows a fettered convict at the foot of the steps leading up to the noose on Viper Island, the site of convict executions. It is possible that this picture was set up for the camera.[17] However, in the absence of an accompanying textual description, likely we will never know. Whatever the case, the scene reveals the hanging as an intensely ordered process, and through the imposing figures of the Sikh police force, one underpinned by military structure and discipline. Intriguingly, this photograph does not appear to have been circulated widely, and I have been unable to locate it in any other collection. We might choose to see its relative absence from visual archives of the Andamans as a metaphor for the removal of punishment from public view during the nineteenth century, and its enactment behind the closed doors and high walls of prisons or in even more remote penal locations like the site of secondary punishment for reoffenders, Viper Island.

Elizabeth Edwards has shown that a different kind of Andamans photography, E. H. Man's images of landscape and fauna taken at about the same time as the execution scene, possessed a 'picturesque quality', part of what she describes as a 'conventional European aesthetic response to the majesty of nature'. We even catch a glimpse of this visual approach

[17] Famously, W. W. Hooper, who took the 'X marks the spot' picture of Hope Town, directed an execution by firing squad in Burma, so that he could get a good photograph.

in a seemingly unpromising image of a convict timber yard at Phoenix Bay.[18] As such, Man's photographs form an important backdrop to the later visual representation of the Islands. Indeed, the assassination of the Viceroy and the general interest in the Islands that his death provoked perhaps stimulated the subsequent photographic tour of the Andamans by Calcutta-based photographers Samuel Bourne and Charles Shepherd in the 1880s. Realizing the commercial potential of fascination with the Islands in the aftermath of Mayo's death, they went to the Andamans and took dozens of photographs of landscapes, buildings, convicts and Islanders, and mass-produced them for sale. Some of the photographs were given factual tags, for instance: 'Church At Ross, Port Blair' or 'Viper, Andamans'. In others, the captions incorporated efforts at witty word plays on the low status of convicts and the pre-modernity of indigenous peoples. Thus we see also: 'Prisoners At Dinner' (Indian convicts squatting on the beach eating from tin plates in messes) and 'A Ball in the Andamans' (Islanders dancing). But overall the landscape remained orderly. Islanders, convicts and other settlers were dutiful and well behaved; and with coconut palms swaying in the breeze, the Islands were presented as a space of optimal penal organization and calm.

It is evident that Bourne and Shepherd's photographs were printed in quite large numbers, for like W. W. Hooper's photograph of the landscape of Mayo's assassination, they have found their way into numerous private albums.[19]

The studio production and sale of Andaman photographs also coincided with the growth of the Islands' colonial and military establishment, and the development of Indian tourism, in both of which they found a ready market. After Thomas Cook's first round-the-world tour in 1872, Europeans holidaying in India were encouraged to visit the Andaman Islands. Cook's brochure described them as 'a delightful three weeks' trip' from Calcutta.[20] Photographs of the Islands appeared subsequently in contemporary travel narratives and round-the-world literature, in French as well as English. They were also reproduced in other types of contemporary literature, notably popular British narratives of 'oriental crime' that described the supposedly 'exotic' criminality of Indians. Each

[18] Edwards, 'Science Visualized', 112.

[19] Albums incorporating their prints can be found in archives including the Alkazi Collection of Photography in New Delhi, the British Empire and Commonwealth Museum in Bristol, the National Library of Scotland, the India Office Collections of the British Library, the Smithsonian Institute in Washington, DC, Cambridge University Library and even the Suffolk Regiment Archive in the small English town of Bury St Edmunds.

[20] *Cook's Indian Tours* (London: Thomas Cook and Son, 1887).

Figure 8.3 'Viper, Andamans', photograph by Bourne and Shepherd, 1880s: photographs of the Andaman Islands (308 [541.9] TUS). Courtesy of the Horniman Museum, London.

visualised the Andamans as a penal success, incorporating pictures of orderly landscapes – coconut plantations on drained swamps, barracks, bungalows – but they also represented convicts in pursuits that might amuse the reader: under reformative training with the St John's Ambulance Brigade, for instance, or queuing up to find a partner in the 'marriage parade'.[21]

Travellers and other consumers of Andaman photographs found intriguing the idea that the convicted murderers who constituted the bulk of the convicts were employed as barbers or nannies in the penal colony. German criminologist Robert Heindl visited the Islands at the

---

[21] H. L. Adam, *The Indian Criminal* (London: J. Milne, 1909); H. L. Adam, *Oriental Crime* (London: T. W. Laurie, 1909); *Îles Andaman et Ceylan, Moeurs et Coutumes* (Paris: L. Boulanger, 1880); W. H. Fitchett, *The King's Empire: A Pictorial and Descriptive Record Illustrated from Photographs and Drawings* (London: Cassell and Co., 1906); Mrs Talbot Clifton, *Pilgrims to the Isles of Penance; Orchid Gathering in the East* (London: John Long, 1911); Stanley W. Coxon, *And That Reminds Me; Being Incidents of a Life Spent at Sea, and in the Andaman Islands, Burma, Australia, and India* (London: John Lane, 1915).

turn of the twentieth century, part of a global tour of penal settlements. (Germany never established penal colonies, but having colonized parts of Micronesia at the turn of the twentieth century it was certainly interested in them.) He reproduced an image of an Indian convict shaving a white European (perhaps Heindl himself) with a cutthroat razor, as well as of a Burmese convict holding the hands of two young girls.

Heindl also incorporated into his book pictures of convicts working, bathing and eating in messes; and anthropological photographs of the Islands' indigenous peoples. The latter included pictures of men and women drinking from shells, carrying babies and children, tattooing or being tattooed, and wearing body paint.[22] In some of the penal colony images, there is a visual promise that reaches beyond the desire to amuse the reader. If one looks closely at his picture of a convict nanny, for instance, we see that the two young girls pictured beside him were likely descended from indigenous/Indian parentage. I speculate that this was taken in the Andaman Home orphanage, a place of confinement for indigenous children. Another photograph, from the archival collections of the V&A in London, makes the visual point about *métissage* more explicit still, for it is captioned 'Half Castes'.[23] I find these photographs interesting, because children and adults of mixed heritage in the Andamans are almost completely absent from the colonial archives, as though they never existed.[24] In their absence they constitute a part of the colonial aphasia (that which cannot be said or described) articulated as a concept by Ann Laura Stoler.[25] But photographs like these belie the textual disappearance of mixed race, indigenous children, and this makes them especially powerful. They do not illustrate, represent, destabilize or visually transform that which we can read about in colonial correspondence, personal diaries or convict records (as do the images that we have discussed so far); they *constitute* the archive, marking the presence of people who do not otherwise exist. In so doing, they make an especially poignant point about their social marginality and historical elision.

---

[22] Robert Heindl, *Meine Reise nach den Strafkolonien, mit vielen originalaufnahmen* (Berlin-Wien: Ullstein, 1913).

[23] In the absence of a specific caption, looking at the appearance and dress of its subjects, this image *may* have been taken in the neighbouring Nicobar Islands, which at the time housed a small Andaman convict outpost at Camorta.

[24] There are brief mentions in 'Islands of No Return' by Charles J. Bonington, with accompanying photographs (1937–86), MS380838, 250, Archives and Special Collections, School of Oriental and African Studies; and M. V. Portman, *A History of Our Relations with the Andamanese*, vols. *I* and *II* (Calcutta: Office of the Superintendent of Government Printing, 1899), *passim*.

[25] Ann Laura Stoler, 'Colonial Aphasia: Race and Disabled Histories in France,' *Public Culture* 23, 1 (2011), 121–56.

Der Mörder als Kindermädchen

Figure 8.4 'The murderer as nanny', Robert Heindl, *Meine Reise nach den Strafkolonien, mit vielen originalaufnahmen* [*My global tour of penal colonies, with original photographs*], Berlin-Wien, Ullstein and Co., 1913.

If some of the images discussed above coalesce visually with colonial discourses about the control and discipline of people and landscapes, unusually Donald Stewart's album contains photographs of the everyday, too. These pictures are quite different from the 'tropical' and 'disciplinary' views presented by images that circulated in popular periodicals and other publications during the 1870s. I would like to consider for a moment by way of illustration Stewart's photographs of the Ross Island Bazar, where ticket-of-leave and liberated convicts could buy and sell goods, for the pictures are extraordinary in their very ordinariness. They do not appear on the surface to include convicts at all, and on first viewing they seem unremarkable. And yet we glimpse something disconcerting: one picture is strongly suggestive of the management of the photographic process itself. In the far right, a policeman stands looking beyond the frame of what is available to us, rattan stick in hand. Disconcertingly, the viewer's eye is drawn to what we cannot see: people (convicts?) excluded from the production of the quotidian. Was the armed guard put in place to prevent the touching of the camera or other forms of disruption to the photographic process? Could Stewart not trust those excluded from the image to stand still? Was the street otherwise too crowded to make a pleasing image? Or, did Stewart want the viewer's eye to be drawn to the entrepreneurialism of the (rehabilitated) ex-convict ('self-supporter') milk seller, in the middle of the print? For though photographs freeze a place in time, they were produced within what Felix Driver and Luciana Martins have described as a 'living space of encounter and exchange'. Crucially, subaltern contestation was an element within the production of visual knowledge.[26] Of course, what is intriguing about the circumstances within which this photograph was produced is the fact that we will never know. After all, as historical geographer James Ryan puts it, photographs unsettle the past as much as they fix its truth. They are 'dynamic objects with entangled histories'.[27]

Andaman photograph-objects

In a recent theoretical intervention into reading photographs, it has been suggested that we should see images as *Sensible Objects*, 'things' with meanings that go beyond visual representation.[28] In this interpretation,

---

[26] Driver and Martins, 'Views and Visions of the Tropical World', 5.

[27] James R. Ryan, *Picturing Empire: Photography and the Visualization of the British* (London: Reaktion, 1997), 225.

[28] Elizabeth Edwards, Chris Gosden and Ruth B. Philipps (eds.), *Sensible Objects: Colonialism, Museums and Material Culture* (Oxford: Oxford University Press, 2006).

photographs are three-dimensional objects with relationships to human experience, and they hold extra-visual significance. Think of photographs as objects: they are printed, handled, folded, mounted, gifted, copied, collected, bought, sold, posted, discarded and stored. Note the coalescence of this interpretation with Arjun Appadurai's influential suggestion that objects have cultural and political 'lives'; that there is a history to be written of the *Social Life of Things*.[29] I would like to dwell on these important anthropological/historical interpretations for a moment in further analysis of photographs of the Andaman penal colony. Photograph albums are of especial relevance to this discussion, for they are best understood not solely as sets or associations of prints but as distinct objects in their own right. They have a quite different form to folders, packets or boxes of single images, and as collections of images they constitute something more than sets of individual photographs. They are structured visual displays that can incorporate random selection and mounting, but also careful comparison and sequencing. They can express themes, and the movement of time. They can include and present personally taken photographs as well as bought, mass-produced ones. And, often, the album-maker makes captions, notes and textual interventions of various kinds. They can be enormously tactile objects too; with their juxtaposition of hard covers, thick paper and thin card; and blank sheets framing the visual density of the photographic print.

In the pages that follow, I will centre on collections of photographs that incorporate pictures of the Andamans. I will argue that they could enact visually aspects of colonization, most particularly through the inclusion (and juxtaposition) of particular types of images, and the exclusion of others. I will suggest that accompanying captions to and written descriptions of photographs, often noted many years after the pictures had been taken and the album made, are key to their readability and interpretation. Some of the albums, like that of Donald Stewart that I have already discussed, were quite formally mounted.[30] But I am also interested in less formal albums, as well as the incorporation of photographs into other

---

[29] Arjun Appadurai (ed.), *The Social Life of Things: Commodities in Cultural Perspective* (Cambridge: Cambridge University Press, 1986).

[30] Photographs of the Andamans appear in numerous albums, usually as part of larger collections that include also images of India and Burma. For example: album 95.0026 (Stewart Album) and album 96.390053–58 (unknown provenance), Alkazi Photographic Collection, New Delhi; Photo 447/3 (W.W. Hooper Collection), Photo 355/1 (Dunlop Smith Collection), Photo 252 (Royden Wilkinson [United Provinces police service] Collection), Photo 125/2 (Chief Commissioner R.C. Temple Collection), IOR; The Tuson Albums, Horniman Museum, Forest Hill, London; Photograph Album, c. 1850/60 (F.J. Mouat's album), X821 V&A; Photograph album presented to Lt Colonel and Mrs Michael Lloyd Ferrar by the Girl Guides and Boy Scouts of the Andaman and

colonial objects: their gluing into diaries, their folding into letters, their appending to memoirs or their attachment to convict identification papers, for instance.[31] Thus, I see photographs, albums, groups of photographic prints and written records as part of an archival continuum, and best considered together, in an integrated frame of analysis.

Before I continue, I would like to comment that there are very few colonial-era photographs surviving in the Andamans today, and no complete albums: or at least none that I am aware of. The Andaman and Nicobar Secretariat Archives has made repeated requests for donations or loans of such material, but most colonial records and family papers – including photographs – have been destroyed by earthquakes, fires or during the Japanese occupation of 1942–5. During interviewing work in 2011 and 2012, I was repeatedly told that local-born, convict-descended families living freely in the Islands during the war had thrown away pictures because they were so afraid that the Japanese would accuse them of spying for the British and subject them to torture. Those that do exist are often badly damaged.[32] There is, then, a politics of the visual archive, of which I am deeply mindful.[33] In Chapter 5, I discussed the role that the showing of photographs played in my work with local-born people in the Andamans. I would like to note here that some of the elderly residents of Port Blair became deeply emotional when at this time I shared with them (and later copied and presented to them) images of the Islands from British archives – particularly when they saw pictures of eminent local-born Islanders who have long since died. Despite the general absence of colonial-era photographs in family collections in the Islands, I have, however, located a few amongst family papers now in Britain. They belonged to an Englishwoman who married an Anglo-Indian man stationed in the Islands shortly before the war. This Anglo-Indian family was one of many employed in the jail, telegraph and wireless services at this time.

I begin with a discussion of a photograph album that once belonged to Inspector-General of Prisons Bengal, and head of the 1857 survey party, F. J. Mouat, and which is now in the V&A Archives. It seems most

Nicobar Islands, during Lt Colonel Ferrar's time as Chief Commissioner in the Islands, 1929–31, Ferrar Papers, Box II, CSAS.

[31] E.g. Bonington, 'Islands of No Return'; Dorothy Fullerton Papers, c. 1929–32, MSS/83/ 010, National Maritime Museum; Mrs W. E. Burt manuscript and photographs, Eth. Doc. 1714, Anthropology Library, British Museum.

[32] Interview with Mahomed Abdul Qadir and Sheikh Farooq Alam, 7 December 2011.

[33] Cf. Ann Laura Stoler, *Along the Archival Grain: Epistemic Anxieties and Colonial Common Sense* (Princeton, NJ: Princeton University Press, 2009).

Figure 8.5 Sheikh Farooq Alam's local-born father, Port Blair, n.d.
Sheikh Farooq Alam's private collection, Andaman Islands.

unlikely that Mouat himself mounted the album now attributed to him,
for it was purchased in London (from Wright & Co., Account Book
Manufacturers and General Stationers, 60, Pall Mall) and a typed note
glued into the front cover describes Mouat in the third person and gets

Figure 8.6 Interview with ex-president of the Local Born Association, Mr John Lobo, Port Blair, November 2011. Photograph: Clare Anderson.

his middle initial wrong ('T'). However, it was clearly put together, or possibly remounted from an older album, by somebody who had read his account of the Andamans expedition, for on the inside cover is a brief summary of its content:

'Adventures and Researches among the Andaman Islands' [sic] Pub. London 1863, Hurst & Blackett.
    In November 1857 he was called to form part of an expedition to the Andaman Islands with the object of building a harbour of refuge and establishing a penal settlement. They sailed on Nov. 23rd. he took with him photographic apparatus, and employed a Monsieur Mellite [Mallitte], described as a 'photographic artist of great talent and considerable experience.' They made a large collection of pictures of the country and people. They reached Port Cornwallis on Dec. 11th, and suggested changing its name to Port Blair. They fought with natives: Heathcote was severely wounded, also Mellitte, the bullet being removed by Playfair. They brought back an islander with them.

Despite this textual fanfare, just three photographs are definitely attributable to the Andamans (possibly five, though without captions we cannot be sure), in an album that otherwise contains about sixty photographs, *cartes-de-visite* (visiting or trading cards), greetings cards, paintings and drawings. It is an intensely personal album – more a scrapbook – and includes different types of images of a wide range of subjects. Pictures of Indian buildings and streets, mainly in Calcutta; ships in port; Mouat's house and veranda; Mouat with his wife, friends, servants and pet dog (he had no children) all appear, alongside images of Jesus holding the Cross; Tintern Abbey; Egypt and Sebastopol; and a black-and-white reproduction of a painting of a nautch dance, complete with 'exotic' veils, hookahs and bared breasts.

Reflecting the wide range of visual media in Mouat's album are the disparate origins of the images. Some were perhaps commissioned or taken by Mouat himself. He purchased several famous photographs, such as James Robertson's images of the Battle of Sebastopol and Josiah Rowe's picture of the reading of the 1858 Proclamation in Calcutta, through which India was transferred from East India Company to Crown control.[34] The images are framed textually through three scripts: Mouat's notes on the back of some of the images (e.g. 'My Horse Pilgrim and Harry & the Grooms'; 'View of the Back of Our House'); a handful of contemporary longhand descriptions below the images (e.g. 'Calcutta from Chowringhee Street'), and biro-marked numbering (and a couple of descriptions, e.g. 'Calcutta 1862') evidently added some time after the album's acquisition.

What interests me here is that not one of the three Andaman photographs in Mouat's album is incorporated into the 'official' photographic record that was sent back to London, to the Queen, and is now part of the Royal Collection at Windsor Castle. The *official* photographs of the Islands were, it would seem, taken at the same time as this series of *private* ones, and so they bear close relation to those included in Donald Stewart's album, which I discussed above. I will elaborate further on two of Mouat's images.

The first is not mounted, but was printed on a small piece of thin paper. Pencil-written on the reverse in Mouat's own hand is the description: 'my photographic tent, Port Cornwallis'. The others each show members of the survey party. One is a posed shot, which must have been taken by Mallitte, and like 'my photographic tent' was not mounted on card or thick paper. It still bears the creases of having been folded carefully in such a way as to fit into a small pocket whilst leaving the men's faces uncrumpled. Perhaps Mouat intended to show this picture to Islanders in the event of his capture. After all, the party came under

---

[34] Josiah Rowe was professor of drawing and surveying at Presidency College, Calcutta.

heavy arrow fire, and Heathcote was badly injured.[35] Or perhaps Mouat kept it as a souvenir; ensuring the faces were clear to view so that he could look at and show the image over and over again. Whatever the case, the content and use of the survey party's photographs were dependent on their intended purpose, either for presentation to government or in the case of these two images for personal consumption or display.

This early photograph compels us to think more about how photographs travelled as objects, about how they connected the Andamans to the Indian mainland and to metropolitan Britain, and about their function beyond representation in these respects. Indeed, many penal colony–era photographs – of convicts, landscapes and built structures – were transformed into postcards; transnational objects that were sent and received all over the empire.[36] I have been reminded again and again in my work just how networked this supposedly isolated penal colony was. British officials wrote to and received letters from their families outside the Islands,[37] as did convicts – including Shere Ali, who allegedly read aloud a letter describing the murder of Justice Norman in Calcutta, the night before he killed Mayo.[38] And such letters sometimes enveloped photographs within their pages. E. H. Man – whose picturesque views I mentioned earlier, and who took a number of ethnographic portraits of Islanders[39] – even photographed the chaplain's daughter Maude Warneford with her *ayah* (nursemaid) and dog. Her father sent the tiny, flimsy image to her after she left Port Blair for England, to go to school in the 1870s.

In letters between the two, father and daughter wrote frequently about their exchange of photographs, giving us a fascinating insight into how photographs were sent and received across long distances during periods of separation. Indeed, Warneford's written comments open up interesting insights into how photographs were *used* as household objects, as reminders of looks and markers of adolescence, and also about their visual limitations. 'I think very often of you, and look at your photograph

---

[35] Mouat, *Adventures And Researches*, 247–51.

[36] 'Postcard Views of the Andaman Islands', Photo 775/(1–5), IOR. The circulation of colonial postcards has received relatively little scholarly attention. One exception is Saloni Mathur, 'Wanted Native Views: Collecting Colonial Postcards of India', in Antoinette Burton (ed.), *Gender, Sexuality and Colonial Modernities* (London: Routledge, 1999), 95–115.

[37] Especially the Warneford Papers, Mss Eur F388/1, IOR; Ferrar Papers, CSAS.

[38] Events of assassination, 8–13 February 1872: notes from verbal and written statements made by Major General Stewart, Superintendent of Port Blair, 10 February 1872, Add. Ms 7490 Mayo Papers, 94, Department of Manuscripts, University of Cambridge Library.

[39] Edwards, 'Science Visualized'.

nearly every day. I wish I could see you again, and I hope I shall some day next year', Warneford wrote in mid 1875.[40] He sent photographs of other family members, too, including Maude's mother who had died young in Calcutta: 'it will remind you of her'. After a visit to the mainland, he sent Maude a photograph of her grave.[41] The letters also reflect on the disappointments of photographs, which despite their visual promise did not produce imprints of remembered appearance. 'So you did not like my photograph ... ?' Warneford wrote after receiving one letter from Maude. 'Very well, I will try and get a better one taken another day and send to your ladyship, and then see what you say.'[42] And, a week or so after noting how grown up Maude looked in one picture: 'The more I look at your photograph the less I like it, because the photographer has touched up your eyes and eyebrows and so has taken away your natural expression. He has made you stand stiff.'[43] Subsequently, he sent Maude advice on sitting for the photographer: "Mind you look <u>very nice</u> and don't go screwing up your little nose, like you used to out here, when you were going to be taken.'[44] These photographs also conveyed visual messages. Warneford took great pleasure in seeing Maude wearing the Indian bangles gifted by her mother in one picture.[45] These photographs seem to have facilitated family communication, as time passed, between Britain and India. I propose that looked at repeatedly they held personal meanings about family relationships and carried messages in an effort to breach the physical separation produced through imperial service.

Periodically during the nineteenth century it was lamented that as the penal colony in the Andaman Islands became more widely known – as news travelled back and forth across the Bay of Bengal, and further still – it began to lose its terror. As early as 1877 it was described as 'a haven where prisoners would rather be'. The circulation of images of the Andamans accompanied and perhaps even sustained these connections between Islands, mainland and metropole – and surely played a role in the change in attitudes about the penal colony in the last quarter of the nineteenth century. If we think of Andaman photographs as travelling photograph-objects rather than as representations, and as occupying the spaces between and across the public and private sphere, we move beyond issues of colonial representation to catch a glimpse of this broader cultural importance and impact.

[40] Letter from the Reverend Warneford to Maude, 29 June 1875, Mss Eur F388/1, IOR.
[41] Warneford to Maude, 12 June 1876, Mss Eur F388/1, IOR.
[42] Warneford to Maude, 19 November 1875, Mss Eur F388/1, IOR.
[43] Warneford to Maude, 13 January 1876; 21 Jan 1875, Mss Eur F388/1, IOR.
[44] Warneford to Maude, 13 December 1875, Mss Eur F388/1, IOR.
[45] Warneford to Maude, 5 September 1878, Mss Eur F388/1, IOR.

It is perhaps no coincidence then that during this period photography also acquired a more evidently disciplinary purpose. In the 1870s British penal officers even experimented with it as a way of recording (with the 'stern fidelity' only photography was thought to allow) the individual features and characteristics of convicts, for circulation in their home districts in case of their escape from the penal colony.[46] Such photography – sometimes accompanied by anthropometric measurements – was intended to supplement wider colonial practices of native identification and surveillance. In this it failed miserably, though, for there was a thin representational line between the Indian 'individual' and the more familiar ethnographic 'collective'. The latter, which was often based on caste, relied on social markers including objects associated with particular occupations (e.g. baskets), particular kinds of clothing and jewellery and textual captions. Images of individual convicts were head-to-waist portrait shots, with convicts wearing simple *dhotis* (waist cloths) only. Though during the 1870s, pictures of escaped convicts were circulated near their mainland homes, untrained police officers could not read them. Despite the assumption that the photograph represented a 'true' image of an individual, captured by a technology that demanded a long camera exposure, convicts could subvert the entire process by refusing to sit still or pulling faces. Afterwards, transportation could also effect physical change, including weight loss, or the darkening of skin, which made it hard to recognize a person from their picture.[47] It is difficult to glean insights into convict experiences of this photographic process from European descriptions. In one celebrated case, however, an observer noted the enormous gratification felt by Liaquat Ali, an 1857 rebel who had eluded arrest for over a decade, when he was finally arrested and had his picture taken.[48] We also know that convicts in the Andamans were trained in photography, and used during the anthropometric measurement of the Nicobarese, in the 1920s.[49]

In an effort to restore Indian fears of transportation, in the midst of these circulating photographs, the British constructed the Cellular Jail, completed in 1906, as a place for the probationary confinement of all new arrivals. In the years that followed, it was used also for the incarceration and separate treatment of anti-colonial nationalists, who were made subject to altogether special treatment. The jail was an imposing

[46] The expression 'stern fidelity' was used by the Rev. Joseph Mullins in an 1856 address to the Photographic Society of Bengal. On the 'indexicality' of Indian photographs, see Clare Anderson, *Legible Bodies: Race, Criminality and Colonialism in South Asia* (Oxford: Berg, 2004), 141–2.
[47] For these and related issues, see Anderson, *Legible Bodies*, chapter 5.
[48] *The Times*, 24 November 1871.   [49] Bonington, 'Islands of No Return', 144.

presence, an architectural embodiment of or metaphor for the penal colony, which towered over Port Blair harbour in full view of both town and sea. As such, it was not just as a place of punishment and confinement but also what David Arnold and I described elsewhere as a 'moral object'.[50] Its construction – just after the introduction of the cheap and easy-to-use Kodak Brownie camera, which revolutionized popular photography – perhaps explains why the Cellular Jail was unquestionably the most frequently circulating image of the Islands, for it appears (even under construction) in almost every contemporary publication or album, as either a photograph or unused postcard. This includes albums belonging to Frederic and Katherine Tuson, who were stationed in the Andamans during Frederic's employment as officer in charge of the Andaman Home during 1874–5. Katherine and Frederic's son, K. H. Tuson, donated the albums to the Horniman Museum in Forest Hill, London, in 1980.

The Tuson albums are centrally concerned with the Andamans; they contain only photographs, and their scope extends across the Bay of Bengal to the River Hooghly (Calcutta) and to the neighbouring Nicobar Islands. The images are extremely wide-ranging and include copies of E. H. Man's 'picturesque' photographs as well as a number of the commercially produced Bourne and Shepherd prints discussed above. These include the famous ethnographic picture of Islanders, 'Shooting Fish'. Other photographs of Islanders feature prominently, too, notably turn of the twentieth century ethnographer M. V. Portman's famous head-and-shoulders shots of men and women.[51] As Elizabeth Edwards has shown, these had their antecedents in E. H. Man's presentation of Andamanese culture in 'quasi-quantifiable' ways, in which he positioned individuals' limbs in such a way as to support ideas about their 'physical type'. This mode of representation laid the ground for Portman's well-known and more explicitly anthropometric images, where Islanders' were photographed against the paraphernalia of measuring sticks, callipers and other equipment.[52]

The Tusons themselves evidently took the remainder of the one hundred or so pictures, made possible through developing photographic technology that made the ownership of cameras more widespread. They include views of landscapes, colonial bungalows, officials and servants,

[50] Clare Anderson and David Arnold, 'Visualising the Prison', in Frank Dikötter and Ian Brown (eds.), *Cultures of Confinement: A History of the Prison in Africa, Asia and Latin America* (Ithaca, NY: Cornell University Press, 2007), 304–31.

[51] Falconer, 'Ethnographical Photography'; Sen, 'Savage Bodies, Civilized Pleasures'.

[52] Edwards, 'Science Visualized', 109–10, 116–7.

Figure 8.7 'Andamanese shooting fish', photographer and date unknown. Photographs of the Andaman Islands' (308 [541.9] TUS). Courtesy of the Horniman Museum, London.

and even the Islands' amateur dramatic society, giving an important visual glimpse into elite colonial life. Though they are not the subjects of the photographs, and are unmentioned in the accompanying captions, groups of convicts often appear in the background of the pictures: as boatmen or labourers, or simply observing the photographic process from a distance. In this sense, the absences and elisions of the prints reveal a great deal about colonial power relations and the politics of visual inclusion and exclusion.

There are a few contemporary labels beneath some of the images, but most of the photographs seem to have been mounted by the Tusons, and as such many images were left without annotations, to speak for themselves. But later on, at some unknown date, a somewhat shaky (perhaps elderly) hand intervened in the album to *remember* the scenes depicted in the photographs. Thus beneath a print of the police force are the words: 'Sikh police such as acted as guards in our houses and boats.' And beside a photograph of a group of Europeans: 'Party at Mt Harriet: elephants took some ... up to 1200 ft'. The postcard print of the Cellular Jail has the number '600' beside it, clearly a reference to the number of cells that it contained (See Figure 4.1). There is also a picture of 'Abdul Ameer Khan' (and a second, unnamed man) alongside Katherine and Frederic's son Alan. The colour of his tunic ('red') has been carefully remembered in the note accompanying the black-and-white image, though otherwise there is no indication that he was a convict, as he almost certainly was. Perhaps these additions were made towards the end of its owner's life, before the album was passed down the family or donated to the Horniman Museum. The album was looked at, leafed through, and engaged with textually (possibly verbally, though that we cannot know). It might be described as a site for the inscription of family history and memory.

We see similar family shots and later inscriptions in a photograph album that was compiled by the family of G. E. Wood, an engineer in the Royal Indian Marines who served as port officer at the turn of the twentieth century. There are pictures of officers playing golf, fishing and at the beach. A note added to a photograph of the interior of Christ Church on Ross Island, for instance, reads: 'Defiled by Japs 1942. Mules kept in chancel'.[53] And, in other archives, photographs are inseparable from their descriptive texts. In the personal papers of Dorothy Fullerton, wife of the commander-in-chief of the East Indies, for example, pictures appear between diary entries, dinner invitations, playbills, stamps, postcards and other textual mementoes: sometimes captioned, annotated or written over, and sometimes including extensive notes on the reverse of the prints. These are images of empire at play; fishing and sea bathing, or simply admiring the spectacular Andaman views.[54]

Apart from the image of Abdul Ameer Khan with Alan Tuson, there are only a few pictures in the Horniman Museum album that take convicts as their subject (and none in those compiled by Wood), and those that do exist were likely taken by the Tusons themselves. In part, this reflects the general lack of interest of commercial photographers in convicts, compared to picturesque landscapes and 'exotic', 'authentic' Islanders, which far outnumber them in the archives. There is one print of a convict shaving another convict's throat (strikingly similar to Robert Heindl's photograph of the same) and another of 'servants at dinner' (Burmese convicts squatting on the ground outside, eating from tin plates). These pictures anticipated the visual tropes common in the

[53] Wood Large Andamans Album, British Empire and Commonwealth Museum Collection, 2002/202/181, Bristol Record Office.

[54] Dorothy Fullerton Papers, c. 1929–32, MSS/83/010, National Maritime Museum.

Figure 8.8 'Abdul Ameer Khan; Chota Sahib [Little Man] Alan Tuson 5 years old', photographer and date unknown. Photographs of the Andaman Islands (308 [541.9] TUS). Courtesy of the Horniman Museum, London.

popular turn-of-the century literature discussed above, and perhaps reveal visually a standing colonial joke. There is, though, an evidently 'staged' image of a convict on a flogging triangle. The photograph belies the true violence of the punishment, and resembles the gallows scene discussed earlier, in its portrayal of an orderly and bloodless penal space. This enables us to interpret it within the broader tropes of penal discipline (labour, training, orderly conduct) that suffuse other photographs and derivative engravings.

Finally, there are two other photographs of convicts in the Tuson albums, where they are at work in mangrove swamps. In stark contrast to the convict overseers, St John's Ambulance trainees, barbers and nannies represented in commercial images and criminological and other popular publications, the convicts in these pictures are far from crisp and disciplined. Rather, they are thin, impoverished men and boys standing half-naked and knee-deep in mosquito-infested water. They are surrounded by their overseers, who are marked out visually not only by their physical elevation above the convict working party, but also by their sashes and tunics. I think that Katherine probably took this picture from the shore, for in another image her husband can be seen in the boat on its way to visit the convict party. Exclusively in the albums, these two shots are part of a carefully numerically sequenced though undated set of photographs of a trip made by the Tusons to the Nicobars and back to Calcutta. In the second of the images, a convict overseer, framed by mangrove trees, turns back to stare into the camera. I find this image haunting, for it reverses the usual function of the camera in the penal context. *I* am not looking at *him*; rather, I feel, *he* is looking at *me*.

Figure 8.9 'Mangrove swamps, prisoners at work', photographer and date unknown. Photographs of the Andaman Islands (308 [541.9] TUS). Courtesy of the Horniman Museum, London.

Figure 8.10 'Mangrove swamps', photographer and date unknown.
Photographs of the Andaman Islands (308 [541.9] TUS).
Courtesy of the Horniman Museum, London.

The Tusons' use of sequenced photographs to portray what they saw during a particular journey returns us to Donald Stewart's album, for nestled among copies of Bourne and Shepherd's shots are series of picturesque framings that juxtapose mountain, shoreline and sea in a visually pleasing fashion. Tiny ships appear on distant horizons, glimpsed through bungalows and coconut trees, a visual reminder of the Islands' desired isolation from the mainland. And, in the first of one set of prints mounted on a single page, Stewart himself (or at least a European man) walks up Mount Harriet, flanked by servants. This image is part of a sequence in which Stewart (or this man) retraces the Earl of Mayo's fatal steps of 1872, producing a sort of photographic re-enactment of the assassination. Correspondingly, Hooper's commercial print of Hope Town jetty, the site of the Viceroy's death, appears as the final image in the set.

I close this chapter with a consideration of the private collection of papers of Eileen Arnell. It belonged formerly to her mother, who went out to the Andamans from England at the age of eighteen, before the Second World War, and married an Anglo-Indian man. The collection includes copies of various images, which Eileen has glued onto paper and keeps in plastic pockets in an A4 binder. During my interview with Eileen, it became clear that the compilation of this album has been grounded in her desire to make sense of her past, for she was born in the Andamans and grew up in the Nicobars, only leaving for England at the age of eight. Before her recent death, her mother had refused to talk much about the Islands, or to answer Eileen's questions about them. Eileen speculates that this is because she had married an Anglo-Indian man, but refused to acknowledge the fact. Eileen has embraced her Anglo-Indian heritage through the compilation of this album. It contains lovely, informal shots of her parents, aunt and sister, as well as studio *carte-de-visite* style images. I will show one – frankly astonishing – image here, of a happy family laughing with its convict servants. Eileen is the baby in the picture.

As I thought about and tried to interpret this image, in the context of the post-colonial politics of Eileen's identity as an Andaman-born Anglo-Indian living in Britain today, I was reminded of Ann Laura Stoler and Karen Strassler's work with elderly people in the former Dutch East Indies. Stoler and Strassler were able to interrogate and to note the wide

Figure 8.11 'Our family group with convict servants, 1939'.
Private collection of Eileen Arnell.

gap between colonial memories of great affection for native servants, and native expressions of detachment from the intimacies of the colonial household.[55] However compelling their argument, Eileen and her family, perhaps, occupied the interstices in between these racial spaces; for Anglo-Indians were used as social buffers between the British colonial establishment and the Indian convicts, from the 1860s and right up to 1942. In this context, what intrigues me most about this photograph is not what it may or may not reveal about the constitution of, or affect experienced within, an Anglo-Indian household in the penal colony, for there are no surviving ex-convict servants in the Islands today with whom this might be discussed. Rather, I am compelled by the fact that the dark-skinned man represented in this and other family photographs was important in eventually revealing to Eileen the secret that her family would or could not speak of: being Anglo-Indian.[56] In this way, the visual promise of these images coincides with that of the photographs of mixed-race children and adults that I discussed earlier. They constitute an archive of intimacy that is otherwise textually inaccessible.[57]

Conclusions

In working through the photographic archives of the Andamans penal colony, a series of overlapping questions open up about the visual representation of history *in* the Islands, and about the larger significance of images, in writing histories *of* the Islands. In the nineteenth century, commercial photography and its derivative forms expressed visually the Islands as ready for colonization, and ultimately revealed scenes of penal orderliness and colonial discipline. But photographs hold meanings beyond representation alone, and in people's folding, arranging and sequencing of images, particularly those taken privately, and through textual interventions of various kinds, they transformed them into material objects with quite different meanings. These included their value in the constitution of kinship, in remembering the past, and in forging identity. Privately taken images provide alternative views of peoples and landscapes that belie official views too, and on occasion they open up for discussion aspects of colonial culture and society that were only rarely textualised. In the pictures that I have considered here, this is notable for

---

[55] Ann Laura Stoler and Karen Strassler, 'Castings for the Colonial: Memory Work in "New Order" Java', *Comparative Studies in Society and History* 42, 1 (2000), 4–48.

[56] Interview with Eileen Arnell, Cambridge, 27 June 2011.

[57] On this point, for an important recent intervention, see Elizabeth Edwards and Matt Mead, 'Absent Histories and Absent Images: Photographs, Museums and the Colonial Past', *Museum and Society*, 11, 1 (2013): 19–38.

images of the misery of convict labour; of the existence of mixed heritage people; and of the nature of the colonial family and children. The point is also relevant to our reading of pictures of (dis)orderly convicts, and the framing of everyday street life in the penal colony.

In the remembering of place and experience through images, in the writing of captions and comments, and in their folding up and placing in pockets, photographs and photograph albums also need to be under-stood as intimate, tactile objects that are inextricably connected to the people and places that they represent. In the context of the colonizing survey of the Andamans in 1857 and 1858, privately desired images were produced in parallel to publicly demanded ones. In family letters between the Islands and Britain two decades later, we see an attempt to use photographs to bridge the long separation of father from daughter. And, as past British residents of the Islands looked at photographs upon their return to Europe in the twentieth century, they added texts and inscriptions, which directed them – and us – to 'read' the images in particular ways. In this way, in the final instance, in their visual and textual inclusions, elisions, exclusions and additions, photographs are important reminders that we can never fully 'know' the past.

9 Endangered landscapes, dream destinations: the shifting frames of 'tropicality' in the Andaman Islands

Madhumita Mazumdar

Introduction

Clare Anderson's explorations of the visual archive of the colonial state and representations of the penal colony in particular (Chapter 8) brings into focus the complex and shifting terrain of the Andamanese 'image world'.[1] Her focus on the production, circulation and consumption of a range of images from both official and private collections allow us to rethink not only the politics of representation but what Deborah Poole invokes as the larger 'circulation of fantasies, ideas and sentiments'[2] about the Islands in the public and intimate spaces of empire.

This chapter engages not with any specific photographic archive but with the contemporary image world of the Andaman Islands built around contending visions, ideas and fantasies about the island's 'tropical' endowments. Both chapters in this section seek to draw attention to ways in which the Andaman Islands have been imagined, represented and consumed in different historical contexts and how such visual and social practices reflect the deep ambivalences that have marked successive colonization and developmental projects on the Islands.

The last few decades have seen an enormous investment in the tourist imaging of the Andaman Islands as a prime tropical beach destination.[3] Private tour operators both national and global as well as the Indian state have produced large amounts of visual material to promote the Islands' tropical allure. Images of the Islands' pristine forests, golden beaches and

---

[1] The notion of the 'image world' is derived from the Deborah Poole's invocation of the term in her book *Vision, Race and Modernity: A Visual Economy of the Andean Image World* (Princeton, NJ: Princeton University Press, 1997), 7. Poole argues that the term captured 'the complexity and mulitplicity of the realm of images' and acknowledged 'simultaneously the material and social nature of both vision and representation'.

[2] Poole, *Vision, Race and Modernity*, 6.

[3] In 2004, *Time* magazine drew attention to Radhanagar beach in Havelock Island as one of the best beaches in Asia. This was a rare commendation for a place that had remained well outside the frames of the global tourist imagination. *Time*, 164 (22 November 2004).

emerald waters have become the stock-in-trade of tourist brochures, coffee table books, picture postcards, posters, calendar art, websites and social media. Holiday websites have enriched the genre by uploading personalized tourist images and albums that compete to reveal the unexplored sites of the Islands' tropical landscape, seascape and beaches.

This extravagant celebration of the Islands' tropical landscape, however, has alarmed environmental activists and conservationists who have for years warned the Indian state of the fragility of the Islands' ecology and the dangers presented by tourist intervention. The conservationist argument that peaked in the mid 1990s and culminated in a series of environmental legislation against deforestation and for the protection of indigenous communities, however, seems to have been gradually sidelined.[4] Environmental activists face the relentless opposition of a tourism industry that seeks to subvert the 'endangered Islands' argument by persuasive support for the virtues of their version of ecotourism, that is, a form of tourism responsive to the concerns of the environment. While there are few grounds to believe that mainstream tourist industries promote any meaningful eco-tourist practices on the Islands, there is increasing evidence to show how well tourist interests, both state and private, have sought to neutralize the political edge of the environmentalist lobby and co-opt the 'ecological' framing of the Islands as a means of self-promotion. The focus of this new tourist rhetoric is premised upon a projection of the Islands' 'tropicality' that draws upon the frames of ecology but redefines it on its own terms.

The notion of tropicality, as discussed by historian David Arnold, derives from an understanding of the tropics as a 'conceptual and not just a physical space'. It became a way in which Europe defined, labelled and understood a geographical zone that was both distinctive and alien from what was known as the temperate zones. In its most basic understanding the term 'tropics' referred to those lands that straddled the Equator and were defined by heat, moisture and lush vegetation. Tropical lands were also deemed to be either pestilential or Edenic. Ideas of tropicality, in sum, derived from a range of scientific and scenic ideas and became critical points of reference in colonial encounters in Asia, Africa and the Pacific.[5]

---

[4] For details of the environmentalist movement and the Supreme Court intervention in the Andaman Islands, see, among others, Pankaj Sekhsaria, *Troubled Islands: Writings on the Indigenous People and Environment of the Andaman and Nicobar Islands* (Pune: Kalpavriksh, 2003), 35–41.

[5] David Arnold, *The Tropics and the Travelling Gaze, India, Landscape and Science, 1800–1856* (Seattle: University of Washington Press, 2006), 35.

This chapter draws upon studies that have explored the long and complex history of the discourse of tropicality as it took shape through the mid-eighteenth century in Europe and more generally in the countries of the Global North as they began to colonize countries beyond the equator.[6] In more recent times, Felix Driver and Luciana Martins have observed, 'the discourse of tropicality that took shape under the aegis of colonialism, has further proliferated under the influences of decolonization, developmental discourses, global tourism, commodity advertizing and environmental politics'.[7] To elaborate this point further, I draw attention to Denis Cosgrove's explorations of what he describes as the interplay between 'tropical epistemologies' and the 'ontological tropics'.[8] Cosgrove is interested in the 'historical drift' between the 'tropics' as geographical spaces and 'tropicality' as a set of imagined, pictorial and textual spaces.[9] This focus on the visual and discursive interplay between a physical space and the symbolic values invested in it mark the point of entry to this chapter as it tries to understand how contending discourses on the 'tropicality' of the Andaman Islands (and also in the southern extension of the archipelago, the Nicobars), has been variously configured in post-colonial frames of development, environment and tourism.

This chapter maps the contours of the complex post-colonial ecological/aesthetic discourse that has come to inform debates on tourism and conservation in the Andaman and Nicobar Islands, particularly those that focus on the nature of the Islands' 'tropicality'. It tries to understand how an emerging discourse on 'Island ecology' has opened up a new debate on the inherent fragility of its tropicality. This new tropical epistemology, based squarely on the issues of environment, questioned earlier developmental discourses that took the Islands' 'tropical' fecundity for granted. The chapter considers some of the key environmental reports on the Islands that emerged from the mid 1970s and tries to understand how concerns about the Islands' ecology have been framed around the key argument that colonization, settlement and developmental agendas premised upon an assumption of the Islands' resilient tropicality were deeply flawed. The new environmentalist discourse used an array of empirical data as well as visual evidence to show how environmental degradation had set in in the Islands and imperceptibly

---

[6] See, for instance, Felix Driver and Luciana Martins (eds.), *Tropical Visions in an Age of Empire* (Chicago: University of Chicago Press), 2005.

[7] Felix Driver and Luciana Martins, 'Introduction', in Driver and Martins (eds.), *Tropical Visions*, 3–22, 4.

[8] Denis Cosgrove, 'Tropic and Tropicality', in Driver and Martins (eds.), *Tropical Visions*, 198.

[9] Cosgrove, 'Tropic and Tropicality', 197–216, 198.

endangered their future. While the first such report positioned itself as a purely 'scientific' environmental impact record, subsequent documents emanating both from the Island administration as well as private agencies became more polemical. The Island administration, for instance, took upon itself to sponsor the production of a range of books in visually appealing formats that could convey the environmental concerns of the Islands to a wider public and also present its own responses to it.

I argue that it was the deliberate visual focus on the Islands' endangered tropical ecology that introduced an inadvertent paradox in the debate on development, tourism and conservation. This was particularly evident in the way the visual rhetoric of conservation introduced new modalities of experiencing and engaging the Islands' natural environment. For conservationists, to make the case for the ecologically 'endangered Isles', it was important to document what was truly endangered and what was thence to be conserved. The visuality of conservation thus invariably turned into a pictorial celebration of the Islands' distinctive tropical ecosystems – forest, mangrove and marine. The persistent visual documentation of these ecosystems by conservationists rendered familiar what was hitherto little known and made it seem accessible and open to experience.

It is a central argument of the chapter that the visuality of conservation lent itself to new ways of redefining the Islands' tropicality. The epistemological frame through which conservationists viewed the Islands' tropical ecosystems was gradually jettisoned. In other words, political and economic arguments that historicized the degenerative conditions of the Islands' forest, mangrove and marine resources were systematically downplayed and the Islands' tropical value redefined in purely aesthetic terms. The tourist industry was thus able to draw upon the environmentalist agenda and successfully 'tropicalize' the Andaman Islands on its own terms. I use the term 'tropicalization' to refer to what Krista Thompson describes in the Caribbean context as 'complex visual systems through which (tropical) Islands were imaged for tourist consumption and the social and political implications of these representations on the actual physical space of the Islands'.[10]

While focusing on the visual representations of the Islands' tropical landscapes, the chapter draws also upon Elizabeth Edwards' observation that the visual medium of photography has to be seen beyond its representational values and in conjunction with its textual and material

---

[10] Krista A. Thompson, *An Eye for the Tropics: Tourism, Photography and Framing the Caribbean Picturesque* (Durham, NC: Duke University Press, 2006), 1–26.

frames.[11] From this perspective, it explores how visual and textual trans-actions between discourses of tourism and environment played out within the covers of various coffee table books on the Islands, particularly those that were either directly produced or supported by government agencies.[12]

The chapter invokes the arguments of both Elizabeth Edwards and Deborah Poole to underscore the significance of approaching images as material objects with 'sensuous characteristics of their own' and of their ability to reveal the ways in which 'fantasy and desire enter into the production and consumption of visual images'.[13] It argues that the coffee table format, with its oversized pages, glossy paper, visual excess and limited text, provides an interesting site to examine the political-aesthetic terms in which the debates on Island development, environment and tourism were presented to the public in easily accessible ways. The coffee table book is often treated as a souvenir to be given to dignitaries visiting the Islands or as general publicity material to be put on display in relevant government offices. The coffee table book, in other words, functions as a visual object that is meant to command immediate attention. The study of coffee table books is juxtaposed with government-sponsored studies and other stakeholder reports on the environment. I will show how deeply researched and nuanced arguments on the environmental implications of developmental agendas on the Islands were successfully simplified or neutralized in the course of their presentation within this larger, visually compelling format deliberately designed to generate instant curiosity.

With its focus on both textual and visual sources, the chapter seeks to explore how environmental issues have been framed and represented in the Andaman Islands and more significantly how these have served paradoxically to both challenge and reinforce colonial and neoliberal representations of the Islands as pristine tropical landscapes awaiting exploration, colonization and consumption. The chapter argues that a critical examination of the shifting frames of tropicality opens up possi-bilities of understanding the post-colonial anxieties of the Andaman Islands as it struggles to define a coherent path for its economic and ecological survival.

---

[11] Elizabeth Edwards and Janice Hart, 'Introduction: Photographs as Objects', in Elizabeth Edwards and Janice Hart (eds.), *Photographs Objects Histories: On the materiality of images*, London, 2004, 1–16.

[12] The Andaman and Nicobar Island administration has published coffee table books at various times under the aegis of either department of tourism or the department of environment to showcase various faces of the Islands in response to specific contexts and the needs of the administration.

[13] Poole, *Vision, Race and Modernity*, 12–13.

The environmental anxieties of colonization

As elaborated in Chapter 2, the Shivdasani Report that drew up the post-Partition plans for the colonization and development of the Andaman and Nicobar Islands in 1949 included a programme of refugee rehabilitation based on a massive extension of agriculture in the Islands.[14] It was on the basis of this report that the Andaman and Nicobar administration brought hundreds of refugee families to the Islands in the aftermath of the Partition and particularly in the years after 1949, when large-scale riots in the deltaic districts of East Pakistan forced a huge exodus of agrarian labouring families into refugee camps in West Bengal and other northern and central Indian states.

Seen from the perspective of the larger developmental imaginary that it embodied, the Shivdasani Report, as has been argued in Chapter 2, was in many ways a recapitulation of old colonial ideas about the Islands' development and their key assumptions about land and labour. It drew upon both the immediately preceding plans for post-war reconstruction in the Islands and the older colonization programme of the late 1920s and 1930s. From last British Chief Commissioner N. K. Paterson's development plan of 1946, it took the argument the Islands had undergone acute depopulation, hence they needed to be recolonized with appropriate groups of settlers/colonists.[15] The population had dropped from about 22,000 in 1941 to 14,000 in 1946.[16] The Report also reiterated that an estimated 3,000 acres of cultivable land was lying vacant, abandoned and fallow, and that the Islands had to be turned into a self-sufficient agrarian economy with supplementary investments in plantation and horticulture. Paterson made an emphatic plea in 1946: agriculture was a more viable route to the development and settlement of the Islands because it was the only way of ensuring the growth of a population tied to the land.[17] His view was that the Islands should also be used to absorb any surplus population of India. If one were to trace the lineages of the Paterson Report one could find in it an extension and elaboration of the first major plan for agrarian colonization and development initiated under the aegis of the Islands' Chief Commissioner M. L. Ferrar in the mid 1920s. Like Paterson, Ferrar too premised

[14] H. Shivdasani, 'Report on the Possibilities of Colonization and Development of the Andaman and Nicobar Islands', Government of India, Ministry of Home Affairs, 5 March 1949, V/190/65, IOR.
[15] Kiran Dhingra, *The Andaman and Nicobar Islands in the Twentieth Century: A Gazetteer* (New Delhi: Oxford University Press, 2005), 71.
[16] Dhingra, *The Andaman and Nicobar Islands*.
[17] Dhingra, *The Andaman and Nicobar Islands*.

his scheme of development of the Islands on the vision of a flourishing agricultural colony.

But apart from the continuities that marked the specific proposals of the Shivdasani Report and the earlier programmes of colonization and development set in motion in the 1920s and thereafter again in the immediate aftermath of the British reoccupation of the Islands in 1946, there were more fundamental continuities. These related to the deep anchorage of the Shivdasani Report in an essentially colonial discourse on land and the 'will to improve it'. After all, it was this that was so central to the settlement of Ferrargunj (Chapter 2). Yet notwithstanding its colonial provenance, the Report continued to inform all subsequent plans for resettlement and development of the Islands. The 1964 Plan for the Accelerated Development of the Islands was critical in this regard.[18]

At the time of the redrafting of its objectives in 1964 the Ministry of Rehabilitation was made responsible for the development of 'special areas': those parts of the country where for climatic, geographical or other reasons, economic and social development had been retarded, and which though sparsely populated were richly endowed with natural resources. These areas, it was deemed, had to be put on a course of accelerated development. The first area to be notified in this special areas list was the Andaman and Nicobar Islands. They were considered to be eminently suitable for resource development and for the rehabilitation of migrants from East Pakistan.

Commenting on this development strategy, the 1964 Accelerated Development Plan categorically stated that it would set up long-term goals and delineate special programmes for their achievement. In the case of the Andaman and Nicobar Islands, it would be necessary to take into consideration, it noted, their specific economic and strategic characteristics. The Plan turned unequivocally to the question of land and observed that it was 'the biggest unexploited resource' on the Islands and therefore would occupy a dominant position in the ensuing programme.[19] It emphasized that the present land-use pattern would be directed in future to encourage the opening up of further swathes of virgin land for colonization and in which agriculture and plantations would play a dominant role.

Addressing the specific debate on whether agriculture or forestry should drive developmental agendas on the Islands, the Plan took an interestingly nuanced view. While it acknowledged that there were two

---

[18] *Report by the Inter-Departmental Team on Accelerated Development Programme for the Andaman and Nicobar Islands* (Ministry of Rehabilitation, Government of India, 1964).

[19] *Report by the Inter-Departmental Team on Accelerated Development*, 1, 16.

diametrically opposed views on the subject, one clearly favouring agriculture and the other forestry, it was evident that the demands of development had to weigh out the comparative advantages of both in terms of
the economic promises each held out. The Plan concluded that the
extension of agriculture had to be considered the more viable option at
that moment.[20]

From this it followed that forests should be cleared from all lands
deemed suitable for agriculture and plantations, and their retention
allowed only where agriculture would not be profitable. It addressed
fears of soil erosion with the argument that such had occurred in the past
only because no measures to check it were taken. With the provision of
adequate safeguards, the hazards of soil erosion could be easily averted.
The debate on agriculture versus forestry settled, the newly appointed
office of the Chief Commissioner was directed to open up forest areas,
locate suitable lands for farm and plantation crops, clear jungles, extend
agricultural operations and resettle families of former East Pakistan
migrants, Sri Lankan repatriates and ex-servicemen in selected islands as
part of a new colonization policy based on considerations of skills required
for the implementation of specific developmental projects.[21]

Within a decade, the entire accelerated development project came
under serious government scrutiny. In March 1975, Prime Minister
Indira Gandhi issued directives for a complete halt in deforestation on
the Islands, after the problems of deforestation, soil erosion and waste
began to be noticed in the areas opened up for agricultural extension.
She also called for a study of the environmental and ecological aspects of
the developmental project on the Islands.[22] A multi-disciplinary team
consisting of representatives of Agricultural Science and Technology and
Rehabilitation visited the Islands to recommend interim measures.[23] The
Prime Minister also urged that the problem of deforestation should be
studied in depth by a 'foreign expert' if necessary.[24]

Accordingly, in 1976 the first comprehensive report on the environmental implications of colonization and development in the Andaman
Islands was prepared by D. N. McVean of the International Union for

---

[20] *Report by the Inter-Departmental Team on Accelerated Development*, 17–18.
[21] 'Report on Visit of the Members of the Consultative Committee of the Department of
Rehabilitation to Andaman and Nicobar Islands from 26 February 1976 to 2 March
1976', prepared by Chief Development-cum-Rehabilitation Commissioner, Andaman
and Nicobar Administration Port Blair, A&N Archives, 3.
[22] 'Rehabilitation Programme in the Andaman and Nicobar Islands, presented by Chief
Development-cum-Rehabilitation Commissioner, Andaman and Nicobar Islands',
15 March 1978, 6, A&N Archives (henceforth Rehabilitation Programme, 1978).
[23] Rehabilitation Programme, 1978.   [24] Rehabilitation Programme, 1978, 6, 7.

Conservation of Nature and Natural Resources. Entitled 'Report on Land Use in the Andaman and Nicobar Islands', the document was prepared with financial assistance from the Government of India and the United Nations environmental programme. In a preface, McVean wrote:

The report is required to evaluate the impact of deforestation on the general environment of the Andaman and Nicobar Islands and to formulate guidelines for land use and conservation there. These were a broad set of guidelines issued by the Government of India to a multidisciplinary team of experts in 1975. The team consisted of senior government officials and experts in botany, soil science, soil conservation climatology as well as representatives from the Andaman and Nicobar administration, the Planning Commission and the Department of Rehabilitation. It may be noted at this point that environmental concerns relating to the Andaman and Nicobar Islands were first taken up at the international level in 1969 at the Eleventh Technical Meeting of the IUCN in New Delhi. This meeting acquires significance in the context of the fact that just three years before this the government of India had endorsed an Accelerated Plan for the Development of the Islands.[25]

Indeed, subsequent to the meeting of 1969 four separate ground reports on the Andaman and Nicobar Islands had been prepared by the Forest Research Institute, Dehradun, the National Council of Agricultural and Economic Research (NCAER) and the Ministry of Agriculture.[26] McVean mentioned that though he sought to build upon the findings of these earlier reports, his study was concerned less with economic and administrative aspects and concentrated more on the overall 'ecological' situation in the Islands. The study, he noted, had been conducted over a period of six weeks in early 1976, including four weeks of fieldwork based in Port Blair. Apart from its main findings on the ecological conditions of the Islands, the McVean Report took it upon itself to challenge one of the most enduring beliefs about these tropical Islands: '*the myth that luxuriant tropical forest necessarily indicated immense fertility is a long-standing ecological misconception*'.[27]

The McVean Report suggested that tropical forest soils could be extremely 'impoverished' and were often indistinguishable from more fertile soils, as luxuriant growth was not always indicative of soil fertility. Such growth was possible only because soil nutrients had accumulated over a vast period of time and were kept in brisk circulation between the tree canopy and ground level as a result of leaf fall, rapid decomposition

[25] D. N. McVean, 'Report on Land Use in the Andaman and Nicobar Islands', (Switzerland: Morges, 1976), 17–23, A&N Archives.

[26] McVean, 'Report on Land Use', 1.

[27] McVean, 'Report on Land Use', 17 (emphasis mine).

and nutrient absorption by the surface roots. Random forest clearance broke this cycle and made it almost impossible for the soil to regenerate. The implicit argument in the Report was that all developmental agendas based upon the myth of tropical soil resilience, and therefore the legitimacy of the extension of settlement through forest clearance, had to be radically rethought. Tropical soils were vulnerable to rapid impoverishment and sterility.[28]

As far its main findings were concerned the Report focused on four major areas. It was categorical in its assertion that the Andaman and Nicobar Islands were essentially forest terrain and hence unsuitable for large-scale agriculture or agriculture-based enterprises. The Island economy must, McVean argued, be based on forestry and forest products. If severe damage to the island environment were to be avoided, only subsidiary agricultural and fishery development could be allowed.[29] Following from this initial observation, McVean warned that all further immigration for land settlement was absolutely inadvisable and limits had to be set to any further allocation of land to second-generation settlers, other migrants, or local residents. He recommended an immediate land resource and capability survey, based on what he called a 'high quality aerial survey'.[30]

On the extent of damage already done, the Report stated that so far the most marked had been around the area of Port Blair, Bakultala, Rangat, the Betapur valley and on the islands of Baratang and Neil. The ecological damage in these areas consisted of wasted forest resources, soil loss and reduced availability of surface water. Great forest wastage had also been evident in Katchal in the Nicobars and in Little Andaman. The identification of these areas was significant in light of the fact that these were precisely those areas in which the accelerated push for development had been recommended in the 1966 Report. McVean, however, was quick to qualify his observations of ecological damage around Port Blair by turning to the larger history of British colonization of the region. He argued that accelerated erosion had begun with deforestation around Port Blair over one hundred years previously. The issue was of gradual intensification ever since. There were clear warning signs that soil loss was quickly increasing in the present phase of land development. The gradual yet perceptible drying up of soil moisture and the loss of soil structure were the first indications of what he predicted as 'impending erosion'.[31]

---

[28] McVean, 'Report on Land Use', 1–2.   [29] McVean, 'Report on Land Use', 1.
[30] McVean, 'Report on Land Use', 2.   [31] McVean, 'Report on Land Use', 2.

The McVean Report is particularly noteworthy for its warning against the hazards of rice cultivation. In this, it went against the developmental narrative of the Islands since the 1950s. Throughout the 1950s and 1960s it was widely believed that the Andaman Islands had to invest in agricultural research, particularly in paddy cultivation.[32] The Report argued that the focus on the expansion of the settlement made the investment in paddy cultivation compelling, yet had failed to appreciate that the climate and lack of surface water precluded the possibility of more than one crop per annum. The more suitable soil yields were satisfactory in the first few years but had subsequently fallen sharply, especially with the introduction of improved strands of rice. Because of constantly falling yields even on the more fertile soil, plans for the progressive reduction of rationed rice for settlers had to be abandoned. It was observed that the Islands had never been more than 60 per cent self-sufficient and that this figure would perhaps drop further in future.

Following these observations on the fallacies of the expansion of paddy cultivation on the Islands, the Report concluded that although there may have been some grounds for the opening up of tropical forests for human settlement during earlier years, the continuation of such a policy was bound to be counterproductive. All the previous advantages of virgin terrain, uncomplicated by problems of land ownership, would necessarily have been frittered away by the later push for further settlement. The Report suggested that, clearly, a period of reappraisal and recognition was urgently required. Further immigration would have to be stopped and forest clearance limited to that required to meet the needs of the natural increase of population. The Report further suggested that land allocation should cease and all expansion take place in the wage-earning sector. There was an immediate need for a land capability survey that should have been carried out much earlier, starting with an aerial photographic survey and proceeding by way of a land-use assessment to an overall development plan.[33]

By questioning the overall developmental paradigm in the Islands, focusing particularly on the counterproductive strategies of random forest clearance and paddy cultivation, the McVean Report brought into focus the need for more data on the extent of ecological damage effected on the Islands. The Report however, focused mostly on the terrain,

---

[32] Department of Agriculture reports of this period are replete with recommendations to introduce innovative techniques, including those of Japanese paddy cultivation, to increase productivity. For details, see Office Memorandum from District Commissioner to Agricultural Officer (AO), 30 June 1956, No. 35–31 (5) 56/02, A&N Archives (henceforth District Commissioner to AO).

[33] District Commissioner to AO, 9–11.

particularly on the visible impacts of the expansion of the settlement, namely soil erosion and the rapid denudation of its tropical forest cover. A comprehensive survey of the impact of settlement on the lives of the Islands' indigenous peoples or on its animal life remained outside the purview of the Report. There were, however, concerns expressed about the building of the proposed Grand Andaman Trunk Road connecting South to North Andamans. It was argued that the road would adversely impact the Jarawas if it went thought their territory.[34] Although there were suggestions everywhere of the potentially damaging impact of settlement on the life of the Islands as a whole, the Report seemed to suggest all was not lost. All that was needed at this point was a reappraisal and recalibration of the developmental agenda.

Overall, the McVean Report flagged the major ecological impacts of the settlement initiatives in the Islands but refrained from raising an alarm. It was restrained in its tone and constructive in its suggestions, for it was meant to be 'scientific' and not polemical. Although it suggested the use of aerial photography as a way of assessing the overall impact of forest clearance and cultivation, the Report desisted from the use of any visuals. It is important to make this point because subsequently most environmental literature on the Andaman and Nicobar Islands, either documents and books, or journal articles and reports, made judicious use of a range of images to make their point. The counter-narrative to the officially sanctioned developmental agenda would be shaped largely through a complex matrix of images that would serve to reframe public discourse on the Islands in the years to come.

The endangered Isles

Almost a decade after the publication of the McVean Report, another environmental dossier on the Andaman Islands was prepared by the Indian herpetologist and ecologist, Romulus Whitaker, who worked as a consultant to the Environmental Services Group, World Wildlife Fund (WWF), India.[35] In the preface to this report, he made it clear that 'what was presented in the following pages was not merely an academic study'. Rather, it was a 'powerful appeal' to save an 'endangered group of

---

[34] District Commissioner to AO, 20.
[35] Romulus Whitaker, *Endangered Andamans: Managing Tropical Moist Forests, A Case Study of the Andamans* (New Delhi: Environmental Services Group, World Wildlife Fund, India and MAB India, Department of Environment, 1985). Note: MAB is the shortened title for the programme conducted by the National Committee for 'Man and Biosphere', under the aegis of the Department of Environment, Government of India.

Islands, so near, yet so far'.[36] The Whitaker Report implicitly positioned itself as an updated supplement to the McVean Report. The issues it raised were an elaboration of McVean's study, but its tone and tenor were distinctly polemical. The subtitle of Whitaker's report made it clear that the focus would remain on the Islands' tropical forests and the dangers it faced in the context of colonization, settlement and developmental agendas. From its title to its cover image it was clear that this report demanded no reappraisals but immediate action. The image of an untidy heap of felled trees and tangled branches on the front cover was meant to draw attention to the central focus of the report, but it was clear that the argument presented would go well beyond the forest, and extend to its human and animal habitat.

Two observations in the preface were critical in this respect. Firstly, the Report was to make it clear that the 'greatest single environmental threat to the Andaman and Nicobar Islands was the destruction of their tropical forests for development'.[37] The forest cover continued to be removed officially to meet the timber requirements of the match, paper and plywood industries. Tamil Nadu, it stated, depended on the Andaman Islands for half of its timber needs! Other major projects that had destroyed large tracts of forest cover included clearance of half of Little Andaman for oil palm plantations, the clearance for an airstrip on Great Nicobar, and more significantly the clearance for the building of the Andaman Trunk Road that cut through a large section of Jarawa Reserve Territory.[38] The clearance of mangroves and the felling of several thousand acres of virgin forest for the construction of jetties, airstrips, and roads had resulted, it argued, in numerous 'downstream effects' detracting from the possibility of sustainable future development.[39]

The second significant point made in the preface was about the 'tragic impact' of this development on the Islands' indigenous population. Three of the five tribal groups on the Islands, it argued, faced imminent extinction. It was only the Sentinelese and Jarawas who had resisted contact and therefore enjoyed a greater chance of survival.[40] Unlike the McVean Report, which made references to the impact of Andaman Trunk Road on the Jarawa, the Whitaker Report made the explicit connection between the destruction of the forest with the destruction of the Islands' indigenous communities. The frame of endangerment was meant to underscore

[36] Whitaker, *Endangered Andamans*, 2.   [37] Whitaker, *Endangered Andamans*, 2–3.

[38] Construction work on the Andaman Trunk Road connecting Chidiyatapu in South Andaman to Aerial Bay in the north started in 1958. The estimated length of the road at that point was 343 kilometres. See Draft Annual Plan, 1984–5, PWD File No. D/2165, A&N Archives.

[39] Whitaker, *Endangered Andamans*, 3.   [40] Whitaker, *Endangered Andamans*, 3.

the prospects of imminent danger to the entwined fates of the fragile land and fragile lives of the people on the Islands. The Whitaker Report took the position that if the tropical forests of the Andaman Islands had to be conserved, its indigenous communities had to be protected: the forests and indigenous peoples were symbiotically related.

The Whitaker Report was clear in its recommendations of the need to formulate a decisive policy of conservation and development in the Islands. The focus at that point was on the imperative to conserve the forest cover of the Islands. About 70 per cent of the Andaman Islands was still forested, it claimed, but most of this land consisted of degraded secondary growth. Since the late 1940s, it argued, soil, meteorological and forestry experts had stressed the need to keep the Islands under forest cover, yet the government continued to endorse large-scale felling and plantation projects. In the words of the Report:

A change of policy from revenue earning forestry to conservation management of the forests along with enlightened development based on limited resource utilization would allow the Andamans to remain ecologically stable while supporting a limited human population growth.[41]

What distinguished the Whitaker Report from the McVean Report was its focus on the tribal communities of the Islands and the impact of colonization and development on their lives. This theme was elaborated at the outset of the report, and the colonial project and its impact was described through the polemics of invasion and development and consequent decline of the Islands' tribal populations. Two tables, comparing figures of the decline of tribal populations in the Andamans and in countries such as Brazil, Chile and Australia, were put together to make the point of similar fates of indigenous peoples that faced the consequences of the destructive projects of colonization and development.[42] In the Andaman Islands, Whitaker pointed to the demographic catastrophes faced by the Great Andamanese and the Onges in particular. The so called 'hostile' tribes the Jarawas and the Sentinelese were yet to be accurately enumerated, he noted, but it was clear that their numbers were far better than the ones who were supposedly 'friendly'.[43] If, therefore, there were still possibilities of securing the conditions for the survival of the Onges, the Whitaker Report stressed that any conservation effort had to begin in Little Andaman. It was here that the Onges had been settled and it was here that major projects for plantation, forestry and settlement were underway.

---

[41] Whitaker, *Endangered Andamans*, 4.   [42] Whitaker, *Endangered Andamans*, 7.
[43] Whitaker, *Endangered Andamans*, 7.

The Whitaker Report used limited visual material but it is interesting to note that it was employed. No other report hitherto had used images in an order that would generate the framework for a new visual narrative of the settlement and colonization of the Andamans. The Whitaker Report in a sense set in motion a paradigm shift in politics of visuality in the Andaman Islands wherein the narrative of settlement/development/ improvement was juxtaposed with the narrative of destruction and the concomitant argument for conservation.

The first image in the Whitaker Report was that of an Onge family of three. A father, mother and child stand in a row with baskets and arrows in their hands looking straight into the camera with an air of studied indifference.[44] This was immediately followed in the next page by an image of an Onge couple sitting together in a posture of evident comfort. Their faces were painted in traditional patterns and they seemed to be at ease in front of the camera.[45] There was nothing in these two images suggestive of the ill health of the Onges or any signs of their imminent demographic demise. The pictures that followed thereafter, however, pointed to the possibilities of such a fate if immediate steps were not taken to stop and change the course of development in their habitat of Little Andaman.

The next sequence of images depicted the destruction of forests not only in Little Andaman but throughout the south, middle and northern limits of the Andaman Islands. The first image in this series was titled 'encroachment'.[46] Though blurred, the image was one of a haphazard clearing in the forest with traces of huts at the far end and billowing smoke in the backdrop. The next image, titled 'Mangrove Felling', depicted a similarly cleared patch in the midst of a mangrove forest with four men walking through it. It is not clear if they were forest labourers or just settlers. However, it is important to note that both images were from North Andaman, a place hitherto relatively 'uncolonized', but under threat during the mid 1960s when South Andaman had become heavily populated. A new regime of private forestry in North Andaman Island had already created the context for the extension of settlement in the region.

Much of the Whitaker Report focused on the 'plunder' of the Andaman forests. The Report was scathing in its attack on the purport of forestry as well as the costs of human settlement as a result of it. There were images of 'massive clear felled areas that lay unused', of deforestation on steep slopes, of severe stream erosion, of unplanned urbanization in North

---

[44] Whitaker, *Endangered Andamans*, 8.   [45] Whitaker, *Endangered Andamans*, 8, 10.
[46] Whitaker, *Endangered Andamans*, 17.

Andaman and of threatened flora and fauna.[47] Taken together, the images and their captions became powerful referents to the emerging visual counter-narrative of settlement and colonization in the Andaman Islands. All environmental critiques of the Islands' development would henceforth elaborate this narrative in greater depth and detail.

Significantly, the Whitaker Report also set the tone for a new appraisal of the threatened flora and fauna of the Islands. In a chapter titled 'Threatened Wildlife', it began by stating:

[A]ll this forest flogging poses a great threat to the tropical flora and fauna of the Andamans whose richness deserves special note. The wildlife of the Andamans shows an affinity with that of mainland India, Burma and Malaysia. The Islands' long geographic isolation from the Asian mainland has resulted in a high rate of endemism.[48]

The Report went on to observe that there were 255 species and sub-species of birds including endemics like the Andaman teal and the Narcondam hornbill; 35 species of mammals including the dugong and the Andaman pig; 80 species of reptiles and amphibians including 20 endemics; and 3,000 species of flowering plants, 10 per cent of which were endemics. The numbers were staggering, and Whitaker's focus on endemism would add a new critical element in the discourse of conservation. Whitaker went on to argue that the Andaman and Nicobar Islands had served as a haven for naturalists and work on surveying, collecting and classifying the Islands' flora and fauna had begun in colonial times. He suggested that this early and more recent work had now to be consolidated in terms of drawing out systematic plans for conservation.

Six small national parks and five sanctuaries were established in the Islands when the Wildlife Protection Act of 1972 had come into force in 1973.[49] Yet poaching remained a compelling problem. The Whitaker Report argued that the Government had to attend to the issue of poaching more effectively, as regular incidents were reported from all across the Islands. Police in remote outposts such as the Interview Islands were often offenders, as they had to live off the land for their meat requirements.[50]

A scheme for expanding the scope and activities of the Wildlife Fund for Nature and Wildlife Conservation was submitted to the government for approval. The scheme envisaged establishing sanctuaries, wildlife reserves, biosphere reserves, protection of endangered species and the development of a mini zoo. Studies were to be conducted on the ecology

[47] Whitaker, *Endangered Andamans*, 22–45.   [48] Whitaker, *Endangered Andamans*, 33.
[49] Whitaker, *Endangered Andamans*, 34.   [50] Whitaker, *Endangered Andamans*, 34.

of endemic species such as the Narcondam hornbill, the megapode, the Nicobar macaque and the Andaman teal, among others.[51] The scheme also proposed the protection and maintenance of natural features such as caves, volcanoes and limestone bridges. It suggested the creation of a whole range of protective zones – parks, sanctuaries and reserves – to conserve whatever was left of the Islands' endangered forests, peoples and species. Forests in the North Andaman, Middle Andaman, Little Andaman, Rutland Island and Ritchies Archipelago all warranted protection as biosphere reserves.[52]

In his concluding chapter, Whitaker chose to reiterate the problems posed by what was described as the 'mounting human pressure on the Islands'.[53] He stressed the history of post-Independence colonization and the drive for agrarian extension. He put together a table to chart the incremental growth of agriculture in the Islands from 1931 onwards. He drew upon the McVean Report to show how successive schemes for accelerated growth had generated new pressures on the land, particularly by settlers from East Pakistan, who he argued 'were grabbing whatever land they can'. Continuing his critique of the land-use patterns among newly arrived settlers, Whitaker warned that unless 'basic ecological practices were not observed already evident changes such as soil erosion and infertility and reduced water resources would worsen'.[54] What Whitaker sought to suggest therefore was that if the Islands were to be increasingly targeted for rapid developmental activity, ecological concerns had to be urgently factored in or else the Islands' fragile tropical ecology would be pushed to the brink.

Conservation photography and the shifting frames of tropicality

Soon after the publication of the Whitaker Report, in 1986 Indian Prime Minister Rajiv Gandhi visited the Andaman Islands, in order to push for a new developmental strategy responsive to ecological concerns. He set up a new body: the Island Development Authority.[55] Ironically, the Prime Minister also showed a keen interest in developing a free port in Great Nicobar along the lines of that of Hong Kong.[56] The consequence of this announcement and the promise of new commercial opportunities in both the Andaman and Nicobar Islands unleashed a surge of land

[51] Whitaker, *Endangered Andamans*, 35.   [52] Whitaker, *Endangered Andamans*, 35.
[53] Whitaker, *Endangered Andamans*, 42.   [54] Whitaker, *Endangered Andamans*, 44.
[55] Dhingra, *The Andaman and Nicobar Islands*, 104.
[56] Dhingra, *The Andaman and Nicobar Islands*, 104.

speculation. However, the rapidly growing land prices did not deter the steady flow of new migrants. It was at this point that environmental concerns were raised once again, this time relating to the 'carrying capacity' of the Islands and new threats to its ecology. For the Islands' administration, suggestions to deregularize encroachments by new settlers or to issue valid Island identity cards to *bona fide* settlers were difficult to implement. The population influx continued, and by the early 1990s had crossed the two *lakh* (two hundred thousand) mark, a number that well exceeded the desirable limits.[57]

Environmental concerns also arose from the fact that the Islands' administration wished to encourage new forms of tourism. On the recommendation of the Working Group on Tourism, constituted by the Island Development Authority, tourism was officially declared an industry in 1987.[58] For the Andaman and Nicobar Islands' administration thereafter, the challenge was to manage the requirements of tourism, the presence of settlers and growing concerns about the impact of both on the Islands' ecology.[59] It was in this context that it sought to initiate new strategies of public communication of environmental concerns that would take the findings from the various reports published in the preceding years and present these in an accessible format for a wider audience.

In 1989, Cecil J. Saldanha, 'priest, professor and scientist' best known for his work on the flora of Hassan District in Karnataka and for his passion for conservation photography, was commissioned by the Ministry of Environment and Forests, Government of India, to prepare an illustrated study of environmental impact on the Andaman and Nicobar Islands, including neighbouring Lakshadweep.[60] In his preface to the book Saldanha observed that there was a great deal of apprehension about the fact that the 'unique and fragile ecosystems' of the Andaman and Nicobar Islands had been irrevocably damaged by the developmental frenzy of the last three decades. In view of this, it was felt at the highest levels of government that there was a need for an objective and integrated

---

[57] Dhingra, *The Andaman and Nicobar Islands*, 105.

[58] Harry V. Andrews and Vasumathi Sankaran (eds.), *Sustainable Management of Protected Areas in the Andaman and Nicobar Islands* (New Delhi: ANET, IIPA and FFI, 2002), 64–5.

[59] For details, see *Proceedings of the Third Meeting of the Island Development Authority*, 29 December 1987. It was at this meeting that Cecil J. Saldanha was requested by the Prime Minister to make a presentation on the environmental and ecological features of the Andaman and Nicobar and Lakshwadeep Islands (6). The IDA report was sourced from the personal collection of Shri Samir Acharya, founder of the Society for Andaman Nicobar Ecology (SANE).

[60] Cecil J. Saldanha (ed.), *Andaman, Nicobar and Lakshadweep: An Environmental Impact Assessment* (New Delhi: Ministry of Environment, 1989), Blurb.

appraisal of the situation in these beautiful islands. Saldanha under-scored the need for a holistic and rather than a 'sectoral' approach to appraise the environmental impact on the Islands while keeping in mind that their tropical ecology was distinct from that of the Indian mainland.[61]

Although the broad thrust of its research findings and its critique of the developmental agenda on the Islands drew upon the McVean and Whitaker reports, Saldanha put forth his arguments within a somewhat different, distinctively ecological framework. At the very outset, he chose to emphasize that the Andaman and Nicobar Islands needed to be looked through the lens of specific 'ecosystems'. There were three identified ecosystems in the Islands, he argued: forest, mangrove and marine. Each had its own interlinked sub-systems and was linked to the other ecosys-tems by 'geological and physiographic conditions'.[62]

The protection of these tropical ecosystems was important for the survival of the Islands' human ecosystem; however, the Saldanha Report, unlike the McVean or Whitaker reports, made direct reference to the significance of these for the agenda of both conservation and tourism on the Islands. N. V. Subbarao, (of the Zoological Survey of India) in his chapter in the Saldanha Report, argued that that the rationale for conser-vation could be put under four categories: 'economic, aesthetic, ethical and ecological'.[63] He was clear that the 'economic and aesthetic aspects of conservation' were interrelated.[64] From the logic of this argument it followed that the marine, forest, and mangrove ecosystems each had their distinctive aesthetic appeal, and this was critical to the development of new forms of ecotourism on the Islands.

Coral cities on the seabed, for example, had an enduring aesthetic appeal, Subbarao wrote. However, in order to maintain it, the coral ecosystem had to be preserved as a 'treasure house'.[65] Ecoystems, he argued, ensured the preservation of the diversity of species, and these in all senses should be looked upon as 'islands of science'.[66] Like McVean and Whitaker before him, Saldanha too stressed on the need to establish national parks and sanctuaries on the Islands as a strategic first step

---

[61] Saldanha (ed.), *Andaman, Nicobar and Lakshadweep*, 1. The book was an edited volume with contributions from several scholars from the disciplines of zoology, botany, oceanography and ecology. It was divided into two sections, one with a focus on the Andaman and Nicobars and the other on the Lakshadweep Islands, though it was focused squarely on the former.

[62] Saldanha (ed.), *Andaman, Nicobar and Lakshadweep*, 23.

[63] Saldanha (ed.), *Andaman, Nicobar and Lakshadweep*, 81.

[64] Saldanha (ed.), *Andaman, Nicobar and Lakshadweep*, 81.

[65] Saldanha (ed.), *Andaman, Nicobar and Lakshadweep*, 78.

[66] Saldanha (ed.), *Andaman, Nicobar and Lakshadweep*, 81.

towards the conservation of the Islands' flora and fauna, along with its supporting ecosystems.

Unlike other reports that put an exclusive focus on issues of environmental degradation as a result of the colonization and developmental agendas pursued on the Islands, the Saldanha Report juxtaposed darker images of ecological crisis with the promise of new forms of renewal. This agenda of renewal was to be pursued through shifting focus from the utilization of land resources to those of the sea and also putting in place an agenda of conservation that could accommodate a new kind of tourism on the Islands; one that promised a new adventurous exploration of the island seascape and its varied flora and fauna.

The Saldanha Report was distinctive in its overall production values and its liberal use of visual material. A closer look at the plates allows us to see how an environmental impact assessment report could easily double as a coffee table book. As an oversized book with glossy pages, the Saldanha report was intentionally eye-catching. It was evident that if environmental concerns of the previous reports had to reach a wider public, scientific documents needed a radical visual overhaul.

Among the very first cluster of plates are images of a 'morning view at Port Blair', a view of Little Andaman, a group of images of lush evergreen forests of Bompoka in the Nicobars, and then a cluster of images of the Andaman and Nicobar evergreens and finally the magnificent Galathea River.[67] This collection of images forms a kind of preamble to the narrative of the tropical richness and the sublime beauty of the Andaman and Nicobar Islands. This set of plates is immediately followed by a series more 'scientific' in nature, giving readers a visual tour of the variations within the Andamanese forest ecosystem. There are images of a buttressed tree in a giant evergreen forest, close up shots of virgin evergreen forest in Cinque Islands, patchworks of mangrove, moist deciduous and littoral forests and hilltop greens.[68] This section in a sense is a visual elaboration of foresters G. Champion and S. K. Seth's late 1960s' classification of the Andaman and Nicobar forest system.[69] It was immediately followed by a series of images of the Islands' mangrove ecosystem: Mangroves lining a creek, an embankment of stilted roots and breathing knee roots. These constitute some of the iconic images of what would later become one of the Islands' prime eco-destinations.[70]

---

[67] Saldanha (ed.), *Andaman, Nicobar and Lakshadweep*, plates 1–4.

[68] Saldanha (ed.), *Andaman, Nicobar and Lakshadweep*, plates 1–4, 6–9.

[69] H. G. Champion and S. K. Seth, *A Revised Survey of the Forest Types of India* (Dehradun: Forest Research Institute, 1968).

[70] Saldanha (ed.), *Andaman, Nicobar and Lakshadweep*, plates 13–17.

The natural ecosystems are immediately followed by images of the Islands' indigenous people, most notably, again, the Onges. In this section there is a close-up shot of an Onge couple, with the title, 'civilized Onge'.[71] The fact that the Onge habitat was threatened by encroachments is visually communicated through images of immigrant settlements at Hut Bay in the vicinity of the Onge Reserve.[72] Similar images of lush paddy fields at Ferrargunj in South Andaman Islands and an uneven row of Bengali settlements at Diglipur in North Andaman complete the picture of the extent of the new colonization of the Islands.[73]

The ecological upshot of colonization is then narrated through a sequence of images of a rapidly changing landscape. Under the title 'forestry', the next series of images show the plunder of the forest wealth of the Islands: Towering Gurjan trees followed by massive felling in Rutland Island; elephants loading logs in Little Andaman; a log raft of floaters and sinkers towed to Mayabunder; Chatham Saw Mill; and finally, piles of logs cut for matchbox splinters.[74] The images of the depredation of forestry are violent and evocative.

The theme of environmental degradation is continued in the next pictures, that conveyed in a kind of raw realist vein the darker side of the Government of India's plans for the accelerated development of the Islands. Images of settlements were replaced by images of encroachments onto forest land, of mangroves destroyed for fuel wood, of the uneven extension of marginal agriculture in prime forest land, of deeply eroded hillsides and of cattle with the ubiquitous stephanofilarial hump sore.[75] Saldanha's larger thesis of the fallacies of island development through the rampant exploitation of land-based resources acquired new urgency through this powerful visual data. There was degradation all around with little hope for renewal. Although there is a token appreciation of government initiatives of agricultural research and agro-horticultural practices, with images of hillside orchards and multiple cropping for spices together with the image of a government farm at Jirkatang, the overall sense is one of wariness.[76] The time had come when a new developmental trajectory for the Islands had to be thought out.

Saldanha believed that the Islands' marine resources were yet to be fully utilized, but the turn to the sea had to be informed by a view to conserve its resources, too. The next set of images of the Islands' beaches

---

[71] Saldanha (ed.), *Andaman, Nicobar and Lakshadweep*, plate 19.
[72] Saldanha (ed.), *Andaman, Nicobar and Lakshadweep*, plates 20–1.
[73] Saldanha (ed.), *Andaman, Nicobar and Lakshadweep*, plates 29–30.
[74] Saldanha (ed.), *Andaman, Nicobar and Lakshadweep*, plates 34–6.
[75] Saldanha (ed.), *Andaman, Nicobar and Lakshadweep*, plates 42–3, 46–50.
[76] Saldanha (ed.), *Andaman, Nicobar and Lakshadweep*, plates 51–2.

Figure 9.1 'Eroded hillsides due to intense deforestation', in
Cecil J. Saldanha (ed.). *Andaman, Nicobar and Lakshadweep: An
Environmental Impact Assessment* (New Delhi: Ministry of Environment,
1989), plate 49, 23. Image courtesy of Cecil J. Saldanha.

conveyed this nuanced argument through a deeply evocative visual aesthetic. A picturesque morning on the beach at Cinque Island and a
swathe of sparkling blue waters of the Bay is juxtaposed with images of
fishing boats, fishermen selling their catch and confiscated deep-sea
fishing vessels known to belong to local sea poachers.[77] The marine
ecosystem of the Andamans was rich, unexplored and inviting but it
was also vulnerable to greed and exploitation. Saldanha's last set of
images is of the sheer sensuous beauty of the turquoise waters of the
Bay, and a muted pink and orange sunrise on the skies of Mayabunder.[78]

By the closing chapter, the 'environmental impact' report written by
experts in the field gently mutates into a book celebrating the visual
delights of these tropical Islands. The story of settlement, colonization
and the resultant degradation of the Islands' forest, mangrove and

[77] Saldanha (ed.), *Andaman, Nicobar and Lakshadweep*, plates 54–9.
[78] Saldanha (ed.), *Andaman, Nicobar and Lakshadweep*, plate 60.

marine ecosystems seems hazy. What remains are the images celebrating its marine life, the virgin forests and the stretches of secluded beaches. The iconography of 'Endangered Isles' gives way to the iconography of a tropical beach destination.

The visual tension in the Saldanha Report was reflective of the tension within the emerging developmental imaginary of the Indian state. Even while acknowledging the ecological hazards of settlement and colonization of the Islands, the notion of development was hard to give up. The Islands may not have been suited to a ceaseless expansion of agriculture nor could its forest resources be exploited without hazarding their survival, but there was always the possibility of 'developing' the Islands' natural resources for the sake of tourism: In tourism lay the redemptive possibilities of a island group in imminent crisis.[79]

From the endangered to the picturesque

Lapped by incessant white foam crested waves, the Andaman and Nicobar Islands lies in the centre of the Bay of Bengal. These idyllic islands in the sun are fringed with dazzling white beaches of white sand with richly clad forests forming a backdrop, while colourful beds of coral reefs shimmer through the clear blue turquoise sea water.[80]

These are the opening lines of a blurb from perhaps the first popular travel book endorsed by the Andaman and Nicobar Islands Administration in 1989. Produced by the photographer Ashok Dilwale and the travel writer Ranjana Kaul, it carried an interesting forward by the Lieutenant Governor of the Islands, Retd Lt General T. S. Oberoi. He invoked John Berger to observe that there were many ways of looking at reality.[81] The magic of photography, he argued, was to create visual representations that appear to be reality itself. The book was in his view 'an enchanted voyage through the kaleidoscopic reality of the Islands, among its primeval tribes, and its composite society, its pristine forests and marigold beaches, its emeralds set in the deep blue'.[82]

By the late 1980s, the Island Development Authority had taken the view that tourism on the Islands needed a new and different drive. The environmental issues raised during the previous decade had generated the awareness that conventional modes of resource exploitation (forestry, plantation and agriculture) could not be sustained. The Islands' prime

[79] Saldanha (ed.), *Andaman, Nicobar and Lakshadweep*, 25–6.
[80] Ashok Dilwali and Ranjana Kaul, *Andaman and Nicobar Islands: Islands in the Sun* (New Delhi: Spantech Publishers, 1989), cover blurb.
[81] John Berger, *Ways of Seeing* (London: BBC and Penguin Books, 1972).
[82] Ashok Dilwali, 'Foreword', in Dilwali and Kaul, *Andaman and Nicobar Islands*.

revenue-generating activity would have to be tourism. But this would be tourism informed not only by the concerns of the environment but a new awareness and celebration of the Islands' natural endowments. Tourists would be encouraged to explore the hitherto unknown tropical richness of the Islands and to develop a corresponding commitment towards their conservation. The operative modality of the new tourism would be exploration and discovery of the 'pristine', the 'virgin' and the secluded landscapes of the Andaman and Nicobar Islands.

Ashok Dilwali, in his preface to the book, wrote:

> [T]he Islands are a photographer's delight – a secluded and unexplored world with the blessings of a tropical climate and lush green forests surrounded by the deep blue sea. But if the Islands are an invitation they are also a challenge. One must capture not only the reality but also the dream, the magic and the fantasy that the Islands generate. I hope that the photographs reflect some of my own excitement at the discovery of nature's bounty.[83]

These words were followed by a series of photographs that invoked the picturesque and the tropical as visual frames through which state tourism would literally and figuratively reimage the Andaman Islands at a time when environmental concerns were at their peak. The 'realist' frames of Saldanha's conservation photography were now replaced by the frames of 'dream, magic and fantasy'.[84] Tourist industry supporters in the Andaman and Nicobar Administration, as well as the Island Development Authority in New Delhi, used these concepts and photographs to structure new ways of seeing and experiencing the Islands. This would be a new means of positioning the Islands' unexplored tropicality.

Dilwali and other photographers who followed Saldanha aimed to ensure that in their representations, the Islands offered a feast for a new tropical aesthetic, one that was quite different from colonial depictions of disciplined Andaman penal landscapes and the supposed racial characteristics of their indigenous peoples, as described by Clare Anderson in Chapter 8. Now, photographers pictured the Andamans in such a way that the Islands appeared to possess many of the traits conventionally associated with tropical islands: fertility, exoticism, overabundance of nature and indigenous people. Training their cameras on forms of nature that seemed distinctly tropical, photographers also associated the Islands with naturalists' and nature lovers' expectations of sublime and fantastic tropical nature: lush forests, exotic tribes and idyllic settlements.

---

[83] Ashok Dilwali, 'Photographer's Note', in Dilwali and Kaul, *Andaman and Nicobar Islands*.

[84] Dilwali, 'Photographer's Note'.

Although Dilwali's images begin with those of beautiful sunsets on the beaches of Car Nicobar and Great Nicobar, his dramatic first image of the Andaman Islands is that of a heavily overcast sky hanging over lush green paddy fields.[85] Soon after, there are images of settlers, the Bengalis and Karen, and of children in studio portrait styles.[86] Following these are images of the ruins of Ross Island, former headquarters of the penal colony and the iconic Cellular Jail.[87] This brief visual tour of the Islands' colonial past is immediately followed by a two-page lavish display of tropical flora. Dominant among these are stunning images of Andamanese orchids in brilliant hues and forms.[88] This set of images spills over into another visual spread of trees laden with tropical fruits, including pineapples, papayas, pepper pods and cashew nuts.[89] Forests, fields, orchards and plantations conjure up and in some ways contradict the anxieties about environmental degradation and tropical fragility. The Andaman Islands in Dilwali's book are repositioned in the frames of what Arnold describes as the colonial representation of the '"Edenic" tropics'.[90] Dilwali's book in a way recapitulated some of the tropes of the tropical picturesque elaborated earlier in the colonial visual archives.

There are the usual images of forestry too, of elephants lifting logs in Wimberleygunj and of the Chatham Saw Mill processing woods for making matchstick splinters.[91] These bits of the prosaic realities of the Andamanese forest-based economy, however, quickly pass over into the lesser-photographed terrain of the Islands' indigenous peoples, the Onge and the more recently contacted Jarawa. A full-page portrait of a Jarawa man and woman marks the dramatic entry of Dilwali's lenses into tribal territory. These are images evidently taken in the course of a Jarawa 'contact' mission organized by the Andaman administration. Most of the images are of Jarawas on board the contact vessel. The caption at the bottom of one dramatic close-up shot of a Jarawa man reads 'the physical beauty of the Jarawa is almost palpable'.[92] This is elaborated through another image of a Jarawa woman sitting on the deck of the ship and looking sharply at the camera. For this image, Dilwali's caption was 'beautiful Jarawa woman with ebony skin and luminous eyes – one of

[85] Dilwali and Kaul, *Andaman and Nicobar Islands*, 32–8.
[86] Dilwali and Kaul, *Andaman and Nicobar Islands*, 40–4.
[87] Dilwali and Kaul, *Andaman and Nicobar Islands*, 46–51.
[88] Dilwali and Kaul, *Andaman and Nicobar Islands*, 52.
[89] Dilwali and Kaul, *Andaman and Nicobar Islands*, 53.
[90] Arnold, *The Tropics and the Travelling Gaze*, 35–7.
[91] Dilwali and Kaul, *Andaman and Nicobar Islands*, 60–1.
[92] Dilwali and Kaul, *Andaman and Nicobar Islands*, 73.

the tribe who came on aboard the ship which anchors off the Island every full moon night'.[93]

This is the visual narrative of dreams, fantasies and magic that Dilwali's lens sought to capture as he set about his photographic journey into the Islands. The Jarawa images are followed by those of the Onge in typical poses: hunting, spear fishing and dancing.[94] This is the world of the Andamanese indigenous people who are inaccessible to the ordinary traveller but are constituted as new and exotic objects of tourist interest and imagination. Dilwali's images are ironically a visual invitation to a forbidden world and hence inherently subversive to the government's stated policy of protecting the indigenous peoples of the Islands from the intrusive interest of tourists and outsiders.

The more welcoming areas for the tourist are those of the Islands' celebrated ecosystems. The vast mangrove and forest systems of the Islands are the first in this series of images.[95] These were once again brilliantly photographed images revealing the depth and scale of the mangrove forests lining hundreds and hundreds of miles of the Islands' shores.[96] Dilwali's captions state that the mangroves are not merely a visual treat but are home to an 'infinite variety of flora and fauna'.[97] This is further elaborated in the following set of images of the Nicobar pigeon, the Narcondam hornbill and finally the Andaman eagle.[98]

The final set of images is of the marine ecosystem, or more appropriately, the seascape.[99] There are pictures of beaches, fishermen, jetties, rare and unusual shells all on a single page, culminating in one of the final images of the book, that of a bikini-clad woman lying on the shores of a secluded beach.[100] This closing image seals the Islands as the site for the ideal tropical holiday, the perfect place for western tourists hungry to reach the yet unexplored tropical corners of the world.

The significance of Dilwali's book is not merely that it successfully positioned the Islands as a tropical beach destination replete with images of sun, sand and turquoise waters, but that its camera delved deeper into the interiors of the Islands' ecosystems to reinforce environmentalist images of the Islands as an unexplored natural world to be discovered

[93] Dilwali and Kaul, *Andaman and Nicobar Islands*, 72, 73.
[94] Dilwali and Kaul, *Andaman and Nicobar Islands*, 74. Note Dilwali's recapitulation of an earlier colonial image of Onge spear fishing, mentioned in the previous chapter by Clare Anderson.
[95] Dilwali and Kaul, *Andaman and Nicobar Islands*, 78.
[96] Dilwali and Kaul, *Andaman and Nicobar Islands*, 80.
[97] Dilwali and Kaul, *Andaman and Nicobar Islands*, 84–5.
[98] Dilwali and Kaul, *Andaman and Nicobar Islands*, 78, 80, 84–5.
[99] Dilwali and Kaul, *Andaman and Nicobar Islands*, 89–95.
[100] Dilwali and Kaul, *Andaman and Nicobar Islands*, 89–95, 100.

Figure 9.2 'The beach on Jolly Buoy Island: A tourist's delight', in
Ashok Dilwali and Ranjana Kaul, *Andaman and Nicobar Islands: Islands
in the Sun* (New Delhi: Spantech Publishers, 1989), 98. Image courtesy
of Ashok Dilwali.

with care. This was the official line on tourism as it was debated at the
meetings of the Island Development Authority as well as the Andaman
Nicobar Tourists Guild, a private consortium of tourist enterprises that
drew up the first blueprint for the development of sustainable ecotourism
on the Islands.[101]

The concern for the environment and the deeper understanding of
the Islands' varied ecosystems informed Dilwali's elaboration of a new
tropical picturesque for the Andaman Islands. It picked upon the themes
of the Saldanha Report but carefully edited out the images of environmental degradation of the Islands. The concern for the environment was
articulated not through images of ugly settlements, eroded hillsides or
cattle with hump sores but through images of what remained pristine,

---

[101] Formed in 1990, the Andaman Nicobar Tourist Guild promoted ecotourism by
organizing various information campaigns on the importance of tropical forests, the
value of trees, rubbish disposal and the importance of coral in the primary food chain,
among other topics. Most importantly, the Guild convinced the local government to
position the Islands as a destination for high-end tourists in order to bring money into
the local economy and reduce the pressure on the already scarce resources, by
restricting the number of tourists. Conversation with Samir Acharya, December 2011.

untouched and unexplored. These were the Islands' natural riches waiting to be *explored*, not *exploited*. Dilwali's book provided the template for a new visual repositioning of the Islands in the years to come. Subsequent travel literature produced by the government's department of tourism as well as by travel writers and photographers took visual cues from these early texts combined with environmental concerns of the 1980s and argued for new ways of looking at the Andamans as an emerging site for travel, leisure and consumption.

In 2000, after long years of preparing conditions for the development of 'ecotourism' in the Islands, a new coffee table book was prepared under the aegis of the Ministry of Environment and Forests, by C. P. S. Oberai, a member of the Indian Forest Service.[102] Like Dilwali's book, this too had a foreword and messages from the Lieutenant Governor of the Islands, Shri. I. P. Gupta, as well as the Minister of Environment and Forests, Mr T. R. Baalu. The Lieutentant Governor wrote: 'This archipelago has about 572 islands and islets and has rare idyllic beaches, coves and other scenic formations. It is truly an ecotourist paradise'.[103] To this, the Minister added:

Tourism picks up during December to March – though the other months also have a magical-tropical ambience of torrential rain leading to unparalleled flora and faunal activity ... The book would be a great asset to tourists venturing to peep into the vast herbarium and ethnic assets of these Islands.[104]

Oberai's book offers a visual journey through the Islands' 'herbarium and ethnic assets', taking the reader through descriptions and images of flora and fauna, and the Andamans' avian world, its mammals, reptiles and vertebrates, the dugong, megapode, hornbill and teal, and finally its vast and deep mangroves.[105] Immediately after this is Oberai's chapter on Ecotourism.[106] Particularly interesting is his listing of the prime beach destinations of the Islands.[107] He dedicates an entire chapter to Havelock Island with the very suggestive title, 'Havelock and Ecotourism', as though they were made for each other. The rhetoric is similar to Dilwali's, only in this case Oberai appeals to specific kinds of tourists for specific attractions the Islands offered. In his words:

---

[102] C. P. S. Oberai, *Eco-Tourism Paradise: The Andaman and Nicobar Islands* (New Delhi: B.R. Publishing Corporation, 2000).
[103] Oberai, *Eco-Tourism Paradise*, Foreword.
[104] Oberai, *Eco-Tourism Paradise*, Preface.   [105] Oberai, *Eco-Tourism Paradise*, 1–88.
[106] Oberai, *Eco-Tourism Paradise*, 91.
[107] Oberai, *Eco-Tourism Paradise*, 131–40. Oberai lists thirty-three beaches all over the Andaman Islands, beginning in North Andaman and going southward to Havelock. He suggested that all could be opened up for tourists once adequate infrastructure was in place.

If you are looking for idyllic lush green hills and marigold sunsets, your destination is Havelock. If you have a craving for nature study, zest for wondrous marine life, interest for a peep in the course of the Indian freedom struggle and flair for outdoor life, itinerary Havelock. For students of ethnobotany, marine biology, natural history and oceanography – all roads lead to Havelock.[108]

Even though Oberai notes the historical significance of the Islands in the story of the Indian freedom struggle, the imperatives of framing the Islands as an eco-tourist destination compel him to devote a final solitary section to the historical past of the Islands.[109] Of greater significance perhaps is Oberai's interpretation and narration of this past. There are the usual textual and pictorial references to the penal settlement, with Ross Island and the Cellular Jail taking centre stage.[110] There are also brief paragraphs signposting important events that marked the history of the Islands from colonial times to the present and a final plea for a radical change of perspective on the Islands. The forbidding image of *kala pani* (black waters) had to be replaced, he argued, by the image of the warm-blue waters of *nila pani* (deep blue waters)![111] However, at no point in this book on 'ecotourism' are there any references to the work of environmentalists who sought to bring together the narrative of the history and economy of the Islands with that of its ecology.

If Dilwali's book scripted a new tropical picturesque for the Islands, and Oberai's book on 'ecotourism' discreetly dodged the history of colonization, development and environmental degradation, Priti Singh's sumptuously produced travel book, published shortly after a deadly tsunami lashed the shores of the Andaman and Nicobar Islands on 26 December 2004, tropicalized the Islands in compelling new terms.[112] The Andaman and Nicobar Islands in this book are not merely 'historical places, they are "secluded worlds of enchantment" that are bound to overwhelm the traveller by their "mysterious aura". The Islands' past is "tragic" but its present is promising.'[113] Singh made the point by arguing that while the Islands' monuments make us pause and ponder its tormented past, its natural beauty and the bounty of its open spaces add to our 'sensory' delights.[114] It is to these 'sensory' delights that the book invites its readers. Much of the book's lavish photographic spread follows the organization of Dilwali's book with its sections on the history of the

[108] Oberai, *Eco-Tourism Paradise*, 124.
[109] Oberai, *Eco-Tourism Paradise*, 189–216, Part 7 'Retrospect'.
[110] Oberai, *Eco-Tourism Paradise*, 191–205.
[111] Oberai, *Eco-Tourism Paradise*, Chapter 'From Kala Pani to Nilapaani', 191–205.
[112] Priti Singh, *The Islands and Tribes of Andaman and Nicobar* (New Delhi: Prakash Books, 2006).
[113] Singh, *The Islands and Tribes*, Cover Blurb.   [114] Singh, *The Islands and Tribes*.

penal settlement, followed by the Islands' flora, fauna and indigenous communities, yet it is the final section of the book that puts together a collection of images and a strikingly excessive rhetoric to position the Islands as a 'dream destination'.[115]

Here, Singh offers a visual itinerary for prospective tourists to the Islands: on day one, a visit to the Cellular Jail, the prison at Viper Island and the ruins at Ross Island. Having engaged with the Islands' past, subsequent 'fun' days would be spent venturing beyond Port Blair and into the heart of the Islands' tropical recesses.[116] But Singh, unlike her predecessors, also makes a case for the Islands' tropical beauty in and around the built environs of Port Blair. She put together images and descriptions of Port Blair's 'landscaped' spaces, the gently undulating roads, the numerous terrace gardens, artistically designed ponds brimming with bushes and plants, and the clean and open stretches on the shore drive or the Marina.[117] The bulk of her book, however, follows the visual grammar of Dilwali. The familiar spread of images is of the forest, mangrove and beach. Singh, however, had a deliberate focus on the beach, the iconic site of her 'Island Paradise.'

In this, she followed a tradition of visual representation of tropical island destinations that took shape in the mid 1950s. Several visual icons and trends in touristic representation arose in the era of the growth of mass tourism. As Thompson argues, tropical island images drew upon a select pool of visual tropes of which the sun, sand and the beach became ubiquitous. By the 1950s, it is argued, the beach had moved squarely to the centre of the tropical experience becoming a primary signifier of the tropics from the Caribbean to the Pacific.[118] The descriptions in one of Singh's chapters on the Andaman Islands, suggestively titled *The Paradise: The Dream Destination,* can be convincingly located within this tradition. Her images of the beaches at Corbyn's Cove, and Radhanagar beach at Havelock Island remain the enduring showpieces of the book.

As noted above, Singh's book was published two years after the Asian tsunami of 26 December 2004 left its trail of destruction across several parts of the Andaman Islands. Large stretches of rich coral reefs were destroyed, and mangroves and fields were inundated with debris. The scale of destruction was more devastating still in the Nicobar archipelago,

---

[115] Singh, *The Islands and Tribes*, 178–204.   [116] Singh, *The Islands and Tribes*, 182–3.

[117] Singh, *The Islands and Tribes*, 180–1. These are familiar images of 'tropical modernity' that abound in Pacific and Caribbean islands. For a discussion see, Thompson, *An Eye for the Tropics*, 204–51.

[118] For detailed elaboration of this argument, see Thompson, *An Eye for the Tropics*, 156–203.

where small islands disappeared into the sea.[119] The global fear that the tsunami generated slackened the flow of tourists to the Islands in the years that followed, and relief work took a long time to complete, leaving infrastructural problems long unaddressed. However, within a year of the tsunami, opinion within the island administration veered towards the revival of tourism.[120] Implicit in this new initiative was an acknowledgement that notwithstanding the scale of the devastation that the tsunami wrought, there was still much in the Islands that remained unspoiled. A single natural disaster was not enough to rob the Islands of their tropical riches.

Conclusion

It may be tempting to argue that the imaging of the Andaman Islands as a tropical tourist destination completely subverted the environmentalist agenda on the Islands, but it is important to note that the visual tropes of tropicality that informed the tourist literature drew upon and elaborated what I would like to call the visual grammar of environmentalism. It was the environmentalists' repositioning of the Islands as a distinctive tropical island ecosystem that allowed travel photographers to push their lenses into the hitherto unexplored reaches of the Andaman forests, beaches, mangroves and coral sea beds. It was images like these that catapulted the Islands into a globalized touristscape that could immediately identify in the Andaman and Nicobar Islands a common visual template that linked it to the Caribbean and the Pacific.[121] Environmentalists discussed the tropical landscapes of the Andaman Islands only to warn us of its fragility and vulnerability. However, tourist promoters reinvested in it to open up new forms of consumption. The meanings of the Islands' tropicality remain mired in these conflicting ideological positions and economic rationales for their development continue to befuddle their inhabitants. For the images of a welcoming Andaman Islands resplendent in their tropical richness lies far removed from the pressing and mundane problems of quotidian life. There are serious problems of overcrowding, of inadequate infrastructure, of water supply and power and declining returns from agriculture. Local activists

[119] For studies of the impact of the tsunami in the Andaman and Nicobar Islands see, among others, R. V. R. Murthy, *Andaman and Nicobar Islands: A Geopolitical and Strategic Perspective* (New Delhi: Northern Book Centre, 2007), 51–65.

[120] For a discussion of these new plans for tourism and their environmental implications, see Sunita Reddy, 'Mega-tourism in the Andaman and Nicobar Islands: Some Concerns', *Journal of Human Ecology* 21, 3 (2007), 231–9.

[121] Thompson, *An Eye for the Tropics*, chapter 1, 1–27.

struggle to keep these issues alive, albeit haltingly, as the demands of keeping the Islands' economy afloat supersede concerns about the destruction of mangroves, of sand mining and the slew of environmental offences that flow almost automatically from the dynamics of encroachment and settlement on the one hand and tourism on the other. The first environmental NGO Society for Andaman and Nicobar Ecology, SANE, established in the mid 1980s played a pioneering role in raising awareness about these issues among the local population as well as to visitors from the mainland. It also filed several public interest litigations against the timber lobby in the Islands, eventually succeeding in stopping commercial forestry there. Its founder, Samir Acharya, remains one of the most respected voices in the Islands. In more recent times, Denis Giles and Zubair Ahmed, journalists associated with the local paper *Andaman Chronicle*, continue to play a vital role in arguing against government policies of Island development that threaten the Islands' ecosystems and its indigenous peoples.[122]

Promoters of Island tourism within the Islands' administration need the environmentalists to keep the image of tropicality alive. They understand, as the historian Nancy Ley Stepans argues, that 'photographic representations of the tropics need periodic reinvestments in times of change and challenge or in moments of representational instability when an accepted mode of seeing the tropics is contested or subverted.'[123] In the aftermath of the tsunami, the Andaman and Nicobar administration sought to reinvest the Islands with the image of an unchanging tropics, as if slotting familiar tropical images into tourists' purview would blind them to deeper uncertainties of the island environment. It drew upon environmentalists' discourses of tropicality to address the challenges the Islands faced but also saw in its ecosystems the elusive sources of its survival. It believed that the 'Endangered Islands' discourse had to be jettisoned and the Andaman Islands visually repositioned as a Dream Destination. In effect, its 'tropicality' had to be radically redefined if it had to sustain itself and remain economically relevant to mainland India. It is these shifting tropes of 'tropicality' that remain poignant indicators of the anxieties and aspirations of an Island space fraught with the troubled legacies of colonization and historical marginality.

---

[122] Zubair Ahmed was formerly associated with the *Light of Andamans*, a local fortnightly newspaper that acquired respect not only for its fine journalism but also for being one of the most fearless voices against government policies.

[123] Nancy Leys Stepan, *Picturing Tropical Nature* (London: Reaktion, 2001), 21.

10   Conclusion

*Clare Anderson, Madhumita Mazumdar
and Vishvajit Pandya*

New Histories has brought together a range of disciplinary interests to propose a view of the relationship between history and the present from within the Andaman Islands. We have explored the complexities of the relationship between the Islands and the mainland; the transformation of space and the making of place; and the ways in which history is understood, deployed and contested in the Andamans today. We have examined the colonization of the Islands and the developmental agendas that were formulated both during the colonial period and in the years after the British retreat. A special focus here has been on their implications for Bengali refugees. We have interrogated the history and afterlife of the penal colony and convict society, looking at the peculiar social and cultural structures forged through transportation, and how they have impacted on both community formation and contemporary perspectives of the historical importance of the Islands. Here, we have been concerned to understand how the Islanders have worked with and against mainland ideas about anti-colonialism and nationalism. We have dwelled on the importance of the Japanese occupation of the Andamans during the Second World War, historically, for post-colonial identity formation, and for the making of a history for the new, independent Indian nation. Issues of commemoration and memorialization have lain at the heart of our work. Further, we have analyzed the multilayered relationships between the indigenous peoples of the Islands, with the Indian state on the one hand and with settlers on the other. Our interest has been in the 'in between' spaces in which communities imagine their past, their present and their future; and seek to manage the ontological landscape in which they are located. And, finally, we have investigated how the Islands have been visualized historically and in the present day, and how these projections relate to the colonial desire for an orderly landscape; how they are used for contrary, private purposes; and for post-colonial dreams of ecologically pristine Islands. Here, we have explored images, photographs and tourist brochures, and what they can tell us about our three central points of interrogation:

across Islands and mainland; space and place; and history and the present.

The underpinning interest of the arguments presented in this book has been our belief in the need to understand the linkages between the Islands' colonial and contemporary history, and also the complexities of the relationship between the Andamans and the mainland. In this, we have attempted to construct a history of the present to connect Islanders to each other and to mainland India. We understand the history of the local born of the Islands as linked to that of the Bengali settlers, and that of the Bengali settlers as linked that of the Jarawas. We see important continuities between colonial efforts to colonize, landscape and organize the Islands spatially with post-colonial attempts to manage tribal reservation, settler mobility and community claims to particular forms of political status. There are several levels of entanglements that are of relevance; including the continuation of particular colonial practices in what is now a union territory of the Republic of India, as well as the construction of histories (often contested) of the penal colony and the Second World War. We have sought to unpick these knots through a focus on history in and of the Islands as they played out through its landscape.

The idea of landscape has allowed us to talk to each other's interests in new and surprising ways. Thus we have written of commemoration and memorialization; of dwelling and belonging; of war and reconstruction; of light and darkness; and of images and photography. We have sought points of conversation across history, ethnography and anthropology in order to look for ways in which the Islands' story could be told on its own terms, by interrogating both mainland-generated projects and by retrieving local voices. *New Histories of the Andaman Islands* brings into dialogue these sometimes coherent and sometimes competing agendas: mainland imaginations and practices, and Island perspectives and understandings. Our cartographic gaze has centred the Islands and their Bay of Bengal location at the heart of imperial and independent India. This has produced further points of integration, too; in particular, the need to situate the Andamans in the history and historical geography of islands and island spaces; and within large histories of colonization, empire and decolonization. It is this that gives our work reach and relevance in this and other post-colonial contexts. In our view, to invoke Sujit Sivasundaram's memorable phrase, previously the Andaman Islands have been historiographically 'islanded', and have seldom been accessed by mainstream South Asian or even Southeast Asian studies. With our integrated histories approach, we have addressed this issue. We have located a new way of understanding the Islands: as a place in the making, a rhizomatic space demanding new modes of inquiry and new frameworks of analysis.

Our approach will have relevance to other places with complex histories of migration and settlement, as also to those which are embedded within particular political formations associated explicitly with the aftermath of empire.

The focus on 'entangled landscapes' understood through its broad socio-spatial dialectics remains the organizing theme of this book. The focus on landscape is one way of engaging the criticality of the 'land question' in an island context – where the territorial limits of the land raise an altogether different set of questions pertaining to land in terms of how far one could move on it, how much of it could be transformed and what it could sustain. This is not to suggest any geographically determinist argument in case of islands but to draw attention to the ways in which land and landscape both as material reality and as a representational discourse constitutes a critical point of reference in developing an understanding of the culture, history and society of islands in general and the Andaman Islands in particular.

New Histories has, then, proposed a fresh mode of writing for the history of the Andaman Islands. We acknowledge the Andamans as a place in the making, a place that engages with its isolation and with its connectedness in terms that elude easy formulations. We have sought to add depth to understandings of the Islands as 'mini India', as sites for particular and alternatively convergent and divergent articulations of both cultural, social and religious 'belonging' and the formation of identity networks. Our research has ranged across history and its aftermath in a range of contexts, to interrogate the spatiality of the Islands in relation to the British Empire and its aftermath in South Asia, the links between tribal and settler communities, and the continuities of society and culture across the colonial and post-colonial periods. Our book has focused on the human history of the Islands and its relationship to the making and representation of landscapes of distinction and connection. It articulates the many levels of association that can be made between the history of the Islands' indigenous people, the penal colony, colonial-era migration, jungle clearance and cultivation; the Japanese occupation of the Second World War; refugee resettlement; and indigenous–settler relations. It also brings the archives and the field together, to foreground the contemporary relevance of history in and of the Islands, and especially to tease out Island-centred understandings of Andaman history within the context of the Islands' place in the Indian nation state. Relationality looms large, for we have been especially keen to explore the relationships between tribal peoples and settlers, the relationships between the Islands and the mainland, and the relationships between the past and the present.

Relationality has been key to the production of this book in another way, too. We have pursued a collaborative, multi-disciplinary approach to the archives and to the field, under the firm conviction that only the integration of disciplines and scholarship, the bringing together of related expertise, could underpin such a project. Through an historical, ethnographic and anthropological perspective on the Andamans, through our relationship with each other as scholars, we hope to add a new richness to the hitherto sedimented literatures of indigeneity, migration and place in the Islands. We have argued that the history and social and cultural context of the Andamans cannot be disaggregated from contemporary debates about social justice, conservation, development and land. Our analysis has turned on ideas about the especial importance of island-mainland relations, and the significance of the construction of landscape (or, rather, landscaping) for understanding a society forged through indigenous marginalization and migration. We have urged recognition of the Islands' place in networks of governance, coercion and mobility across and beyond South Asia. We have suggested that the Islands' colonial and post-colonial history needs to be reconceptualized within a framework of relationality that focuses on the Islands-mainland dialectic. We have pushed for an understanding of the dynamics of history making in the Islands, to show that since Independence, history has been and continues to be narrated, represented and contested in particular ways within the context of larger post-colonial projects of nation building. These include not just the symbolic importance of the Andamans for the making of the Indian nation, but the drawing out of aspects of Island distinction, particularly with respect to the Japanese occupation of the Second World War, and the Islands' concentration of local-born residents and refugee settlers. The relationship between Islands and mainland; the transformation of space and the making of place; the debates about history: *New Histories of the Andaman Islands* offers new ways of understanding the Bay of Bengal, the dynamics of island societies and empire and its aftermath. It looks outward, across land and sea, from a series of vantage points that link the local to the (post)colonial to offer a different perspective on history and after, and compels us to shift the way in which we think about the past and its relevance for the world in which we live today.

Bibliography

NEWSPAPERS AND PERIODICALS

Andaman Sheekha, 13 February 2012, 10 March 2012, 27 August 2012.

The Daily Telegrams, 28 January 2010.

The Graphic, 16 March 1872.

The Illustrated London News, 18 May 1867, 24 February 1872.

Indian and Foreign Review, 15 May 1966.

The Light of Andamans (Vol. 34) No. 16, November 13 2009.

Time, 164, 22 November 2004.

The Times, 24 November 1871.

The Times of India, 19 June 1946; 18 October 1948.

ALKAZI COLLECTION OF PHOTOGRAPHY, NEW DELHI

Andamans Album, provenance unknown. 95-0026.

W. W. Hooper's album, 1870s. 95.0004.

ANDAMAN AND NICOBAR ADMINISTRATION ARCHIVES, SECRETARIAT COMPLEX, PORT BLAIR (A&N ARCHIVES)

'Bhantu petitions for return', File no. 11-4-1947.

Hindustan Times clipping, File no. 1-225-46.

Home Department, 1945, 1947, 1948, 1957, 1969, 1971, 1972, 1974, 1975.

Jails Department, 1942, 1943, 1945.

Judicial and Revenue Department, 1950, 1952, 1953, 1970.

Major Barker's Report, 20 July 1925, Law (General) 1925, File no. 485.

D. N. McVean, *Report on Land Use in the Andaman and Nicobar Islands*, Morges, Switzerland, June, 1976.

Note of DC, Kishen Singh, dated 20.7.1945, File no. 11-4-49.

Note on the Bhantus, File no. 11-4-1947.

Office Memorandum from District Commissioner to Agricultural Officer, 30 June 1956, File no. 35–31 (5) 56/02.

Petition for the restoration of lands, 1946, File no. 11-4-49.

Public Department, 1957, 1960, 1961, 1962, 1967, 1970, 1972, 1973, 1974.

Public Works Department: Draft Annual Plan, 1984–5, File no. D/2165.

Records of Pradesh Council (local body), 1987.

Rehabilitation Programme in the Andaman and Nicobar Islands, presented by Chief Development–cum-Rehabilitation Commissioner, Andaman and Nicobar Islands, 15 March, 1978.

Report on Visit of the Members of the Consultative Committee of the Department of Rehabilitation to Andaman and Nicobar Islands from 26th February 1976 to 2nd March 1976, prepared by Chief Development-cum-Rehabilitation Commissioner, Andaman and Nicobar Administration Port Blair.

Surajit Sinha, 'Resettlement of East Pakistan Refugees in Andaman Islands: Report on Survey of Further Possibilities of Resettlement: January – May 1952' (Alipore: Superintendent of Government Printing, West Bengal Government Press, 1953).

BRISTOL RECORD OFFICE, BRITISH EMPIRE AND COMMONWEALTH MUSEUM COLLECTION

2002/202, Wood Large Andamans Album.

BRITISH LIBRARY: INDIA OFFICE LIBRARY (IOR)

Bengal Judicial Consultations 1794.

Copy of the first part of a report from Major Kyd relative to the Settlements at Prince of Wales Island and the Andamans with its appendix [Reports of the surgeons at Port Cornwallis during the years 1793 and 1794], 4 March 1795. G/34/1 ff. 379–518.

Home (Port Blair) Proceedings, 1874, 1877, 1878, 1882, 1890, 1891, 1895, 1896, 1914, 1915, 1919, 1921.

India Judicial Consultations, 1858.

Photo 447/3 (W. W. Hooper Collection).

Photo 355/1 (Dunlop Smith Collection).

Photo 252 (Royden Wilkinson [United Provinces police service] Collection).

Photo 124/2 (Portraits of Bengal types, trades and castes).

Photo 125/2 (Chief Commissioner R.C. Temple Collection).

Photo 127/(96 & 99) (Album of cartes de visite portraits of Indian rulers and notables).

'Report on the Reform of the Andaman Penal Settlement' by Lieut.-Col. M. W. Douglas, C.I.E., I.A., Superintendent, Port Blair and Chief Commissioner, Andaman and Nicobar Islands (New Delhi: Superintendent Government Printing, 1919), P/10592.

Selections from the Records of the Government of India (Home Department) No. XXV: The Andaman Islands, with Notes on Barren Island, Calcutta, 1859, V/3199.

Shivdasani, H. 'Report on the Possibilities of Colonization and the Development of the Andaman and Nicobar Islands', Government of India, Ministry of Home Affairs, 5 March 1949, V/190/65.

Warneford Papers, Mss Eur F388/1.

BRITISH MUSEUM, ANTHROPOLOGY LIBRARY

Mrs W. E. Burt manuscript and photographs, Eth. Doc. 1714.

CELLULAR JAIL MUSEUM LIBRARY, PORT BLAIR (CJML)

Government of India Home (Port Blair) proceedings, June 1876.

Krishna, Rama. *The Andaman Islands Under Japanese Occupation, 1942-1945*, unpublished manuscript.

R. C. Temple's 1908 Andaman Gazetteer, draft typescript.

HORNIMAN MUSEUM, FOREST HILL, LONDON

Photographs of the Andaman Islands, 308 (541.9) TUS.

IMPERIAL WAR MUSEUM

JFU416: video footage of Andaman reoccupation, 1947.

PERSONAL COLLECTION, MUKESHWAR LALL (PCML)

Misc. papers, Local Born Association.

PERSONAL COLLECTION, KEITH WILSON (PCKW)

D. M. Deakes' letters, 1949.

'I was there', by Mrs D. M. Deakes, age 65, 1960.

UNIVERSITY OF CAMBRIDGE

Box II, Photograph album presented to Lt. Colonel and Mrs Michael Lloyd Ferrar by the Girl Guides and Boy Scouts of the Andaman and Nicobar Islands, during Lt. Colonel Ferrar's time as Chief Commissioner in the Islands, 1929–31, Ferrar papers.

Centre of South Asian Studies (CSAS)

Ferrar Collection (small box collection 10) 1926–32.

University of Cambridge Library, Department of Manuscripts

Events of assassination, 8–13 February 1872, Add. Ms 7490 Mayo Papers.

SCHOOL OF ORIENTAL AND AFRICAN STUDIES, ARCHIVES AND SPECIAL COLLECTIONS

Charles J. Bonington, Islands of No Return with accompanying photographs (1937–86), MS380838.

THE NATIONAL ARCHIVES, KEW

Andamans and Nicobar Islands, 'A Paradise on Earth', Mr H. V. R. Iengar's broadcast talk, All India Radio, 3 January 1949, 9.40pm, DO142/373.

Calcutta Special Report No. D.H.C. 28 (Secret), 11 February 1949, DO133/39.

Report on a Tour to the Andamans by Mr A. J. Brown from the 22nd to the 29th July 1950 (secret), D133/39.

NATIONAL ARCHIVES OF INDIA, NEW DELHI

Home (Port Blair) 1860, 1896.

NATIONAL LIBRARY OF AUSTRALIA, CANBERRA

Rex Nan Kivell Collection: Robert Hyde Colebrooke, Fort Cornwallis, Andaman Islands, c. 1790, PIC T2940 NK170LOC 6102–5.

NATIONAL MARITIME MUSEUM, GREENWICH

Dorothy Fullerton Papers, c. 1929–32, MSS/83/010.

MISCELLANEOUS ONLINE RECORDS

Advice No. 2/A&N/2009, National Commission for Backward Classes, A&N Bench, http://ncbc.nic.in/Pdf/Andaman%20&%20Nicobar%20Islands/2.pdf (accessed 16 May 2013).

Andaman and Nicobar Administration, 'Basic Statistics of Andaman and Nicobar Islands 2010–1', www.and.nic.in/stats/

BasicStatistics/basicstat%20PDF/03%20Demography.pdf (accessed 2 August 2014).

Arrangement between the Government of Japan and the Government of India Regarding Settlement of Certain Indian Claims, 14 December 1963, www.gwu.edu/~memory/data/treaties/India.pdf (accessed 11 September 2012).

Article 6, Treaty of Peace Between Japan and India, ratified and signed into force, 27 August 1952, www.gwu.edu/~memory/data/treaties/India.pdf (accessed 19 March 2012).

Bag, Shamik. 'OBC Job Quota Move Casts Shadow Over "Caste-less" Andamans', *The Indian Express*, 20 June 2006, http://archive.indianexpress.com/news/obc-job-quota-move-casts-shadow-over–casteless–andamans—/6887/0 (accessed 31 July 2014).

'Bahadur Shah Zafar's Ghazal', www.bestghazals.net/2007/06/bahadur-shah-zafars-ghazal.html (accessed 14 September 2014).

Basu, Soma.'OBC Satus for Bengali Settlers in A&N' (blog), http://deshlai.wordpress.com/2011/12/26/obc-status-for-bengali-settlers-in-an/ (accessed 25 June 2014).

British House of Commons debates, 18 February 1924, volume 169, c1282: Moplah rebellion (prisoners) http://hansard.millbanksystems.com/commons/1924/feb/18/moplah-rebellion-prisoners (accessed 13 April 2012).

Gandhi: The Mahatma, www.youtube.com/watch?v=3yQKgRRUsfw (accessed 28 June 2012).

Gupta, Jayanta. 'Mamata gets Matua Membership', *The Times of India*, 6 December 2009, http://timesofindia.indiatimes.com/city/kolkata/Mamata-gets-Matua-membership/articleshow/5306294.cms (accessed 23 July 2014).

National Commission for Backward Classes, A&N Bench, Advice No. 2/A&N/2009, http://ncbc.nic.in/Pdf/Andaman%20&%20Nicobar%20Islands/2.pdf (accessed 16 May 2013).

War Crimes Studies Center, University of California Berkeley, http://wcsc.berkeley.edu/world-war-ii-document-archive/pacific-theater-document-archive/ (accessed 21 May 2013).

ROYAL GEOGRAPHICAL SOCIETY, LONDON (RGS)

Selections from the Records of the Government of India (Foreign Dept), 24, John Gray, 'Calcutta Gazette' Office, 1858, Survey of the Andamans, Report of Archibald Blair, 27 May 1793.

Extracts from report of Captain Blair, 14 Dec. 1789, JMS/18/45 1859.

V&A MUSEUM ARCHIVES

Photograph Album, c. 1850/60 (F.J. Mouat's album) X821.

QUEEN'S COLLECTION, WINDSOR CASTLE

Photographic Drawings of the Andaman Islands (1857–8).

PUBLISHED MATERIAL, PRE-1945

'A Savage Archipelago'. *Chambers' Journal*. Reprinted in *The Eclectic Magazine* (November 1863).

Adam, H. L. *The Indian Criminal* (London: J. Milne, 1909).

Adam, H. L. *Oriental Crime* (London: T. Werner Laurie, 1909).

Bonington, M. C. C. *Census of India, 1931, Volume II: The Andaman and Nicobar Islands* (Calcutta: Government of India Central Publication Branch, 1932).

Booth-Tucker, Frederick. *Criminocurology or the Indian Crim, and What to Do with Him: Being a Review of the Work of The Salvation Army amongst the Prisoners, Habituals and Criminal Tribes of India* (Simla: Liddell's Printing Works, 1916).

Clifton, Mrs Talbot. *Pilgrims to the Isles of Penance; Orchid Gathering in the East* (London: John Long, 1911).

Cook's Indian Tours (London: Thomas Cook and Son, 1887).

Coxon, Stanley W. *And That Reminds Me; Being Incidents of a Life Spent at Sea, and in the Andaman Islands, Burma, Australia, and India* (London: John Lane, 1915).

Dass, F. A. M. *The Andaman Islands* (Bangalore: Good Shepherd Convent Press, 1937).

East India (Jails) Committee: Report of the Indian Jails Committee, 1919–20 (London: H.M.'s Stationery Office, 1921).

Evans-Pritchard, E. E. *The Nuer: A Description of the Modes of Livelihood and Political Institution of a Nilotic People* (Oxford: Clarendon Press, 1940).

Fitchett, W. H. *The King's Empire: A Pictorial and Descriptive Record Illustrated From Photographs and Drawings* (London: Cassell and Co., 1906).

Heindl, Robert. *Meine Reise nach den Strafkolonien, mit vielen originalaufnahmen* [*My Global Tour of Penal Colonies, with Original Photographs*] (Berlin-Wien: Ullstein and Co., 1913).

Hunter, W. W. *Rulers of India: The Earl of Mayo* (Oxford: Clarendon Press, 1891).

Iles Andaman et Ceylan, Moeurs et Coutumes (Paris: L. Boulanger, 1880).

Lowis, R. F. *Census of India, 1911, Volume II: The Andaman and Nicobar Islands* (Calcutta: Superintendent of Government Printing, 1912).

Lowis, R. F. *Census of India, 1921, Volume II: The Andaman and Nicobar Islands* (Calcutta: Superintendent of Government Printing, 1923).

Mouat, F. J. *Adventures and Researches among the Andaman Islanders* (London: Hurst and Blackett, 1863).

Portman, M. V. *A History of Our Relations with the Andamanese, Vol. I* (Calcutta: Superintendent of Government Printing, 1899).

Radcliffe-Brown, A. R. *Andaman Islanders* (New York: Free Press, 1922).

Radcliffe-Brown, A. R. *The Andaman Islanders: A Study in Social Anthropology* (Cambridge: Cambridge University Press, 1922).

Report on the Administration of the Andaman and Nicobar Islands and the Penal Settlement of Port Blair for 1921–22 (Calcutta: Superintendent of Government Printing, 1922).

Report of the Administration of the Andamans and Nicobar Islands and the Penal Settlement for 1925–6 (Calcutta: Government of India Publications Branch, 1927).

Report on the Administration of the Andaman and Nicobar Islands and the Penal Settlement of Port Blair for 1927–28 (Calcutta: Government of India Press, 1929).

Report on the Administration of the Andaman and Nicobar Islands and the Penal Settlement of Port Blair for 1929–30 (Calcutta: Government of India Press, 1931).

Report on the Administration of the Andaman and Nicobar Islands and the Penal Settlement of Port Blair for 1935–36 (New Delhi: Government of India Press, 1936).

Report on the Administration of the Andaman and Nicobar Islands and the Penal Settlement of Port Blair for 1936–37 (New Delhi: Government of India Press, 1937).

Report on the Administration of the Andaman and Nicobar Islands and the Penal Settlement of Port Blair for 1937–38 (New Delhi: Government of India Press, 1938).

Ritchie, John. 'An Unpublished 18th Century Document about the Andamans'. *The Indian Antiquary* **30** (1901).

Sheard, Major Edwin H. 'Reforming Robbers in the Andamans'. *The Officers' Review* (November 1937).

Statistics of the Population Enumerated in the Andamans, 17th February 1881 (Calcutta: Superintendent of Government Printing, 1883).

Temple, R.C. *Census of India, 1901, Volume III: The Andaman and Nicobar Islands* (Calcutta: Superintendent of Government Printing, 1903).

[Temple, R. C.] *Imperial Gazetteer of India, Provincial Series: Andaman and Nicobar Islands* (Calcutta: Superintendent of Government Printing, 1909).

Woolley, J.M. 'Convict Marriages in the Andamans'. *Indian Medical Gazette* 47, 3 (1912).

PUBLISHED MATERIAL, POST-1945

Adams, Paul C., Steven D. Hoelscher and Karen E. Till. *Textures of Place: Exploring Humanist Geographies* (Minneapolis, MN: University of Minnesota Press, 2001).

Aggarwal, A. N. *The Heroes of Cellular Jail* (Patiala: Publication Bureau, Punjabi University, 1995).

Aiken, Robert S. 'Images of Nature in Swettenham's Writings: Prolegomenon to a Historical Perspective on Peninsular Malaysia's Ecological Problems'. *Asian Survey* **11**, 3 (1973), 135–49.

Amin, Shahid. *Event, Metaphor, Memory: Chauri Chaura 1922–1992* (New Delhi: Oxford University Press, 1995).

Amrith, Sunil S. *Crossing the Bay of Bengal: The Furies of Nature and the Fortunes of Migrants* (Cambridge, MA: Harvard University Press, 2013).

Amrith, Sunil S. 'Tamil Diasporas across the Bay of Bengal'. *American Historical Review* **114**, 3 (2009), 547–72.

Ananthamurthy, U. R. *"Literature in the Indian Bhashas: Frontyards and Backyards"*, in Paranjpye Makarand and G.J.V Prasad (eds) Indian English and Vernacular India, Delhi, Chennai, Hyderabad, Pearson, 2002, pp 149–52.

Anderson, Benedict. *Imagined Communities* (London: Verso, 1983; 2nd Revised edn 1991; new edn 2006).

Anderson, Clare. 'After Emancipation: Empires and Imperial Formations'. In Catherine Hall, Nicholas Draper and Keith McClelland (eds.) *Emancipation and the Remaking of the British Imperial World* (Manchester: Manchester University Press, 2014), 113–27.

Anderson, Clare. 'Colonization, Kidnap And Confinement in the Andamans Penal Colony, 1771–1864'. *Journal of Historical Geography* **37**, 1 (2011), 68–81.

Anderson, Clare. *The Indian Uprising of 1857–8: Prisons, Prisoners and Rebellion* (London: Anthem, 2007).

Anderson, Clare. *Legible Bodies: Race, Criminality and Colonialism in South Asia* (Oxford: Berg, 2004).

Anderson, Clare. 'Oscar Mallitte's Andaman Photographs, 1857–8'. *History Workshop Journal* **67**, 1 (2009), 152–72.

Anderson, Clare. *Subaltern Lives: Biographies of Colonialism in the Indian Ocean World, 1790–1920* (Cambridge: Cambridge University Press, 2012).

Anderson, Clare and David Arnold. 'Visualising the Prison'. In Frank Dikötter and Ian Brown (eds.) *Cultures of Confinement: A History of the Prison in Africa, Asia and Latin America* (Ithaca, NY: Cornell University Press, 2007), 304–31.

Andrews, Harry V. and Vasumathi Sankaran (eds.). *Sustainable Management of Protected Areas in the Andaman and Nicobar Islands* (New Delhi: ANET, IIPA and FFI, 2002).

Appadurai, Arjun (ed.). *The Social Life of Things: Commodities in Cultural Perspective* (Cambridge: Cambridge University Press, 1986).

Arnold, David. 'The Self and the Cell: Indian Prison Narratives as Life Histories'. In David Arnold and Stuart H. Blackburn (eds.) *Telling Lives in India: Biography, Autobiography, and Life History* (Bloomington: Indiana University Press, 2004), 29–53.

Arnold, David. *The Tropics and the Travelling Gaze, India, Landscape and Science, 1800–1856* (Seattle: University of Washington Press, 2006).

Ausubel, H. 'General Booth's Scheme of Social Salvation'. *American Historical Review*, **56**, 3 (1951), 519–25.

Bachelard, Gaston. *Psychoanalysis of Fire* (Boston MA: Beacon Press, 1968).

Baldacchino, Godfrey. 'Studying Islands: On Whose Terms? Some Epistemological and Methodological Challenges to the Pursuit of Island Studies'. *Island Studies Journal* **3**, 1 (2008), 37–56.

Baldacchino, Godfrey and Eric Clark. 'Guest Editorial Introduction: Islanding Cultural Geographies'. *Cultural Geographies* **20**, 2 (2013), 129–32.

Bandopdhyay, Sekhar. *Caste, Culture and Hegemony: Social Dominance in Colonial Bengal* (New Delhi: Sage Publications, 2004).

Bandopdhyay, Sekhar. *Caste, Protest and Identity in Colonial India: The Namasudras of Bengal, 1872–1947* (Richmond: Curzon Press, 1997).

Bandopdhyay, Sekhar. 'Popular Religion and Social Mobility in Colonial Bengal: The Matua Sect and the Namasudras'. In Rajat Kanta Ray (ed.) *Mind, Body and Society: Life and Mentality in Colonial Bengal* (Calcutta: Oxford University Press, 1995), 155–92.

Bandopdhyay, Sekhar. 'Social Mobility in Colonial Bengal: The Namasudras'. In Ishita Banerjee-Dube (ed.) *Caste in India* (New Delhi: Oxford University Press, 2008), 181–96.

Banivanua Mar, Tracy, and Penny Edmonds (eds.). *Making Settler Colonial Space: Perspectives on Race, Place and Identity* (Basingstoke: Palgrave, 2010).

Barlow, H. S. '*Swettenham, Sir Frank Athelstane (1850–1946)*' *Oxford Dictionary of National Biography* (Oxford: Oxford University Press, 2004).

Basso, Keith. *Wisdom Sits in Places: Landscape and Language among the Western Apache* (Albuquerque, NM: University of New Mexico Press, 1996).

Bayly, Christopher and Tim Harper. *Forgotten Armies: The Fall of British Asia 1941–5* (London: Penguin, 2004).

Bayly, Christopher and Tim Harper. *Forgotten Wars: The End of Britain's Asian Empire* (London: Allen Lane, 2007).

Bender, Barbara. *Landscape, Politics, Perspectives* (Oxford: Berg, 1993).

Berger, John. *Ways of Seeing* (London: BBC and Penguin Books, 1972).

Bhattacharya, S. K. *Sagarkanya Andaman* (Calcutta: Swati Prashani, 1983).

Bhattacharya, S. K., P. C. Dutta and S. Bhattacharya. 'The Migrant Oraon in the Amdaman: Demographic Aspects'. *Journal of Indian Anthropological Society* **20**, 1 (1985), 86–92.

Biswas, Swapan Kumar. *Colonization and Rehabilitation in the Andaman Islands* (New Delhi: Abhijeet Publications, 2009).

Bose, Sugata. *His Majesty's Opponent: Subhas Chandra Bose and India's Struggle Against Empire* (Cambridge, MA: Harvard University Press, 2012).

Briggs, Asa. *The Age of Improvement 1783–1867* (London: Longman, 1959).

Burton, Antoinette (ed.). *Gender, Sexuality and Colonial Modernities* (London: Routledge, 1999).

Byrne, David and Aidan Doyle. 'The Visual and the Verbal: The Interaction of Images and Discussion in Exploring Cultural Change'. In Caroline Knowles and Paul Sweetman (eds.) *Picturing The Social Landscape: Visual Methods and the Sociological Imagination* (London: Routledge, 2004), 166–77.

Carter, Paul. *The Road to Botany Bay: An Exploration of Landscape and History*, (Chicago: University of Chicago Press, 1987).

Chakraborty, Dilip K. *The Great Andamanese, Struggling for Survival* (Calcutta: Seagull Books, 1990).

Champion, H. G. and S. K. Seth. *A Revised Survey of the Forest Types of India* (Dehradun: Forest Research Institute, 1968).

Chatterjee, Indrani and Richard M. Eaton (eds.). *Slavery and South Asian History* (Bloomington, IN: Indiana University Press, 2006).

Chatterji, Joya. 'Dispositions and Destinations: Refugee Agency and "Mobility Capital" in the Bengal Diaspora, 1947–2007'. *Comparative Studies in Society and History* **55**, 2 (2013), 273–304.

Chaudhuri, Sabyasachi Basu Ray. 'Exiled to the Andamans: The Refugees from East Pakistan'. In Pradip Kumar Bose (ed.) *Refugees in West Bengal: Institutional Processes, Contested Identities* (Calcutta: MCRG, 2000), 131–9.

Coomar, Palash Chandra. *Migration and Social Change: A Study of the Bhantus of the Andaman Islands* (Calcutta: The Anthropological Society of India, 1997).

Coomar, Palash Chandra. *Tradition and Transformation in an Immigrant Island Society: The Karen of Andaman Islands* (New Delhi: Abhijeet Publications, 2009).

Coomar, Palash Chandra and Manis K. Raha. 'Family among the Bhantu of Andamans'. *Journal of the Indian Anthropological Society*, **24**, 2 (1989), 121–8.

Cosgrove, Denis. 'Modernity, Community and the Landscape Idea'. *Journal of Material Culture* **11** (2006), 49–66.

Cosgrove, Denis. *Social Formation and the Symbolic Landscape*, 2nd edn (Madison, WI: University of Wisconsin Press, 1998).

Cosgrove, Denis. 'Tropic and Tropicality'. In Felix Driver and Luciana Martins (eds.) *Tropical Visions in an Age of Empire* (Chicago: University of Chicago Press, 2005), 197–216.

Dasgupta, Jayant. *Japanese in the Andaman and Nicobar Islands* (New Delhi: Manas Publications, 2000).

Daston, Lorraine and Peter Galison. 'The Image of Objectivity'. *Representations* **40** (1992), 81–128.

Deleuze, Gilles and Felix Guattari. *A Thousand Plateaus: Capitalism and Schizophrenia*, trans. Brian Massumi (Minneapolis, MN: University of Minnesota Press, 1987).

Dhingra, Kiran. *The Andaman and Nicobar Islands in the Twentieth Century: A Gazetteer* (New Delhi: Oxford University Press, 2005).

Dilwali, Ashok and Ranjana Kaul. *Andaman and Nicobar Islands: Islands in the Sun* (New Delhi: Spantech Publishers, 1989).

Drayton, Richard. *Nature's Government: Science, Imperial Britain and the Improvement of the World* (New Haven, CT: Yale University Press, 2000).

Driver, Felix and Luciana Martins (eds.). *Tropical Visions in an Age of Empire* (Chicago: University of Chicago Press, 2005).

Driver, Felix and Luciana Martins. 'Views and Visions of the Tropical World'. In Felix Driver and Luciana Martins (eds.) *Tropical Visions in an Age of Empire* (Chicago: University of Chicago Press, 2005), 3–22.

Edwards, Elizabeth. 'Science Visualized: E.H. Man in the Andaman Islands'. In Elizabeth Edwards (ed.) *Anthropology and Photography, 1860–1920* (London: Royal Anthropological Institute, 1994), 108–21.

Edwards, Elizabeth, Chris Gosden and Ruth B. Philipps (eds.). *Sensible Objects: Colonialism, Museums and Material Culture* (Oxford: Oxford University Press, 2006).

Edwards, Elizabeth and Janice Hart. 'Introduction: Photographs as Objects'. In Elizabeth Edwards and Janice Hart (eds.) *Photographs Objects Histories: On the Materiality of Images* (London: Routledge, 2004), 1–16.

Edwards, Edwards and Matt Mead. 'Absent Histories and Absent Images: Photographs, Museums and the Colonial Past.' *Museum and Society*, **11**, 1 (2013), 19–38.

Etherington, Philip J. 'Placing the Past: "Groundwork" for a Spatial Theory of History'. *Rethinking History: The Journal of Theory and Practice* **11**, 4 (2007), 465–93.

Falconer, John. 'Ethnographical Photography in India 1850–1900'. *Photographic Collector* 5, 1 (1984), 16–46.

Falconer, John. 'Photography in Nineteenth-Century India'. in C. A. Bayly (ed.) *The Raj: India and the British 1600–1947* (London: National Portrait Gallery, 1990).

Field, Steven and Keith Basso (eds.). *Senses of Place* (Santa Fe, CA: School of American Research Press [Seattle], Distributed by the University of Washington Press, 1996).

Gellner, Ernest. *Nations and Nationalism* (Ithaca, NY: Cornell University Press, 1983).

Glover, William J. 'Objects, Models, and Exemplary Works: Educating Sentiment in Colonial India'. *Journal of Asian Studies* 64, 3 (2005), 539–66.

Ghosh, A. K. *Census of India, 1951, Volume XVII: The Andaman and Nicobar Islands* (Calcutta: Government of India Press, 1955).

Handler, Richard. *Critics Against Culture: Anthropological Observers of Mass Society* (Madison, WI: University of Wisconsin Press, 2005).

Harper, Tim and Sunil Amrith (eds.). 'Sites of Asian Interaction'. *Modern Asian Studies* 46, special issue 02 (2012), 273–304.

Harvey, David. *Spaces of Global Capitalism: Towards a Theory of Uneven Geographical Development* (London: Verso, 2006).

Hobsbawm, Eric. *Nations and Nationalism Since 1780: Programme, Myth, Reality* (Cambridge: Cambridge University Press, 1990).

Ingold, Tim. *The Appropriation of Nature: Essays on Human Ecology and Social Relations* (Iowa City: University of Iowa Press, 1987).

Ingold, Tim. *The Perception of the Environment: Essays on Livelihood, Dwelling and Skill* (London: Routledge, 2011).

Iqbal, Rashida (ed.). *Unsung Heroes of Freedom Struggle in Andamans: Who's Who* (Port Blair: Directorate of Youth Affairs, Sports and Culture, Andaman and Nicobar Administration, 1998).

Iqbal, Rashida. 'Back To My Roots,' *Light of Andaman*, n.d.

Jess, Pat M. *A Place in the World? Places, Cultures and Globalization* (Oxford: Oxford University Press, 1995).

Joshi, A. K. *Emigration and Social Change: A Sociological Study of Early Emigrants of the Andamans* (New Delhi: Rawat Publications, 2005).

Joshi, Ratanlal (ed.). *The Martyrs* (Bombay: Udbodhak Granthmala, 1994).

Kailash, 'Peaceful Coexistence: Lessons from Andamans'. *Economic and Political Weekly* 35, 32 (2000), 2859–65.

'Kala Pani: A Forgotten History'. BBC Radio 4 (21 April 2010).

Lall, B. B. *A Regime of Fears and Tears: History of the Japanese Occupation of the Andaman Islands* (New Delhi: Farsight Publishers, 1992; 2000; 2001).

Lamb, D. C. 'Booth, (William) Bramwell (1856–1929)'. Rev. L.E. Lauer, *Oxford Dictionary of National Biography* (Oxford: Oxford University Press, 2004), online edn, September 2012, www.oxforddnb.com/view/article/31969 (accessed 17 September 2014).

Leach, Edmund. *Political Systems of Highland Burma* (London: LSE Monograph on Social Anthropology No. 44, 1954).

Lebra, Joyce C. *Japanese-Trained Armies in Southeast Asia* (New York: Columbia University Press, 1977).

Lefebvre, Henri. *The Production of Space* (Oxford: Blackwell, 1991).

Lester, Alan. 'Spatial Concepts and the Historical Geographies of British Colonialism'. In A. Thompson (ed.) *Writing Imperial Histories* (Manchester: Manchester University Press, 2013), 118–42.

Li, Tania Murray. *The Will to Improve: Governmentality, Development, and the Practice of Politics* (Durham, NC: Duke, 2007).

Macintyre, Stuart and Anna Clark. *The History Wars* (Melbourne: Melbourne University Press, 2003).

Martins, Susanna Wade. *Coke of Norfolk, 1754–1842* (Woodbridge, Suffolk: Boydell Press, 2009).

Massey, Doreen. *For Space* (London: Sage, 2005).

Massey, Doreen and Pat M. Jess. *A Place in the World? Places, Cultures and Globalization* (Oxford: Oxford University Press, 1995).

Mathur, L. P. *Kala Pani: History of Andaman and Nicobar Islands with a Study of India's Freedom Struggle* (New Delhi: Eastern Book Corporation, 1985).

Mathur, Saloni. 'Wanted Native Views: Collecting Colonial Postcards of India'. In Antoinette Burton (ed.) *Gender, Sexuality and Colonial Modernities* (London: Taylor and Francis, 1999), 95–115.

Mauss, Marcel and Henri Beuchat. *Seasonal Variations of the Eskimos: A Study in Social Morphology* (London: Routledge and Kegan Paul, 1979).

Mohanraj, Prashanth and K. Veena Kumar. 'Lt.Colonel M.L. Ferrar: The "Butterfly Mad" Chief Commissioner of the Andaman and Nicobar Islands'. *Current Science* **87**, 10 (2004), 1467–9.

Mujtaba, Ahmad. *The Silent Past of Andamans: Few Freedom Fighters of 1857* (Pamphlet: 2004).

Mukherjee, Madhusree. *The Land of Naked People: Encounters with Stone Age Islanders* (Boston, MA: Houghton Mifflin, 2003).

Murphy, Kate. 'The Modern Idea is to Bring the Country to the City: Australian Urban Reformers and the Ideal of Rurality, 1900–1918'. *Rural History* **20**, 1 (2009), 119–36.

Murthy, R. V. R. *Andaman and Nicobar Islands: A Geopolitical and Strategic Perspective* (New Delhi: Northern Book Centre, 2007).

Nicholas, Ralph W. *Rites of Spring: Gajan in Village Bengal* (New Delhi: Chronicle Books, 2008).

Nigam, Sanjay. 'Disciplining and Policing The "Criminals By Birth", Part 1: The Making of a Colonial Stereotype – The Criminal Tribes and Castes of North India'. *Indian Economic and Social History Review* **27**, 2 (1990), 131–64.

Nigam, Sanjay. 'Disciplining and Policing The "Criminals By Birth", Part 2: The Development of a Disciplinary System, 1871–1900'. *Indian Economic and Social History Review* **27**, 3 (1990), 257–87.

Oberai, C. P. S. *Eco-Tourism Paradise: The Andaman and Nicobar Islands* (New Delhi: B.R. Publishing Corporation, 2000).

Pandya, Vishvajit. *Above the Forest: A Study of Andamanese Ethnoanemology, Cosmology, and the Power of Ritual* (New Delhi: Oxford University Press, 1993).

Pandya, Vishvajit. 'Forest Smells and Spider Webs: Ritualized Dream Interpretation among Andaman Islanders'. *Dreaming: Journal of the Association for the Study of Dreams* **14**, 2–3 (2003), 136–50.

Pandya, Vishvajit. *In the Forest: Visual and Material Worlds of Andamanese History, 1858–2006* (Lanham MD: University Press of America, 2009).

Pandya, Vishvajit. 'In Terra Nullius: The Legacies of Science and Colonialism in the Andaman Islands'. Public Lecture Series, 'Science, Society and Nature' (New Delhi: Nehru Memorial Museum and Library, Teen Murti, 22 May 2013).

Pandya, Vishvajit. 'Movement and Space: Andamanese Cartography'. *American Ethnologist* **17**, 4 (1990), 775–97.

Pandya, Vishvajit. 'Sacrifice and Escape as Counter-Hegemonic Rituals: A Structural Essay on an Aspect of Andamanese History'. *Journal of Social Analysis* **41**, 2 (1997), 66–98.

Panikkar, K. N. *Against Lord and State: Religion and Peasant Uprisings in Malabar* (New Delhi: Oxford University Press, 1990).

Parker, R. A. C. 'Coke of Norfolk and the Agricultural Revoltuion'. *Economic and Social History Review* **2**, 8 (1955), 155–66.

Paterson, Noel, *Experiences of a District Officer: Andaman and Nicobar Islands, The Reoccupation 1945–47*, unpublished manuscript in the authors' possession.

Pinney, Christopher. *Camera Indica: The Social Life of Indian Photographs* (London: Reaktion, 1997).

Poole, Deborah. *Vision, Race and Modernity: A Visual Economy of the Andean Image World* (Princeton, NJ: Princeton University Press, 1997).

Portelli, Alesandro. 'History-Telling and Time: An Example from Kentucky'. *Oral History Review* **20**, 1 (1992), 51–66.

Pred, Allan. *Even in Sweden: Racism, Racialized Spaces, and the Popular Geographical Imagination* (Oakland, CA: University of California Press, 2000).

Radhakrishna, Meena. 'Colonial Constructions of a Criminal Tribe: Yerakulas of Madras Presidency'. *Economic and Political Weekly* **35**, 28/29 (15–21 July 2000), 2553–63.

Radhakrishna, Meena. *Dishonoured by History: 'Criminal Tribes' and British Colonial Policy* (New Delhi: Orient Blackswan, 2001).

Reddy, Sunita. 'Mega-tourism in the Andaman and Nicobar Islands: Some Concerns'. *Journal of Human Ecology* **21**, 3 (2007), 231–9.

Report by the Inter-Departmental Team on Accelerated Development Programme for the Andaman and Nicobar Islands, Ministry of Rehabilitation (Government of India, 1964).

Rizvi, S. A. A. and Moti Lal Bhargava. *Freedom Struggle in Uttar Pradesh: Source-Material* [five volumes] (Lucknow: Publications Bureau, Information Department, 1957–61).

Rosaldo, Renato I. *Ilongot. Headhunting 1883–1974: A Study in Society and History* (Stanford, CA: Stanford University Press, 1980).

Roy, Priten and Swapnesh Choudhary. *The Lost Horizon: A Tale of Ross: The Deserted Island's Citadel* (New Delhi: Farsight Publishers, 2002).

Roy, Sanjib K. 'India Shuns Last Survivors of Andaman Tribe' (Port Blair: Reuters, 18 May 2007).

Roychowdhury, Jyotirmay. *Andamaner Bangali: Sanskritir Binimay* (Kolkata: Sahitya Prakash, 2004).

Roychowdhury, Rabin. *Andaman and Nicobar: The Untold Islands* (New Delhi: Manas Publications, 2011).

Roychowdhury, Rabin. *Black Days in Andaman and Nicobar Islands* (New Delhi: Manas Publications, 2004).

Roychowdhury, Sabyasachi Basu. 'Exiled in the Andamans: The Refugees of East Pakistan'. In Pradip Kumar Bose (ed.) *Refugees in West Bengal: Institutional Processes and Contested Identities* (Calcutta: Calcutta Research Group, 2000).

Royle, S. A. 'Postcolonial Culture on Dependent Islands'. *Space and Culture* **13**, 2 (2010), 203–15.

Ryan, James R. *Picturing Empire: Photography and the Visualization of the British* (London: Reaktion, 1997).

Saldanha, Cecil J. (ed.). *Andaman, Nicobar and Lakshadweep: An Environmental Impact Assessment* (New Delhi: Ministry of Environment, 1989).

Saral, Shrikrishan. *Indian Revolutionaries: A Comprehensive Study, 1757–1961* (New Delhi: Ocean Books Pvt. Lts., 1999).

Sareen, Tilak Raj. *Japanese Occupation of the Andaman and Nicobar Islands 1942–5* (New Delhi: Pragun Publications, 2012).

Savarkar, V.D. *The Indian War of Independence, 1857* (Bombay: Phoenix Publications, 1947).

Scott, James C. *Seeing Like the State: How Certain Schemes to Improve the Human Condition have Failed* (New Haven, CT: Yale University Press, 1998).

Sekhsaria, Pankaj. *Troubled Islands: Writings on the Indigenous People and Environment of the Andaman and Nicobar Islands* (Pune: Kalpavriksh, 2003).

Sekhsaria, Pankaj and Vishvajit Pandya (eds.). *The Jarawa Tribal Reserve Dossier: Cultural and Biological Diversity in the Andaman Islands* (Paris: UNESCO, 2010).

Sen, Probhat Kumar. *Land and People of the Andamans* (Calcutta: The Post-Graduate Book Mart, 1958).

Sen, Satadru. *Disciplining Punishment: Colonialism and Convict Society in the Andaman Islands* (New Delhi: Oxford University Press, 2000).

Sen, Satadru. 'Domesticated Convicts: Producing Families in the Andaman Islands'. In Indrani Chatterjee (ed.) *Unfamiliar Relations: Family and History in South Asia* (New Brunswick: Rutgers University Press, 2004), 261–91.

Sen, Satadru. *Savagery and Colonialism in the Indian Ocean: Power, Pleasure and the Andaman Islanders* (Oxford: Routledge, 2010).

Sen, Satadru. 'Savage Bodies, Civilized Pleasures: M. V. Portman and the Andamanese'. *American Ethnologist* **36**, 2 (2009), 364–79.

Sen, Uditi. 'Dissident Memories: Exploring Bengali Refugee Narratives in the Andaman Islands'. In Panikos Panayi and Pippa Virdee (eds.) *Refugees and the End of Empire: Imperial Collapse and Forced Migration in the Twentieth Century* (Basingstoke: Palgrave, 2011), 219–44.

Shanks, G. Dennis and David J. Bradley, 'Island Fever: The Historical Determinants of Malaria in the Andaman Islands'. *Transactions of the Royal Society of Tropical Medicine and Hygiene* **104**, 3 (2010), 185–90.

Sheard, Major Edwin H. 'Reforming Robbers in the Andamans'. *The Officers' Review* (November 1937), 535–40.

Sheard, Major Edwin H. *Sergeant-Major in the Andamans: Kanhaiya Gariba* (St Albans: Campfield Press, 1957).

Sherman, Taylor C. 'From Hell to Paradise? Voluntary Transfer of Convicts to the Andaman Islands, 1921–1940'. *Modern Asian Studies* **43**, 2 (2009), 367–88.

Singh, Kumar Suresh (ed.). *People of India: Andaman and Nicobar Islands, Volume XII* (New Delhi: Anthropological Survey of India, 1994).

Singh, Priti. *The Islands and Tribes of Andaman and Nicobar* (New Delhi: Prakash Books, 2006).

Sinharay, Praskanva. 'Caste, Migration, Identity'. *Seminar* **645** (May 2013), 56–7.

Sivasundaram, Sujit. 'Ethnicity, Indigeneity, and Migration in the Advent of British Rule to Sri Lanka'. *American Historical Review* **115**, 2 (2010), 428–52.

Sivasundaram, Sujit. *Islanded: Britain, Sri Lanka and the Bounds of an Indian Ocean Colony* (Chicago: University of Chicago Press, 2013).

Soja, Edward W. 'The Socio-Spatial Dialectic'. *Annals of the Association of American Geographers* **70**, 2 (1980), 207–25.

Sponz, Paolo, Chui Sponz and Shanchulla Sponz. *Tangkhul: Head Hunting Nagas* (New Delhi: India Research Press, 2007).

Srivastava, M. P. *Freedom Fighters of Indian Mutiny 1857* (Allahabad: Chugh, 1997).

Srivastava, Pramod Kumar. 'Resistance and Repression in India: The Hunger Strike at the Andaman Cellular Jail in 1933'. *Crime, History and Societies* **7**, 2 (2003), 81–102.

Stepan, Nancy Leys. *Picturing Tropical Nature* (London: Reaktion, 2001).

Stoler, Ann Laura. *Along the Archival Grain: Epistemic Anxieties and Colonial Common Sense* (Princeton, NJ: Princeton University Press, 2009).

Stoler, Ann Laura. 'Colonial Aphasia: Race and Disabled Histories in France'. *Public Culture* **23**, 1 (2011), 121–56.

Stoler, Ann Laura and Karen Strassler. 'Castings for the Colonial: Memory Work in "New Order" Java'. *Comparative Studies in Society and History* **42**, 1 (2000), 4–48.

Talbot, Ian. 'The Punjab Under Colonialism: Order and Transformation in British India'. *Journal of Punjab Studies* **14**, 1 (2008), 3–10.

Thompson, Krista A. *An Eye for the Tropics: Tourism, Photography and Framing the Caribbean Picturesque* (Durham, NC: Duke University Press, 2006).

Tolen, Rachel J. 'Colonizing and Transforming the Criminal Tribesmen: the Salvation Army in British India'. *American Ethnologist* **18**, 1 (1991), 106–25.

Tranter, Bruce and Jed Donoghue. 'Convict Ancestry: A Neglected Aspect of Australian Identity'. *Nations and Nationalism* **9**, 4 (2003), 555–77.

Treveleyan, Raleigh. *The Golden Oriole: The Two Hundred Year History of an English Family in India* (London: The Long Rider's Guild Press, 2007).

Tuan, Yi-fu. *Space and Place: The Perspective of Experience* (Minneapolis, MN: University of Minnesota Press, 1977).

Vaidik, Aparna. *Imperial Andamans: Colonial Encounter and Island History* (Basingstoke: Palgrave, 2010).

Vaidik, Aparna. 'Settling the Convict: Matrimony and Domesticity in the Andamans'. *Studies in History* **22**, 2 (2006), 221–50.

Vaidya, Suresh. *Islands of the Marigold Sun* (London: The Travel Book Club, 1960).

van der Beek, Zita and Marcel Vellinga. 'Man the Collector: Salvaging Andamanese and Nicobarese Culture through Objects'. *Journal of the History of Collections* **17**, 2 (2005), 135–53.

Venkateswar, Sita. *Development and Ethnocide: Colonial Practices in the Andaman Islands* (Copenhagen: IWGA, 2004).

Verma, O. P. 'The Working Composition of the Ranchi Tribal Labourers in Andaman and Nicobar Islands: A Case Study of Baratang Island'. *Journal of Social Research* **19**, 2 (1976), 114–24.

Waterton, Emma. 'Landscape and Non-Representational Theories'. In Peter Howard, Ian Thompson and Emma Waterton (eds.) *The Routledge Companion to Landscape Studies* (London: Routledge, 2013), 66–75.

Watt, Carey A. 'The Promise of "Character" and the Spectre of Sedition: The Boy Scout Movement and Colonial Consternation in India, 1908–21'. *South Asia: Journal of South Asian Studies* **22**, 2 (1999), 37–62.

Whitaker, Romulus. *Endangered Andamans: Managing Tropical Moist Forests, A Case Study of the Andamans* (New Delhi: Environmental Services Group, World Wildlife Fund, India and MAB India, Department of Environment, 1985).

Wintle, Claire. *Colonial Collecting and Display: Encounters with Material Culture from the Andaman and Nicobar Islands* (Oxford: Bergahan, 2013).

Withers, C. W. J. 'Place and the "Spatial Turn" in Geography and in History'. *Journal of the History of Ideas* **7**, 4 (2009), 637–58.

Wolfe, Patrick. *Settler Colonialism and the Transformation of Anthropology* (London: Cassell, 1999).

Wood, Conrad. 'The First Moplah Rebellion against British Rule in Malabar'. *Modern Asian Studies* **10**, 4 (1976), 543–56.

Wylie, John. *Landscapes, Key Ideas* (London: Routledge, 2007).

Zehmisch, Philipp. 'Freedom Fighters or Criminals? Postcolonial Subjectivities in the Andaman Islands, South-East India'. In Paula Pannu (ed.) *Kontur Nr. 22 'Colonial and Post-Colonial Subjectivities'*, (2011), 4–16.

Index

For EU product safety concerns, contact us at Calle de José Abascal, 56–1°,
28003 Madrid, Spain or eugpsr@cambridge.org.

.

www.ingramcontent.com/pod-product-compliance
Ingram Content Group UK Ltd.
Pitfield, Milton Keynes, MK11 3LW, UK
UKHW020455240426
470322UK00016B/353